**ADMINISTRATION
FOR THE
HUMAN SERVICES**

Harper Series in Social Work, Werner W. Boehm, Series Editor

WALTER H. EHLERS
MICHAEL J. AUSTIN
JON C. PROTHERO

Florida State University

ADMINISTRATION FOR THE HUMAN SERVICES

An Introductory Programmed Text

HARPER & ROW, PUBLISHERS
New York, Hagerstown, San Francisco, London

Sponsoring Editor: Alvin A. Abbott
Project Editor: Pamela Landau
Designer: Emily Harste
Production Supervisor: Stefania J. Taflinska
Compositor: Maryland Linotype Composition Co., Inc.
Printer and Binder: The Murray Printing Company
Art Studio: J & R Technical Services Inc.

ADMINISTRATION FOR THE HUMAN SERVICES
An Introductory Programmed Test

Copyright © 1976 by Walter H. Ehlers, Michael J. Austin, and Jon C. Prothero

Library of Congress Cataloging in Publication Data

Ehlers, Walter H.
    Administration for the human services.

    (Harper's series in social work)
    Includes bibliographies.
    1. Social work administration—Programmed
instruction. I. Austin Michael J., joint author.
II. Prothero, Jon C., joint author. III. Title.
[DNLM: 1. Social service—Programmed texts.
2. Social welfare—Programmed texts. 3. Organi-
zation and administration—Programmed texts. HV40
E33a]
HV41.E37   658'.91'3610077   75-34374
ISBN 0-06-041868-0

Contents

Introduction

In recent years, administration has come to be viewed as a subject of instruction essential for social work and other human service personnel. In the absence of a text capable of reaching such personnel on either or both the undergraduate or graduate levels, it was difficult to effectively acquaint students with appropriate concepts and techniques. The present text seeks to fill this gap. It is placed in the Harper Series in Social Work because the major purpose of this series is to make available texts for students who prepare for professional positions in social work and related human services. An additional purpose of the series is to make available teaching and learning materials also to professionals on the job via staff development channels. This text serves both these purposes; it manages to provide users with an opportunity to minister to their own learning needs by enabling them to gauge their progress through the intermediary of programmed instruction. The text, thus, seeks at one and the same time to meet the needs of the advanced as well as the beginning student.

As the chapter titles indicate, this work embodies a comprehensive approach to administration viewed as a professional activity. For the beginner, the programs will serve both as introduction and test of accomplishment. For the more advanced student, and the professional in service, they provide an opportunity for reviewing, deepening, and further developing essential components of administration.

The Harper Series in Social Work is pleased to be able to pioneer with a text on administration which seeks to bring pertinent knowledge and skill to this vital realm of human services.

Rutgers University   **Werner W. Boehm**

Foreword

The authors of this programmed text have made an original and innovative contribution to the study of the administration of human services.

The human services today are the most significant part of our governmental programs, both in terms of their significance and importance to the people of the United States and in terms of their cost. Approximately one-half of the total budget of the federal government is devoted to the human services, and in many of our states the newly created Offices of Human Services or Departments of Human Services take from one-third to one-half of the state budgets.

The administration of these huge programs is complicated and important, and the training of persons in the art and skill of administration, specifically geared to the administration of the human services, is an extremely important and significant contribution.

Those who have worked with programmed materials and programmed texts such as this are, I believe, becoming increasingly convinced that it is one of the most effective ways of presenting both factual materials and conceptual approaches to subjects such as administration.

The programmed text covers the important and relevant areas of administration; it ties them to the special requirements of the human services; and, it contributes an excellent textbook for courses in this area. In addition, the book should commend itself to teachers who will find in it ways of presenting material that is normally extremely difficult to communicate to students who have had little administrative experience.

All in all, I consider this approach a real contribution to the literature of administration.

Brandeis University   **Charles I. Schottland**

Preface

This programmed text resulted from the authors' interest in developing a book that would meet the needs of administrators in various human service agencies, such as day care, public assistance, vocational rehabilitation, psychiatric half-way houses, mental retardation, mental health, corrections, and similar types of services. It was designed to answer the need for a basic introductory text which had some elements of the recipe or "cookbook" style and could also be used in a "self-instruction" mode for those who wanted to learn by themselves some of the basic principles of administration.

The book covers nine specific areas labeled as functions of administration in a number of textbooks: communication, planning, organizing, staffing, directing, coordinating, reporting, budgeting, and evaluating. Henri Fayol is credited with identifying the management functions as five in number: planning, organizing, commanding, coordinating, and controlling. Luther Gulick, in 1937, identified seven functions: planning, organizing, staffing, directing, coordinating, reporting, and budgeting. He also devised the acronym POSDCORB to represent the seven functions. We have chosen to add two additional functions, communicating and evaluating, two functions vital to a dynamic administrative process. Employees as well as clients are becoming involved in the decision making process. The communication process must be understood thoroughly by all parties concerned if any messages are to get through at any level. Likewise, evaluation is a concern not only of management but also of the employees and, increasingly, of the clients.

There are no easy answers on how to perform the principles of administration. The best that can be said is that there are some preferred approaches based on experience, new knowledge, and practice wisdom. This book has been designed to explore these preferred approaches. Readers are led into preferred answers throughout the book as a way of supplying a factual base upon which to build their knowledge of administrative principles.

Although this programmed text has been designed primarily to be used as self-instruction, it is best used with an instructor present to discuss problems that go beyond the text. The content in this text is designed to "flag" or alert the reader to key aspects of the administrative process from a very practical perspective. As a result, experienced workers should be able to logically disagree with some of our statements and to justify their position in light of their own experience and current administrative constraints. To facilitate this possibility, at the end of each unit we have brought together a summary that looks at the content area and suggests additional readings and new concepts that could be explored in order to round out one's knowledge. Such suggestions include, but are not limited to, the further development of organizational theory, conflict management and resolution, labor relations, evaluative research, social policy analysis, communications theory, and the more advanced technology of the management sciences.

Both the learner and the instructor need to be cautioned further that there are additional areas of current administrative concern with which the authors do not deal. For example, institutional racism and equal opportunities for all, regardless of sex or race, have raised difficult new and unresolved problems for administrators. Never before has the question of who to retain and who to let go in a tight financial situation been fraught with so many value decisions. More and more cases are being brought before the United States Equal Employment Opportunity Commission (EEOC), cases that involve judgments made by administrators. For the human services administrators we might go one step further to indicate that in-depth knowledge will be required in the whole area of institutional racism and sexism in order to function effectively in tomorrow's administrative world. At this point there are only some speculative notions about how this knowledge may be acquired and used in the administrative setting. Certainly no theoretical concepts have as yet gained wide enough acceptance to be called established practice. Nevertheless, we put out the caution flag here for the learner and instructor alike and indicate that here is an area you will want and need to discuss.

In our search of the literature on administration and our own administrative experience, we found that many arbitrary decisions were required in order to select concepts and principles relevant to human service administration. As a result, each of the units in this text represents entire fields of study and could be easily expanded into several college courses. For example, in an area of study such as evaluation, we selected only a few key techniques of program and organizational evaluation out of a growing body of literature in the fields of operational research and evaluative research. This example highlights the important and strategic role of the instructor in the use of this text. While the learner is expected to proceed through this text at his own pace, his understanding of the material will be considerably enhanced through discussion sessions led by instructors who can bring to the learning situation their own experiences and skills in the art of administration. Our experience with over 100 students using this text indicates that much can be learned from a programmed text which emphasizes the practical aspects of administration. Pre- and post-tests were utilized. For pre-tests all questions with a difficulty index of below .3 or above .8 were examined and revised or eliminated. For post-tests all questions with a difficulty index below .8 were examined, and either the questions were revised and/or the text corresponding to the questions was improved to facilitate learning or to clarify unclear segments. Students found themselves engrossed in the material as demonstrated by the numerous questions brought to the discussion sessions each week.

We have also found it profitable to supplement this text with simulations of current agency practices requiring administrative expertise. The simplest and most immediate technique for feed- back is the "in-basket" technique. This involves the instructor in the development of situations confronting an administrator and the drafting of the situations in the form of two or three sentences on an index card that students then draw out of simulated in- baskets, commonly found on the desks of administrators. Students select a card and respond spontaneously to the situation presented based on their understanding of the principles of administration found in this text.[1] Needless to say, the role of the instructor is crucial in order to guarantee the integration of programmed in- structional content into the practice and skill development of current and/or future administrators. The specific objectives that appear at the beginning of each lesson provide the instructor and reader with suggestions for using practical examples in applying the content of the lesson to everyday issues.

ACKNOWLEDGMENTS

Acknowledging the many people who contributed to the develop- ment of this text requires us to express our appreciation to agency representatives, colleagues, and students. We owe a con- siderable amount of gratitude to the U.S. Department of Health, Education and Welfare, Social and Rehabilitation Service, which encouraged the development of this text (#20-P-20009). Special thanks go to Eulene Hawkins, Regional Staff Development Spe- cialist for the Social and Rehabilitation Service in Atlanta, Georgia, for her continuous support and encouragement. We are also indebted to our colleagues for their help in the early stages of the development of the text, Alexis Skelding, Margaret Bell, and Judith Garrett. We are also grateful to Dean Diane Bernard at the Florida State University School of Social Work for her sup- port of this text. Our thanks also go to our patient and outstanding secretaries, Sharon Hudson, Beverly Harness, Nancy Holaday, Lana Gardner, and Anita Rosenberg.

Our students provided us with our most important source of criticism, for this we are grateful to: George Bird, Tom Bishop, Vivian Bryant, Betty Carley, Michael Collins, Pete Evans, Dollie

[1] For in-basket situation ideas, see Harry A. Schatz, *A Casebook in Social Work Administration* (New York: Council on Social Work Education, 1970).

Franklin, Margaret Hargrove, Andy Harshbarger, Tom Herndon, Pat Hicks, Mark Hopkins, Alice Jackson, Marie Jackson, Yang Koh, Richard Matus, Barbara McCullough, Linda Padgett, Joe Spierer, Janie Whitfield, Susan Yelton, Dan Blackstock, Patricia Boylan, Dan Brady, Valerie Camp, Donna Foster, Bruce Griffith, Jim Hermans, Gail Hinson, Tom Long, Gil McDaniel, Bob McTague, Gail Matteson, Delores Moore, Mahmoud Nofallah, Dorothy Ogburn, Sean O'Sullivan, Gary Robinson, Sandy Rubin, Mike Russell, Fred Seamon, Gerard Verzaal, John Whiddon, Les Wyche, Marianne McAulliffe, John Dow, Jay Hyman, Ree Sailors, Lindon Storm, Danna Vaught, Lydia Atkins, Francine Barnes, Don Blinzinger, Jerry Bowman, Jerome Corley, Dana Cozad, Linda Darden, Diana DiNitto, Margaret Ellis, Jean Frankel, Maureen Gaboury, James Godwin, Sandra Goss, Marianne Hurkes, Spurgeon Johnson, Don King, Lynn Kothe, Raphael Lago, Glen Lamb, Van Lear Logan, Bob Lombardo, Laura McKinley, Kitty Majors, Don Michaels, Richard Peterson, Ruth Peterson, Evelyn Phillips, Sheila Rymberg, Susie Schneider, Bob Sharpe, Larry Shirley, Paulette Simmons, Linda Smith, Vince Smith, Daniel Sokol, Susan Thomas, Theodore Thomas, Teadie Tunsil, Carol Abercrombie, Sharleen Baker, Barbara Blume, Lenora Bragg, Greg Bundrick, Josie Colston, James Dama, Deborah Holtzman, Beth Hull, Ginny Kennedy, Fran Kling, Bob McGuire, Mike Neidig, Cynthia Norton, Stan Peacock, Steve Preisser, Keith Shroyer, Jack Ahearn, Jerry Bradley, Loretta Bussiere, Susan Chilcote, Lucia Droege, Becky Dunitz, Bob Hodnette, Dan Kirchner, Seaborn O'Neal, Joan Patrick, John Phelps, Mike Robichaud, Angie Rodriguez, Luis Rodriguez, Sharon Savage, Guy Spearman, Earline Wesley, and Andrea Wood.

And finally we want to express a special word of appreciation for our wives, Sabine, Sue, and Prue, who have so graciously tolerated the numerous evenings and weekends required to complete this book. In addition, Sabine edited our first rough draft—a major job—for which we owe her a debt of thanks.

Tallahassee, Florida   **Walt, Mike, and Jon**

Instructions
to the User

This book must be read differently than the traditional books to which you are accustomed. It is not a textbook but an instructional program that may be used as a "self-instructional" text, although in a class in which there is a teacher you may be referred to other written materials, instructional films, slides, slide-tapes, or other instructional aids.

Each lesson in this book is made up of two parts and should be read and followed as directed. Each unit begins with a listing of objectives which specifies exactly what you are expected to be able to do at the conclusion of the lesson. A programmed lesson follows the learning objectives, which presents the content related to the objectives, and requires responses to questions with immediate feedback. The feedback is given when you turn to the answer of your choice. This technique, called the "scrambled text," may bother you at first, BUT IF YOU FOLLOW THE DIRECTIONS GIVEN BELOW, you will find that reading this portion is interesting and challenging. In addition, at the end of each unit there are review questions enabling you to test yourself.

DIRECTIONS

Throughout this entire program you will be sent to different frames labeled M, Q, or A followed by a number. A frame may contain content material (M1, M2), a question (Q1, Q2), or an answer (A1, A2). From every frame you will be referred to another frame (For example, turn to A1). Follow the directions carefully to avoid any unnecessary page turning, which might interfere with your learning. You have now completed frame Mii (see frame number in right hand margin of the page).

Continue with frame Miii

Many items throughout this program will ask you to make some **Miii** form of response. In most cases, such responses will require that you choose one of several given alternatives. In a few cases, you will be asked to give a word, phrase, sentence, or short description. Be sure to follow directions and when asked to write a response do so in the spaces provided. This method will lead to the most effective learning.

Since this program has been empirically tested on a large number of students, we know that you should be able to answer most questions provided you have consistently and diligently studied the material.

Because this program is designed to facilitate learning through the presentation of a wide variety of material, do not spend time attempting to write perfect answers. In those few cases where it is required, answer each question as best you can and move on.

Continue with Qo

If you apply yourself diligently to this material, you will   **Qo**

A. Be unable to answer most questions . . . . *Ao*
B. Be able to answer most questions . . . . *Aoo*

If you have turned to this frame, then you either have not read the **Ao** *material carefully or you have little confidence in your own abilities, since you have said that you will be unable to answer most questions if you apply yourself diligently to the material presented in this program.*

Whatever the case, this is an incorrect answer. If, during the program, you should choose the wrong answer to a question, you will be told either to review the material and/or answer the question and/or be given further information to clarify any misunderstanding or be told to review the material you missed. Return now to Qo and answer this question correctly.

Yes, you have answered Qo correctly. You will be able to answer **Aoo** *most questions if you carefully study the material presented in this program.*

Continue with Miv

You should be able to finish each programmed lesson during one **Miv** study session. However, if you find that you must take breaks during a lesson, try to make them short. It is recommended, for most effective learning, that you do not wait more than a day between study sessions for any single programmed lesson.

Continue with Mv

In introducing this program, we begin by looking at the life-long **Mv** goal and the end-of-program objective. To further acquaint you with each unit and each lesson, we state unit objectives for each unit, and specific and enabling objectives at the beginning of each lesson. The program material that follows immediately has been written to cover each of the instructional objectives. The objectives may also be used as a study guide. After you have learned the enabling objectives under any specific objective, you should be able to meet the specific objec-

tive, and after all the specific objectives for a unit have been learned,   **Mv**
then you will be capable of accomplishing the unit objective. When
you have completed all the unit objectives, you should be capable of
accomplishing the end-of-course objective. The accomplishment of the
long-range goal of this program is primarily your responsibility. This
program merely helps you get started in the right direction toward
that goal, the rest is up to you.

Upon completion of this program, you will be able to demonstrate
an understanding of the administrative process. You will also be able
to demonstrate an understanding of the communication process as it
applies to the administration of human service agencies or programs.
Lastly, you will have acquired basic skills in each of the eight major
areas of responsibility in which the executive must function effectively.

Begin with Lesson One

UNIT I
ADMINISTRATION

LESSON 1
Theoretical Approaches to Administration

UNIT I OBJECTIVE—ADMINISTRATION

After completing this unit, you will be given an administrative problem to solve, and you will be able to demonstrate your understanding of the basic administrative philosophies, concepts, and functions of an executive.

The first specific objective, and its enabling objectives are presented below. After you have read them, proceed to M1 and begin the programmed material corresponding to the enabling objectives.

Specific Objective

Given a description of an agency that is functioning inefficiently, you will be able to make decisions regarding changes in the administrative philosophy or approach that would lead to a more effective agency.

Enabling Objective 1
You will be able to define the term *administration* as it applies to human service agencies.

Enabling Objective 2
Given a description of one of three distinctive characteristics of human service agencies, you will be able to explain the possible problems that may result from mismanagement and how the executive might avoid or minimize them.

Enabling Objective 3
Given a description of one or more of the characteristics of a philosophy of administration or administrative approach, you will be able to identify the type of philosophy or approach described.

Enabling Objective 4
Given the name of an administrative philosophy or approach, you will be able to state the problems or current developments that might threaten the effective functioning of an agency operating under a particular administrative approach or philosophy.

Enabling Objective 5
You will be able to explain the key element of the administrative philosophy or approach that the competent executive should employ.

Continue with M1

ADMINISTRATION—WHAT IS IT?

M1

Administration has been described in many different ways—as a process, as a method, as a set of relationships with and between people working toward common objectives. However, the most succinct definition for the purposes of this text is as follows:

Administration is a method of practice that is concerned primarily with the following activities:[1]

1. Translating societal mandates—such as changes in laws, technical knowledge, administrative ruling—into organizational (agency) goals and operational policies to guide organizational behavior.
2. Designing organizational structures and procedures or processes through which the goals can be achieved.
3. Securing resources in the form of materials, staff, clients, and societal legitimation necessary for goal attainment and organizational survival.
4. Selecting and engineering the necessary technologies.
5. Optimizing organizational behavior directed toward increased effectiveness and efficiency.
6. Evaluating organization performance to facilitate systematic and continuous problem solving.

Continue with Q1

Q1

Administration, viewed as a method, includes six major activities. Circle the letters below corresponding to those activities that are included in the administration of human service agencies. Check your answer by turning to A3.

[1] Rosemary C. Sarri, "Administration in Social Welfare," *Social Work Yearbook*, 16th ed., vol. 1 (New York: National Association of Social Workers, 1971), pp. 42–43. Other sources that might add to your understanding of this concept include: Harleigh B. Trecker, *Social Work Administration, Principles and Practices* (New York: Association, 1971), see esp. pp. 22–24; and Harry A. Schatz, *Social Work Administration: A Resource Book* (New York: Council on Social Work Education, 1970).

A. Securing resources.

**Q1
cont.**

B. Designing agency structures and processes.
C. Avoiding the use of technology as dehumanizing.
D. Evaluating the agency's performance thereby facilitating problem solving.
E. Increasing the effectiveness and efficiency of the agency by optimizing organizational behavior.
F. Translating societal mandates into organizational goals.

Continue with M2

**DISTINCTIVE
FEATURES OF
HUMAN SERVICE
ORGANIZATIONS**

In order for you to gain a more comprehensive understanding of administation as it applies to human service agencies, you should be aware of the distinctive features that differentiate these organizations from other organizations. Sarri has described three such features as follows:

M2

1. The clients of human service organizations—such as mothers on welfare, children in day care, juveniles on parole—are both the major input and output, the raw material and the product.
2. The great reliance on human relations technologies (such as counseling, teaching, casework, group work), with considerable freedom to apply these techniques and, therefore, a heavy reliance on professionals to legitimize the programs and services.
3. The high proportion of nonroutine events (family crises, emergency health problems, housing evictions) confronted by staff in human service organizations. The behavior of these clients under stress is often disruptive and unpredictable, a fact that poses problems in control and goal attainment for the staff.[2]

Continue with Q2

According to Sarri, there are three distinctive features of human service agencies. Underline the proper words appearing in brackets below and then turn to A5.

Q2

A. The clients of human service organizations (are/are not) the major input and output.
B. The great reliance on human relations technologies (with/without) considerable freedom to apply these technologies.
C. A (high/low) proportion of (routine/nonroutine) events confront staff members.

Each of the three features of human service agencies should be explained further.[3] The attainment of the social goals of human service agencies is made difficult for three reasons:

M3

1. The clients served are both the major input and the major output of the agency in contrast to industrial organizations, where raw materials are the inputs and finished products are the outputs. But too often no agreed upon model exists for the worker who is attempting to process or change behavior.

[2] Sarri, "Administration in Social Welfare," pp. 43–44.
[3] Ibid.

2. Some goals vary in ambiguity, or are potentially contradictory; they may both be ends in themselves, or means to ends (For example, protection, custody, treatment, and rehabilitation are typical goals found in prisons, mental hospitals, and sheltered workshops, that may be both means and ends).

3. It is very difficult to distinguish clearly between output goals for clients and agency maintenance goals (that is, has the client improved or simply completed an agency's treatment program?).

M3 cont.

Continue with Q3

Attaining human service agency goals is a difficult task for three major reasons. Circle the letters corresponding to the reasons listed below then check your answers by turning to A1.

Q3

A. Goals such as treatment, protection, custody, and rehabilitation are very similar.

B. The clients served by agencies are both the major input and output of the agency.

C. Clear distinctions between output goals for clients and agency maintenance goals are difficult to draw.

D. Although clients are the input of the agency, agency maintenance goals are the output.

E. Many goals of human service organizations are potentially contradictory.

ADMINISTRATIVE APPROACHES

Every age develops an administrative approach or an organizational form peculiar to it. There are two major theoretical approaches, namely, bureaucratic or formal and democratic or informal. There is also a third approach that is presently evolving. This approach has been referred to as *adhocracy*.[4] We shall first describe the characteristics of the two major theoretical approaches and then present the most recent approach that represents a combination of the formal and the informal.

M4

Continue with Q4

There are two major theoretical approaches to administration. These are the

Q4

A. Bureaucratic and adhocracy *A4*

B. Bureaucratic and democratic *A8*

BUREAUCRACY[5]

The bureaucratic approach to administration was perfected during the Industrial Revolution to organize and direct the activities of a business. The key feature of this approach is a chain of command

M5

[4] See Alvin Toffler, *Future Shock* (New York: Random House, 1970), pp. 124–151.
[5] For a more comprehensive discussion of this approach, see Max Weber, *The Theory of Social and Economic Organization*, trans. A. M. Henderson and Talcott Parsons (Glencoe, Illinois: Free Press, 1946); and Peter M. Blau, *Bureaucracy in Modern Society* (New York: Random House, 1966).

structured on the lines of a pyramid. In addition, it is composed of the **M5 cont.** following elements:

1. A pre-set system of procedures and rules for dealing with all contingencies relating to work activities.
2. A division of labor based on specialization.
3. Promotion and selection based on technical competence.
4. Impersonality in human relations.[6]

Continue with Q5

The key feature of bureaucracy is: **Q5**

A. A division of labor *A6*
B. A pyramidal chain of command *A11*
C. Close personal relationships *A14*

Other elements of a bureaucratic form of administration include **Q6** which of the following?

A. Close personal relationships *A9*
B. Promotion and selection based on varied abilities *A12*
C. A division of labor based on specialization *A15*

DEMOCRATIC ADMINISTRATION

The key feature of the democratic approach to administration is **M6** employee participation and sharing.[7] Therefore, important characteristics of a democratic administration, which follow from this key feature, include:[8]

1. Decisions regarding goals and objectives, plans and procedures are made by all concerned persons or their selected representatives.
2. Cooperation of staff, board, and committees is cultivated in order to establish a smooth working relationship.[9]
3. Promotion or selection for new or different work opportunities based on the varied abilities and experiences of the worker, with an eye toward their personal development as well as the good of the agency.
4. Warm, friendly, cooperative relationships, based on group or team spirit concepts, are encouraged.

Continue with Q7

The key feature of a democratic approach to administration is: **Q7**

A. Close personal relationships *A13*
B. Participation by and sharing among employees *A16*
C. Pyramidal chain of command *A19*

[6] John S. Morgan, *Improving Your Creativity on the Job* (New York: American Management Association, 1968), pp. 149–150.
[7] For a fuller discussion of this concept, see Chester I. Barnard, *Functions of the Executive* (Cambridge, Mass.: Harvard University Press, 1968); and Ordway Tead, *Democratic Administration* (New York: Association, 1945), esp. pp. 57–75.
[8] Ray Johns, *Executive Responsibility*, rev. ed. (New York: Association, 1966), pp. 35–36.
[9] Trecker calls this, "The Principle of Purposeful Relationships." See Harleigh B. Trecker, *Social Work Administration*, p. 188.

Therefore, which of the following would be another component of   **Q8**
the democratic approach to administration?

A. Impersonality in human relations **A17**
B. Promotion and selection based on varied abilities **A21**
C. Work assignments based on specialization **A23**

Besides "promotion and selection based on varied abilities," there   **Q9**
are three additional major characteristics of the democratic approach
to administration. Take a moment to recall them now and then circle
the letters below corresponding to the key words representative of
these three characteristics before turning to A10.

A. Pre-set procedures and rules.
B. Cooperation.
C. Decisions regarding goals, procedures, and rules are a concern of
   all employees.
D. Division of labor based on specialization.
E. Cooperative relationships and team play are encouraged.

THEORY INTO   Either of the two major theoretical approaches to administration dis-   **M7**
PRACTICE   cussed so far may work in agencies where the conditions are ideal
                    and include the following:[10]

1. Moderate changes taking place in services needed.
2. Small size.
3. Little diversity of specialized knowledge needed by executives and
   staff.
4. Executives with a high degree of managerial skill and forceful personalities.

However, in actual practice, few, if any, of these conditions prevail.
Communities are constantly changing, thus requiring the need for
more and different types of services. Agencies must expand to meet
these needs, and personnel with more specialized knowledge are
required. The executive must be constantly aware of the complex and
shifting needs of his staff members, whose growth is as important as
the growth of the agency's clients. The executive must be able to
consider the opinions of other executives, staff members, and members of the community at large, and he must rely on their expertise,
especially in areas where his experience is lacking.

Therefore, a purely bureaucratic or a purely democratic approach
to administration are the two ideal types, but, in actual practice, elements of both approaches are found.

Continue with Q10

There are four conditions that must prevail so a purely bureau-   **Q10**
cratic or a purely democratic form of administration can exist in an
agency. Circle the letters corresponding to these conditions listed
below and then check your answer by turning to A18.

A. Constant changes in services.
B. Great diversity of specialized knowledge needed by executives and
   staff.

[10] Morgan, *Improving Your Creativity*, p. 150.

C. Small size.

D. Moderate changes in services.

E. Large size.

F. Executives with a high degree of managerial skill.

G. Little diversity of specialized knowledge needed by executives and staff.

Q10
cont.

In actual practice, an agency managed along the lines of either a purely bureaucratic or a purely democratic approach to administration is the norm.

Q11

A. Yes A20

B. No A24

Blending of Two Major Approaches

In actual practice what usually occurs is a blending of both theoretical approaches resulting in current administrative practices.[11] However, in the administration of human service agencies, where the growth and well-being of all participants should be a central controlling consideration, the approach employed by the agency should incorporate more _____ than _____ characteristics. (In order of appearance.)

Q12

A. Democratic; bureaucratic A22

B. Bureaucratic; democratic A25

The agency executive must, of course, have an administrative approach or philosophy that is consistent with forwarding the work of the agency and allowing for the growth and well-being of the entire staff.

M8

Victor Thompson reminds us that we live in an age of specialization when cooperation has become a highly needed and valuable ingredient without which all efforts at coordination will fail. Specifically, he says, "Co-operation implies an attitude toward co-ordination, which is the formalized regulation of interdependence. It is an attitude of agreement to the system of co-ordination, of willingness to be co-ordinated."[12]

The ability of the executive to achieve a cooperative attitude among those essential to the enterprise makes cooperation a key factor if the executive is to work effectively with staff, committees, legislative bodies, boards of directors, and community groups.

Continue with Q13

The ability to achieve a _____ attitude among groups with whom the executive works is a key factor.

Q13

A. Competitive A27

B. Coordinative A29

C. Cooperative A2

[11] For a fuller discussion of modern approaches to administration, see: James D. Thompson, *Organizations in Action* (New York: McGraw-Hill, 1967); Harleigh B. Trecker, *Social Work Administration*; and Victor A. Thompson, *Modern Organization* (New York: Knopf, 1961).

[12] Thompson, *Modern Organization*, pp. 179–180.

In all agencies, work groups are formed to work toward the com- **Q14**
mon purpose of the agency. Circle the letters below corresponding
to examples of these work groups, and then turn to A26.

A. Staff members.
B. Committees.
C. Executive director.
D. Board of directors or legislative body.
E. Community groups.

MODIFIED ORGANIZATIONAL STRUCTURE

In order to allow for the required cooperative activity in which the **M9**
specialized talents of various individuals and groups are brought together to achieve the agency's common purpose, it is necessary to
arrange these individuals and groups into a form of organization or
structure that will allow people and groups to be interconnected and
in communication with each other.

A modified organizational structure including a blend of bureaucratic and democratic characteristics with a strong democratic emphasis is often created in human service agencies to serve this function.
This structure includes the hierarchical or pyramidal chain of command used for establishing authority and defining the agency's official
position. However, this structure is modified through a tempering of
the authority of the executives by reason, by reality, and by the
acceptance of the interdependencies of individuals and work groups.[13]

Continue with Q15

A modified agency structure, including a blend of bureaucratic and **Q15**
democratic characteristics with a strong democratic emphasis, is required to foster cooperative efforts. Which of the following does such
a structure include?

A. A hierarchical chain of command *A28*
B. A tempering of executive authority by reason, reality, and the ac-
   ceptance of the interdependence of work groups *A30*
C. Both of the above *A7*

The sound agency administrative approach, which often evolves **M10**
in actual practice, includes a blend of democratic and bureaucratic
characteristics with a strong democratic emphasis.

[13] For a detailed discussion of the possibilities of modified structures see,
Dorothy Smith, "The Mental Hospital as a First Line Organization," *Administrative Science Quarterly* (December, 1965): 381–399.

You should have circled B, C, and E. If you did, then continue with **A1**
M4. If not, return for a review to M3.

Excellent! A key factor in the administrative approach or philosophy **A2**
of the competent executive is the ability to achieve a cooperative atti-
tude among those essential to the effective running of the agency.

Continue with Q14

You should have circled A, B, D, E, and F. Concerning answer C, **A3**
selection of the necessary technologies should not be avoided by
human service administrators. Technological advances need not be
dehumanizing—witness the typewriter!

Continue with M2

One of the major theoretical approaches to administration is the **A4**
bureaucratic. However, adhocracy is only emerging as a significant
approach for the future.
Return to M4 for a review, then choose the correct answer to Q4.

You should have underlined: **A5**

1. are *the major input and output.*
2. with *considerable freedom.*
3. high *proportion of nonroutine events.*

Continue with M3

A division of labor based on specialization is one of the elements of a **A6**
bureaucratic form of administration, but it is not the key feature.
Return to M5 and review the material presented there before select-
ing the correct answer to Q5.

You are correct! A modified agency structure, which is the norm **A7**
at present, is composed of a hierarchical or pyramidal chain of com-
mand with executive authority being tempered by reason, reality,
and acceptance of the interdependencies of individuals and work
groups. Well done.

Continue with M10

Yes, both the bureaucratic and the democratic approach to admin- **A8**
istration have been the dominant approaches. New approaches are,
however, emerging, along with societal changes.

Continue with M5

No, close personal relations is not one of the elements of a bureauc- **A9**
racy. The nature of a bureaucracy creates a climate of impersonality.
Return to M5, and review the material presented there before
answering Q6 correctly.

Did you circle letters B, C, and E? Good for you! If you had any **A10**
trouble with this question return to M6, if not, continue with M7.

Right you are! The key feature of a bureaucracy is a pyramidal chain of command.   **A11**

Continue with Q6

If you have chosen this answer you need a review. Promotion and selection based on varied abilities of an individual is not one of the elements of a bureaucratic form of administration. Such selection and promotion is based on technical competence.   **A12**
Return to M5 for a review and then answer Q6 correctly.

Close personal relationships is one of the features of the democratic approach to administration, but it is not the key feature. Return to M6 for a brief review, then answer Q7 correctly.   **A13**

This is rarely the case. In a bureaucracy, human relations tend to be impersonal due to the organizational structure.   **A14**
Return to M5 and review the material presented there before correctly answering Q5.

This is the correct answer. One of the elements of a bureaucratic form of administration is a division of labor based on specialization.   **A15**
Can you name the other three major elements of the bureaucratic approach to administration? If not, you need a review, so return to M5 before continuing with M6. If you have no trouble recalling the three elements, continue with M6.

This is correct. Employee participation and sharing is the key feature of the democratic approach to administration.   **A16**

Continue with Q8

Sorry. Impersonality in human relations is a component more often present in bureaucratic administration but hopefully not in democratic administration.   **A17**
Return to M6 for a review before responding correctly to Q8.

You should have circled letters C, D, F, and G. In other words, the ideal conditions that must prevail so an agency may be governed by a purely bureaucratic or a purely democratic approach to administration include: **A18**

1. Moderate change.
2. Small size.
3. Little diversity of specialized knowledge.
4. Forceful executives with a high degree of managerial skill.

If you need a review, return to item M7. If not, continue with Q11.

A chain of command structured along the lines of a pyramid is the key element of the bureaucratic administrative approach, not the democratic approach. Return to M6 for a review, then answer Q7 correctly.   **A19**

You have stated that, in actual practice, it is normal for an agency to be managed along the lines of a purely bureaucratic or a purely democratic approach to administration, you have missed the point here. Return to M7 for a review and then answer Q11 correctly.   **A20**

This is absolutely correct. In a democratic agency employee selections and promotions are based mainly on varied abilities and experiences instead of on specialized knowledge alone as in bureaucratic organizations.   **A21**

Continue with Q9

Yes, the human service agency executives should attempt to incorporate more democratic than bureaucratic characteristics in the management of the agency since humanistic assumptions should be at the foundation of all human service agencies.   **A22**

Continue with M8

This answer is incorrect. Work assignments based mainly on specialization is an aspect of a bureaucratic not a democratic form of administration.   **A23**

Return to M6 for a review

This is correct. In real life, few, if any agencies are managed according to a purely bureaucratic or a purely democratic approach to administration.   **A24**

Continue with Q12

No, human service agencies are obliged by their very nature to be more humanistic than other organizations. Therefore, the administrative approach should be more in line with this underlying consideration.   **A25**
Return to Q12 and select the correct answer.

The correct answers are A, B, D, and E. Work groups include staff, board of directors or a legislative body, committees, community groups, and the like.   **A26**

Continue with M9

Although competition is a fact of life in business and industry, it would only inhibit attainment of goals in a human service agency.   **A27**
Return to M8 for a brief review before answering Q13 correctly.

This is correct so far as it goes, but it does not go far enough! In order to bring about cooperative effort among employees and work groups in an agency, the hierarchical chain of command must be tempered by reason, reality, and interdependencies.   **A28**
Return to Q15 and select the correct answer.

Coordination of activities is a very important aspect of administration but will not occur without cooperation among workers.   **A29**
Return to Q13 and select the correct answer.

This is a very important aspect of the modified agency structure   **A30**
if cooperative effort is to be achieved. However, it is only a part of
the structure.
    Return to M9 for a review and then answer Q15 correctly.

UNIT I
ADMINISTRATION

LESSON 2
Executive Administrative Functions

This lesson will deal with the second specific objective presented below. Once you have learned the enabling objectives you should have no trouble accomplishing the second specific objective.

Specific Objective

Given the name of one of the eight major executive functions, you will be able to describe the function and explain how the executive could most effectively fulfill the executive function cited.

Enabling Objective 1
You will be able to name the eight administrative functions that the executive should master.

Enabling Objective 2
Given a description of an activity involved in one of the eight major executive functions, you will identify the function.

Enabling Objective 3
Given the name of one of the eight major executive functions, you will be able to describe the function.

Enabling Objective 4
Given a description of one of the methods used by an executive to effectively fulfill one of the eight major executive functions, you will be able to identify the function.

Enabling Objective 5
Given the name of one of the eight executive functions, you will briefly describe a method by which the executive could fulfill the function.

Continue with M1

EXECUTIVE ADMINISTRATIVE FUNCTIONS

As you learned in the first lesson, administration refers to the process of setting agency objectives and policies, creating and maintaining an organization, making plans, carrying them out, and evaluating the results. In order to accomplish these activities, the executive must be competent in the eight major skills that are related to those skills mentioned in the definition of administration. **M1**

In future lessons you will be given the opportunity of learning to develop a beginning competency in all eight of these skills. However, it will be helpful for you to first learn what the skills are and the process by which they may be effectively performed in an agency setting.

The first step will be for you to learn the significance of the acronym POSDCORBE.[1] The letters refer to each of the eight functional activities that must be performed by the executive, especially the chief executive or the executive director, of an agency or program. These activities include:

PLANNING
ORGANIZING
STAFFING
DIRECTING
COORDINATING
REPORTING
BUDGETING
EVALUATING

Continue with Q1

List below the eight executive functions that are represented by the letters in the acronym POSDCORBE and then turn to A3. **Q1**

A.
B.
C.
D.
E.
F.
G.
H.

First, the eight executive functions will be described; then a brief description of the method(s) by which they may be carried out by the executive will be presented. Planning includes the following activities: **M2**

[1] This acronym, not including the word *evaluating*, is further described in an article by Luther Gulick entitled "Notes on the Theory of Organization," in Luther Gulick and L. Urwick, *Papers on the Science of Administration* (New York: Institute of Public Administration, 1937), pp. 3–45.

1. Determining the purposes, aims, and objectives of the agency.
2. Stating the tasks or activities that must be performed in order to accomplish the purposes, aims, and objectives.
3. Describing the methods to be used in performing the tasks.[2]

M2 cont.

Continue with Q2

Are you ready for this one? Which of the following activities are involved in planning?

Q2

A. Stating the tasks that must be done to accomplish the agency's purposes *A1*
B. Determining the agency's purposes *A4*
C. Describing the methods to be used to perform the tasks . . *A6*
D. All of the above *A9*

The second executive function is organizing. This refers to the establishment of the formal structure of authority through which work subdivisions are arranged, defined, and coordinated so as to accomplish agency purposes, aims, or objectives.[3]

M3

Continue with Q3

The next executive function, staffing, includes the entire personnel function and has three major aspects:[4]

M4

1. Hiring and firing the staff members.
2. Training the staff members.
3. Maintaining favorable work conditions.

Continue with Q4

Organizing refers to:

Q3

A. Establishing agency purposes and policies *A2*
B. Establishing a formal structure of authority *A5*
C. Establishing methods for accomplishing agency purposes . *A7*

Circle the letters below that correspond to those aspects of the staffing function for which the executive director is responsible.

Q4

A. Planning.
B. Hiring.
C. Establishing a structure.
D. Training.
E. Firing.
F. Delegating.
G. Maintaining favorable working conditions.

Turn to A8 to see how well you did.

The fourth letter in the acronym POSDCORBE stands for what function? Write the answer on page 16 and then turn to M5.

Q5

[2] Ibid., p. 13.
[3] Ibid.
[4] Ibid.

The fourth executive function is directing or serving as the leader of **M5** the agency. In order to serve in the capacity of leader, an executive must continuously make decisions and carry out the tasks necessitated by these decisions either by himself or by delegating them to subordinates.[5]

In addition, the executive must learn to foster individual and collective creativity within the agency.[6]

Continue with Q6

The fifth executive function is coordinating. Coordinating is the **M6** all-important function of interrelating the various parts of the work of an agency in order to reduce or eliminate inter- and intradepartmental friction, and thereby create an efficient organization.[7]

Is the above similar to your conception? If so, move on to Q7. If not, take a few moments to reread the above and rethink your conception; then turn to Q7.

In order to fulfill his directing function, the executive must serve **Q6** as the leader of the agency. In order to competently direct and lead an agency, which of the activities listed below must the executive perform? Circle the letters corresponding to those activities that apply. To check your answers, turn to A10.

A. Make competent decisions based on facts.
B. Carry out all tasks by himself.
C. Delegate all tasks to subordinates.
D. Be able to distinguish between those tasks he must carry out himself and those he can best delegate.
E. Foster individual creativity in the agency.
F. Foster collective creativity (synergism) in the agency.

It is time for a brief review. Fill in the spaces below and then turn **Q7** to A11 to check your answers.

The acronym representing the eight major executive functions is

_____.

The function that refers to the establishment of the formal structure of authority is called _____.

_____ is hiring and training of agency personnel.

The executive must function as the leader of an agency in order to fulfill the _____ function.

When the executive decides he will be unable to carry out a task himself, or when it would be more efficient or effective if accomplished by others, _____ it to one of his subordinates would be required.

---

[5] Ibid.

[6] See John S. Morgan, *Improving Your Creativity on the Job* (New York: American Management Association, 1968).

[7] Gulick and Urwick, *Papers on the Science of Administration*, p. 13.

Determining the purposes of an agency is one aspect of the _____ _____ function.

Inter- and intradepartmental friction can be ameliorated or eliminated by effective _____ of an agency.

Q7 cont.

The sixth executive function is _____. (What does the R represent in POSDCORBE?)

If you wrote reporting, you were correct. In order to fulfill this function, the executive must inform all those individuals to whom he is responsible (funding agency representatives, board of directors or legislative body, entire staff, and so forth) about agency activities and progress.[8]

M7

Continue with Q8

The last two executive functions are budgeting and evaluating.

Budgeting, of course, refers to the planning and controlling of agency finances. There are three essential elements involved in budgeting. These elements include:[9]

M8

1. A sound organization plan.
2. Financial planning.
3. Control of financial operations.

Evaluating or appraising the performances of agency personnel, the programs of the agency, as well as the overall results in relation to the established purposes of the agency is the last major executive function.[10]

Continue with Q10

Which of the following executives is properly fulfilling his reporting function?

Q8

A. Art A. has informed his entire staff and his superiors of a new program to be established *A14*
B. In order to avoid problems with her superiors, Jane R. has begun a new program before discussing it with those she thinks will fight its creation *A16*

The last two executive functions are self-evident and need little explanation. However, performing them is no easy task.

What are the last two executive functions? Name them below and then continue with M8.

Q9

1.
2.

Circle below the letters corresponding to the major elements in agency budgeting. To check your answers, turn to A12.

Q10

A. Financial planning.
B. Fund raising.

[8] Ibid.
[9] Ray Johns, *Executive Responsibility* (New York: Association, 1966), pp. 119–120.
[10] Ibid., p. 108.

C. Controlling financial operations.
D. A sound organizational plan.
E. Assessing personnel performance.
F. Reducing costs.

Q10
cont.

List below the eight major executive functions and as you are
listing them take a moment to think of the activities involved in
performing each. Check your answers by turning to A13.

Q11

1. P
2. O
3. S
4. D
5. Co
6. R
7. B
8. E

**EIGHT MAJOR
ADMINISTRATIVE
FUNCTIONS
Planning**

Planning, as you may recall, is the first executive function mentioned
in this text. It includes determining agency purposes, stating the tasks
to be performed, and the methods used for performing these tasks.

M9

The purposes of human service agencies are initially described in
general terms, when the agency is established. In the case of public
agencies, the purposes are described in the authorizing legislation. In
private agencies, the purposes are described in the constitution or in
the bylaws and in the articles of incorporation or charter.[11]

Continue with Q12

However, the general descriptions of agency purposes are made
explicit as the work of the agency takes form.[12] As is evident, the
necessary methods for accomplishing the tasks must change along
with changing purposes.

M10

It is, therefore, imperative for the executive to keep abreast of the
emerging purposes and subpurposes as they become explicit and to
plan for the necessary tasks and related methods required for the
accomplishment of the emerging purposes.

Continue with Q14

Organizing

The second executive function, organizing, requires the establishment of the formal structure through which work subdivisions are
arranged, defined, and coordinated. When roles and responsibilities are
not kept clear, friction results among agency employees, leading to
an inefficient and ineffective agency. The structure of an agency is
usually described in general terms, in the provisions of the constitution and bylaws, or in the manual of operations.[13]

M11

---

[11] Ibid., p. 32.
[12] Ibid.
[13] Ibid.

In order to keep the structure strong and viable, the executive must make sure it is clearly understood by all employees and is revised to keep pace with changes in agency purposes and subsequent changes in the required tasks and methods for accomplishing the purposes.

M11 cont.

Continue with Q16

The purposes of a private agency are usually described in the

Q12

A. Authorizing legislation *A15*
B. Constitution or bylaws *A17*
C. Articles of incorporation or charter *A19*
D. B and C above *A22*
E. A, B, and C above *A24*

State below where the purposes of a public agency are described and then turn to A18 to check your answer.

Q13

Agency purposes are made explicit

Q14

A. When the agency is established *A21*
B. As the work of the agency takes form *A23*

As agency purposes change and become explicit, so must the relevant tasks and methods for accomplishing these purposes change. What must the executive do in order to help assure that the changing purposes will be accomplished?

Q15

A. Be aware of emerging purposes and subpurposes *A20*
B. Plan for the necessary methods to accomplish tasks . . . *A25*
C. Plan for any new tasks that will be required for accomplishing the agency purposes *A27*
D. A and C above *A30*
E. A, B, and C above *A32*

An agency's formal structure of authority and responsibility is usually described, in general terms, in which of the following? Circle the letter(s) corresponding to the proper answer(s). Then check your answer by turning to A26.

Q16

A. Provisions of the agency's constitution and bylaws.
B. Agency's articles of incorporation.
C. Agency's manual of operations.
D. Authorizing legislation of the agency.

Circle below the results that often occur when the roles and responsibilities of agency employees are hazy due to a faulty organizational structure. To check your answer see A31.

Q17

A. Cooperation.
B. Friction between employees.
C. Clear lines of communication.

D. Efficiency.

E. Inefficiency.

F. An ineffective agency.

Q17
cont.

Bill B., the director of a welfare agency, always makes sure that the structure is clearly understood by all his employees. In doing so Bill is fulfilling his organizing responsibility as it relates to keeping the agency structure strong and viable.

Q18

A. Yes A28

B. No A33

There are four methods by which the executive may strengthen an agency's structure and keep it up to date:[14]

M12

1. Setting up and keeping current an organizational chart that defines the "work units" (branches, divisions, and/or departments) and indicates the lines of responsibility and authority between such work units.
2. Writing guidelines to agency committees and staff members defining responsibilities more explicitly.
3. Keeping the respective roles of all associate executives clear.
4. Clearly stating the relationships and responsibilities of the chief executive officer (executive director) and, in the case of private agencies, the chairman of the board of directors; and seeking restatements and revisions as needed.

Continue with Q19

Creating and keeping current an organizational chart to define work units and indicate lines of responsibility and authority between such units is one method of strengthening an agency's structure and keeping it up-to-date. In the space below, cite other methods which, if employed by an executive, will help keep an agency efficient and effective and strengthen its structure. To check your answer see A29.

Q19

[14] The core of these ideas are developed by Ray Johns in his book *Executive Responsibility*, p. 32.

Staffing

Staffing consists of three activities, as you previously learned. List **Q20**
these activities, then check your answer by reading M13.

1.

2.

3.

The three activities included in staffing are hiring and firing, train- **M13**
ing the staff members, and maintaining favorable conditions of work.
First we shall consider the hiring and firing responsibilities of the
executive and then focus on the training and maintaining aspects of
staffing.

The board of directors of a private agency, or the federal or state
authorities (legislative body and governor) in the case of a public
agency, select and hire the executive director. The board, governor, or
president then delegates the responsibility of hiring the associate executives and the regular staff members to the executive director.

Concerning the firing policy of agencies, it is difficult to state just
how any agency fulfills this responsibility. In most cases, the board
or legislative body retains the power to fire the executive director and
delegates firing responsibilities of all other staff members to the executive director.

Continue with Q21

The responsibility for hiring and firing all agency staff members, **Q21**
including associate executives, is delegated to the _____
_____ by the _____.
(In order of appearance)

A. Executive director; board of directors or state or federal authorities *A34*
B. Personnel director; executive director *A36*
C. Personnel director; board of directors or state or federal authorities *A38*

The competent executive director will attempt to select only com- **M14**
petent associate executives. However, since he realizes the importance
of competent associates and he is aware of his own fallibility, he may
obtain the approval of the board of directors or legislative body on
each selection.

Concerning the hiring of regular staff members, the executive director often delegates this responsibility to a subordinate executive, such
as the personnel director or the assistant director, and requires that
the personnel director obtain his approval only when selecting supervisory level personnel.

In addition to hiring employees, the executive director is responsible
for their training and for maintaining favorable working conditions.
These two tasks are usually delegated to the personnel director or the
assistant director, who may, in turn, delegate these tasks to one or
more of his subordinates, caseworkers, personnel workers, or training
supervisors.

Continue with Q22

In most agencies, the actual task of training staff members and maintaining favorable working conditions is ultimately left to which of the following persons?

Q22

A. Executive director A35
B. Personnel director A37
C. Caseworkers, personnel department, or training supervisors . A39

No matter who ends up with the actual task of training staff members, the best method for carrying out this task is through the establishment of effective training programs.

M15

The best method for maintaining favorable working conditions is to keep the lines of communication open among all members of the agency so that interpersonal friction can be ameliorated or eliminated before it causes a breakdown in the delivery of services. This communication should be two-way—from top executives to staff members and from staff to top executives.

Continue with Q23

An effective method for training staff members is to _____ _____ and an effective method to help maintain favorable conditions of work in an agency is to _____.
(In order of appearance)

Q23

A. Keep the lines of communication open; establish effective training programs A40
B. Establish effective training programs; keep the lines of communication open A44

Directing

The executive director and his associate executives must be leaders in order to effectively direct the agency by demonstrating their ability to:

M16

1. Make reasonable decisions after considering all the relevant facts at hand.
2. Demonstrate an active interest in and commitment to fulfilling the purposes of the agency.
3. Give other employees credit for their contributions and help raise their status in the agency.
4. Delegate responsibility and authority effectively, which includes how, when, and to whom delegations should be made. Delegating responsibility without the requisite authority needed to fulfill the responsibility is the sign of an irresponsible executive.
5. Foster individual and collective creativity.

Continue with Q24

Since the major direction in an agency must be provided by the executives, they must become leaders. From the descriptions of abilities listed below, circle the letters corresponding to those the executive must be able to demonstrate in order to provide leadership to an agency. After you have completed this task, turn to A42.

Q24

A. Effectively delegate responsibility and authority.   Q24
B. Point out subordinates' shortcomings in an aggressive manner.   cont.
C. Foster creativity.
D. Give credit to deserving employees and help raise their status in the agency.
E. Always subordinate individual interests to group interests.
F. Base decisions on facts.
G. Make decisions based on personal prejudices.
H. Demonstrate a commitment to fulfilling agency purposes.

Before going on to the method by which coordination may be   Q25
achieved by an executive, take a few moments to review in your mind
the methods already described for the first four executive functions.
Take them one at a time. To check your answer, see A45.

First—Planning
Second—Organizing
Third—Staffing
Fourth—Directing

Coordinating   State below, in your own words, what is meant by the coordinating   Q26
function. If you are satisfied with your statement, continue with M17.

Coordinating is the all-important function of interrelating the various   M17
parts of the work of an agency.
Once again effective channels of communication among the various
staff members (executives and regular staff) and among the various
departments within the agency must be created and maintained in an
agency if the executive is to fulfill his coordinating function.[15]
The method most widely used to help create and maintain effective
channels of communication thereby effecting coordination, is the creation and utilization of committees.

Continue with Q27

[15] Ibid., p. 33. See also: Herbert A. Simon, *Administrative Behavior*, 2d ed.
(New York: Free Press, 1965); Harleigh M. Trecker, *Social Work Administration, Principles and Practices* (New York: Association, 1971), especially the
discussions on communications and coordination.

If the executive is to fulfill his coordinating function, he must set up   Q27
and maintain

A. Effective   services *A41*
B. Effective channels of communication *A43*
C. Effective personal relations with the community *A46*

The method most widely used by the executive to help facilitate   Q28
coordination within an agency is the creation and utilization of
—————————————. Fill in the blank and then turn to A49.

Committees[16]

Committees are created by and responsible to some authoritative in-   M18
dividual or group of individuals. The executive director of an agency
often creates a committee to solve a specific problem or to work on a
specific activity requiring the input of different individuals and time
for its solution. The purpose of the committee should always be clearly
defined in writing.[17] Similarly, the board of directors of a private
agency makes extensive use of committees. There is little board activity that does not depend upon the work of committees.

There are two types of committees, standing and special. Special
committees are short term and often called ad-hoc committees (meaning, for this particular purpose). Standing committees deal with problems of activities of a continuous nature such as program, personnel,
finance, or property. Special committees are appointed to adjust or
study an immediate problem situation or an occasional activity that can
be accomplished in a short period of time.[18]

Continue with Q29

The method you would use to deal with long-range personnel prob-   Q29
lems is the (standing/special) committee. Underline the proper word
in the parens and then turn to A47.

Reporting

In order to fulfill his function of reporting, the executive must keep   M19
the agency staff, the board of directors or the legislative body, the
local community, and the funding agency informed about what is
occurring within his agency. The only way the executive is able to
inform these groups is to keep himself/herself and the associate
executives informed of agency progress.[19]

There are three major activities that should be carried out in order

[16] For further information concerning committee usage see: Audrey Trecker
and Harleigh Trecker, *Committee Common Sense* (New York: Whiteside,
1954), pp. 69–155; William Tuck, *Step by Step in Better Board and Committee
Work* (New York: Association, 1962); Roy Sorenson, *The Art of Board Membership* (New York: Association, 1950).

[17] Committee meetings, however, can be great time wasters, especially if they
are inadequately directed, poorly staffed, and with unclear direction. See
Peter F. Drucker's succinct remarks in, *The Effective Executive* (New York:
Harper & Row, 1966), pp. 44–45.

[18] Tuck, *Better Board and Committee Work*, pp. 67–70.

[19] See also materials usually found under the heading Communications; For
example, Trecker, *Social Work Administration*, pp. 131–136.

to keep the executive director and the associate executives up-to-date on agency activities. These include:

M19 cont.

1. Record keeping.
2. Regular inspections.
3. Research.

Continue with Q30

The executive director and his associates must keep up-to-date on agency activities so that he is able to report responsibly to the staff, the board of directors or legislative body, community groups, and so forth. Circle the letters corresponding to the activities listed below that should be performed to assist the director in fulfilling the reporting function.

Q30

A. Maintain effective channels of communication.
B. Keep records.
C. Conduct regular inspections.
D. Improve working conditions.
E. Create committees.
F. Perform research.

Check your answer by turning to A50

Record keeping for assisting in the reporting function should include records of all the agency activities, including the activities of agency committees as well as case histories of clients and personnel records. These records will help reveal the progress of staff members in delivering services to clients.

M20

Regular inspections of the agency by the executive director and/or the associate executives will help the executive obtain an over-all picture of how the agency is functioning and help reveal needed areas for improvement. This over-all picture is an important aspect of the reports that the executive director must deliver to all superiors.

Research should be carried out within the agency to help reveal:

1. How well the agency's services are being performed.
2. Whether or not current services are necessary.
3. Whether or not new services are needed.
4. Methods for delivering services more effectively.

The results of research are also a vital part of the executive director's reports to superiors.

Continue with Q31

This activity helps the executive director obtain an over-all picture of how the agency is functioning.

Q31

A. Regular inspections *A48*
B. Research *A51*
C. Record keeping *A54*

Circle the letters corresponding to the purposes listed below that may be fulfilled by research in an agency. To check your answer turn to A55.

Q32

A. Reveal the need for new services.
B. Establish whether or not current services are necessary.
C. Establishing new programs.
D. Discovering methods for delivering services more effectively.
E. Discovering how well present services are being performed.

Q32 cont.

Budgeting

As you learned earlier, budgeting is composed of three essential elements, a sound organizational plan, financial planning, and _____ _____. Fill in the final element, then check your answer by turning to M21.

Q33

Sound financial administration (budgeting) is composed of the following elements:

M21

1. A sound organizational plan.
2. Financial planning.
3. Control of financial operations.

Let's take these elements one at a time and see how the executive may best fulfill his budgeting function.

First, the executive director must make sure that the organizational structure, discussed in an earlier section, is sound from a budgetary standpoint. This may be accomplished if the structure clearly defines the basis of authority and responsibility for authorizing and making expenditures in all agency departments.[20]

Continue with Q34

The major responsibilities for the last two elements of budgeting— financial planning and accounting (control)—are usually delegated by the executive director to an associate director (here to be referred to as the finance director).

M22

Financial planning, which includes planning for current operations as well as for long-term goals, should be based on a budget policy.[21]

A budget policy includes the following major elements:

1. Wage and salary schedules.
2. Methods of securing income.
3. Methods for controlling expenditures.

Continue with Q35

An agency's organizational structure is sound from a budgetary standpoint if the structure:

Q34

A. Is clearly understood by all agency employees A52
B. Clearly defines the methods for obtaining agency funds . . A57
C. Clearly defines the basis of responsibility and authority for making all agency expenditures A59

[20] Johns, *Executive Responsibility*, p. 119.
[21] Ibid., p. 120.

Financial planning should be based on budget policy. Circle the letters corresponding to the components of the budget policy listed below. Check your answer by turning to A53. **Q35**

A. Methods for controlling expenditures.
B. Employee work schedules.
C. Methods of securing income.
D. Wage and salary schedules.
E. A sound agency structure.

It is, therefore, the responsibility of the executive director, or a delegated associate, to make sound financial plans based on the budget policy and the needs of the agency as described in the budget. **M23**

Lastly, the executive director or the finance director has the over-all responsibility for controlling the agency's financial operations through financial records (accounting methods).

Continue with Q36

There are three essential elements involved in budgeting, as well as different methods for fulfilling each of these elements. Choose the answer below that correctly matches the elements with the respective methods for accomplishing them. **Q36**

A. A sound organization plan.

1. Budget policy used as a guide in developing a budget.

B. Financial planning.

2. Accurate financial records (accounts).

C. Control of financial operations.

3. A structure that clearly defines the basis of authority and responsibility for authorizing and making expenditures.

A. A1, B2, C3 . . . . *A56*
B. A3, B1, C2 . . . . *A58*
C. A2, B3, C1 . . . . *A60*

Evaluating[22]

Evaluating entails the appraisal of over-all results in relation to the established purposes of the agency. In order to evaluate the accomplishment of agency purposes or objectives, the executive may apply the following two measures:[23] **M24**

1. An effectiveness measure: an assessment of the degree to which agency services have been accomplished in relation to the need for such services.
2. An efficiency measure: an assessment of the degree to which agency services have been accomplished in relation to the available resources.

In order to help the executive effectively fulfill the evaluation function, attempts should be made to foster a climate throughout the

[22] For further consideration of the problems of evaluation see, Trecker, *Social Work Administration*, pp. 167–184.
[23] Johns, *Executive Responsibility*, p. 116.

agency in which the employees feel free to make evaluations and suggestions concerning any agency function or program.   **M24 cont.**

Continue with Q37

An assessment of the degree to which agency services have been accomplished in relation to the available resources is an: **Q37**

A. Effectiveness measure *A61*
B. Efficiency measure *A64*

Explain below what an effectiveness measure assesses and then turn to A62.   **Q38**

Which of the following executive behaviors would tend to foster the fulfillment of the evaluating function? Circle the letter(s) corresponding to those that apply and then turn to A63.   **Q39**

A. Rejection of suggestions.
B. Warm reception of comments.
C. Consideration of criticisms.
D. Hostility.
E. Need for acceptance of own ideas without discussion.
F. Encourage discussion across as well as up and down the organizational structure.
G. Good listener.
H. Requires acceptance of decisions with little or no discussion by those involved.

You have now completed this lesson. Since it was a long lesson designed to briefly cover all the eight executive functions, you may need a review of these functions. If so, you should consult the frames listed below beside each of the functions. In these frames are the descriptions as well as the methods for accomplishing each function. Once you have done this, go on to the end of this unit and answer the review questions. Also, be sure to check out the summary and suggested readings at the end of this unit.   **M25**

Function	Description and Methods
Planning	M9 and M10
Organizing	M11 and M12
Staffing	M13 and M15
Directing	M16
Coordinating	M17
Reporting	M19 and M20
Budgeting	M21 and M22
Evaluating	M24

SUMMARY

We have described administration as a method that involves a set of activities and relationships with and between people working toward common objectives. Formal, informal and ad hoc approaches to administration were indicated and discussed.

We also discussed administration as a process involving the setting of objectives and policies, creating and maintaining an organization, making plans, implementing them into action, and evaluating results. We used the acronym POSDCORBE to indicate the eight functional activities: planning, organizing, staffing, directing, coordinating, reporting, budgeting, and evaluating.

SUGGESTIONS FOR
FURTHER STUDY

The materials presented in this unit are based on traditional principles of administration. Much modern management theory has expanded these principles and represents more advanced concepts beyond the scope of this introductory text. For example, the planning function has been refined through the technique of management by objectives (MBO), and management by objectives and results (MOR), and in planning, programming, and budgeting systems (PPBS).

New management theory is concerned with how groups affect the formal and informal structure of an organization. The behavioral science approach to groups, leadership, and group dynamics has its historical roots in the now famous Hawthorne studies. The management implications of the human relations approach to administration require study in terms of such organizational restructuring concepts as project structures and free form and matrix designs. These concepts also involve the basic functions of planning, organizing, and staffing.

Administrators certainly have to face a future filled with uncertainty, change, and conflict. This ought to be accepted as a "given" by any modern administrator. New ideas and challenges will produce new methods. Job environment, job satisfaction, new theories of motivation and leadership will need to be studied and understood.

Human service administrators will want to become very familiar with the works of Rensis Likert, Peter Drucker, Chris Argyris, and Douglas McGregor, to name only a few of the creative writers in this area. Other authors are suggested in the following list of selected references.

SUGGESTIONS FOR
FURTHER READING

Argyris, Chris. *Organization and Innovation.* Homewood, Ill.: Irwin, 1965.

Ammer, Dean S. "What Businessmen Expect from the 1970's." *Harvard Business Review*, January–February 1971: 41–52.

Avots, Ivans. "Why Does Project Management Fail?" *California Management Review*, Fall 1969: 77–82.

Blake, Robert R., and Mouton, Jane S. "The Managerial Grid in Three Dimensions." *Training and Development Journal*, January 1967: 2–5.

Cleland, David I., and King, William R. *Systems Analysis and Project Management.* New York: McGraw-Hill, 1968.

Drucker, Peter F. "New Templates For Today's Organizations." *Harvard Business Review*, January–February 1974: 45–53.

Haire, Mason. *Modern Organization Theory*. New York: Wiley, 1959.

Kazmier, Leonard S. *Principles of Management: A Program for Self-Instruction*. New York: McGraw-Hill, 1969.

Likert, Rensis. *New Patterns of Management*. New York: McGraw-Hill 1961.

———. *The Human Organization*. New York: McGraw-Hill, 1967.

Luthans, Fred, and Hodgetts, Richard M. *Social Issues in Business*. New York: Macmillan, 1972.

Luthans, Fred. *Organizational Behavior: A Modern Behavioral Approach to Management*. New York: McGraw-Hill, 1973.

Maslow, Abraham H. *Eupsychian Management*. Homewood, Ill.: Irwin and Dorsey Press, 1965.

Morrisey, George L. *Management By Objectives and Results*. Reading, Mass.: Addison-Wesley, 1970.

Newman, William H. *Administrative Action: The Techniques of Organization and Management*. Englewood Cliffs, N.J.: Prentice-Hall, 1951.

Odiorne, George S. *Management by Objectives*. New York: Pitman, 1965.

Titmuss, Richard M. *Commitment to Welfare*. New York: Pantheon, 1968.

Wortman, Max S., Jr., and Luthans, Fred, eds. *Emerging Concepts in Management*. New York: Macmillan, 1969.

Wren, George R. "Can Business Benefit from New Organizational Patterns?" *Atlanta Economic Review* 21, no. 1 (January 1971): 14–17.

Young, Stanley, D. *Management: A Systems Analysis*. Glenview, Ill.: Scott, Foresman, 1966.

Directions: For the following questions, as well as all the rest of the questions presented at the end of each unit, circle the *LETTERS* corresponding to the answers of your choice. The correct answers are presented on the last page of each unit—check answers before proceeding to the next lesson.

1. Administration is a method concerned primarily with which of the following activities?

   A. Securing resources.
   B. Selecting and engineering necessary technologies (counseling, group work).
   C. Designing organizational structures and processes.
   D. A and C above.
   E. A, B, and C above.

2. Three distinctive features of social services agencies are

   A. Potentially contradictory goals; evaluating staff performances, and high proportion of nonroutine events.
   B. Expectations; minimum progress and rapid turnover.
   C. High caliber employees; longevity and age requirements.
   D. Evaluating staff performances; rapid turnover and potentially contradictory goals.

3. Agency goals are difficult to attain because

   A. Some agency goals are potentially contradictory.
   B. Distinctions between output goals for clients and agency maintenance goals are difficult to draw.
   C. Agency clients are both the major input and output of the agency.
   D. B and C above.
   E. A, B, and C above.

4. What are the two major theoretical administrative approaches prevalent today?

   A. Uniform and collective.
   B. Bureaucratic and democratic.
   C. Autocratic and facilitative.
   D. Bureaucratic and ad hoc.

5. The key feature of the bureaucratic approach to administration is

   A. Chain of command.
   B. Close personal relations.
   C. A division of labor based on specialization.
   D. Promotion and selection based on technical competence.

6. One of the components of the democratic approach to administration is

   A. Competitiveness.
   B. Promotion and selection based on varied abilities.
   C. Work assignments based on specialization.
   D. A chain of command.

7. Which policy is likely to be the key to successful administration for an agency executive?

   A. Authoritarian.
   B. Cooperation.
   C. Determination.
   D. Competitiveness.

8. Which of the following is (are) considered one of the work group(s) formed to work toward the common purpose of an agency?

   A. Board of directors.
   B. Community groups.
   C. Committees.
   D. A and C above.
   E. A, B, and C above.

9. In order to allow for the cooperative activity required to achieve an agency's purpose, a modified structure is necessary. Which of the following should such a structure include?

   A. A chain of command.
   B. A tempering of authority by the acceptance of interdependencies of individuals and work groups.
   C. A tempering of authority by reason and by reality.
   D. B and C above.
   E. A, B, and C above.

10. Which of the following is often created in social service agencies to allow for the necessary cooperation to achieve agency purposes?

    A. A blend of democratic and bureaucratic with emphasis on the bureaucratic.
    B. A blend of democratic and bureaucratic with emphasis on the democratic.
    C. A blend of democratic, bureaucratic, and autocratic.
    D. A blend of democratic, bureaucratic, and ad-hocratic.

11. Which of the following contains the proper executive functions referred to by the acronym POSDCORBE?

    A. Planning, organizing, staffing, directing, coordinating, operating, budgeting, evaluating.
    B. Planning, organizing, staffing, directing, coordinating, reporting, budgeting, evaluating.
    C. Planning, organizing, staffing, decision making, cooperating, reporting, budgeting, evaluating.
    D. Planning, organizing, staffing, directing, coordinating, research, budgeting, evaluating.

12. Which of the following activities is not involved in planning by the executive?

    A. Stating the tasks that must be done to accomplish the agency's purposes.
    B. Determining the agency's purposes.
    C. Establishing methods for accomplishing agency purposes.
    D. Establishing favorable working conditions.

13. Organizing refers to the executive function of

    A. Establishing agency purposes and policies.
    B. Establishing a formal structure of authority.
    C. Establishing methods for accomplishing agency purposes.
    D. Establishing favorable working conditions.

14. The element not considered one of the three essential involved in budgeting is

    A. A sound organizational plan.
    B. Sound statistical procedures.
    C. Financial planning.
    D. Control of financial operations.

15. The executive may strengthen an agency's structure and keep it up-to-date by

    A. Keeping an organizational chart.
    B. Written commissions.
    C. Keeping respective roles of associate executives clear and clearly stating and revising executive and staff relationships and responsibilities.
    D. A and C above.
    E. A, B, and C above.

16. Which of the following behaviors exemplifies leadership ability?

    A. Makes decisions based on facts.
    B. Delegates responsibility but not the necessary authority.
    C. Fosters creativity.
    D. A and C above.
    E. A, B, and C above.

17. Training and maintaining favorable work conditions are activities included in which executive function?

    A. Directing.
    B. Organizing.
    C. Staffing.
    D. Planning.

18. The board of directors of private agencies or the state or federal authorities of public agencies hire

    A. All the top executives of the agency.
    B. The executive director of the agency.
    C. All agency staff members.
    D. None of the above.

19. Associate executives of a public agency are usually selected and hired by the

    A. Board of directors.
    B. Legislative body.
    C. Executive director.
    D. Personnel director.
    E. None of the above.

20. The method most widely used for creating and maintaining effective channels of communication is

    A. Evaluation.
    B. A hierarchical chain of command.
    C. Creation and utilization of committees.
    D. Information dissemination.

21. The executive fulfills his reporting function by

    A. Keeping his staff informed.
    B. Keeping the board or legislative body informed.
    C. Keeping the local community informed.
    D. A and B above.
    E. A, B, and C above.

22. A budget policy includes

    A. Wage and salary schedules.
    B. Methods of securing income.
    C. Methods of controlling expenditures.
    D. A and B above.
    E. A, B, and C above.

23. The reporting function is facilitated through

    A. Regular inspections.
    B. Research.
    C. Record keeping.
    D. A and C above.
    E. A, B, and C above.

24. The measure used to assess the degree to which agency services have been accomplished in relation to the need for such services is referred to as a (an)

    A. Efficiency measure.
    B. Effectiveness measure.
    C. Estimated measure.
    D. Performance measure.

See the last page of this unit for the answers.

Yes, stating the tasks that must be performed to accomplish the agency's **A1**
purposes is one aspect of the planning function, but there are others.
   Return to M2 for a review before selecting the correct answer to Q2.

   Sorry, but you botched this one! You have said that organizing **A2**
refers to establishing agency purposes and policies. However, this is a
planning activity.
   Return to M3 and review the material presented there, then turn to
Q3 and select the correct answer.

   POSDCORBE stands for **A3**

Planning
Organizing
Staffing
Directing
Coordinating
Reporting
Budgeting
Evaluating

   How well did you do? You will now learn more about each of these
functions as you proceed through this program.

                                                   Continue with M2

   You are correct in saying that one of the activities involved in plan- **A4**
ning is the determination of the agency's purposes, but this is only
one aspect of this executive function.
   Return to item M2 for a review and then select the correct answer
to Q2.

   Well done! Organizing refers to the establishing of a formal struc- **A5**
ture of authority through which work subdivisions are arranged, de-
fined, and coordinated so as to accomplish agency purposes.

                                                   Continue with M4

   Determining and/or describing the methods to be used to perform **A6**
the necessary tasks is but one aspect of the planning function—there
are others. You did not look far enough for the correct answer.
   Return to M2 for a review and then choose the correct answer to
Q2.

   You'll receive no prize for this answer! You have said that estab- **A7**
lishing methods for accomplishing agency purposes is an organizing
activity, which demonstrates that you need a review.
   Return to M3 and learn what is meant by the function of organizing,
then turn to Q3 and select the correct answer.

   The staffing function includes: **A8**

B. Hiring.
D. Training.
E. Firing.
G. Maintaining favorable work conditions.

                                                   Continue with Q5

35

You've turned to the right answer. The planning function includes **A9**
determining agency purposes, stating the tasks to be performed, and describing the methods used to perform the tasks leading to the accomplishment of the agency's purposes.

Continue with M3

You should have circled letters A, D, E, and F. The executive should **A10**
become the leader of the agency by continuously making decisions based on facts and then by making sure the tasks necessitated by those decisions are carried out. The executive should be able to distinguish between those tasks that can best be accomplished and those that should be delegated.

Continue with M6

The correct answers to the questions in Q7 are as follows: **A11**

POSDCORBE—M1
Organizing—M3
Staffing—M4
Directing—M5
Delegating—M5
Planning—M2
Coordinating—M6

How well did you do? If you missed any of the above, return to the item(s) listed beside those you missed and review the material presented there and then continue with the material presented in frame M7.

The three essential elements of budgeting include: **A12**

A. Financial planning.
C. Control of financial operations.
D. Sound organizational plans.

Continue with Q11

The eight major executive functions are: **A13**

1. Planning—M2
2. Organizing—M3
3. Staffing—M4
4. Directing—M5
5. Coordinating—M6
6. Reporting—M7
7. Budgeting—M8
8. Evaluating—M8

If you missed any of the above functions or if you had trouble remembering the activities corresponding to any of them, make sure that you review the material presented in the items listed beside those you missed.
If you have satisfactorily completed the above, you may be a little tired. If so, this is a good spot to take a break before forging ahead to M9.

The executive is expected to inform all those groups and/or in-   **A14**
dividuals to whom he is responsible concerning the activities and
progress of the agency. This is the reporting function. Art has fulfilled
his responsibility in this case and you are correct in choosing this
answer.

Continue with Q9

No, the purposes of a public not a private agency are usually de-   **A15**
scribed in the authorizing legislation.
Return to M9 for a review before answering Q12 correctly.

Jane will only intensify, not avoid, problems by pursuing this course   **A16**
of action and she is certainly not fulfilling the reporting function by
neglecting to inform all those affected by the new agency activity.
Return to M7 for a review and then answer Q8 correctly.

Yes, the purposes of a private agency are usually described in the   **A17**
agency's constitution or bylaws, but these purposes are also found in
another agency document.
Return to M9 for a review before answering Q12 correctly.

If you said that the purposes of a public agency are usually de-   **A18**
scribed in the authorizing legislation, you are absolutely correct.

Continue with M10

Yes, the purposes of a private agency are usually described in the   **A19**
agency's articles of incorporation or charter, but these purposes are
also described in another agency document.
Return to Q12, and answer the question correctly.

It is necessary to be aware of emerging purposes and subpurposes   **A20**
if the executive is to help assure that they will be accomplished. How-
ever, he must do more than be aware of them.
Return to M10 for a brief review, then correctly answer Q15.

You have these confused. Initially, when the agency is established,   **A21**
agency purposes are described in general terms and are made explicit
later.
Return to Q14 and select the correct answer.

The purposes of a private agency are generally described in the   **A22**
constitution and bylaws and in the articles of incorporation or charter.
You have done well!

Continue with Q13

Right you are! The purposes of an agency become explicit as the   **A23**
work of the agency takes form and the input from the agency board,
executives, staff, clients, and local community has been considered.

Continue with Q15

No, this is only partially correct. The purposes of a private agency are not described in the authorizing legislation, although they are described in the other two documents.

Return to Q12 and select the correct answer.

A24

The executive must plan for the necessary methods for accomplishing tasks related to purposes, but this is only part of the responsibility related to carrying out the purposes of the agency especially as this relates to planning.

Return to M10 for a review, then correctly answer Q15.

A25

You should have circled letters A and C. An agency's formal structure of authority is usually described, in general terms, in the provisions of the agency's constitution and bylaws, or in the manual of operations.

Continue with Q17

A26

The executive must plan for any new tasks that will be required for accomplishing new purposes and subpurposes. However, there are other elements that must also be considered by the executive in planning for new purposes.

Return to M10 for a review, then correctly answer Q15.

A27

You have said that Bill's responsibility has been fulfilled if his employees understand agency structure, but you forgot that keeping the structure up-to-date and revising it if necessary is also important.

Return to M11 and reread the material presented there; then choose the correct answer to Q18.

A28

Beside maintaining an up-to-date organizational chart, the three methods, if employed by an executive, that will help keep an agency effective and strengthen its structure include:

A29

1. *Written guidelines to agency committees and staff members that explicate their responsibilities.*
2. *Clear statements of the relationships and responsibilities of the executive director and, in the case of a private agency, the chairman of the board of directors.*
3. *Clear statements of the roles of the associate executives.*

If you had any trouble stating any of the above methods, take a moment to review them before continuing with Q20.

Both awareness of emerging purposes and plans for those tasks required to accomplish those new purposes are required; but there is one further element you have missed if you chose this answer.

Return to Q15 and select the answer that includes that missing element.

A30

You should have circled letters B, E, and F. When roles and responsibilities are unclear, the resulting friction among agency employees will lead to an inefficient and ineffective agency.

Continue with Q18

A31

You have chosen the correct answer—well done. The executive should keep up-to-date on emerging agency purposes and subpurposes and plan for the new tasks required to fulfill these new purposes as well as the necessary methods to accomplish the new tasks.

A32

Continue with M11

This is correct. Bill's responsibility does not end with the assurance that the structure is understood by agency employees. The executive's role in keeping the agency's structure strong and viable is to make sure that it is clearly understood by all concerned employees and revised to keep pace with changing agency purposes, as well as subsequent changes in methods for accomplishing the purposes.

A33

Continue with M12

The board of directors or, in the case of a public agency, the state or federal authorities (legislative body), delegate to the executive director of the agency the responsibility for hiring and firing all staff members including associate executives. The executive director may then delegate the responsibility for hiring the regular staff members to the personnel director or, in small agencies, the assistant director. However, the director often retains the power to fire any employees. Since you have chosen the correct answer you may continue.

A34

Continue with M14

No, in most agencies the executive director delegates the responsibility of training staff members and maintaining favorable working conditions to one of the top executives, especially if there is a director of training.
Return to M14 and review the material presented there, then return to Q22 and answer it correctly.

A35

This is incorrect. The executive director may delegate the responsibility for hiring staff members to the personnel director or, in the case of a small agency, the assistant director. But the responsibility for hiring and firing the associate executive is not delegated.
Return to M13 for a brief review before correctly answering Q21.

A36

Although the personnel director is often delegated the responsibility for training staff and maintaining favorable working conditions, much of the responsibility for these tasks is delegated to a special staff assigned to perform these functions.
Go back to M14 for a review, then answer Q22 correctly.

A37

This answer is only partially correct. The board, or legislature in the case of a public agency, delegates all hiring and firing responsibilities to the executive director, who may in turn delegate part of this responsibility to the personnel director or assistant director.
Return for a review to M13 before answering Q21 correctly.

A38

Yes, the actual task of training staff members and maintaining favorable working conditions often rests with the caseworkers, personnel department, or others assigned these special functions. It must be

A39

remembered, however, that, as with all delegations, the personnel director is still responsible to the executive director, in turn, the executive director is responsible to his superiors such as a board of directors to accomplish the delegated task no matter who actually performs the task.

**A39
cont.**

Continue with M15

Sorry, you have them reversed! Return to M15 for a review before answering Q23 correctly.

A40

No, effective services are one of the results, not the cause, of effective coordination.
Return to M17 for a brief review, then answer Q27 correctly.

A41

The letters you should have circled include A, C, D, F, and H. If you were able to identify the proper abilities, continue with Q25. If you missed any of the five abilities, return to M16 for a brief review before answering Q24 correctly.

A42

Exactly! Maintaining effective channels of communication among the various staff members as well as among the various departments within an agency is necessary if the executive is to fulfill his coordinating function.

A43

Continue with Q28

We agree! An effective method for training staff members is to establish excellent training programs; a useful way to help maintain favorable working conditions is to keep two-way lines of communication among all agency employees.

A44

Continue now with M16

If you had trouble recalling the methods for any of the first four functions, review the material in the frames listed beside each function you missed and then continue with Q26.

A45

Planning—M9
Organizing—M11
Staffing—M13
Directing—M16

Although effective community relations is an important aspect in the effective implementation of agency services, it is not central to the executive's coordinating functions within the agency.
Return to M17 for a review, then correctly answer Q27.

A46

If you underlined standing you were absolutely correct. Standing committees deal with problems or activities of a continuous nature, including program, personnel, finance, and property, while special committees deal with immediate problems or an occasional activity, such as planning for a meeting or arranging for a banquet or for the arrival of a speaker.

A47

Continue with M19

Precisely! Regular inspections are performed to help the executive director obtain an over-all picture of how the agency is functioning. This is an important aspect of reporting to superiors.   **A48**

Continue with Q32

The most widely used method to facilitate coordination in an agency is the creation and utilization of committees.   **A49**
Continue with M18 for a brief description of the two major types of committees.

You should have circled letters B, C, and F. The three activities that should be performed to assist the executive in fulfilling the reporting function include: **A50**

1. Record keeping.
2. Regular inspections.
3. Research.

Continue with M20

No, research has many purposes but it does not necessarily reveal an over-all picture of agency functioning.   **A51**
Return to M20 for a brief review of the three major activities included in reporting and then answer Q31 correctly.

Although this is important, merely understanding the agency structure will not ensure that the structure is sound fom a budgetary standpoint.   **A52**
Return to M21 for a brief review and then answer Q34 correctly.

You should have circled letters A, C, and D. The three components of the budget policy include: **A53**

1. Wage and salary schedules.
2. Methods of securing income.
3. Methods of controlling expenditures.

Continue with M23

Sorry, but obtaining an over-all picture of agency functioning is not one of the objectives of record keeping.   **A54**
Return to M20 for a brief review before answering Q31 correctly.

You should have circled letters A, B, D, and E. Research plays a vital role in helping pinpoint needed improvements in agency services by revealing the effectiveness of and need for current services as well as the need for new services. The executive director must report the results of such research to superiors in a clear and readily understandable form.   **A55**

Continue with Q33

You have the budgeting elements and their methods of accomplishment confused.   **A56**
Return to M21 and review the lesson from that point on, then continue with Q36 and answer the question correctly.

No. Although the methods for obtaining agency funding are im-   **A57**
portant, they are not usually described in the structure of the agency.
Return to M21 for a brief review before answering Q34 correctly.

Excellent! You have correctly matched the three budgeting ele-   **A58**
ments with their respective methods of accomplishment.
Continue with M24 and learn about methods for performing the
last executive function, namely, evaluation.

This is the correct answer. An executive should first make sure that   **A59**
the agency structure clearly defines the basis of authority and respon-
sibility for authorizing and making expenditures in all departments of
the agency.

Continue with M22

You are off the mark if you chose this answer.   **A60**
Return to M21 and review the lesson from that point on, then con-
tinue with Q36 and answer the question correctly.

Sorry about that, but you need a review! An assessment of the   **A61**
degree to which agency services have been accomplished in relation to
the available resources is an efficiency measure and not an effective-
ness measure.
Return to M24 and review the material presented there before cor-
rectly answering Q37.

An effectiveness measure is an assessment of the degree to which   **A62**
agency services have been accomplished in relation to the need for
such services.

Continue with Q39

The executive should foster the establishment of a climate in which   **A63**
the employees feel free to comment on and make evaluations of any
agency program. If such a climate exists, the fulfillment of the evaluat-
ing function will be greatly facilitated. Therefore, the letters B, C, F,
and G should have been circled.

Continue with M25

Well done! An assessment of the degree to which agency services   **A64**
have been accomplished in relation to the available resources is an
efficiency measure.

Continue with Q38

**ANSWERS TO
REVIEW QUESTIONS**

The following are the correct responses to questions for Unit I.

Questions	Answers	Questions	Answers
1	E	14	B
2	A	15	E
3	E	16	D
4	B	17	C
5	A	18	B
6	B	19	C
7	B	20	C
8	B	21	E
9	E	22	E
10	B	23	E
11	B	24	B
12	D		
13	B		

If you answered 20 of these questions correctly, you have completed this unit.

If you answered less than 20 correctly, review this unit briefly before taking a break or before going on to Unit II.

UNIT II
COMMUNICATION

LESSON 1
The Essential Elements of Communication

Effective communication is an essential ingredient in the accomplishment of each of the eight major executive functions mentioned in the first unit. Therefore, we are elaborating on the subject of communication in this unit before continuing with a more detailed discussion of the executive functions.

UNIT II OBJECTIVE— COMMUNICATION

Following this unit, you will demonstrate, by your responses to a decision making situation, your ability to apply the principles of communication in maintaining effective communcation within an agency.

Specific Objective

Given a situation involving faulty executive communication, you will be able to point out the missing elements that are causing the faulty communication and explain how the communication could be improved.

Enabling Objective 1
You will be able to define, in your own words, what is meant by the concept "communication."

Enabling Objective 2
You will be able to name and describe the three major factors essential to effective communication in an agency.

Enabling Objective 3
You will be able to explain the meaning of noise and distortion and state the three sources of noise and distortion in communication.

Enabling Objective 4
Given the name of one of the three sources of distortion in communication, you will be able to cite three ways in which the source cited may contribute to distortion.

Continue with M1

THE MEANING OF COMMUNICATION

M1

The concept of communication has taken on a different meaning for different people. However, the most common misconception among many executives, although they are certainly not alone in this, is that they are communicating when they are actually only informing. The basic distinction here is that informing is but one form of communication and a form that is inherently faulty. Communication, to be effective, must be two-way. Any attempt at communication that does not allow for possible feedback may jeopardize the communication process. Both speaker and listener must be able to hear, understand, record, and feed back information if communication is to be effective.

For our purposes, the concepts developed by Bellows and others have relevance for human service agencies if restated as follows:

Communication is a two-way channel directed to all staff and/or board members for transmitting ideas, plans, commands, reports, and suggestions concerning all appropriate agency tasks, goals, and objectives which are to be met. Communication is, therefore, the vital link that unites executives, board members, employees and clients of an agency or a program, and establishes a liaison between the agency, the government representatives, and the concerned members of the community.[1]

Continue with Q1

Which of the following is the most accurate statement regarding effective agency communication? **Q1**

A. A channel for transmitting ideas, plans, reports, and so on, from executives to subordinates A2
B. A channel for transmitting ideas, plans, reports, and so on, from subordinates to executives A6
C. A two-way channel for transmitting ideas, plans, reports, and so on, among all agency personnel, board members, and others . . A8

Explain below one of the two major purposes served by effective communication in agencies, then check your answer by turning to A4. **Q2**

[1] See Roger Bellows, "Communication and Conformity," *Personnel Administration* 23 (September–October, 1960): 21–28, in which Bellows develops the concept of communication and refers to the work of John A. Strubin, and an article by E. Petersen and E. G. Plowman.

ESSENTIAL COMPONENTS OF COMMUNICATION

Communication is, therefore, a primary administrative tool. In order for it to be effective, communication must include not only the carefully planned sending of a message by a source or sender, but also the clear reception of that message by the receiver. Clear reception requires feedback or the ability of the receiver to ask the sender for clarification, if needed.

M2

Communication, then, is composed of three essential elements:[2]

1. The source or sender.
2. The message.
3. The receiver.

Continue with Q3

John C., the executive director of an agency, sends a memo to his assistant director, Jill R.

Q3

In the space below, identify the three major elements of this communication. Check your answers by turning to A1.

1. Jill R. is the _____.
2. John C. is the _____.
3. The memo is the _____.

Communication Barriers: Noise, Filtering, Interference, Distortion

The communication process may be altered or impeded by noise, filtering, or interference.[3] In the case of a spoken message, extraneous noise such as hammering, street noises, or loud music, may actually impede the process of communication. The filtering process may also lead to distortion. There is selective interpretation of the message due to the receiver's "experience filter" of prejudices, preconceptions, and snap judgments regarding message significance.[4] Interference may alter the message by creating confusion regarding what the sender is intending to transmit. The sender therefore needs to be aware of and to allow for interference and to adjust his message accordingly.[5]

M3

Specifically, the sender or source may also contribute to alteration or distortion of a message by failure in four areas:

1. Failure to carefully plan his communication with a specific purpose in mind.

[2] George deMare, *Communication for Leadership—A Guide for Executives* (New York: Ronald, 1968), p. 236, (The reader is referred to the deMare book for practical, down-to-earth illustrations of how to communicate at all levels. For the beginner, it will be exceedingly helpful; for the rest, it will be a refresher.) For further discussion of what is involved in listening and communicating, see: Larry L. Barker, *Listening Behavior* (Englewood Cliffs, N.J.: Prentice-Hall, 1971).

[3] For a complete development of the subject of communication barriers, see: de Mare, *Communication for Leadership*, pp. 231–236; Ernest G. Bormann et al., *Interpersonal Communication in the Modern Organization*, (Minneapolis: University of Minnesota Press, 1969), pp. 145–166; Ray Johns, *Executive Responsibility* (New York: Association, 1954), pp. 167–169; Gordon Wisemann and Larry L. Barker, *Speech/Interpersonal Communication*, 2d ed. (San Francisco: Chandler, 1974), pp. 39–40.

[4] Roger M. D'Aprix, *How's That Again?* (Homewood, Ill.: Dow Jones-Irwin, 1971), p. 11.

[5] Wisemann and Barker, *Speech/Interpersonal Communication*, p. 39.

2. Failure to remove egocentric material from the message.　　**M3**
3. Failure to communicate because of the overuse of technical jargon　**cont.**
   that has no meaning for the receiver. (The message has become
   more important than the understanding of it.)
4. Failure to allow for a plan for necessary feedback.

Continue with Q4

Circle the letters corresponding to the three elements of communica-　**Q4**
tion and cross out the term that impedes communication. Check your
answer by turning to A3.

A. Message.
B. Receiver.
C. Distortion, noise, interference.
D. Sender.

Circle the letters corresponding to the ways in which a sender may　**Q5**
contribute to alteration or distortion. Check your answer by turning
to A7.

A. Writes or orally delivers his communication with a vague purpose
   in mind.
B. Is receiver oriented.
C. Is message oriented.
D. Fails to plan his communication with a specific purpose in mind.
E. Allows for feedback whenever necessary.
F. Is source oriented (uses egocentric materials).

The second source of distortion is the message itself. The message　**M4**
may create distortion if it:

1. Is written or spoken in terms that are vague or confusing and may,
   therefore, be misunderstood by the receiver.
2. Includes contradictions.
3. Is sent to the wrong person or persons.
4. Is sent via an inappropriate medium.

Continue with Q6

The second source of distortion that can cause communication break-　**Q6**
down may be created by the _____ itself. Fill in
the blank and then answer the question below.
   Circle the letters corresponding to the ways in which this second
source of distortion can create communication barriers and check your
answer by turning to A5.

A. Is conveyed in clear terms.
B. Is sent to the wrong person(s).
C. Is sent at the proper time.
D. Is relayed by telephone but should have been delivered in person.
E. Includes contradictions.
F. Is phrased in professional terms and sent to a layman.

The third and final source of distortion, therefore, is the receiver, **M5**
who may create communication barriers if he:
1. Fails to listen to or disregards the message.
2. Fails to obtain clarification if necessary.
3. Has negative feelings toward the sender.

Continue with Q7

From the list below, circle the letters corresponding to the ways in **Q7**
which the receiver may create barriers to communication and then
check your answer by turning to A9.

A. Is ego oriented.
B. Dislikes the source.
C. Concentrates on other business while receiving the message.
D. Files the message in a wastebasket.
E. Is confused and asks for clarification.

ANSWERS

Jill R. *is the* receiver.   **A1**
John C. *is the* source *or* sender.
The memo is the message.

No, a channel of communication from executives to subordinates   **A2**
often creates large gaps in the transfer of meaning and/or intent. One
is not truly communicating, merely informing, when the communication is only one-way.
Return to M1 for a brief review, then answer Q1 correctly.

You should have circled letters A, B, and D and crossed out the   **A3**
term distortion *since this impedes the passage of the message from
sender to receiver.*

Continue with Q5

Communication is a vital link that serves two major purposes in an   **A4**
agency:

1. Unites executives, employees, and clients and board members.
2. Establishes a liaison between agencies, government, and the public.

Continue with M2

Did you write in the word message? The second source of com-   **A5**
munication distortion is the message itself. The letters you should have
circled are B, D, E, and F.

Continue with M5

No, a channel of communication from subordinates to executives is   **A6**
only half of an effective communication network. The executives are
not able to lead if their ideas, plans, commands, and the like are not
being received by their subordinates. Such a faulty network would
quickly paralyze the agency.
Return to M1 for a brief review, then answer Q1 correctly.

You should have circled letters A, C, D, and F. The sender may   **A7**
contribute to alteration or distortion when he:

1. Writes or orally delivers his communication with a vague purpose
   in mind.
2. Is message oriented.
3. Fails to plan his communication with a specific purpose in mind.
4. Is source oriented.

Continue with M4

Excellent! If it is to be effective, communication must be two-way   **A8**
among all agency personnel, board, and others. Possible distortions in
meaning are significantly reduced if communication is two-way, an
important element in getting messages across.

Continue with Q2

Letters B, C, and D should have been circled. The receiver may   A9
create distortion by:

1. Failing to listen to or to heed the message.
2. Failing to clarify misunderstandings and give and obtain the neces-
sary feedback.
3. Having negative feelings toward the sender.

You may be able to think of other ways in which these three sources
of distortion create barriers to communication—we have not listed all
of them, by any means.

You have now reached the end of the first lesson in Unit II. The
next two lessons in this unit will explain the reasons for communica-
tion in an agency as well as describe how you may improve your com-
munication techniques as both sender and receiver by reducing the
factors of noise, interference, and distortion mentioned in this lesson.

UNIT II
COMMUNICATION

LESSON 2
Improving Sender Communication

Specific Objective

Given the need to foster effective agency communication, you will be able to write such a message and explain why you used a particular medium in sending the message.

Enabling Objective 1
You will be able to name five major purposes of agency communication.

Enabling Objective 2
You will be able to explain what you would do, as the sender of a communication, to avoid distortion of your message.

Enabling Objective 3
You will be able to list the four major steps that should be taken when planning a communication.

Enabling Objective 4
Given a description of one of the four steps that should be followed in planning a communication, you will be able to explain what is involved in planning for the given step.

Enabling Objective 5
Given an agency situation requiring communication, you will be able to name the most effective medium of communication to use in the situation.

Enabling Objective 6
Given a description of a situation requiring communication, you will be able to state the four important aspects that should be remembered when delivering the communication.

Continue with M1

PURPOSES OF AGENCY COMMUNICATION

An agency executive must communicate constantly with his fellow employees and with his superiors as well as with the public. According to Trecker, there are six major purposes of administrative communication. These include: **M1**

1. To clarify what is to be done, how, and by whom.
2. To reinforce identity with agency purposes.
3. To transmit problems, suggestions, ideas.
4. To report progress.
5. To promote participation.
6. To promote social interchange or provide recognition.[1]

Continue with Q1

A list of purposes of administrative communication are given below. Circle the letters corresponding to Trecker's views, then check your answers by turning to A6. The purposes are: **Q1**

A. To clarify the tasks to be accomplished.
B. To encourage participation in decision making.
C. To obtain funding.
D. To see that there are opportunities for social interchange.
E. To promote social action.
F. To create the agency's structure.
G. To identify problems, ask for or submit suggestions and ideas.
H. To evaluate performances of staff and board members.
I. To attempt strengthening identity with agency purposes.

As an executive, you will always have a reason for communicating to someone. Let's assume that you have received a memo from an associate executive that informs you of a problem situation to which you must respond in some way in order to solve the problem.   **Q2**

Such a situation may be presented as follows:

You receive a message from X. You read the message. You communicate to Y.

If you simply repeat the message, verbatim, will Y necessarily understand all you want to convey? Check your answer by turning to A7.

The sender must be receiver oriented in order to successfully reduce communication noise or distortion coming from the source or sender. For example, if the recipient of the communication (Y) has a different background than you, the sender, your message would need to be (similar/different) than if Y's background is similar to yours. (Underline the proper word in parens and check your answer by turning to A2.)   **Q3**

[1] Harleigh Trecker, *Social Work Administration, Principles and Practices* (New York: Association, 1971), p. 132.

If Y already understands the nature of the problem to be discussed, **Q4**
your message will require (more/less) information to enable someone
to act on it, than a person who has had no contact with the problem.
(Again underline and check the correct answer by turning to A4.)

Therefore, all communication between a sender and a receiver must **M2**
consist of two elements as follows:[2]

1. The basic item of information to be transferred.
2. Whatever extra details are necessary to make that basic information understandable and will produce the action required of the
   recipient.

Continue with Q5

The amount of extra detail necessary in each communication, there- **Q5**
fore, depends primarily on the person who is:

A. Sending the communication A3
B. Receiving the communication A8

In order to assess how many or how few extra details are required for **M3**
any communication, you, the sender, must ask yourself four questions.
The first two questions have already been presented: What is the
receiver's background of experience? How much does he know about
the subject to be discussed? The remaining questions are:

1. How capable is the receiver of taking action based upon the
   communication?
2. How will the receiver expect me to write or speak? What are his
   conceptions of me and how will this affect the way the receiver will
   expect me to communicate, that is, formally or informally?

Continue with Q6

In a memo to one of your subordinates, you have included extra **Q6**
details based on the subordinate's experience and knowledge about
the subject under consideration, but you have not taken any other
elements into consideration.
Name the two missing elements below, then check your answers
by turning to A5.

A.
B.

PLANNING YOUR   Once you have a reason or purpose for communicating, you must plan **M4**
COMMUNICATION   your communication before delivering it. Basically, there are four steps
                           that should be followed in planning communication. These include:

1. Decide who will be the recipient of the communication.
2. Decide what you will say in general terms.

[2] Learning Systems Limited, *Effective Communication for all Executive Directors
and Other Managers* (Elmsford, N.Y.: Pergamon, 1969), p. 8.

3. Decide when to communicate.   **M4**
4. Decide how your communication will be sent, the most appropriate   **cont.**
   medium.[3]

Continue with Q7

The planning of effective communication must proceed through a   **Q7**
four step decision making process. Circle the letters corresponding to
these steps below, then check your answer by turning to A1.

A. Who will receive it?
B. What will you say?
C. When will you send it?
D. Where will you send it?
E. How will you send it?
F. Why will you send it?

WHO—THE RECEIVER   Deciding who, ultimately, is to receive your communication is only   **M5**
part of the job concerning this first step. In order to avoid confusion
and misunderstandings, in most situations, you should adhere to the
following rules of communication:

1. If you want a superior to receive the content of your communication,
   you should always communicate with your immediate superior.
2. If you wish to reach a subordinate, you should communicate with
   your immediate subordinate.
3. If the recipient is on the same level as you, then you should communicate with him/her directly.
4. If your communication involves the work of other employees, then
   you must keep them informed also.

Continue with Q8

If this were the structure of your agency and a problem concerning   **Q8**
a caseworker's handling of a client was brought to you, who would
you contact first?

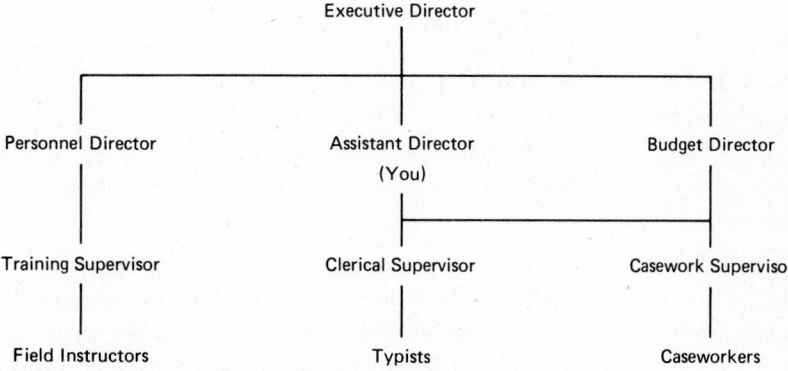

State your answer below and then check by turning to A9.

---

[3] Ibid., pp. 16–30.

This was discussed earlier. State below the two elements involved **Q9** in the message, then check your answer by turning to A14.

A. The basic _____.

B. The _____ _____ required to make the communication clearly understandable to the receiver.

TIMING THE MESSAGE

You must choose the appropriate moment for communication by con- **M6** sidering the readiness of the receiver as well as the conditions relevant to the content of the communication. Deciding when to communicate will also determine the final decision in the planning process, namely, how you will communicate.

TYPES OF MEDIA

The choice of medium is made, in most cases, depending upon the urgency of the situation. The following media, along with when they may be used, are cited only as suggestions, not as hard and fast principles to follow. The first three media are:

1. Telephone—the quickest medium, and feedback is immediate.
2. Face to face—fairly quick if the recipient is readily available. Feedback is immediate.
3. Special messenger—for urgent internal (but between separate buildings), written communication. Feedback is not immediate but often quick.

Continue with Q10

Circle the letters corresponding to the types of media that may be **Q10** used when urgency and/or immediate or quick feedback is necessary, then turn to A11.

A. Special messenger.
B. Meeting.
C. Report.
D. Telephone.
E. Letter.
F. Face to face.

The four remaining media or methods for delivering communication **M7** are used if urgency and/or feedback is less important. These media include:

1. Meetings—social agencies use these more than most other organizations. These include staff, board, committee, council, and annual meetings, among others. Meetings are used for group communication and are essential for making plans, transmitting information, and developing and maintaining a sense of working together. They are not for quick communication but provide for immediate feedback.
2. Reports—these are one of the most useful means of communicating in an agency. This is the major method by which the staff keeps the executive in touch with the progress of their work. Reports are

widely used by the executive to communicate with the board, the legislative body, and the agency constituency. They are a slow means of communication but dispense a large amount of information.   **M7 cont.**

3. Letters—used for external nonurgent communication. Feedback is, of course, greatly impeded and slow.
4. Memos—used for internal nonurgent communication. Feedback is also very slow.

Continue with Q11

Circle below the letters corresponding to the major types of media used when urgency and/or immediate feedback is not of prime importance, then check your answers by turning to A13.   **Q11**

A. Meetings.
B. Face to face.
C. Reports.
D. Letters.
E. Special messenger.
F. Memo.
G. Telephone.

It should be remembered that in preparing reports and writing letters and memos, the sender must be especially careful to focus on the recipient since these media tend to be a one-way form of communication with little, if any, feedback to help clarify the sender's meaning to the receiver.   **Q12**

An urgent situation has just been brought to your attention and must be imparted to a subordinate who must understand the urgency of the situation. Name below a communication media that you should use in this situation, then check your answer by turning to A10.

After you decide you have a reason for communicating and before you begin to communicate, you must make a brief and rapid plan based on what four decisions? State them below, then check your answer by turning to A12.   **Q13**

A.
B.
C.
D.

EFFECTIVE DELIVERY OF COMMUNICATIONS

Delivery is, of course, vital to effective communication. As an agency executive you should keep five important points in mind whenever you are attempting to communicate or deliver a message. These points include:[4]   **M8**

[4] Ibid., p. 30.

1. Address written messages (letters, memos, special messenger) correctly.
2. Include the date of the communication and name of sender's agency.
3. Clearly state the reason for the communication.
4. State your message including any additional details required to make your message clear to the receiver, considering his background experience, knowledge, capabilities, and expectations.
5. Provide for adequate feedback when you realize that the receiver is not understanding your message.

M8 cont.

Continue with Q14

Assume that you must send a letter to an individual concerning an agency matter. Fill in the blanks below for the five points that you should follow if your communication is to be effective, then check your answer by turning to A16.

Q14

A. The _____ should be correct.
B. The _____ of the communication and the _____ _____ of your agency.
C. The _____ for your communication should be clearly stated at the _____ of the letter.
D. The body of the letter should contain your _____ including any extra details necessary for clarifying your meaning to the receiver.
E. Explain how the receiver should obtain and/or send _____ _____ and/or the necessary follow-up information.

Which of the following addresses is correct?

Q15

A. Mr. Fred H. Stein, Bureau of Family Services, Welfare Administration, U.S. Department of HEW, Washington, D.C. . . . *A15*
B. Mr. Fred H. Stein, Director, Bureau of Family Services, Welfare Administration, U.S. Department of HEW, Washington, D.C. . *A19*

The following memo contains (sufficient/insufficient) information to make it an example of an efficient communication. Underline the proper answer, then check your answer by turning to A22.

Q16

Dear Sally,

Concerning our conversation yesterday, the answer is, let's try it.

Sincerely,
Joan

Assume now that you must telephone Mrs. Ruby, a casework supervisor in a Social Welfare Department, concerning one of her caseworkers. Explain below how you would proceed in developing effective communication by numbering the topics listed below in proper order from 1 to 6, then check your answers by turning to A20.

Q17

_____ Ask for Mrs. Ruby by name.
_____ Make sure you are calling the proper agency.
_____ Make sure you are talking to the proper person (Mrs. Ruby in this case), and state your name and agency.
_____ Explain your message adding the necessary extra details.
_____ Allow for feedback.
_____ State the reason for your call.

Now suppose you were unable to reach Mrs. Ruby. Explain below at least two courses of action that you could take, then check your answer by turning to A17.

Q18

A.

B.

If you are able to think of other courses of action cite them below and then turn to A17.

C.

D.

Feedback

There is one key way to find out whether or not our communication has been effective. This is through feedback. Obtaining feedback is, of course, far more difficult when the communication is written. However, your communication should request feedback, otherwise the communication will be only half-effective. Feedback, therefore, should always be requested by the sender, no matter what media of communication is used. In the following message, underline the sentence requesting feedback.

Q19

MEMORANDUM

TO: Joe Phillips, V. P. of Corporation
FROM: Me, President of Corporation
RE: Need for in-service training program

Some of my recent observations have led me to see the need for an in-service training program focused on developing administration skills.
I would like to have you develop such a program.
Please send me a memo outlining your ideas and we will set up an appointment to discuss the proposed program.

Check your answer by turning to A25.

If you have communicated by letter and feedback has been unfavorable, what could you do to rectify the situation?

Q20

A. Send a more detailed letter *A18*
B. Telephone the receiver *A21*
C. Both of the above *A23*

If the feedback is favorable and your communication has been correctly interpreted and will be acted upon properly, what should you do?

Q21

A. Add more information *A24*
B. End the communication *A26*

Whether your communication is written or oral, you must do several things. Check your answers by turning to A27.

Q22

I. *Plan your communication in four steps as follows:*
   A.
   B.
   C.
   D.

II. *Deliver your communication by following four major guides as*   Q22
follows: cont.

    A.

    B.

    C.

    D.

ANSWERS

The key components of communication planning are as follows: **A1**

A. Who—the recipient.
B. What—the message.
C. When—timing.
D. How—the medium.

Continue with M5

You should have underlined different.   **A2**

Continue with Q4

No, the sender, who is source oriented, causes communication dis-   **A3**
tortion by focusing on his own problems and by not considering the
background of information possessed by the receiver. This distortion
can only be reduced by considering the background of the receiver.
Return to Q5 and answer the question correctly.

The proper word is less.   **A4**

Continue with M2

The two missing elements are: **A5**

A. *The receiver's ability to take the proper action.*
B. *The receiver's expectations concerning how you, the sender, should*
   write to him.

Continue with M4

Although we changed the wording, you should have been able to   **A6**
recognize that the letters A, B, D, E, G, and I correspond to the items
quoted from Trecker. How did you do? Return to M1 if you need a
review, otherwise continue with Q2.

The answer is no. If you wish to communicate effectively you must   **A7**
make an effort to carefully plan your communication to insure that it
is understood by Y (the receiver).

Continue with Q3

Right, the sender must consider the background of the receiver in   **A8**
order to avoid the creation of communication distortion.

Continue with M3

You should contact the casework supervisor since he is the immediate   **A9**
subordinate responsible for the performance of the caseworker.

Continue with Q9

You should use the telephone or face-to-face communication if the   **A10**
subordinate is readily available.

Continue with Q13

Telephone, face-to-face, special messenger.   **A11**

Continue with M7

A. *Who—the recipient.* A12
B. *What—the message.*
C. *When—timing.*
D. *How—the medium.*

Continue with M8

A. *Meetings.* A13
C. *Reports.*
D. *Letters.*
F. *Memos.*

Continue with Q12

The two elements involved in the message include: A14

A. *The basic information.*
B. *The extra details required to make the communication clearly understandable to the receiver.*

Continue with M6

Sorry, but this address is improperly written since the title of the A15
receiver is missing. Titles, especially in large agencies, are important
in order to eliminate the possibility of the letter becoming lost. It is
also poor manners to leave off titles.
Return to Q15 and select the correct answer.

A. *The address should be correct. It should include:* A16
  1. *The name of the person you want to reach.*
  2. *The title of this individual.*
  3. *The full name of his agency or company as well as the complete address.*
B. *The date of the communication and the name of your agency.*
C. *The reason for your communication should be clearly stated at the beginning of the letter.*
D. *The body of the letter should contain your message, including any extra details necessary for clarifying your meaning to the receiver, with his background taken into consideration.*
E. *An explanation of how the receiver should obtain, and/or send feedback and/or the necessary follow-up information.*

Continue with Q15 after you clearly understand the above points.

There are four acceptable courses of action, namely: A17

A. *Phone back later.*
B. *Request Mrs. Ruby to call you back when she gets in.*
C. *Ask for her immediate superior or subordinate.*
D. *Give the reason for your communication and ask who is available to help you.*

How well did you do? If you wrote three or four choices, then you
have already acquired some very useful skills in the use of the tele-
phone. If you only wrote one or two courses or action, take a moment
to review those you missed.

Continue with Q19

This is only partially correct. You could send a more detailed letter to help rectify unfavorable feedback, but you could also telephone the receiver.
Return to Q20 and select the correct answer.

A18

Yes, the title of the receiver is missing in address A. The inclusion of titles helps to eliminate the possibility that the letter may get lost or fall into the wrong hands, especially in large agencies where there may be two persons with the same or similar names. It is also poor manners to omit titles.

A19

Continue with Q16

Your answers should have been 2, 1, 3, 5, 6, 4. When telephoning you should contact the correct person by:

A20

1. *Making sure you telephone the right agency (social welfare department, in this case), by checking the number and dialing it correctly or having your secretary do so.*
2. *Asking for Mrs. Ruby by name and title, especially if this is the first time you have called her.*
3. *Ascertaining whether or not she is indeed Mrs. Ruby, and then giving your name and agency. (At this point it is polite to ask if it is convenient for her to receive your communication.)*
4. *Stating the reason for your call and being sure she understands the reason.*
5. *Explaining your message and adding any extra details that may be needed to clarify your message.*
6. *Allowing for feedback from Mrs. Ruby throughout the conversation.*

Continue with Q18

Although this may be the best way to rectify this situation, it is not the only way listed in the answer in Q20. Return there now and answer the question correctly.

A21

Insufficient. Only if Sally personally receives the memo could it be considered a fairly adequate memo, although feedback will be required for pinpointing the "it" in the memo and for follow-up. However, if Sally is absent her secretary would not know what the memo is about or who else, if anyone, could act on it.

A22

Continue with Q17

Exactly! Both of these methods could be used to rectify this situation.

A23

Continue with Q21

No. This particular communication is now completed. You would want to go on to a new subject area for your next communication.
Return to Q21 and select the other answer.

A24

The sender will find out if Mr. Phillips has understood his message and whether or not his communication has been effective by Mr. Phillips' response to the statement, "Please send me a memo and we will set up an appointment."

A25

Continue with Q20

*Exactly. This particular communication should end once the re-   A26
ceiver has understood the message and has shown that he will act upon
it in a proper manner.*

Continue with Q22

Planning   A27

A. *Who—the receiver.*
B. *What—the message.*
C. *When—timing.*
D. *How—the appropriate medium.*

Delivery

A. *Correct address or person.*
B. *State the reason.*
C. *State the message including any extra details necessary considering
the background of the receiver.*
D. *Provide for feedback.*

UNIT II
COMMUNICATION

LESSON 3
Improving Receiver Communication

This lesson deals with the methods by which the receiver is able to improve communications.

Specific Objective

Given a faulty communication, you will be able to identify the reasons for the distortion and explain how you, as the receiver, could help eliminate the distortion, and thereby improve the communication.

Enabling Objective 1
You will be able to list three ways in which the receiver of a communication may contribute to communication distortions.

Enabling Objective 2
You will be able to describe the five actions that the receiver may take in order to help improve communication.

Enabling Objective 3
Given a description of a faulty communication, you will be able to identify the cause of the distortion.

Enabling Objective 4
Given a description of a faulty communication, you will be able to explain what the receiver can do to help improve the communication.

Continue with M1

**THE RECEIVER
AS A SOURCE
OF INTERFERENCE**

As you learned in Lesson One, there are three major sources of com-   **M1**
munication distortion or interference, the sender, the message, and the
receiver. Lesson Two presented ways in which the interference
created by the sender and the message could be reduced or eliminated,
thereby reducing communication barriers. In this lesson, several ways
of eliminating interference created by the receiver will be discussed.

Communication distortion is created by the receiver when he:

1. Fails to listen to or heed the message.
2. Fails to clarify any aspects of the message that he does not
   understand.
3. Has negative feelings toward the sender that obstructs his reception
   of the message.

Continue with Q1

Circle the letters corresponding to those persons who are creating   **Q1**
interference in the communication.

A. Dick, when talking to his boss, often neglects to ask for information
   he may have missed.
B. Hanna listens intently to her superiors but rarely follows up on
   requests.
C. Although Bill dislikes Phil, he pretends that these feelings are not
   involved when receiving messages from Phil or his associates.
D. Joan carries out her responsibilities after listening closely to messages from her boss.

Check your answers by turning to A4.

Improving Reception

The sender of a message should, of course, follow the points discussed   **Q2**
in Lesson Two. However, in actuality, most individuals do not follow
these simple rules. When you receive a faulty message, it is your
responsibility to help clarify the communication. This is true for both
written and oral communication. Upon receiving a message that you
are unable to understand, you should:

A. Disregard it A2
B. Attempt to improve it A5

There are essentially five actions you, as the receiver, should take to   **M2**
help improve communication. These include:

1. Finding out who is communicating with you.
2. Examining your feelings toward this individual and attempting to
   overcome any negative biases you may have toward him.
3. Finding out the reason for the communication.
4. Making sure you understand the message and can act on it, if
   necessary.
5. Confirming the action you are going to take, if any.[1]

Continue with Q3

[1] Learning Systems Limited, *Effective Communication for all Executive Directors
and Other Managers* (Elmsford, N.Y.: Pergamon, 1969), p. 65.

Although the remainder of this lesson will focus on oral communica- **Q3** tion, where it is easier to provide the feedback necessary for improving communication, written communications may also have comprehension gaps that you, the receiver, should fill either by your answering letter or memo or by telephone.

Suppose you receive a call from an individual whose voice you do not recognize and who fails to identify himself. What should you do? Write answer below, then check your answer by turning to A1.

After he gives his name, you may find that you are unable to **Q4** concentrate on his message. What could be causing this? Explain below at least one reason for your reaction, then check your answer by turning to A6.

If you realize you have some negative feelings toward the sender, **Q5** you could face them quickly, accept them, and return your attention to the message (a skill essential for a professional in any field).

If you actually do have urgent business to conduct or if you are in conference with a client, what action should you take? Explain your action below, then check your answer by turning to A3.

After you know who the sender is and have been told his agency **Q6** and function or position, what is the next point that you should make sure you understand? Write your answer below and check it by turning to A9.

Consider the following case in which the sender neglects to tell   **Q7**
Bob the reason for his call.

Assume Bob receives this call from Jim, a fellow executive, "Hello,
Bob, How are you? I've been trying to contact you for quite a while
but couldn't get through. I guess you've been pretty busy. When can
we get together?"

Explain below the corrective action that Bob should take in this
situation, then check your answer by turning to A7.

Let's consider a situation in which the sender does give you his   **Q8**
reason for calling but you are unfamiliar with the situation. For
example:

You are the executive director of a private agency and have received a call from a board member, Mrs. Olds. You do not know to
whom Mrs. Olds is referring when she says, "It has come to my attention that a member of the board is having a problem communicating
with you. Let's set up a meeting with her to discuss it."

What corrective action should you take in this situation? State
answer below, then check your answer by turning to A11.

After the caller has stated his reason for calling and you understand   **Q9**
it, he should then proceed to his message.

During this part of the communication, what action can you, as the
receiver, take to improve the effectiveness of the communication? Explain your action below and check your answer by turning to A13.

Assume you are the director of a newly formed program and you   **Q10**
receive the following call.

"Hello, I'm calling on behalf of a local community organization. We
have heard about your new program and wish to find out more about
it. Do you have any pamphlets? Perhaps you or a member of your
staff could discuss your program with us?"

Have you received enough information to enable you to act on this
communication?

A. Yes *A10*
B. No *A14*

If the caller fails to give you sufficient information to enable you   **Q11**
to act on his communication, you should:

A. Try to figure it out yourself *A8*
B. Wait for the necessary information to come out during the course
   of the communication *A12*
C. Ask the caller for more information as soon as possible . . *A16*

Another situation that often occurs during the course of conversa-   **Q12**
tion and that rarely, if ever, occurs when the communication is in
written form, is that the caller strays from the point of the communication. When this occurs you, the receiver, should recognize it, keep your
mind on the reason for the communication, and try to bring the caller
back to the topic as soon as possible. Assume you are the receiver of
the following call from a friend who works at another agency.

"I want to talk to you about Mr. Stickinthemud. You know, the
president of the local men's club who seems to be against everything
we are trying to accomplish in this community? Oh, by the way, I
saw your wife the other day at Macy's and she looks great! Has she
been on vacation without you? I know how hard you work but can't
you get some time off to go with her? My wife and I are planning a
trip to Honolulu in April. Well, I've got to get to lunch. Will I see you
tomorrow?"

Explain below what you should ask your friend before the conversation is ended, then check your answer by turning to A17.

Consider this example of a telephone communication: **Q13**

"I'm not free to go to the community planning meeting next Monday
at six at the Hilton. I want you to go in my place to represent the
agency. Can you make it?"

How would you end this communication assuming that you are free
to go and can fill in for the caller? State your reply below, then check
your answer by turning to A19.

You may, however, need further information, such as what room in   **Q14**
the Hilton, the agenda, and your role at the meeting, among other
things.

How would you obtain any extra information needed? Write answer
below, then check your answer by turning to A18.

After you have understood the reason for a communication and you **Q15** are clear as to the message and the action, if any, that you are to take, what should you do, other than say goodbye, before the communication ends? Explain what you would do below, then check your answer by turning to A15.

In the spaces below, explain the four actions you can take to im- **Q16** prove the effectiveness of communications you receive be they written or oral and then check your answer by turning to A20.

A.

B.

C.

D.

You have now reached the end of the programmed section of **M3** Unit II. The remaining eight units will cover the eight major executive functions that were briefly described in Lesson Two, Unit I.

After reviewing our suggestions for further study, answer the review questions at the end of this unit.

SUMMARY

In this unit we have emphasized the essentials of communication. The fact that communication is a two-way process was stressed. Communication was seen as related to leadership and as a necessary tool of administration. Barriers to communication were explored and ways to remove them examined.

Techniques for improving communication by both the sender and the receiver were discussed. A series of how-to-do-it memos were used to clarify each specific point. Five essential actions for the receiver, were stressed: 1. Find out who is communicating with you; 2. Overcome negative biases; 3. Ask yourself the reason for the communication; 4. Make sure you understand the message and can act on it, and; 5. Confirm the action you are going to take, if any.

SUGGESTIONS FOR FURTHER STUDY

The student should be aware that some very sophisticated approaches have been developed to analyze communications. The cybernetic-mathematical approach of information theorists owes its origins to Norbert Wiener and Claude Shannon. This highly technical approach will undoubtedly win many adherents as computer knowledge becomes more widespread. What is envisioned is the possibility of developing a computer language and the technology for instant communication, immediate feedback, and controls. That this is not some impractical notion is already evident in the computerized communication systems in use by the airlines, hotels, police departments, and others.

Another approach to understanding and developing better communications involves the study of network systems. This is not a new approach but has been underway for over twenty years. For example, network research has examined the structures of groups and concluded that they have an important affect on both performance and satisfaction. Some of the common communication networks examined have been the circle, chain, "Y," wheel, and all-channel. Studies by Alex Bavelas, Harold Leavitt, Harold Guetzkow, Herbert A. Simon, and Robert Dubin, to name a few of those engaged in network analysis, will provide the reader with a worthwhile insight into this aspect of communication.

A third approach, the interpersonal communication process, while dealt with to some extent in this text is certainly open to more exploration. The interpersonal communication approach is more behaviorally oriented, assumes much more is possible in person-to-person contact, and can be productive. This approach, which is congenial to the human services agencies, emphasizes listening sensitivity, nonverbal communications, immediate feedback, and the modification of communication through the interaction of both sender and receiver. The built in difficulties of this approach are obvious and should be the subject of much more research than is presently being conducted. Theodore Caplow in his book, *Principles of Organization*, when discussing "The Importance of Communication," stresses that distortion in any communication results whenever messages are exchanged between persons of different statuses. Harold H. Kelley analyzes the problem from the point of view of differences in communication in experimentally created hierachies of high and low statuses. The above are only indicative of some of the data that must be examined in order to understand both the difficulties and opportunities inherent in the interpersonal communications approach.

Finally, further study is certainly recommended in the general area of horizontal and upward communication. The usual triad consists of downward, horizontal, and upward communication. Most of the literature on communication has, in the past, dealt essentially with the downward aspects of communication. In today's world of more employee involvement, of worker's pods, of management by objectives and similar employee inputs, greater attention has to be paid to both horizontal and upward communication. Suggested readings in this area should provide stimulating class discussions on this important subject.

SUGGESTIONS FOR FURTHER READING
Mathematical-Cybernetic Approach

Bello, Francis. "The Information Theory." *Fortune*, December 1953.

Gallager, Robert G. *Information Theory and Reliable Communication.* New York: Wiley, 1968.

Pierce, J. R. *Symbols, Signals and Noise: The Nature and Process of Communication.* New York: Harper & Row, 1961.

Shannon, Claude E., and Weaver, Warren. *The Mathematical Theory of Communication.* Urbana, Ill.: University of Illinois Press, 1949.

Wiener, Norbert, *Cybernetics, or Control and Communication in the Animal and the Machine*. New York: Wiley, 1948.

——. *The Human Use of Human Beings*. 2d ed. rev. Garden City, N.Y.: Doubleday, 1954. Originally published in Boston in 1950 by Houghton Mifflin Company.

Communications Networks Research

Bavelas, Alex. "Communication Patterns in Task-Oriented Groups." In *Group Dynamics: Research and Theory*, edited by C. Cartwright and A. F. Zander, 2d ed., pp. 669–683. New York: Harper & Row, 1960.

Burgess, Robert L. "Communication Networks: An Experimental Re-evaluation." *Journal of Experimental Social Psychology*, July 1968.

Dubin, Robert. "Stability of Human Organizations." In *Modern Organization Theory*, edited by Mason Haire, pp. 218–253. New York: Wiley, 1959.

Guetzkow, Harold, and Simon, Herbert A. "The Impact of Certain Communication Nets upon Organization and Performance in Task-Oriented Groups." *Management Science*, April–July 1955.

Leavitt, Harold J. "Some Effects of Certain Communication Patterns on Group Performance." *Journal of Abnormal and Social Psychology*, January 1951: 38–50.

Interpersonal Communication

Caplow, Theodore, and McGee, Reece J. "How Vacancies Occur." In *The Academic Marketplace*. New York: Basic Books, 1958.

Gellerman, Saul W. *Management by Motivation*. New York: American Management Association, 1968.

Ronken, Harriet O., and Lawrence, Paul R. *Administering Change: A Case Study of Human Relations in a Factory*. Boston: Harvard Graduate School of Business Administration, 1952.

Sigband, Norman B. *Communication for Management*. Glenview, Ill.: Scott, Foresman, 1969.

Horizontal and Upward Communication

Flippo, Edwin B. *Management: A Behavior Approach*. 2d ed. Boston: Allyn & Bacon, 1970.

Katz, Daniel, and Kahn, Robert L. *The Social Psychology of Organizations*. New York: Wiley, 1966.

Landsberger, Henry A. "The Horizontal Dimension in Bureaucracy." *Administrative Science Quarterly*, December 1961.

Luthans, Fred. "Modern Organization Theory" and "The Organizational Communication Process." In *Organizational Behavior: A Modern Behavioral Approach to Management*. New York: McGraw-Hill, 1973.

Maier, Norman R. F.; Hoffman, L. Richard; Hooven, John J.; and Read, William H. *Superior-Subordinate Communication in Management*. New York: American Management Association, 1961.

Nichols, Ralph G. "Listening is Good Business." *Management of Personnel Quarterly*, Winter 1962.

Simpson, Richard L. "Vertical and Horizontal Communication in Formal Organizations." *Administrative Science Quarterly*, September 1959.

Once again, circle the answers of your choice.

1. Which of the following would be considered a purpose of agency communication?

   A. To promote participation by all agency employees.
   B. To reinforce staff identity with agency purposes.
   C. To provide recognition and promote social interaction.
   D. A and B above.
   E. A, B, and C above.

2. Which of the following is (are) essential element(s) of communication?

   A. The source.
   B. The receiver.
   C. The message.
   D. A and B above.
   E. A, B, and C above.

3. This creates barriers to effective communication.

   A. Feedback.
   B. Evaluation.
   C. Reinforcement.
   D. Distortion.

4. Current communication theory maintains that provision for _____ _____ is a necessary feature of effective communication.

   A. Distortion.
   B. Evaluation.
   C. Reinforcement.
   D. Feedback.

5. The source, the message, and the receiver may all contribute to:

   A. Feedback.
   B. Distortion.
   C. Reinforcement.
   D. Evaluation.

6. An agency executive must communicate constantly with:

   A. His subordinates.
   B. His superiors.
   C. The general public.
   D. A and B above.
   E. A, B, and C above.

7. If you wish to communicate effectively, you must make an effort to carefully plan your communication. Which one of the following elements of communication is the key element to your communication process?

   A. The source.
   B. The receiver.
   C. The message.
   D. The medium.

8. The sender may reduce interference in communication if he:

   A. Is source oriented.
   B. Is message oriented.
   C. Curtails feedback.
   D. Is receiver oriented.

9. The sender should be sure to include this in his communication if it is to be understood by the receiver.

   A. A greeting.
   B. The correct address.
   C. Extra details.
   D. Distortion.

10. As the sender of a communication, you have obtained favorable feedback and the receiver has interpreted your message correctly and will act upon it properly.

    A. Add more information.
    B. End the communication.
    C. Ask for confirmation.
    D. Repeat your message.

11. Through which of the following elements should the planning of effective communication proceed?

    A. The recipient.
    B. The message.
    C. The medium.
    D. The timing.
    E. All of the above.

12. When urgency is great and immediate feedback is necessary, which medium should be used?

    A. A memo.
    B. A special messenger.
    C. Telephone.
    D. A meeting.

13. Which of the ways listed below describe how the receiver may contribute to communication distortions?

    A. Fails to listen to or heed the message.
    B. Fails to ask for clarification of any aspects of the message he does not understand.
    C. Has negative feelings toward the sender.
    D. A and B above.
    E. A, B, and C above.

14. In a communication, if the sender fails to give you sufficient information to enable you to act on his communication, you should:

    A. Try to figure it out yourself.
    B. Wait for the necessary information to come out during the course of the communication.
    C. Ask the caller for more information as soon as possible.
    D. Take no action.

15. As the receiver of a message by telephone from a former colleague you have understood the reason for the communication and you are clear as to the message. Before the communication ends, you should:

A. Verify the sender's name and title.
B. Confirm the action you are to take.
C. Write the message down.
D. Plan a future meeting date.

See the last page of this unit for answers.

As soon as possible, ask him his name as well as the name of the agency **A1** he represents and his position or function in the agency ("I'm not sure I know who you are."). Avoid the temptation of trying to figure out who he is during the conversation since you will be concentrating on this task instead of the message.

Continue with Q4

If you disregard a faulty message, you are only increasing the **A2** problem. This is not an acceptable way for a responsible executive to act.
Return to Q2 and select the correct answer.

You should explain that you are very busy and ask the caller to call **A3** you back at some specified time or agree to call him when you have time and have finished your task. Note: This kind of a response does not necessarily indicate a negative feeling. You just may be busy!

Continue with Q6

The letters you should have circled are A, B, and C. The receiver **A4** who fails to listen, to clarify the message, or to recognize his negative feelings toward a sender, is creating communication interferences.

Continue with Q2

Of course, the responsible executive should attempt to improve **A5** faulty communication whether he is the sender or the receiver.

Continue with M2

Possibly you have negative feelings toward the sender. You may also **A6** have some urgent task that must be completed, and you do not have time to talk. In either case, you must take some action to help eliminate distractions.

Continue with Q5

Bob should say something like, "Jim, I'm afraid I am unaware of **A7** what it is that needs our attention. Could you fill me in?"

Continue with Q8

Although this is the first temptation of everyone due to his fear **A8** of sounding uninformed or ignorant, it usually results not only in communication failure but also in negative relationships, often with those who can either hurt or help our project or agency depending upon our relationship with them.
Return to Q11 and select the correct answer.

The third aspect of the communication that you, as the receiver, **A9** should be sure you understand is the reason for the call.

Continue with Q7

No, you must still find out the caller's name, the name and address **A10** of the organization he represents, and possibly why the organization is interested in your program.
Return to Q10 and answer this question correctly.

You should attempt to clarify Mrs. Olds' reason for calling with a polite question such as, "Are you referring to Mrs. Knowitall?" or some similar probing question relevant to the situation.

A11

Continue with Q9

By waiting and hoping that the necessary information will come out later, you run the risk of never obtaining it, becoming absorbed in listening for this information, and missing other important aspects of the communication.
Return to Q11 and select the correct answer.

A12

You should make sure that you understand the message and are able to act on it, if necessary. Therefore, you should give feedback by asking for more details, when necessary, to help clarify your understanding of the message and the actions you are expected to take.

A13

Continue with Q10

Exactly. You must still find out the caller's name, the name and address of the organization he represents, and possibly why the organization is interested in your program.

A14

Continue with Q11

You should confirm the action you are to take, if any.

A15

Continue with Q16

Exactly! By asking the caller for the necessary clarification as soon as possible, you are supplying the vital ingredient of all effective communication, namely, feedback. You are also preventing communication breakdown, and, in some cases, helping eliminate the creation of negative relationships with individuals who may be able to help improve your program or agency.

A16

Continue with Q12

Before he hangs up you should ask him what he wanted to tell you about Mr. Stickinthemud.

A17

Continue with Q13

Immediately ask the caller to send you any information that you will need in order to fulfill the request.

A18

Continue with Q15

To what seems like a clear and to the point message, you might say, "Sure, I'll be able to go to the planning meeting next Monday at 6 at the Hilton." But is that all you need to know?

A19

Continue with Q14

A. *Find out who is communicating with you.*
B. *Find out the reason for the communication.*

A20

C. *Make sure that you have the necessary information to enable you to act on a communication if this is necessary.*

D. *At the end of the communication, confirm the action you are to take.*

A20 cont.

Continue with M3

ANSWERS TO REVIEW QUESTIONS

The following are the correct responses to the questions for Unit II.

Questions	Answers	Questions	Answers
1	E	9	C
2	E	10	B
3	D	11	E
4	D	12	C
5	B	13	E
6	E	14	C
7	B	15	B
8	D		

If you missed more than three (3) questions, you should briefly review those areas that gave you trouble before going on to Unit III.

UNIT III PLANNING

LESSON 1
Service Planning

Three types of planning will be discussed in the next three lessons: service or program planning, project planning, and personal planning.

Specific Objective

Given an agency description, you will be able to describe in detail the plans necessary to effectively control its resources.

Enabling Objective 1
You will be able to state the five major components of a plan.

Enabling Objective 2
You will be able to list the six important characteristics that should be present in the plans if the agency goals are to be reached.

Enabling Objective 3
You will be able to list the four categories of resource planning.

Enabling Objective 4
You will be able to describe briefly the three phases of resource planning.

Enabling Objective 5
Given one of the four categories of resource planning, you will be able to describe the techniques used to plan for the cited resource.

Continue with M1

WHAT IS A PLAN?

Planning is the very essence of administration. A plan is a course of   **M1**
action for reaching a goal beginning now or at any predetermined
time in the future.[1]

Planning is merely a systematic way of achieving an objective or goal.

**ESSENTIAL
COMPONENTS
OF A PLAN**

A plan should consist of the following five major elements.

1. What is to be accomplished—the goal of the plan.
2. How the goal is to be accomplished—resources and procedures or
   methods to be used.
3. Who is responsible for accomplishing the goal.
4. What methods of evaluation and review will be utilized.
5. Under what future anticipated conditions will the plan need to
   operate.[2]

These five components should be included in every plan be it short-
term, intermediate, or long-range.

Continue with Q1

After an agreement has been reached on the major goal of a new   **Q1**
agency by you, as the new director of that agency, the board of
directors, and various community representatives, your next step will
be to develop a _____ or a course of action for achieving the
goal. Fill in the blank, then check your answer by turning to A3.

Some plans include only a description of the goal, that is, what is   **Q2**
to be accomplished by the plan. Circle below the letters corresponding
to the other elements that should be included in a well-developed plan,
then check your answers by turning to A7.

A. Identify anticipated future conditions.
B. Identify the person(s) responsible for goal accomplishment.
C. Specify the methods to be used for accomplishing the goal.
D. Specify the time limits of the plan.
E. Clearly state the evaluation and review methods to be used.

In the space below, describe, in your own words, what a plan is,   **Q3**
then check your answer by turning to A2.

**MAKING AGENCY
AND PROGRAM
PLANNING
EFFECTIVE**

Planning is a dynamic process and, in a human service agency or pro-   **M2**
gram, it must be flexible in order to respond to changes within the
agency or program, as well as within the community served. There-

[1] Joseph Cooper, *How to Get More Done in Less Time* (Garden City, N.Y.:
Doubleday, 1962), p. 58.
[2] Ray Johns, *Executive Responsibility* (New York: Associated, 1954), pp. 40–41.

fore, if the goals of the agency or program are to be reached, its plans must be:[3] **M2 cont.**

1. Flexible.
2. Consistent with
   a. human needs,
   b. available funds and personnel,
   c. welfare and agency philosophy.
3. Based on accurate and imaginative community research.
4. Acceptable to the community.
5. Easily communicable.
6. Progressive—forward looking.

Continue with Q4

In order to make the planning process in a human services agency   **Q4** or program dynamic, it must be:

A. Able to respond to changes in the agency and the community *A4*
B. Flexible *A6*
C. Both of the above *A9*

In addition to flexibility, the plans of human service agencies and   **Q5** programs, to be effective, must be designed with other attributes in mind. Circle the letters corresponding to these attributes, then check your answers by turning to A1.
Agency plans must be:

A. Oriented to the present and past.
B. Consistent with human needs, available funds, and agency philosophy.
C. Readily communicable.
D. Consist of idealistic goals.
E. Progressively oriented.
F. Acceptable to the community.
G. Based on accurate research on the community.
H. Based on theory.

The major type of planning in any organization, including human   **M3** service agencies or programs, is resource planning.
There are four categories of resources that require planning. These include:[4]

1. Finances.
2. Facilities and equipment.
3. Supplies.
4. Personnel (manpower).

Continue with Q6

---

[3] Harleigh Trecker, *Social Work Administration, Principles and Practices* (New York: Association, 1971), p. 144.
[4] Russell L. Ackoff, *A Concept of Corporate Planning* (New York: Wiley-Interscience, 1970), p. 65.

The major type of planning in any organization is: Q6

A. Personnel (manpower) planning A33
B. Supplies planning A5
C. Resource planning A8
D. Facilities and equipment planning A11

Circle the letters corresponding to the categories of resources that   Q7
require planning, then check your answers by turning to item A32.
Resources requiring planning are:

A. Financial.
B. Manpower or personnel.
C. Community.
D. Supplies.
E. Training programs.
F. Facilities and equipment.

PHASES OF AGENCY AND PROGRAM RESOURCE PLANNING

There are three phases of resource planning. The first phase is com-   M4
posed of three following decisions:[5]

1. Determining the amount required yearly in each of the four categories of resources during the planning period (finances, manpower, supplies, and facilities equipment).
2. Determining the amount in each category of resources that will
be available for each year.
3. Determining the amount in each category of resources that must
be acquired during each year.

The second phase of the resource planning process should focus on
determining whether the additional required resources can be
acquired and how.[6] If these additional resources cannot be acquired
or generated, then it is necessary to modify, in some manner, the
goal of the original plan in order to reduce the resource requirements
to a level that can be reached.

The third phase of the resource planning process involves the allocation of resources expected to be available to the programs that will
require them.[7]
Although such an allocation is usually called budgeting, and budgeting is often restricted to the allocation of money or finances, all
four types of resources should be considered.

Continue with Q8

During the first phase of the resource planning process, three major   Q8
decisions must be made. Which of the following encompasses all
three decisions?

A. Determining the amount of money, facilities, supplies, and manpower required, the amount available for each year in the planning
period, and whether the necessary resources can be acquired   A34

[5] Ibid.
[6] Ibid.
[7] Ibid., p. 66.

B. Determining the amount of each type of resource required, the amount that will be available, and the amount that must be acquired during each year of the planning period *A10*

C. Determining the amount of each type of resource that will be required, the amount that must be acquired, and how the additional resources will be acquired *A13*

Q8
cont.

After the three decisions are made in the first step, that is, when the amount of each resource that must be acquired is determined, what is the next or second step in the resource planning process?

A. Allocating the resources *A12*

B. Determining whether the additional resources can be acquired and how *A16*

C. Determining the amount in each category that will be available when needed *A20*

Q9

Explain below the action that must be taken if it is determined that additional resources cannot be acquired, then check your answer by turning to A15.

Q10

Circle the letter corresponding to the third and final step of the resource planning process, then check your answer by turning to A14.

Q11

A. Determine how required resources can be acquired.

B. Determine how resources will be used.

C. Allocate resources.

D. Modify the goal to reduce the resource requirements.

Now let's briefly review. The three phases of agency or program resource planning include:

M5

1. Determining the amount for each of the four types of resources (finances, facilities and equipment, supplies, and personnel) required during each year of the planning period, the amount of each resource that will be available, and the amount of each resource that must be acquired or generated.

2. Determining whether the additional required resources can be acquired and how.

3. Allocating available resources to the programs and/or departments that will use them.

Continue with M6

THEORIES AND TECHNIQUES FOR RESOURCE PLANNING
Financial Planning[8]

Successful financial planning requires the ability to forecast the financial position of the agency or program for each year in the planning period. A financial model of the agency or program is essential for this purpose. The agency accounting system is such a model, but computerization is necessary if it is to be used for rapid manipulation of data. A computerized accounting system makes it possible to

M6

[8] See Ibid., pp. 66–67, for further discussion of these theories and techniques.

determine on short notice how much of a money surplus or shortage can be projected or determined.

If a shortage of funds is projected, then there are two options that may be taken in advance:

1. Reducing the amount of funds needed by modifying the plans, that is, by reducing the number or breadth of services rendered or by laying off marginal personnel.
2. Generating or acquiring the needed funds through community fund drives; leasing or selling facilities or equipment; donations from businesses or increases in state or federal funding.

These alternatives should be evaluated so that an effective choice can be made. Additional information concerning agency and program budgeting will be presented in Unit IX.

Continue with Q12

What financial model may be used to help implement financial planning, including projected financial surpluses or shortages in a human service agency or program? Name the model, then check your answer by turning to the appropriate number.

A. Computer system *A17*
B. Accounting system *A19*
C. Auditing system *A21*
D. Computerized accounting system *A23*

Circle the letters corresponding to the functions that are fulfilled by a computerized accounting system, then check your answer by turning to A18.

A. Enhances the ability to predict the available and required amount of money during each year of the planning period.
B. Replaces financial planners.
C. Reduces the budget.
D. Makes it possible to determine shortages or surpluses of funds in advance.
E. Assists in making advance plans for overcoming problems associated with shortages.

If you, as an agency financial planner, discovered that there would not be enough funds for the ensuing year and the executive director of the agency did not want to eliminate any services or fire any of the agency personnel, what might you suggest as a possible alternative?

State a possible course of action below, then check your answer by turning to A25.

Facilities and Equipment Planning

In many human service agencies and programs, this is probably the least important aspect of resource planning since many such agencies rarely need to acquire buildings and equipment. A large percentage of the required facilities are often leased. However, the decisions as to whether or not to lease or buy must be carefully considered. If facilities and/or equipment are purchased, then maintenance and replacement must be carefully planned. **M7 cont.**

The techniques involved in the planning of facilities and equipment are well developed. Most of these techniques have evolved from operations research, the systematic application of research method to facilitate organizational planning.[9] A more complete discussion of this subject appears in Unit X on evaluation.

Continue with Q15

The second resource planning category is facilities and equipment planning. What major decision must be made when planning for needed facilities and equipment? **Q15**

A. Cost benefits A22
B. Whether to lease or buy A24
C. Whether maintenance or replacement is required A26

Many techniques have been developed to assist the agency or program facilities and equipment planner. Most of these approaches have used operations research. Which of the following is the best definition of operations research? **Q16**

A. The systematic application of the scientific method to reduce the costs of operations of organizations A27
B. The systematic application of research methods to facilitate organizational planning A30

Supplies Planning

The supplies required for the operation of any agency or program usually present little or no problem to agency planners. Supplies refer to any items that are constantly being used up and/or replaced such as paper goods, pencils, pens, record folders, and so forth. **M8**

Obtaining these items should become a routine operation and the funds for their purchase must be taken into consideration by agency planners so that the funds will be available whenever they are needed.

Personnel Planning

Since the problems involved with staffing will be considered more fully in Unit V, we shall present here only the major questions of personnel planning.

The three major questions that face personnel planners include:[10]

1. What is the minimal *number of employees by type* (for example, professional, paraprofessional, clerical) that are required to meet the agency's goals?
2. What number of employees by type should be recruited in each year of the planning period?
3. How should newly hired personnel be allocated to the departments within the agency or positions in the program?

Continue with Q17

[9] Russell L. Ackoff and Patrick Rivett, *A Manager's Guide to Operations Research.* (New York: Wiley, 1963). See especially Chapter 2, for a nontechnical discussion of operations research.
[10] Ibid., pp. 68–86.

Circle the letters below corresponding to the major questions that   **Q17**
the agency or program planner must face when planning for personnel, then check your answers by turning to A29.

A. Where are the people located who are the best future employees?
B. What is the minimum number of employees needed to meet the
   goals of the agency?
C. How many employees must be hired during each year of the
   planning period?
D. What will be the projected turnover rate for each year in the
   planning period?
E. How should new employees be allocated to agency departments?
F. How often will new employees be hired and for what reasons?

Equally relevant problems that are often overlooked include: **M9**

1. How should personnel be selected in order to hire the most qualified
   employees?
2. How much training should each type of personnel receive in order
   to maximize their ability to serve the agency program as well as
   satisfy their own needs and desires?
3. How can the work environment (physical, economic, and social)
   be improved so that each individual is motivated to develop to his
   fullest capabilities?

Continue with Q18

State below one of the important problems often overlooked in   **Q18**
personnel planning and then turn to A28.

This lesson has focused on three major aspects of program or agency   **Q19**
planning. As a brief review, think through the answers to the following questions. If you are unable to answer any question, return
to the frame cited after the question.

1. What are the ways to make agency or program planning effective?
   You should be able to cite at least four such methods. If not,
   return to M2 for a review and then continue with question 2.
2. What are the three phases of agency or program resource planning? If you are unable to remember, go back to M4 for review.
3. What method is best used for agency or program financial planning? Do you recall this method? If not, restudy M6.
4. Can you now recall the two courses of action that may be taken
   if a shortage of funds is predicted in advance? If not, reread M6.

Now proceed to Q20

State below the important decision that must be made concerning   **Q20**
facilities and equipment and then explain the meaning of operations
research.

Check your answer by turning to A31.

Decision—

Operations research—   Q20
                                                              cont.

Think about the necessary considerations that must be undertaken   Q21
by agency planners concerning supplies planning. If your mind is
blank, return to M8 for a review before going on to the next question
below.

What are the three important questions that planners must take into
consideration when planning for personnel? If you have trouble recalling any of these questions, return to M8.

If you are confident that you have an acceptable grasp of this lesson, then you have successfully completed it. Continue now with
Lesson Two, Planning a Project.

ANSWERS

You should have circled letters B, C, E, F, and G. To be effective a **A1**
plan should be flexible as well as:

Consistent with human needs, with available funds and personnel, as
   well as with welfare and agency philosophy.
Based on accurate community research.
Acceptable to the community.
Easily communicable.
Progressive.

Continue with M3

A plan is a course of action for reaching a specified goal. (A well- **A2**
designed plan will specify in detail the ways in which the goal(s) may
be reached.)

Continue with M2

If you wrote in the word plan you are absolutely correct! After **A3**
agreeing on the goals for an agency, a plan must be devised that will
lead to their achievement.

Continue with Q2

Yes, but you have only indicated a partial answer. To be dynamic, **A4**
agency planning processes must be responsive to agency and community changes. However, this process must also be flexible in order
to respond to these changes.
Return to Q4 and select the proper answer.

This is not the major type of planning but one of the categories **A5**
of the major type.
Return to M3 for a brief review, then answer Q6 correctly.

This is correct, but there is a more complete answer to this ques- **A6**
tion. Flexibility is required for an agency planning process to be
dynamic, but the process must also be able to respond to changes in
the agency and the community.
Return to Q4 and select the proper answer.

Letters A, B, C, and E should have been circled. A well-developed **A7**
plan includes not only a description of the goal and who is responsible
for its accomplishment, but also how the goal will be accomplished,
including the necessary resources and methods to be used, and a
description of the methods used to review the progress toward the
goal and evaluate how well the goal has been accomplished. Time
limits are not usually specified when dealing with agency goals, but
often they are an important detail of short range objectives.

Continue with Q3

Quite right! The major type of planning in any organization is **A8**
resource planning.

Continue with Q7

Exactly! In order to make the planning process in a social service **A9**
agency or program dynamic, it must be flexible so that it can respond
to changes within both the agency or program and the community
served.

Continue with Q5

Yes, you're right! The first phase of the resource planning process **A10**
requires determining the amount of each of the four resources re-
quired, the amount of each available, and the amount of each that
must be acquired.

Continue with Q9

No, facilities and equipment planning is a category of the major **A11**
type of organizational planning, but not the major type.
Return to M3 for a brief review before answering Q6 correctly.

This is incorrect. Allocation of resources is the final stage in the **A12**
planning process.
Return to M4 for a review before answering Q9 correctly.

You are only partially correct if you chose this answer. The first **A13**
phase of resource planning does require determining the amount of
each resource that will be required, and the amount that must be
acquired, but determining how and whether these additional resources
can be acquired is one of the major decisions of the second phase of
resource planning.
Return to M4 and review the decisions that must be made during
the first phase, then return to Q8 for the correct answer.

You should have circled letter C. The third and final phase of **A14**
agency or program resource planning involves the allocation of avail-
able resources to the various programs or departments.

Continue with M5

If it has been determined that the required additional resources **A15**
cannot be obtained, it is necessary to modify the goal so as to reduce
the resource requirements to a level that can be reached.

Continue with Q11

This is correct. After the amount of additional resources that must **A16**
be acquired has been determined, the planners must decide whether
these resources can be generated or acquired and how.

Continue with Q10

No, although a computerized system is needed for projecting finan- **A17**
cial surpluses and shortages, you have not identified what type of
computerized system.
Return to M6 for a brief review and then answer Q 12 correctly.

You should have circled letters, A, D, and E. A computerized ac- **A18**
counting system greatly enhances the ability of the agency financial

planners to predict the available and required amount of money during each year of the planning period. This makes it possible to determine any surplus or shortage of funds in advance, and to make plans to overcome the problems associated with such shortages.

A18 cont.

Continue with Q14

Although an accounting system is the proper type of system for use as a financial model, such a system must be computerized to allow for proper future predictions needed for rational planning.
Return to Q12 and select a more correct answer.

A19

No, the amount of resources available when needed should be determined before the amount to be acquired is determined.
At this point a brief review might be helpful, so return to M4 before answering Q9 correctly.

A20

No, an auditing system would not be used as a model for financial planning.
Return to M6 for a review before answering Q12 correctly.

A21

No, cost benefits of needed facilities and equipment, although necessary, is not the major decision to be made when planning for needed facilities and equipment.
Return to Q15 and select the correct answer.

A22

Yes! An agency or program accounting system is vital to financial planning. If such a system is computerized then planning effectiveness is greatly increased.

A23

Continue with Q13

This is correct. The major decision that must be made whenever facilities or equipment are needed is whether to lease or to buy the required facilities or equipment.

A24

Continue with Q16

You could, for example, suggest the lease or sale of used facilities or equipment or a community fund drive or a solicitation of funds from business and/or government. Did you also have some other ideas?

A25

Continue with M7

No, another decision needs to be made first—whether to lease or buy the needed equipment or facilities. Maintenance and/or replacement decisions and plans are avoided if equipment and facilities are leased.
Return to Q15 and answer the question correctly.

A26

This is incorrect. Sorry! Operations research does not have as its goal the reduction of costs, although this may result from its application.
Return to Q16 and select the correct answer.

A27

Problems related to the human aspect of personnel include: **A28**

The manner in which to hire the best personnel.
The training necessary to help personnel serve the agency to their
maximum capacity as well as to satisfy their own needs.
The environmental conditions required to motivate each employee to
reach his capabilities.
Before continuing with Q19, take a moment to think about these
three overlooked aspects and how you as an executive could take them
into consideration when planning for personnel in your agency.

Letters B, C, and E should have been circled. The major questions   **A29**
regarding personnel planning include:

What is the minimal number of employees by type required to meet
the agency's goals?
How many employees by type should be hired during each year of the
planning period?
How should new employees be allocated to agency departments?

Continue with M9

Good! This is the correct definition. Operations research is the   **A30**
systematic application of research methods to facilitate planning in
organizations.

Continue with M8

The important decision is whether to lease or purchase facilities   **A31**
and/or equipment.
Operations research refers to the systematic application of research
methods aimed at facilitating organizational planning. The most
widely used techniques that have evolved from OR include PERT
or Program Evaluation and Review Technique and CPM or Critical-
Path Method.

Continue with Q21

You should have circled letters A, B, D, and F since the categories   **A32**
of resources include:

Finances.
Manpower or personnel.
Supplies.
Facilities and equipment.

Continue with M4

Although this is one category of the major type of planning in any   **A33**
organization, it is not the major type.
Return to M3 for a review, then answer Q6 correctly.

This answer is only partially correct, since it encompasses two of   **A34**
the three decisions that should be made in the first phase of resource
planning, namely, determining the amount of each type of resource
required, and the amount that will be available, and one of the major
decisions to be made during the second phase, namely, whether the
necessary additional resources can be acquired.
Return to M4 and review the first phase of resource planning.

UNIT III
PLANNING

LESSON 2
Planning
a Project

This lesson will focus on the essential aspects of planning individual and group projects.

Specific Objective

Given a description of an individual or group project, you will be able to describe a plan for its accomplishment.

Enabling Objective 1
You will be able to give two reasons for planning an individual or group project and three additional reasons for planning a group project.

Enabling Objective 2
You will be able to describe briefly the seven stages through which an individual project should proceed.

Enabling Objective 3
You will be able to describe the one extra stage (in addition to the seven) that is required for a group project.

Continue with M1

**WHY PLAN
A PROJECT?**

There are many reasons for setting up a plan when embarking on a project. However, the two major reasons are:[1]   **M1**

[1] Joseph D. Cooper, *How to Get More Done in Less Time* (Garden City, N.Y.: Doubleday, 1962), pp. 68–69.

94

1. The quality of the effort will be better than if one plunges directly into the work. **M1 cont.**
2. It will take less time to complete the project.

Therefore, whether it is an individual or group project, the failure to plan in advance often results in poor allocation of time for each stage as well as possible improper sequencing of activity.

The failure to plan group projects often results in three additional pitfalls including:[2]

1. Confusion and overlapping of effort.
2. No accomplishment by anyone.
3. Contradictions in approach.

Continue with Q1

If you move directly into a project without making plans you are likely to: **Q1**

A. Do a superior job faster A5
B. Do an inferior job in more time A9

Failure to plan an individual project often results in: **Q2**

A. Poor allocation of time and improper sequencing of activity . A3
B. Confusion and overlapping of effort A7

For all projects, both individual and group, the unplanned activity **M2** is usually characterized by lack of control. Cooper reminds us that, "Not having thought it through in advance, you are not quite clear as to the points at which you should check yourself."[3]

Continue with M3

**STAGES OF
A PROJECT**

A properly planned project should proceed according to a certain **M3** sequence, if it is to be successfully completed at the least cost and within the time limits. The properly planned project will usually include eight stages, seven of which are related to individual projects, with the additional one for group projects.[4] The first four stages are as follows:

1. Recognition and clarification of the project requirements.
2. Fact gathering, using such techniques as prior experience, research, and qualified opinions.
3. Tentative decision as to the basic approach to be followed, including identifying the main assumptions, limitations, and unknowns.
4. Laying out the basic plan of action, including those tasks to be done in sequence and those in parallel (at approximately the same time), as well as a summation of the requirement for each phase together with the criteria for accomplishment.

Continue with Q3

[2] Ibid., p. 69.
[3] Ibid.
[4] Ibid., pp. 69–70.

The first stage in planning a project is: **Q3**

A. Fact gathering *A1*
B. Recognition and clarification of the project requirements . *A4*
C. Tentative decision as to the basic approach to be followed . *A8*

Give the second stage of project planning below and explain what   **Q4**
is included in this stage, then check your answer by turning to A2.

Which stage in the planning process includes setting up a basic plan   **Q5**
of action?

A. The third stage *A6*
B. The fourth stage *A10*

Circle the letters below corresponding to the elements that must be   **Q6**
identified in order to competently perform the major task of the third
stage of project planning, then check your answer by turning to A14.

A. Identifying relevant research.
B. Identifying relevant, qualified opinions.
C. Identifying the main assumptions.
D. Identifying the limitations and unknowns.
E. Identifying relevant prior experience.

Arrange the four stages of project planning listed below by writing   **Q7**
the proper number for each stage beside the stage. Check your
answers by turning to A12.

_____ Fact gathering.
_____ Laying out the basic plan of action.
_____ Tentative decision concerning the basic approach to be
         followed.
_____ Recognition and clarification of the project requirements.

The last four stages of project planning are as follows:[5]   **M4**

5. Review of the project plan. It is best to have some other person or
   persons not related to the project perform this task, since they are
   better able to make objective critical contributions.
6. If it is a group project, discuss and assign tasks during this stage,
   and a project starting date or "kickoff" should be set.
7. Monitoring of the project at predetermined control stages in accordance with previously established criteria of performance. Make
   decisions concerning revisions in approach needed to accomplish
   the goals within the limits of time and funds.
8. Decide on the completion dates and how the report is to be delivered. If the project is to be reported to someone, then its delivery
   to that person is important (by whom and when and with all
   details completed).

Continue with Q8

[5] Ibid., see pp. 69 and 70 for Cooper's presentation of the eight stages.

The fifth stage of project planning involves a review of the project plan. Who should perform this review? Write your answer below, then check by turning to A11.   **Q8**

The one stage of project planning that applies only to group projects is the :   **Q9**

A. Review stage A13
B. Discussion and assignment of tasks stage A15
C. Monitoring stage A17

Explain below the monitoring stage of project planning, then check your answer by turning to A16.   **Q10**

There are seven stages that should be followed in individual project planning, and an eighth stage that is especially crucial for group projects. Please list all eight stages below (as a kind of review), then check your answers by turning to A18. If you have any trouble remembering the stages return to M3 and M4 to review the material.   **Q11**

Describe below at least four pitfalls of failing to plan a group   **Q12**
project, then check your answers by turning to A19.

1.
2.
3.
4.

You have now completed an overview of the requirements in-   **M5**
volved in planning an individual or group project. You should find
this outline helpful, although you do need to see it as only an outline
and with many details absent. Later on, in Unit X, Lesson Three, we
will deal with the methodology known as PERT which we feel will
be of great assistance to you in learning how to do agency planning
and evaluating.

No, fact gathering is the second stage in project planning. **A1**
Return to M3 and review the first four stages that should be followed in sequence when planning a project.

Fact gathering is the second stage of project planning and includes **A2**
prior experiences, research, and qualified opinions, among other methods.

Continue with Q5

Exactly, poor allocation of time to the various project stages as well **A3**
as improper sequencing of activity are often the results of failure to plan.

Continue with M2

Right you are! The first stage of project planning is recognition and **A4**
clarification of the requirements of the project.

Continue with Q4

You have said that you may accomplish a project in less time and **A5**
with superior results if you avoid taking time to plan the project. However, in the vast majority of cases, this is not true. It is just as wasteful to try to start a new project without some planning in proportion to the complexity of the project as it would be for a builder to try to put up an original house without blueprints.
Return to Q1 and select the correct answer.

You have stated that the third stage in the planning process includes **A6**
setting up a basic plan of action. However, this is the fourth stage, not the third. The third stage involves making a tentative decision of the basic approach to be followed by identifying the main assumptions, limitations, and unknowns.
Return to Q5 and select the correct answer.

No, confusion and overlapping of effort, contradictions in approach, **A7**
and no accomplishment by anyone are typical of unplanned group projects.
Return to M1 and review the material presented there before answering Q2 correctly.

Sorry about this one, but you have chosen the third stage in project **A8**
planning.
You need a review so return to M3 and study the first four stages of planning a project before attempting to answer Q3.

You are correct in selecting this answer since it is just as wasteful **A9**
to try to start a new project without some planning (in proportion to the complexity of the project) as it would be for an airplane manufacturer to attempt to construct a plane with no detailed blueprints.

Continue with Q2

Yes, stage four includes setting up a basic plan of action, including **A10**
those tasks to be done in sequencing and those in parallel, as well as
the requirements for each phase and the criteria for accomplishment.

Continue with Q6

The project plan should be reviewed by someone who can be ob- **A11**
jective. If it is an individual project and you are unable to obtain
outside opinions, then you should detach yourself from the project for
a short period of time before reviewing the plan yourself.

Continue with Q9

The four stages of project planning in proper sequence are: **A12**

1. *Recognition and clarification of the project requirements.*
2. *Fact gathering.*
3. *Tentative decision concerning the basic approach to be followed.*
4. *Laying out the basic plan of action.*

Continue with M4

No, the review stage applies to both individual and group projects. **A13**
Return to M4 for a review before answering Q9 correctly.

You should have circled letters C and D, since the third stage of **A14**
project planning involves making a tentative decision concerning the
basic approach to be followed. In order to competently perform this
task, the main assumptions, limitations, and unknowns must be identi-
fied. (The other answers related to fact gathering.)

Continue with Q7

Right-o! The stage of project planning that applies only to group **A15**
projects involves the assignment and discussion of tasks as well as the
project starting date.

Continue with Q10

Stage seven in planning a project involves monitoring the project **A16**
at predetermined control stages. Decisions should be made during this
stage to make any necessary revisions in approach, and thus accom-
plish the project goal within limits of time and funds.

Continue with Q11

No, the monitoring stage is applicable to both individual and group **A17**
projects. Return to M4 for a review and then answer Q9 correctly.

The eight stages are as follows: **A18**

1. *Recognition and clarification of the project requirements.*
2. *Fact gathering.*
3. *Tentative decision regarding the basic approach to be followed.*
4. *Laying out the plan of action.*
5. *Review of the project plan.*
6. *Discuss and assign tasks for a group project.*

7. *Monitor the project at predetermined periods.*   **A18**
8. *Decide on the completion dates and manner of delivery of finished*   **cont.**
   report.

Continue with Q12

Failure to plan a group project often results in: **A19**

1. *Poor allocation of time to the various stages.*
2. *Improper sequencing of activities.*
3. *Confusion and overlapping of effort.*
4. *Unassigned and unaccomplished tasks.*
5. *Contradictions in approaches.*

Continue with M5

UNIT III
PLANNING

LESSON 3
Personal Planning

Specific Objective

Given a situation requiring a decision to accept or reject a new personal project or activity, you will make the decision and explain why you made it, and, if applicable, how you plan to carry out the new personal project.

Enabling Objective 1
You will be able to list and briefly describe the four key elements involved in personal planning.

Enabling Objective 2
You will identify or describe two estimates that should be taken before deciding whether or not to accept a new personal task or project.

Enabling Objective 3
Given that you, the executive, have accepted a new task, you will be able to explain three ways that the new task could be fitted into your schedule.

Continue with M1

THE MEANING OF PERSONAL PLANNING

As the executive director, you not only have the responsibility for the over-all planning of agency programs and projects, but you also must learn to plan your own personal tasks. This involves looking ahead,   **M1** determining your goals and objectives, and writing down the course of action on which you have decided.

Continue with Q1

Explain below, in your own words, what is meant by personal planning, then check your answer by turning to A4.   **Q1**

KEY ELEMENTS OF PERSONAL PLANNING

Planning is, of course, a future oriented activity. In planning, you constantly make assumptions concerning the conditions you will find in the future as well as about the consequences of the actions to be taken.   **M2**

There are four key elements that you must, therefore, keep in mind when planning for the fulfillment of personal goals.[1]

The first key element is to understand the limiting and fixed factors that must be incorporated into your plan: the time in which you must achieve your goal, the resources available to you, the obstacles, the unknowns, and the anticipated actions of others that might have an effect on what you are doing.[2] You must, therefore, be able to anticipate the necessary changes in your plan even as you perform under it.

Continue with Q2

The first key element in personal planning involves an understanding of certain limiting and fixed factors that must be incorporated into your plan. Circle below such factors and then turn to A6.   **Q2**

A. Obstacles.
B. Actions of others that may affect what you will be doing.
C. Unknowns.
D. Available resources.
E. Time limits.

The second key element in personal planning is to design your plan using your own or others' prior experience with similar tasks or projects. If there is no available experience, you must try to simulate it by analogy to other things of which you have knowledge.   **M3**

Continue with Q3

---

[1] Joseph D. Cooper, *How to Get More Done in Less Time* (Garden City, N.Y.: Doubleday, 1962), p. 61.

[2] For a discussion of techniques of forecasting events as well as the behavior of people, see Joseph D. Cooper, *The Art of Decision-Making* (Garden City, N.Y.: Doubleday, 1961), especially Chapter XII, "Crystal-Balling the Future."

Explain below the element upon which you should draw when **Q3** designing your plan of action to reach a personal goal, then check your answer by turning to A2.

After grasping and accounting for future factors and then designing **M4** the plan, the third key element in personal planning is to find out if the plan is feasible. Feasibility includes frank answers to two questions:

1. Can the goal be achieved considering the resources and time available to you?
2. If you have the requisite time and resources, do you have the capability of achieving the goal?

If you find that either of these questions should be answered in the negative, then you should modify the goal in some manner to make it more feasible. However, if a modified goal is still found to be un-attainable, it would be more prudent to make plans toward a different goal than to continue toward the goal that is unattainable.

Continue with Q4

The third key element in personal planning is to determine the **Q4** feasibility of your plan. Circle the letter(s) below corresponding to those statements that reflect the need for modifying a personal plan.

A. You have insufficient time available.
B. Your resources seem to be in short supply.
C. You have the capability to achieve the goal, although resources seem to be inadequate.
D. Considering the available resources and time, you can achieve the goal.
E. You are capable of achieving the goal and you seem to have sufficient time and resources.

Check your answers by turning to A1.

The final key element of personal planning involves the identification **M5** of check points in your plan for the purposes of future control. As you approach these check points, you should evaluate your progress and make revisions in your plans, if necessary.

Continue with Q6

If you find that your goal calls for more resources than are available **Q5** to you, what courses of action are open to you?

A. Go on with the plan and hope that the resources will become available in the future *A3*
B. Modify the goal *A7*
C. Plan another goal *A10*

Four key elements of personal planning have been presented in this lesson. Circle the letters below corresponding to these elements, then check your answers by turning to A5. **Q6**

A. Design your plan based on predicted future problems.
B. Identify logical check points for control purposes.
C. Determine the feasibility of the plan.
D. Design your plan based on prior experience.
E. Take limiting and fixed factors into account.
F. Determine the cost of the plan and its accomplishment.

TAKING ON NEW TASKS

Many executives have trouble turning down new tasks, especially those related to community welfare. However, if you will follow some helpful hints, you may be able to avoid the embarrassments that occur from an overloaded schedule and the resulting unfulfilled commitments. **M6**

Assuming that your schedule is full, what actions can you take to plan for the acceptance and accomplishment of important new tasks. The following actions are only suggestions—you may have others to add to this list which are as good or better. They include:[3]

1. Estimate your on-going work load.
2. Estimate the time that the new task will consume.
3. Decide whether or not to accept the new task based on the conclusions derived in (1) and (2) above, or else agree to just monitor the task.
4. If accepted, fit the new task into your schedule. It could take the place of a task that will be completed soon or you could, of course, work overtime on it. Another solution would be to defer another less important task.

Continue with Q7

SUGGESTIONS FOR ACCEPTING A NEW TASK

The following suggestions may be helpful when you are presented with the decision to accept a new task. **M7**

1. Make your own time estimates and then double them. Do not accept the estimate of those who are making the request.
2. Obtain in writing specifically what is expected of you and the assistance you should expect to receive.
3. Avoid taking on too many outside activities simultaneously.
4. Attempt to reduce your responsibility related to task achievement as a condition of acceptance.[4]

Continue with Q9

Upon which estimates should a decision to accept a new task be based? Circle those letters below corresponding to those estimates upon which this decision should be based. Check your answer by turning to A8. **Q7**

A. An estimate of the cost of accomplishing the task.
B. An estimate of your on-going work load.
C. An estimate of the time the new task will consume.

[3] Ibid., pp. 62–65.
[4] Ibid., pp. 67–68.

After deciding to accept a new task, how could this task be in-   **Q8**
cluded in your schedule?

A. By working overtime *A9*
B. By deferring another less important task *A11*
C. By phasing out another task *A12*
D. A, B, and C above *A14*

Circle below the letters corresponding to those suggestions that may   **Q9**
be helpful when you are taking on a new task, then check your answers
by turning to A13.

A. Do not take on too many outside activities simultaneously.
B. Accept the time estimate of the person making the request since
   he knows more about it than you do.
C. Be sure to get verbal agreement regarding what it is that you will
   be expected to do.
D. Attempt to reduce your responsibilities related to the task as a
   condition of acceptance.
E. Make your own time estimates and then double them.
F. Make sure to get written agreement of what it is that you will be
   expected to do.

You have now been introduced to three specific types of planning   **M8**
including agency, project, and personal planning. How well do you
think you could set up a plan? If you have any doubts, it may be best
for you to briefly review the three lessons in this unit before going on.

If you believe that you understand this unit, congratulations are
in order and it is time for a review. First, read our suggestions for
further study and then answer the review questions at the end of
this unit.

SUMMARY

Planning is very often regarded as the essence of administration
and involves the systematic setting of goals and objectives. We
have detailed the major elements in planning for short term, intermediate, or long-range goals and objectives. We discussed the
importance of understanding the phases of planned change with
examples from resource and project planning. Personal planning
was also stressed, including the planning of your own work as an
executive with suggestions for avoiding the pitfalls of overcom-
mitment, overwork, exhaustion, and general inefficiency.

SUGGESTIONS FOR FURTHER STUDY

Although planning is regarded as a crucial activity of administration, few studies move us beyond the present frontiers of knowledge. Two major concepts, however, are beginning to command
attention: planned change and the planning component of MBO
(Management by Objectives), MOR (Management by Objectives
and Results), and PPBS (Planning, Programming, Budgeting Systems). These planning techniques reflect a new management
interest in control functions.[1]

[1] George L. Morrisey, *Management by Objectives and Results* (Reading, Mass.:
Addison-Wesley, 1970), p. 15.

Planned change as a management concept requires further study.[2] Administrators in human service agencies should be familiar with the basic research in planned change in order to avoid the potentially unsettling results of unplanned change on personnel. Chin referred to this problem of planned change in an organization as a human relations problem requiring administrative awareness and responsible action.[3] "No change without pain" might indeed be a watchword for all executives.

We need to point also to the fact that, increasingly, planning is being perceived as a top management function. Management and administrative functions are being divided, with top management assuming the functions of planning and controlling, and middle management assuming the administrative functions of organizing, directing, and staffing.[4] Planning as a top management function also requires predictions and forecasts. Therefore, special techniques of forecasting need to be examined, including the Delphi technique, brainstorming, game planning, and computer assisted simulations of planning.

SUGGESTIONS FOR FURTHER READING

Ackoff, Russell Lincoln. *A Concept of Corporate Planning*, New York: Wiley-Interscience, 1970.

Argenti, John. *Corporate Planning: A Practical Guide*. Homewood, Ill.: Dow Jones-Irwin, 1969.

Bard, Ray, et al. *Planning for Change*. Washington, D.C.: Education, Training, and Research Associates, 1971.

Bell, Daniel. *The Coming of Post-Industrial Society; A Venture in Social Forecasting*. New York: Basic Books, 1973.

Bell, Wendell, and Mau, James A. eds., *The Sociology of the Future; Theory, Cases, and Annotated Bibliography*. New York: Russell Sage, 1971.

Bennis, Warren G.; Benne, Kenneth D.; and Chin, Robert. *The Planning of Change*. New York: Holt, Rinehart & Winston, 1962.

Brady, Rodney H. "MBO Goes to Work in the Public Sector" (HEW). *Harvard Business Review*, March–April 1973: 65–74.

Branch, Melville Campbell. *The Corporate Planning Process*. New York: American Management Association, 1962.

Cotton, Donald B. *Company-Wide Planning; Concept and Process*. New York: Macmillan, 1970.

De Boer, John C. *Let's Plan; A Guide to the Planning Process for Voluntary Organizations*. Philadelphia: Pilgrim Press, 1970.

Elliott-Jones, M. F. *Economic Forecasting and Corporate Planning*. New York: Conference Board, 1973.

Ewing, David W. *The Human Side of Planning*. New York: Macmillan, 1969.

[2] One of the classics in the area of planned change is: Warren G. Bennis, Kenneth D. Benne, and Robert Chin, *The Planning of Change* (New York: Holt, Rinehart & Winston, 1962), especially Parts 3 and 4.

[3] Robert Chin, "Human Relations: A New Discipline or Integrative Force," in Bennis, Benne, and Chin, *Planning of Change*, pp. 69–73.

[4] See Robert M. Fulmer and Leslie W. Rue, "Competence: The Cohesive of Future Organizations," *Atlanta Economic Review* (March–April 1974): 49; also, Harold Koontz and Cyril O'Donnell, *Principles of Management*, 4th ed. (New York: McGraw-Hill, 1968), p. 1.

Ewing, David W., ed. *Long-Range Planning for Management.* 3rd ed. New York: Harper & Row, 1972.

Fulmer, Robert, and Rue, Leslie W. "Competence: The Cohesive of Future Organizations." *Atlanta Economic Review,* March–April, 1974: 46–51.

Department of Health, Education and Welfare. *Community Planning for Health, Education and Welfare: An Annotated Bibliography.* June 1967: BPS 13–31.

Kahn, Alfred J. *Planning Community Services for Children in Trouble.* New York: Columbia University Press, 1963.

Kahn, Herman, and Bruce-Briggs, B. *Things to Come; Thinking About the Seventies and Eighties.* New York: Macmillan, 1972.

Koontz, Harold, and O'Donnell, Cyril. *Principles of Management.* 4th ed. New York: McGraw-Hill, 1968.

Lande, Henry F. *How to Use the Computer in Business Planning.* Englewood Cliffs, N.J.: Prentice-Hall, 1969.

Mayer, Robert R. *Social Planning and Social Change.* Englewood Cliffs, N.J.: Prentice-Hall, 1972.

Michael, Donald N. *On Learning to Plan and Planning to Learn.* San Francisco: Jossey-Bass, 1973.

Miller, Ernest Charles. *Advanced Techniques for Strategic Planning.* New York: AMA, 1971.

Morrisey, George L. *Management by Objectives and Results.* Reading, Mass.: Addison-Wesley, 1970.

Morrow, James Earl "A Delphi Approach to the Future of Management." Ph.D. dissertation, Georgia State University, 1971.

Sackman, Harold, and Citrenbaum, Ronald L. eds. *On Line Planning: Towards Creative Problem-Solving.* Englewood Cliffs, N.J.: Prentice-Hall, 1972.

Simon, Herbert A. *Administrative Behavior.* 2d ed. New York: Free Press, 1965.

Steiner, George Albert. *Top Management Planning.* New York: Macmillan, 1969.

Toffler, Alvin. *The Futurists.* New York: Random House, 1972.

Trecker, Harleigh B. *Social Work Administration, Principles and Practices.* New York: Association, 1971.

Tudor, Dean. *Planning-Programming-Budgeting Systems (A Bibliography).* Monticello, Ill.: Council of Planning Librarians, 1970 (Exchange bibliographies #121 and #183).

Urwick, L. "The Functions of Administration." In Gulick, Luther, and Urwick, L. eds. *Papers on the Science of Administration.* New York: Institute of Public Administration, 1937.

Wilson, Ian H. "Socio-Political Forecasting: A New Dimension to Strategic Planning." *Michigan Business Review* 26 (July 1974): 15–25.

Remember to circle the answers of your choice.

1. Which of the following is not a major element of a plan?

   A. Methods to be used for evaluation and review.
   B. The amount of staff time required.
   C. The goals and objectives.
   D. The person(s) responsible for the accomplishment of the plan.

2. In order to facilitate the accomplishment of agency goals, agency planning must be:

   A. Acceptable to the community.
   B. Progressive.
   C. Easily communicable.
   D. A and C above.
   E. A, B, and C above.

3. The major type of planning in any organization, including social service agencies or programs, is:

   A. Planning daily work patterns.
   B. Resource planning.
   C. Proper time planning.
   D. Scheduling.

4. The four categories of agency resource planning include:

   1. Finances.
   2. Supplies.
   3. Services.
   4. Consultants.
   5. Equipment and facilities.
   6. Personnel.

   Choose your answer from those presented below:

   A. 1, 2, 5, 6
   B. 1, 2, 3, 4
   C. 1, 2, 4, 5
   D. 1, 4, 5, 6

5. Once the amount of required additional resources has been determined, the planners, to accomplish the first phase of resource planning, must determine:

   A. The amount of resources that will be available.
   B. Whether the additional required resources can be acquired.
   C. Those resources that must be acquired.
   D. A and B above.
   E. B and C above.

6. What is the third or final phase of agency or program resource planning?

   A. Allocation of resources.
   B. Obtaining required resources.
   C. Discovering availability of resources.
   D. None of the above.

7. What financial model may be used to help implement financial planning in a social service agency or program?

   A. Forecast model.
   B. Accounting system.
   C. Legislative system.
   D. Fiscal model.

8. Supplies planning is:

   A. A long-range operation.
   B. The most difficult type of resource planning.
   C. A routine operation in most agencies.

9. Failure to plan an individual project often results in:

   A. Poor allocation of time and improper sequencing of activity.
   B. Confusion and overlapping of effort.
   C. A decrease in completion time.
   D. A reduction in effort.

10. The failure to plan group projects often results in:

    A. Poor allocation of time.
    B. Overlapping of effort.
    C. Contradictions in approaches.
    D. A and B above.
    E. A, B, and C above.

11. What is the first step in planning a project?

    A. Fact gathering.
    B. Recognition of the project requirements.
    C. Tentative decision as to the basic approach to be followed.
    D. Set up a basic plan of action.

12. The planning stage that applies only to group projects is the:

    A. Monitoring stage.
    B. Assignment of tasks and project kickoff stage.
    C. Review stage.
    D. Tentative decision stage.

13. Understanding and taking into account the relevant limiting and fixed factors, design, feasibility, and identification of logical check points are all key elements in:

    A. Personnel planning.
    B. Resource planning.
    C. Personal planning.
    D. Financial planning.

14. Phasing out tasks, working overtime, and deferring less important tasks are all possible ways of:

    A. Getting ahead.
    B. Getting fired.
    C. Fitting a new task into a full schedule.
    D. Planning for new tasks.

15. When accepting a new task you should:

    A. Accept the time estimates of others.
    B. Make your own time estimates and then double them.
    C. Attempt to reduce your responsibility as a condition of acceptance.
    D. A and C above.
    E. B and C above.

16. The stage of project planning in which the decision concerning revisions in approach is made is the:

    A. Recognition and clarification stage.
    B. Monitoring stage.
    C. Tentative decision stage.
    D. Laying out a basic plan of action stage.

See the last page of this unit for the answers.

The two questions pertaining to feasibility include: A1

1. *In light of the resources and time available, will I be able to achieve the goal?*
2. *In light of my own capabilities, is it possible to achieve the goal?*

Therefore, you should have circled letters A, B, and C since these indicate a need to modify the plan.

Continue with Q5

When designing a personal plan, you should draw on your own or others' prior experiences and knowledge or, when this is absent, simulate analogous experiences. A2
How well did you do? If you had any trouble return to M3 for a review. If not, continue with M4.

This would be very risky and usually results in a great deal of wasted time and energy! A3
The responsible executive would not take such risks.
Return to Q5 and select a better answer.

Did you say something like: personal planning refers to looking ahead, settling on the goals and objectives (determining what goals and objectives are feasible), and then designing or agreeing on a course of action that will make it possible for you to accomplish your objective? If so, you have a good grasp of the meaning of personal planning, and you should go right on to M2. If not, review this definition before proceeding to M2. A4

You should have circled letters B, C, D, and E. The four key elements of personal planning include: A5

1. *Understanding and taking into account the limiting and fixed factors that should be included in your plan; that is, time, resources, obstacles, unknowns, and the actions of others.*
2. *Design your plan based on prior experience.*
3. *Determine whether the plan and its achievement is feasible.*
4. *Identify logical check points for control purposes. Evaluate your progress at these points and make any necessary revisions.*

Continue with M6

You should have circled all factors named. Limited and fixed factors that should be understood and taken into account in personal planning include: A6

1. *Time limits.*
2. *Available resources.*
3. *Obstacles.*
4. *Unknowns.*
5. *Actions of others that might affect what you are doing.*

Continue with M3

Good. The responsible executive would modify his goals if available resources and/or time and/or his own capabilities were in shorter supply than called for by the plan. A7

Continue with M5

The correct letters are B and C. You should base your acceptance **A8**
of a new task on the estimates of your on-going work load and on the
time the new task will consume.

The major question here is, "Does the task warrant the time to be
spent on it in relation to your other tasks?"

Continue with Q8

Yes, a new task could be included on your schedule if you are **A9**
willing to work overtime. However, this is only one way—there are
others mentioned in the responses to this question, so return to Q8
and select the correct answer.

You could follow this course of action. However, it would probably **A10**
be best if you first attempted to modify the goal to fit the available
resources.

In some cases, however, even the modified goal may be unattain-
able in light of the available resources, and, in this case, it would be
foolhardy to continue toward the goal.

Return to Q5 and select a better answer.

Although you could defer another task in order to fit a new one into **A11**
your schedule, this is not the only way mentioned in the responses
to Q8, so return there now and choose the correct answer.

By phasing out another task it would be possible to include a new **A12**
task on your schedule. However, this is only one possible method
you could use—there are others mentioned.

Return to Q8 and select the best answer.

You should have circled letters A, D, E, and F. When making a **A13**
decision to accept a new task, you should be sure to follow these
suggestions:

1. *Do not overburden yourself with too many outside activities.*
2. *Attempt to reduce your responsibilities related to the achievement*
   of the task as a condition of acceptance.
3. *Make your own time estimates of how long the task will take and*
   then double this estimate.
4. *Obtain in writing specifically what is expected of you and the*
   assistance you should expect to receive.
   Return now to M8 and complete this lesson.

This is the correct answer. A new task may be placed on your **A14**
schedule by possibly:

1. *Phasing out another task.*
2. *Working overtime.*
3. *Deferring another less important task.*

Continue with M7

The following are the correct responses to questions for Unit III.

Questions	Answers	Questions	Answers
1	B	9	A
2	E	10	E
3	B	11	B
4	A	12	B
5	D	13	C
6	A	14	C
7	B	15	E
8	C	16	B

If you answered less than twelve (12) questions correctly, you need a brief review of those areas that gave you trouble before proceeding to Unit IV.

If you answered fifteen (15) or more correctly, congratulations, you are now ready for Unit IV.

UNIT IV
ORGANIZING

LESSON 1
Organization as Both Structure and Process

UNIT IV OBJECTIVE—ORGANIZING

Given a problem-solving, decision making situation requiring the use of organizational skills, you will be able to demonstrate your emerging organizational skills by making the necessary decisions leading to a solution of the problems presented.

Specific Objective

Given a description of the formal and informal organization of an inefficient agency, you will be able to explain the changes needed to improve the formal and informal organizational structure, thereby enhancing agency efficiency.

Enabling Objective 1
You will be able to state the two essential features of sound organization.

Enabling Objective 2
You will be able to define, in your own words, the meaning of organization.

Enabling Objective 3
You will be able to identify where an agency's organizational structure is described.

Enabling Objective 4
You will be able to design an organizational chart, given a description of an agency.

115

Enabling Objective 5
You will be able to state the three major responsibilities of the executive director regarding agency organization.

Enabling Objective 6
You will be able to distinguish between formal and informal organization within an agency.

Enabling Objective 7
You will be able to explain how the formal and informal structures and procedures are arranged in efficient agencies.

Move right on to M1

THE MEANING OF ORGANIZATION

In Lesson Two, Unit I, you learned that organization refers to the establishment of the formal structure through which work is arranged, defined, and coordinated. According to Friedlander, organization is the means by which staff members' duties are defined and clarified.[1] An organization also reflects a process. Highlighting its two essential features, Jay Urice defines organization as follows:

> Organization is the process and structure that defines and gives direction to the cooperative relationships of people in the formulation of objectives, policies and plans and in carrying them into effect.[2]

Organization in an agency, then, refers to both the process and the structure through which relationships are established that permit employees to work together most effectively in formulating and accomplishing agency objectives, policies, and plans.

M1

Continue with M2

AGENCY STRUCTURE

The first major task in creating any organization is to set up a structure or framework within which the organization will function. As you learned in Unit I, the structure of a human service agency is usually described in general terms in the provisions of the agency's constituition and by-laws in the manual of operations.

M2

In general, an agency structure ordinarily consists of the following:

1. A board of directors, in the case of a private agency, or a legislative body, in the case of a public agency.
2. Committees, standing or special, district or departmental, appointed by the board and/or the executive director.
3. Provisions for an executive director (senior executive).
4. Provisions for associate executives (finance, program, personnel, service, and directors, especially in larger agencies).
5. Provisions for supervisors and regular staff positions.

Continue with Q1

[1] Harleigh Trecker, *Social Work Administration, Principles and Practices* (New York: Association, 1971), p. 38.
[2] Jay Urice, "Developing and Maintaining an Effective Organization," in *The Executive Role in Y.M.C.A. Administration,* ed. Gren O. Pierrel (New York: Association, 1951), p. 110.

Organization refers to: **Q1**

A. Structure *A9*
B. Process *A1*
C. Both structure and process *A5*

If a new executive director wanted to obtain a general description **Q2**
of the structure of the agency, he would find it in:

A. The job description provided by the agency *A3*
B. The agency's constitution and by-laws or in the manual of operations *A4*

What group(s) of individuals are missing from the following struc- **Q3**
ture of a large private agency? Write in the two groups that are
missing.

Board of directors.
Committees.
Executive director.
Regular staff.

Check your answer to this question by turning to A8.

Which of the following groups of individuals are present in the **Q4**
structure of a public agency but not a private agency?

A. Board of directors *A7*
B. Legislative body *A6*
C. Committees *A2*

**THE
ORGANIZATIONAL
CHART**

An organizational chart is used to depict the formal relationships be- **M3**
tween agency employees and functions. Such a chart would include,
in most agencies, the five groups of individuals mentioned earlier.
It is important here to note that organizational structures vary for all
types of human service agencies.[3]

Depending upon the size of the agency and the different services
rendered, the number of committees and the type of staff would, of
course, vary. If the agency is small, then an assistant director could
handle most of the matters that the executive director was unable to
handle. As the agency expands, additional assistant directors would
be needed to take over such responsibilities as finance, personnel,
services, and training programs, or any other major departments. The
chart on M4 is typical of the organization of a medium-size private
agency; the chart on M5 is typical of a large public agency. After
reviewing these two charts continue with Q5.

---

[3] See Trecker, *Social Work Administration*, p. 142, for a description of those
aspects that should be considered when developing a structure to facilitate
the agency program and to make the agency politically effective.

Organizational Chart for a Medium-Sized Private Agency

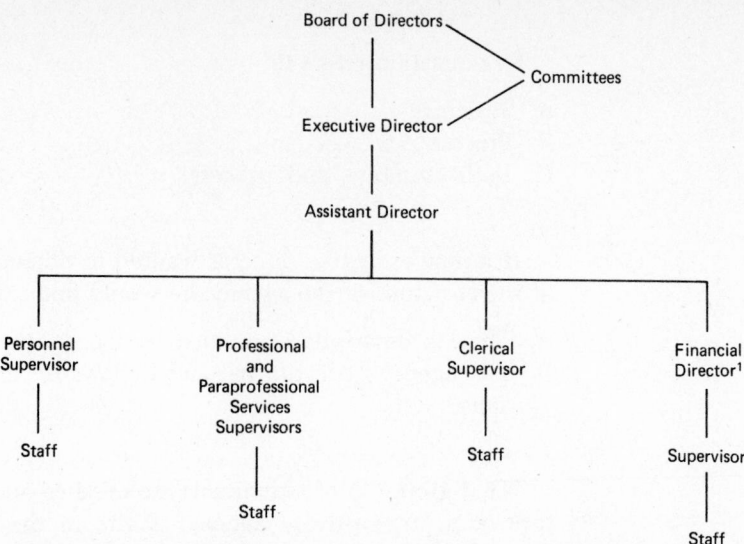

[1] Although the budgetary responsibility may be assumed by the executive director or his assistant, these responsibilities are often delegated to other staff due to the heavy responsibilities involved in directing the other areas of the agency.

Organizational Chart for a Large Public Agency

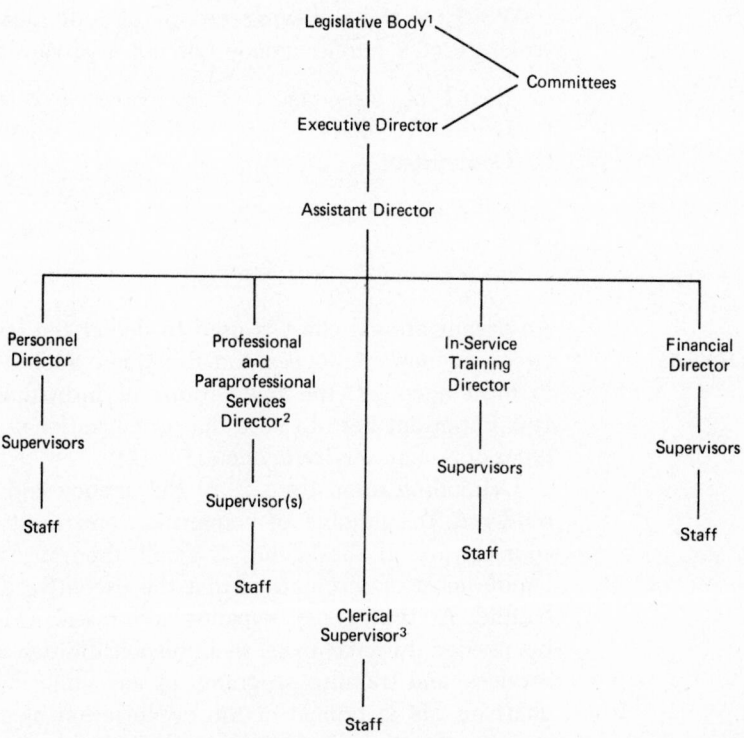

[1] Some large public agencies have a "board" similar to that of private agencies in addition to the legislative which regulates the agency and is interposed between the legislature and the executive.

[2] In many cases, only the services department may need supervisors. However, when the agency becomes large, as in this case, the other departments also may need supervisors or an assistant supervisor.

[3] The clerical department rarely requires a director—a supervisor is usually sufficient.

Continue with Q5

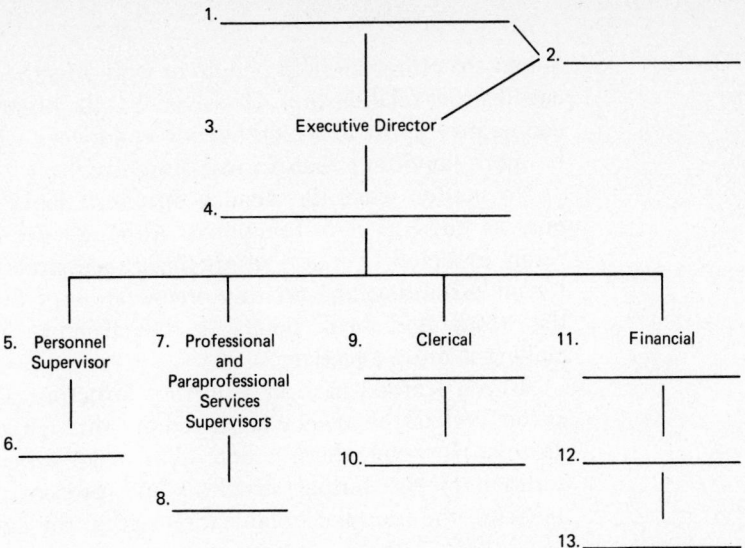

Although most executives find an organization in existence when **Q5** they accept their position, assume that you are given the task of creating a new agency, and that one of your first tasks is to develop the formal organizational structure for the agency. Assume you are working for a medium-sized private agency. In the chart above, fill in the vacant positions. After you have completed the chart, check your answers by turning to A10.

Now assume you have the responsibility of developing an organi- **Q6** zational structure for a large public agency. In the chart below, fill in the positions that are vacant. After you have completed the chart, check your answers by turning to A17.

Organizational Chart

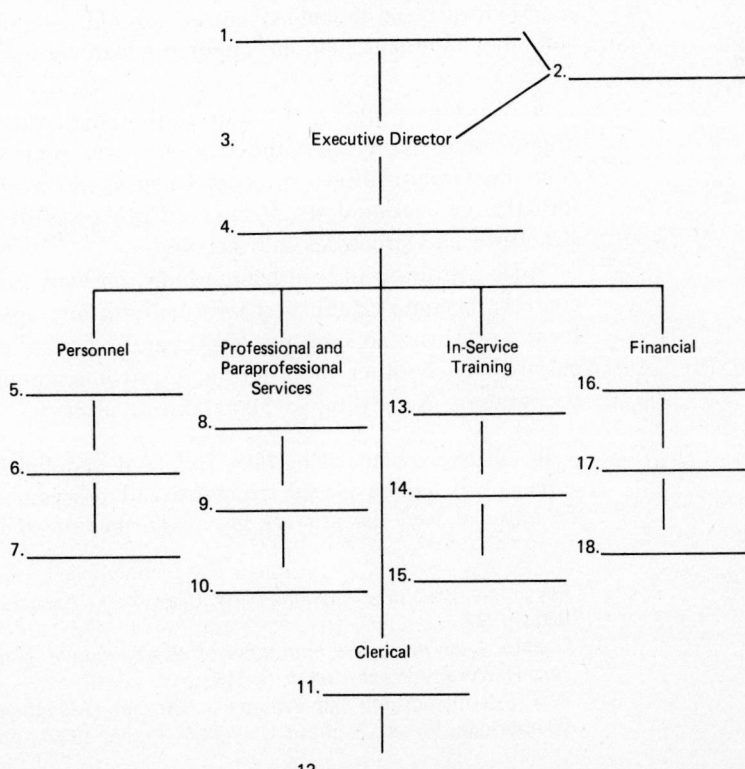

ORGANIZATION AS PROCESS

Sound structure can help people to work together, but faulty structure   **M6**
can obstruct relationships. However, it is the organization process or the
cooperative spirit in which agency employees work together that can
be more important than formal structure.[4]

No matter what the agency structure looks like on paper, it is
only as good as it is functional. Although the executive director is
rarely expected to create an organizational structure, he is responsible
for understanding the existing organization of the agency, identifying
the strong and weak points in the structure and process, and for
making it more effective.[5]

As you learned in Unit I, agency structure is made more explicit
as the work of the agency is carried out through an established, formal
process. However, there is one other major aspect of organization, in
addition to the formal structure and process, that emerges in all
agencies: the informal organization within the agency.

Continue with M7

INFORMAL ORGANIZATION

An informal organization is created among agency employees. Accord-   **M7**
ing to Barnard, informal organization is the aggregate of the personal
contacts and interactions and the associated groupings of people.[6]
According to Roethlisberger and Dickson, the formal agency structure
shows,

> . . . the functional relationships between working units, but they do not
> express the distinctions of social distance, movement, or equilibrium . . . .
> The formal organization cannot take into account the sentiments and
> values residing in the social organization by means of which individuals or
> groups of individuals are informally differentiated, ordered, and integrated
> . . . Without them, formal organization could not survive for long. Formal
> and informal organization are interdependent aspects of social interaction.[7]

A prime example of the impact that the informal relationships in
organizations have upon the structure and process is the employee's
councils. Organizations, in order to survive, have had to adjust their
formal organizational structures and processes to take these informal
structures and processes into account.

Since attitudes and understandings, as well as customs and social
controls, become established informally in any agency, it is important
for the executive to keep the formal and informal organization consistent with each other in order to improve communication and foster
cooperation. According to Scott and Lynton,

> In efficient organizations they [informal and formal organization] cor-
> respond closely; the formal structures and procedures reflect and sustain
> the informal, and the primary groups are integrated in an effective social

---

[4] Ray Johns, *Executive Responsibility* (New York: Association, 1966), p. 54.
[5] Ibid., p. 52.
[6] Chester I. Barnard, *The Functions of the Executive* (Cambridge, Mass.: Harvard University Press, 1942), p. 115.
[7] F. J. Roethlisberger, and William J. Dickson, *Management and the Worker*
(Cambridge, Mass.: Harvard University Press, 1939), pp. 559–560, 562.

institution. In other organizations the formal and informal arrangements   **M7**
diverge, and failure to cooperate tends to result.[8]   **cont.**

Continue with Q7

You have been appointed executive director of an established   **Q7**
agency. Which set of the following items are your major responsibilities?

A. Understanding the existing organizational structure and process
   of the agency; documenting the organizational structure; and
   strengthening the structure and process, if necessary, to make
   it more effective *A15*
B. Understanding the existing organizational structure and process
   of the agency; identifying the strong and weak points of the
   organizational structure and process; and strengthening the structure and process, if necessary, to make it more effective . *A11*

_____ organization is described in the articles of   **Q8**
incorporation and by-laws or in the manual of operations and maintained by the board and the executive, while _____
organization is created among the employees as they begin to work
together toward fulfilling the goal of the organization.
   In order of appearance:

A. Informal; formal *A12*
B. Formal; informal *A14*

The executive should attempt to keep the formal and informal orga-   **Q9**
nizations within an agency consistent in order to:

A. Foster cooperation by improving communication between individual employees and between groups of employees . . . *A16*
B. Facilitate record keeping procedures of the operation of the organization *A13*

[8] Jerome Scott and R. P. Lynton, *The Community Factor in Modern Technology*
(Paris, France: United Nations Educational, Scientific, and Cultural Organization, 1952), p. 122.

Yes, organization is a process, but it also requires a structure. Review **A1**
the material on organization, M1. Then answer Q1 again.

Committees, standing and/or special, district and/or departmental, **A2**
are present in both public and private agencies. Return to Q4 and
select another answer.

Sorry! The job description spells out the necessary details of the **A3**
job only. It would not be an appropriate vehicle for detailing the
structure of an agency. Return to Q2 and select another answer.

Yes, a general description of the structure of an agency is usually **A4**
found in the agency's constitution and by-laws or in the manual of
operations.

Continue with Q3

This is correct. Organization refers to a process and it requires a **A5**
structure—these are its two essential features.

Continue with Q2

Excellent—a legislative body is usually responsible for overseeing **A6**
the administration of a public agency while a board of directors over-
sees the administration of a private agency. Committees are, of course,
present in all agencies, public and private.

Continue with M3

No, a board of directors oversees the administration of a private **A7**
agency. Return to Q4 and select another answer.

Two groups of individuals found in most agencies are missing from **A8**
the structure: associate executives and supervisors. If you missed this
question, review the material on agency structure M2 before answering
Q3 correctly.

Continue with Q4

Yes, organization does require structure, but this is only part of the **A9**
meaning of organization. Return to Q1 and select another answer.

1. Board of directors.   *9. Clerical supervisor.*   **A10**
2. Committees.   *10. Staff.*
4. Assistant director.   *11. Financial director.*
6. Staff.   *12. Supervisor.*
8. Staff.   *13. Staff.*

If you missed any of these answers, review the material presented
on M3 and M4 before attempting to answer Q5 again.
If you had no trouble here continue with Q6.

That's correct. Your responsibilities would include the following: **A11**

A. Understanding the existing organizational structure and process
of the agency.

B. *Identifying the strong and weak points of the organizational struc-*   **A11**
   ture and process.   **cont.**
C. *Strengthening the structure and process, if necessary, to make it*
   more effective.

Continue with Q8

No, you have them reversed. Formal organization is described in   **A12**
the articles of incorporation and by-laws or in the manual of operations. It is maintained by the board and executives of the agency.
Informal organization emerges as the employees begin to work together in their formal roles. Return to Q8 and select the correct answer.

You have not chosen the correct answer. Review the material in M7   **A13**
before attempting to answer Q9 again.

Exactly. Formal organization is first described in the articles of   **A14**
incorporation and by-laws or in the manual of operations. It is main-
tained by the board and executives of the agency. As employees begin
to work together in their respective formal roles, an informal organiza-
tional pattern emerges based on individual and group sentiments and
values.

Continue with Q9

No, you need to review M6 before attempting to answer Q7 again.   **A15**

The formal and informal organizational patterns within an agency   **A16**
should be kept as consistent as possible in order to foster cooperation
by improving communication between individual employees and be-
tween groups of employees.

Continue with Lesson 2

		A17
1. *Legislative body.*	10. *Supervisor.*	
2. *Committees.*	11. *Staff.*	
3. *Assistant director.*	12. *Director.*	
4. *Personnel director.*	13. *Supervisors.*	
5. *Supervisors.*	14. *Staff.*	
6. *Staff.*	15. *Director.*	
7. *Directors.*	16. *Supervisors.*	
8. *Supervisor(s).*	17. *Staff.*	
9. *Staff.*		

If you missed any of these answers, review M3 and M5 before
continuing with M6.

UNIT IV
ORGANIZING

LESSON 2
Principles and Practices of Sound Organization

Specific Objective

Given a description of an agency organization, you will be able to identify the principles that are not being followed and to explain ways of strengthening the organization of the agency.

Enabling Objective 1
You will be able to list the ten essential principles and practices involved in sound organization that, in varying degrees, apply to all types and sizes of agencies and that provide a basis for executives to examine the existing organizational structure and processes as well as to plan steps for strengthening them.

Enabling Objective 2
Given an identifying description of one or more of the ten essential principles and practices involved in sound organization, you will be able to briefly discuss the meaning and purpose of each specified principle or practice.

Enabling Objective 3
Given a description of an organizational structure in one or more areas in an agency relating to one or more of the principles or practices involved in sound organization, you will be able to identify areas of weakness in the structure and explain how the weak areas may be strengthened.

Continue with M1

ORGANIZATIONAL PRINCIPLES AND PRACTICES

The ten principles and practices involved in sound organization to be discussed in this lesson apply, in varying degrees, to all types and sizes of agencies.[1] These principles and practices provide a basis for the agency executive to examine existing organizational structures and processes and thereby identify any weak points that may need strengthening in order to improve the organization of the agency. The first of these is units of work.

M1

Units of Work

Suitable units of work, based on similarities, must be established in all organizations. Such units of work are established for two major reasons: 1. to get all the jobs accomplished, and 2. to help employees develop greater skill so that they are able to concentrate on one task or a set of related or similar tasks.[2]

According to Scott, there are three components of every job: 1. authority to act officially, 2. accountability to the next level of command, and 3. responsibility to perform successfully.[3]

Every employee in an agency will be better able to perform his tasks efficiently if he clearly understands these three components. Each will, therefore, have a better chance of being successful if the tasks to be performed on each job are similar in nature and if the employee is given the authority needed to fulfill his responsibilities and has a clear understanding of the person(s) to whom he is accountable.

Continue with Q1

Two reasons for establishing suitable units of work based on related or similar tasks are:

Q1

A. To get all the tasks accomplished and to get them accomplished more efficiently *A28*
B. To help employees improve their skills and to get all the tasks accomplished *A7*
C. To facilitate the preparation of charts depicting organizational activities and to facilitate the actual completion of these activities   *A1*

Name the three major components of every job that must be clearly understood by an employee if he is to successfully accomplish his job. Check your answer by turning to A26.

Q2

A.
B.
C.

Jobs in an agency are most likely to be successfully performed by each employee if:

Q3

A. Job descriptions are available for each employee—jobs are commensurate with each employee's ability *A20*

---

[1] Ray Johns, *Executive Responsibility* (New York: Association, 1966), p. 58.
[2] Ibid.
[3] Arthur Zich, "The Management Trainer with a Twist—Man on the Move/Don Scott," *Signature* 7 (January, 1972): 37.

B. Employees understand their responsibilities and act accordingly A11

C. Tasks are similar in nature and employees understand their responsibilities and authority as well as the person(s) to whom they must account A17

Q3 cont.

DEFINITE ASSIGNMENTS

The next practice of sound organization is to clearly define the responsibilities and relationships of each staff position and each committee. Clearly defined assignments are based on a clear conception of the agency's structure and will help eliminate uncertainties and misunderstandings among agency employees.[4]

M2

Two methods that are often used to help clarify task assignments include: 1. written assignments or guidelines to staff and/or committee members, and 2. an organizational chart depicting relationships and lines of responsibility.[5] Written assignments or guidelines will be most effective when they are developed jointly by those issuing them and by those to whom they are addressed. In this manner, the recipient(s) are more likely to take the important factors into account and accept their responsibility more readily.

An organizational chart depicts the formal system of communications flow. It is not a hierarchy. Responsibility and authority generally flow downward, and accountability generally flows in both directions. This means that the lines of communication established by an organizational chart are two-way, not just one-way.[6]

Organizational charts are useful in providing a base for definite assignments, but they have limitations. Such charts show accurately only one of the three sets of important employee relationships, namely, the formal positions, their titles, and the formal links among them. However, the actual prestige and authority of the various positions shown and of the individuals who hold them, as well as the actual lines of person-to-person contact in the process of getting the job done, may only be inferred from the organizational chart.[7]

Continue with Q4

In order to reduce or even eliminate misunderstandings and uncertainties among staff and committee members:

Q4

A. Responsibilities and relationships of staff and committee members should be clearly defined A8

B. Each employee should be provided with a written job description A3

C. Staff organizational meetings should be held on a regular basis   A27

Name two methods that are often used to help clearly define staff and committee member's responsibilities and relationships. Check your answer by turning to A9.

Q5

A.

B.

[4] Johns, *Executive Responsibility*, p. 58. See especially, "Essentials of Sound Organization."

[5] Ibid., p. 59.

[6] Don Scott, as quoted in Zich, "Management Trainer with a Twist," p. 37.

[7] Johns, *Executive Responsibility*, p. 59.

Written assignments or guidelines will be most effective if they are developed: **Q6**

A. By those issuing them *A4*
B. Jointly by those issuing and by those receiving them . . . *A18*

Organizational charts are useful in providing a base for definite assignments, but then only one of the three sets of important employee relationships are shown accurately. The relationships that such charts accurately show are: **Q7**

A. The actual prestige and authority of the various agency positions *A35*
B. The lines of person-to-person contact *A24*
C. The formal agency positions, their titles, and the links among them *A22*

CLEAR LINES OF RESPONSIBILITY

One of the most important responsibilities of the executive director is to insure that the responsibilities and authorities of every member of the agency are established, understood, and observed. The basic rule to follow in order to facilitate the establishment, understanding, and observation of clear lines of authority in an agency is: "One person responsible to one person," or single lines of accountability.[8]   **M3**

The typical lines of authority in a human service agency are as follows:

1. The articles of incorporation and the constitution of the agency confer its primary legal authority to act upon the board of directors for a private agency or the legislative body, in the case of a public agency. These are ultimately responsible for agency performance.
2. The senior executive (executive director) derives his responsibility and authority from the board or the legislative body.
3. Committees receive their authority from the individual or group appointing them, that is, the board, the legislative body, and/or the executive director.
4. The senior executive delegates responsibility and authority to all professional staff members.

Continue with Q8

A sound organization is based on clear lines of responsibility. Which of the following best describes the executive director's role regarding this important principle?   **Q8**

A. The executive director must insure that the responsibilities and authorities of every member of the agency are clearly documented and distributed to each employee *A12*
B. The executive director must insure that the responsibilities and authorities of every member of the agency are firmly established, clearly understood, and consistently observed within the agency . *A23*

[8] Ibid., p. 60.

In order to facilitate the establishment of clear lines of authority, **Q9** the following rule should be followed by the executive director:

A. "One person responsible to one person," or single lines of accountability *A29*
B. Multiple lines of accountability in the event that an employee fails to carry out the responsibility delegated to him *A32*

The original source of authority from which all other authority in **Q10** an agency is derived is:

A. The board of directors or legislative body *A15*
B. The articles of incorporation and the constitution *A19*
C. The executive director *A10*

All professional staff members are delegated their responsibility **Q11** and authority from the:

A. Board of directors or the legislative body *A2*
B. Executive director *A30*

Fill in the blanks below with the titles of the individuals or groups **Q12** delegating and receiving responsibility and authority. Check your answers by turning to A21.

The articles of incorporation and the constitution of an agency confer legal authority on the _____ or _____ _____, who confer the responsibilities and authority required to run the agency upon the _____ _____ who, in turn, delegates the necessary responsibility and authority to the _____ of the agency.

Committees appointed by the board of directors receive their authority from the _____, while committees appointed by the executive director receive their authority from the _____.

EFFECTIVE COMMUNICATION

This essential practice has already been discussed in Unit II. However, **M4** it should be stated that organizational structure and processes or procedures must provide for a free two-way flow of ideas. Planned methods of communication, up and down as well as across levels, are a necessity.[9]

DISTRIBUTION OF RESPONSIBILITY

In order to promote efficient operations and high morale in an agency, it is best to adopt a combination of both centralization and decentralization of responsibility. Review and final approval or disapproval of fundamental matters as well as the accounting of both financial and program services should be centralized, that is, reserved for the primary responsible individual and bodies.

However, decentralization may be promoted by locating the plan-

[9] Ibid.

ning of projects as close as possible to the points of responsibility for **M4** performance and by encouraging the delegation of responsibility **cont.** throughout the agency.[10] The efficient operation and high morale of an agency are best promoted by adopting a combination of centralization and decentralization of responsibility.

Continue with Q13

Two methods by which the executive may help promote decentral- **Q13** ization of responsibility in an agency are:

A. Allowing those responsible for carrying out a project to be involved in the planning of the project, and encouraging delegation of responsibility throughout the agency A37
B. Assuring that a project is not completed by those who planned it, and discouraging delegation A36

You have now reviewed the first five essential principles and prac- **Q14** tices of sound organization. List these principles and practices in the space below. Check your answer by turning to A6.

A.
B.
C.
D.
E.

COORDINATION OF The work of an agency must be divided and coordinated. Coordina- **M5**
UNITS OF WORK tion ". . . may be achieved in two primary ways . . . (1) by organiza-
AND EMPLOYEES tion . . . interrelating the subdivisions of work . . . (2) by the dominance of an idea . . . the development of a singleness of purpose . . . of those who are working together as a group . . ."[11]

Cooperative thinking, planning, and action are fundamental to effective coordination. Coordination as an executive function will be discussed in Unit VII. The sixth principle of sound organization mentioned in this lesson is the coordination of work units and employees who perform the work.

SPAN OF CONTROL Optimum span of control varies with agencies and with individuals. The number of staff members who report directly to any one executive or the number of committees that report directly to the board, executive director, or legislative body, should, of course, be kept within manageable limits. When the agency is running smoothly, agency personnel are well seasoned, and there are few new developments, the span may be widened. However, when executives have many other responsibilities, the span should then be reduced correspondingly. It has been found that, under most conditions, a man-

[10] Ibid., p. 61.
[11] Luther Gulick and L. Urwick, eds., *Papers on the Science of Administration* (New York: Institute of Public Administration, 1937), p. 6.

ageable and effective ratio is from six to twelve persons to one executive.[12]

M5
cont.

Continue with Q15

Two ways in which coordination may be achieved are: Q15

A. Organizing or interrelating work subdivisions, and the dominance of an idea leading to singleness of purpose among agency employees *A14*
B. Discouraging the dominance of any single idea in the agency, thereby avoiding a singleness of purpose among agency employees and keeping work subdivisions independent *A38*

A practical span of control is considered to be from _____ to _____ persons responsible to one executive.   Q16

A. One to three *A25*
B. Six to twelve *A34*
C. Ten to twenty *A16*

STANDARDIZED PRACTICES

There are many tasks that can be more accurately managed in less time using standardized practices. Such tasks are 1. purchase of supplies, 2. schedules of work, 3. use of equipment and facilities, 4. payment of bills, and 5. making records of services and funds.[13]   M6

PROVISIONS FOR EXCEPTIONS

The ninth essential organizational practice includes the establishment of specific methods and authorities for making exceptions to established agency policies and practices, such as extensions of sick leave under unusual circumstances. The conditions under which exceptions can be made and the persons who may authorize these exceptions should be defined and clearly understood by staff members.[14]

ACCURATE RECORDS

Keeping adequate records and reports is the final essential element of sound organization. Such records and reports may be used by staff members for the following purposes: 1. to furnish a basis for planning; 2. to note strengths and weaknesses within the agency; and 3. to measure progress.[15]

It should be noted here that suggestions for the necessary records and reports, as well as useful forms and procedures, have been developed by most of the national human service agencies and should be used, with adaptations, by all local agencies.

Continue with Q17

---

[12] Johns, *Executive Responsibility*, p. 62.
[13] Ibid.
[14] Ibid.
[15] Ibid., pp. 62–63.

Which of the following best defines the organizational principle **Q17**
"provisions for exceptions":

A. Stating the procedure for making exceptions *A33*
B. The establishment of the specific methods and authorities for making exceptions to established agency policies and procedures *A39*

In the space below, list five agency tasks that can be more efficiently **Q18**
managed by using standardized practices than by not using such
practices. Check your answer by turning to A31.

A.
B.
C.
D.
E.

Assume that you are given the task of establishing provisions for **Q19**
exceptions to the many different agency policies and practices. In the
space below, explain the two aspects that should be defined so that
they will be clearly understood by all agency personnel. Check your
answer by turning to A5.

A.

B.

Adequate records and reports have three major uses. List these uses **Q20**
in the space below. Check your answer by turning to A13.

A.
B.
C.

How well do you understand the ten essential principles or practices **Q21**
of sound organization? Find out by stating the meanings, purposes,
and/or important aspects as requested in the next ten questions.

I.   *Units of Work*
     Purposes:
     A.
     B.

If you had trouble stating these two purposes, return to M1 before
continuing with Q22.

II. *Definite Assignments*   **Q22**
     A. Purpose
     B. Methods used to help clarify task assignments
        1.
        2.

If you had trouble with A and B, then return to M2 for a review
before continuing with Q23.

III. *Clear Lines of Responsibility and Authority*   **Q23**

    A. The basic rule to follow to facilitate the establishment, understanding, and observation of clear lines of authority in an agency is as follows:

    This rule is cited in M3. Review M3 now if you were unable to state it.

    B. State below beside each group or individual the source from which they receive their authority in social agencies:
      1. Board of directors—
      2. Legislative body—
      3. Committees appointed by the board—
      4. Committees appointed by the executive director—
      5. Executive director (senior executive)—
      6. Professional staff members—

Did you miss any of the above? If so, return to M3. If not, continue with Q24.

IV. *Effective Communication*   **Q24**
What type of communication must be encouraged in a human service agency if it is to be effective? State your answer below and then, if you had any trouble, return to M4 for a review, then continue with Q25.

V. *Distribution of Responsibility*   **Q25**
In order to best promote efficient operations and high morale, a combination of centralization should be adopted. What are two major ways that the executive may distribute responsibility (decentralize responsibility) in an agency?

    A.
    B.

If you had any trouble citing these two methods, return to M4 for a review, then continue with Q26.

VI. *Coordination of Units of Work and Employees*   **Q26**
The work of an agency must be divided and coordinated. Explain below two ways in which this coordination may be achieved.

    A.
    B.

Did you write both methods? If not, return to M5. If yes, continue with Q27.

VII. *Span of Control*   Q27
      State the most practicable span of control which, under most
      conditions, is a manageable and effective ratio.

You probably had no trouble answering this question, but if you did
and feel you need a review of the principle, return to M5 and then
continue with Q28.

VIII. *Standard Practices*   Q28
      State at least four agency tasks that may be more efficiently and
      effectively managed using standard practices.

      A.
      B.
      C.
      D.

Return to M6 if you had any trouble here, or continue with Q29 if
you had no trouble.

IX.   *Provision for Exceptions*   Q29

      A. Meaning—
      B. Two aspects requiring definition when establishing pro-
         visions for exceptions:
         1.
         2.

Did you do well on A and B? If not return to M6. If you are satisfied with your answers, continue with Q30.

X.   *Adequate Records*   Q30

      A. Purposes of records and reports:
      1.
      2.
      3.

Check your answers by turning to A0.

You have reached the end of this lesson. If you believe that you   M7
have a firm grasp of the ten principles and practices of sound organization presented in this lesson, continue with Lesson Three. If not,
briefly review this lesson before going on.

Records and reports are used by staff members to: **A0**

1. *Provide a basis for planning.*
2. *Measure agency and employee progress.*
3. *Identify agency strengths and weaknesses.*

Return now to M7

Although establishing units of work based on related tasks might **A1** *facilitate the preparation of organizational charts, there are more important benefits that will result from this practice. Review M1, then select a more appropriate answer for Q1.*

No, the board of directors or the legislative body confers the re- **A2** *sponsibility and authority needed to run the agency upon the executive director, who, in turn, delegates the required responsibilities to his professional staff members. Return to Q11 and select the correct answer.*

This may reduce misunderstandings and uncertainties to some ex- **A3** *tent, but after reviewing M2 you may be able to detect a more appropriate answer for Q4.*

Although guidelines developed only by those persons or groups **A4** *issuing them may be very effective, the assignment will be better accomplished if the recipients are also involved in this development. Return to Q6 and select a more appropriate answer.*

Provisions for exceptions should include the following: **A5**

A. *Clear definitions of the conditions under which exceptions can be made for each policy and practice, and*
B. *The titles of the person(s) who may authorize the exceptions for each policy and practice.*

Continue with Q20

The first five essential principles and practices of sound organiza- **A6** *tion, and the frames in the text where these are discussed are:*

A. *Units of work* *M1*
B. *Clear lines of responsibility and authority* *M3*
C. *Definite assignments* *M2*
D. *Effective communication* *M4*
E. *Distribution of responsibility* *M4*

If you had any trouble remembering the important points of any of these principles, return to the frames listed beside them before going on to the sixth principle. When you think you have mastered these five principles, continue with M5.

This is correct. Establishing units of work based on related or sim- **A7** *ilar tasks will help employees improve their skills, as well as enable them to get the tasks accomplished.*

Continue with Q2

Correct. Misunderstandings and uncertainties in task performance are reduced and often eliminated through clear definitions of the responsibilities and relationships of staff and committee members.   **A8**

Continue with Q5

The two methods include the following: 1. written assignments or guidelines, and 2. an organizational chart.   **A9**

Continue with Q6

Caught you napping! The executive director receives his authority from the board or legislative body. Return to M3 for a review before answering Q10 correctly.   **A10**

Although employees' understandings of job responsibilities increase the probability that a job will be performed successfully, there are other important factors involved. Review M1, then select a more appropriate answer for Q3.   **A11**

This is not the best answer. Review M3 and then try to answer Q8 again.   **A12**

Adequate records and reports are used: **A13**

A. As a basis for planning.
B. For measuring agency and employee progress.
C. To discover agency strengths and weaknesses.

Continue with Q21

Yes. Coordination may be achieved by 1. organization or interrelated work subdivisions, and 2. the dominance of an idea leading to a singleness of purpose among agency employees.   **A14**

Continue with Q16

No, the board or legislative body derives their authority directly from the original source of authority. Return to M3 for a review before attempting to answer Q10 again.   **A15**

A ratio of ten to twenty persons responsible to each executive is too large, in most cases, to be very effective unless the agency is running smoothly, the personnel being supervised by the executive are well seasoned, and few new developments are occurring to take up the executive's time. Return to Q16 and select the correct answer.   **A16**

Correct! The jobs in an agency will have the best chance of being successfully performed if the tasks are similar in nature and if the employees clearly understand their responsibilities and authority, as well as the person(s) to whom they are accountable.   **A17**

Continue with M2

Yes, jointly developed assignments have a better chance of being accomplished in a competent manner since the person(s) or group(s) receiving them will better understand and accept them if they are involved in their development. **A18**

Continue with Q7

That's right! The agency's articles of incorporation and constitution are the original sources of all authority within the agency. **A19**

Continue with Q11

Undoubtedly, jobs accompanied by descriptions have a higher probability of being accomplished to the satisfaction of the employer than those jobs not accompanied by such a description. However, there are other factors that increase the probability that jobs in an agency will be performed successfully. Review M1, then select a more appropriate answer for Q3. **A20**

The answers are as follows: **A21**

Board of directors.
Legislative body.
Executive director (senior executive).
Professional staff.
Board of directors.
Executive director.

Continue with M4

Very good. Organizational charts accurately show the formal agency positions, their titles, and the formal links among them but not the actual prestige and authority of each position nor the actual person-to-person contact. **A22**

Continue with M3

That's right! The executive director must insure that the responsibilities and authorities of every member of the agency are firmly established, clearly understood, and consistently observed. **A23**

Continue with Q9

The organizational chart does not accurately show the actual lines of person-to-person contact in an agency. Return to M2 and review the material presented there before answering Q7 again. **A24**

No, a ratio of one to three persons for every executive is too small to be effective. Such a span is usually too costly unless the executive is burdened with an overload of additional responsibilities. Return to M5 for a review, and then answer Q16 correctly. **A25**

The three major components of every job are: 1. authority to act officially; 2. accountability to the next level of command; and 3. responsibility to perform successfully. **A26**

Continue with Q3

Regular staff meetings will certainly serve to decrease the number   **A27**
of misunderstandings that tend to occur among staff and committee
members. However, after reviewing M2, you may be able to detect a
more appropriate answer for Q4.

Establishing units of work based on related or similar tasks will   **A28**
undoubtedly permit tasks to be accomplished efficiently. However,
there is also another benefit that accrues from this practice. Read M1
again, then select a more appropriate answer for Q1.

That's right! The simple rule to follow is, "One person responsible   **A29**
to one person," or single lines of accountability.

Continue with Q10

Exactly! The executive director delegates the required responsibil-   **A30**
ities and authority to the members of his professional staff.

Continue with Q12

Standardized practices will improve efficiency when performing   **A31**
such agency tasks as:

A. *Work scheduling.*
B. *Record keeping.*
C. *Purchasing supplies.*
D. *Payment of bills.*
E. *Equipment and facilities usage.*

Continue with Q19

This is not the best answer. Review M3 and then try to answer Q9   **A32**
again.

The definition includes more than just a statement of procedures.   **A33**
Review M6, then try to answer Q17 again.

Yes. A ratio of six to twelve persons to each executive has been   **A34**
found to be the most practical span under most conditions.

Continue with M6

Actual prestige and authority of the various agency positions may   **A35**
only be inferred from the organizational chart. Therefore, the organi-
zational chart does not show these relationships accurately. Return
to M2 and review the material presented there before attempting to
answer Q7 again.

This approach may cause a number of problems. Review M4 and   **A36**
then answer Q13 again.

Right! Decentralization is promoted by 1. allowing those responsi-   **A37**
ble for carrying out a project to be involved in the planning of the
project, and by 2. encouraging delegation throughout the agency.

Continue with Q14

This probably would not achieve the desired effect. Review M5   **A38**
and then answer Q15 correctly.

You are right—well done! Provisions for exceptions refers to the   **A39**
establishment of the specific methods and authorities for making ex-
ceptions to established agency policies and practices.

Continue with Q18

UNIT IV
ORGANIZING

LESSON 3
Performing Board and Committee Functions

Specific Objective

Given a description of one function performed by a board of directors, you will be able to cite at least one method by which a board performs this function and designate which committee should be appointed to fulfill said function.

Enabling Objective 1
You will be able to state the three major purposes of boards.

Enabling Objective 2
You will be able to give the five major functions of boards.

Enabling Objective 3
Given the name of one of the two major types of committees, you will be able to identify the general types of problems with which the committee deals.

Enabling Objective 4
You will be able to name the five major types of standing committees appointed in most human service agencies.

Enabling Objective 5
Given the name of a major standing committee, you will be able to explain the three types of functions that such a committee would perform.

Enabling Objective 6
You will be able to name the four major functions performed by special committees.

Continue with M1

As a preface to this lesson, it should be mentioned that although the purposes, functions, and methods of the boards of private, voluntary agencies, may vary, the board of a public agency must function within the framework of prescribed policies. However, most national private organizations do prescribe or recommend some policies and operating procedures that affect local boards.[1]

M1

Many of the issues cited in this lesson in relation to voluntary agencies also apply to the operation of city councils, or county commissions in the public sector.

BOARD OF DIRECTORS

In general, the three primary purposes of boards are as follows:[2]

1. To bring about citizen participation in the work of an agency. This creates public confidence and acceptance, which, in turn, assists the agency with its public relations.
2. To assure effective administration of the agency. Although boards delegate the day-to-day responsibility of administration to the executive director, they are ultimately responsible for agency performance.
3. To lend continuity to the agency. Although the executive director or other personnel may come and go, the board remains.[3]

Continue with Q1

One of the purposes of boards is to secure the effective administration of the agency. However, regardless of delegation the ultimate responsibility for agency performance falls upon the:

Q1

A. Executive director *A1*
B. Board of directors *A3*

In addition to assuring the effective administration of the agency, the board has other primary purposes. The two remaining purposes of boards are:

Q2

A. Improving public relations between the agency and the community and providing continuity to the work of the agency . . . *A4*
B. Providing job descriptions for each employee in the agency and serving as a disciplinary body when an employee fails to perform his duties in accordance with his job description *A2*

[1] See Roy Sorenson, *The Art of Board Membership* (New York: Association, 1950), pp. 24–26.
[2] See Ray Johns, *Executive Responsibility* (New York: Association, 1966), p. 66.
[3] For a more comprehensive description of the specific purposes of boards, refer to the programmed manual by William C. Tuck, *Step by Step in Better Board and Committee Work* (New York: Association, 1962). This programmed manual is based on the previously mentioned book by Roy Sorenson, *The Art of Board Membership.*

FUNCTIONS OF THE BOARD

In order to fulfill the three purposes just described, boards perform   **M2** the following functions for their agencies:[4]

1. Establish general policies and services.
2. Oversee the operation of the agency.
3. Help raise funds.
4. Validate agency services.
5. Improve agency public relations by:
    a. Interpreting the work of the agency to the community, and
    b. Interpreting community attitudes and problems to staff members and planning groups.

Boards use different methods when performing their functions. First, in order to perform the function of establishing general policies and services, boards:[5]

1. Review and advise concerning statements of proposed policies and plans.
2. Approve basic policy documents.
3. Make ongoing policy decisions (that is, policies that effect the future).
4. Approve plans to establish new services and adapt existing ones.

Therefore, the board utilizes methods such as reviewing, advising, and approving basic and present policies and plans, and approving decisions regarding future policies when performing the function of establishing agency policies and services.

In order to perform their second function of overseeing the operation of the agency, boards use such methods as:[6]

1. Appointing the senior executive (executive director) and major committees.
2. Approving the appointment of associate executives.
3. Authorizing, approving, and adopting budgets and other important plans.
4. Investing and safeguarding capital funds.

In performing their function of fund raising, board representatives, as well as agency executives, negotiate financial allocations with funding agencies.[7]

Agency services are validated by board members as they lend their personal prestige by participating in the work of the agency and by commending its work to community leaders.[8]

Improving agency public relations is the final board function. Through their personal contacts and the public relations plans they approve, board members interpret the agency's purposes and services to community leaders as well as interpret community attitudes and problems to agency personnel and planning groups.[9]

Continue with Q3

[4] Johns, *Executive Responsibility*, p. 67.
[5] Ibid.
[6] Ibid.
[7] Ibid.
[8] Ibid.
[9] Ibid.

Which of the following is *not* one of the functions of a board? **Q3**

A. Provide agency funds A20
B. Establish policies A17
C. Interpret the work of the agency to the community . . . A32

Which of the following is included in the public relations function **Q4**
of the board?

A. Surveying community attitudes and problems and interpreting
   these attitudes and problems to agency personnel A18
B. Interpreting the work of the agency to community leaders and
   interpreting community attitudes and problems to agency personnel A7
C. Fund raising and allocating these funds A10

Circle the letter(s) below that correspond to board functions: **Q5**

A. Help secure or raise funds.
B. Oversee agency operations.
C. Interpret the work of the agency to the community.
D. Establish agency policies and services.
E. Validate agency services.

Check your answer by turning to A34.

Name the five major functions of the agency board. Check your **Q6**
answer by turning to A13.

1.
2.
3.
4.
5.

Which of the following methods are used by boards when per- **Q7**
forming the function of establishing agency policies and services?

1. Review and advise on statements of proposed policies and plans.
2. Approve plans to establish new services.
3. Approve basic policy documents.
4. Appoint the executive director.
5. Make ongoing policy decisions.
6. Guide agency services.

A. 1, 3, 4, and 6 . . . . A23
B. 1, 2, 3, and 4 . . . . A35
C. 1, 2, 3, and 5 . . . . A5

Which of the following methods does the board use in performing **Q8**
its function of overseeing the operation of the agency?

A. Guiding the agency's services A15
B. Appointing all agency personnel A9
C. Authorizing, approving, and adopting agency budgets . . A26
D. A and C above A27
E. All of the above A21

Three other major methods the board uses to perform its function **Q9** of overseeing agency operations are:

A. Appointing the executive director and the major committees, approving the appointment of associate executives, and investing and safeguarding capital funds *A24*
B. Appointing supervisors, approving staff, and investing and safeguarding capital funds *A28*
C. Appointing the executive director and major committees, approving the appointment of associate executives, and serving as a disciplinary body *A12*

Which of the following methods is used by boards to secure or **Q10** raise funds?

A. Make public appearances *A8*
B. Represent the agency in negotiations with funding agencies *A25*
C. Select senior executives to represent the agency in negotiations with funding agencies *A36*

When board members lend their prestige to agencies by participating in agency work and commending the agency to community **Q11** leaders, which function are they performing?

A. Overseeing the operation of the agency *A14*
B. Validating agency services *A29*
C. Securing or raising funds *A11*

Which of the following two basic methods does the board utilize **Q12** when performing its function of improving agency public relations?

A. Approving public relations plans and basic policy documents *A30*
B. Establishing personal contacts and initiating fund raising activities *A33*
C. Establishing personal contacts and approving public relations plans *A22*

As a brief review of the functions of the board and the methods **Q13** used to perform them, match the functions and methods by choosing one of the answers presented below.

Functions

A. Establish agency policies and services.
B. Oversee agency operations.
C. Help secure or raise funds.

Methods

1. Negotiate with funding agencies.
2. Authorize agency budgets.
3. Review, advise, and approve plans.
4. Appoint executive director and major committees.
5. Participate in the work of the agency.

I. A3, A5, B1, B4, and C2 . . . . *A6*
II. A3, B2, B4, and C1 . . . . *A16*
III. A3, B4, C1, and C2 . . . . *A19*

There are two remaining functions performed by boards in addition to establishing policies and services, overseeing agency operations, and securing or raising funds. Cite these two functions below and the methods used by boards to perform them before turning to A31.

Q14

1. Function—
   Methods—

2. Function—
   Methods—

COMMITTEES

As you learned in Unit I, Lesson Two, committees are created by and are responsible to some authoritative individual or group of individuals. In human services agencies, the board makes the most extensive use of committees to help fulfill its functions while the executive director only rarely appoints a committee to solve a specific problem or work on some specific activity that is too large or complex to be accomplished by one or more associate executives and/or staff members. There is, however, one exception to this general rule; namely, the large agency that frequently needs ad-hoc committees to solve specific problems![10] Some agencies and often health and welfare councils are organized in this fashion.

M3

"Committees are ordinarily related to the basic functions of the agency, and should be established only when there is a specific responsibility to be carried."[11] Committees are, therefore, responsible groups established to carry specific responsibilities for the agency. In human services agencies committees are appointed to carry out three major functions: 1. explore problems, 2. develop plans, and 3. formulate recommendations.

Continue with Q15

As you learned in Unit I, there are basically two types of committees. List them below. Check your answer by turning to A43.

Q15

A.
B.

Both types of committees are usually appointed to fulfill three major functions. List these functions below. Check your answer by turning to A44.

Q16

A.
B.
C.

Standing committees deal with problems or activities of a continuous nature. The major committees in human service agencies include:

M4

[10] Alvin Toffler, *Future Shock* (New York: Random House, 1970), pp. 132–151. See Toffler's idea on ad-hocracy.
[11] Johns, *Executive Responsibility*, p. 70.

1. An executive committee that acts as a central planning group and **M4**
functions for the board between board meetings. **cont.**
2. Finance or business committee that deals with budgetary problems,
plans and recommendations.
3. Personal committee that deals with problems, plans, and recommendations related to agency employees.
4. Public relations committee that is appointed to explore problems,
develop plans, and formulate recommendations concerning agency-community relations.
5. Program committees related to specific areas, for example, casework, youth program, adult programs. These committees are appointed to explore problems, develop plans, and formulate recommendations related to agency services.

Continue with Q17

The committee that acts as a central planning group is called the: **Q17**

A. Personnel committee *A46*
B. Executive committee *A39*
C. Program committee *A41*

Which of the following are the three functions of the public rela- **Q18**
tions committee?

A. Exploring problems, initiating fund raising activities, and serving
as a disciplinary body *A42*
B. Exploring problems, formulating recommendations, and serving
as a disciplinary body *A47*
C. Exploring problems, developing plans, and formulationg recommendations *A38*

To which committee would you assign the task of exploring the **Q19**
feasibility of creating a marital counseling service in your agency?

A. Casework committee *A37*
B. Public relations committee *A45*
C. Adult program committee *A40*

Special committees are appointed to carry out responsibilities on **M5**
behalf of the board or the executive director dealing with terminal
assignments. Their duties include one of the four major functions
listed below:[12]

1. Activity functions such as an annual meeting, a reception, a
luncheon. A special committee is appointed to determine what
must be done, how to do it, and to see that everything is carried
out.
2. Adjusting functions such as conflicts of interest within the agency
or between the agency and other groups. The special committee
would be expected to adjust such conflicts and eliminate them.
3. Study functions that arise when the board confronts problems
that need more information.
4. Selection and nominating functions that arise when a new executive

[12] See Roy Sorenson, *Art of Board Membership*, pp. 126–127.

director or a new board officer must be selected or elected. The
special committee would be appointed to make recommendations
to the board and contact the possible candidates.

M5
cont.

Continue with Q20

Standing committees deal with assignments of a _____
_____ nature, while special committees deal with _____
assignments.

In order of appearance:

A. Terminal; continuous A48
B. Continuous; terminal A50

Q20

Which type of committee would be appointed to perform the following functions? State the type of committee, special or standing, in
the space provided beside each function listed below. If it is a standing committee also state the specific name of the committee, financial,
executive, and the like.

Q21

A. Recommendations regarding the election of a new board officer.
   Committee _____.
B. Resolving an immediate board problem when the board cannot
   meet.
   Committee _____.
C. Recommendations for a change in the length of sick leave for
   employees.
   Committee _____.
D. Plans for a program to work with juveniles.
   Committee _____.
E. Recommendations for the purchase of a new office building.
   Committee _____.
F. A luncheon for a guest speaker must be arranged.
   Committee _____.

Check your answer by turning to A49.

SUMMARY

The administrative function of organizing was described in terms
of being both the structure and the process through which worker
relationships are established for the effective and efficient functioning of an agency. The structure of most human service agencies was described as following the usual functional design, including a board of directors or legislative body, committees,
departments, the supervisors, and the workers. Typical organization charts were explained.

Although structure is important, it was pointed out that the
process of organizing is even more important. Many agencies
appear to be poorly structured but have good morale, a cooperative spirit, and dedication to the task that makes the agency
effective in spite of its inadequate structure! Most often, what
has been described as the "informal organization" is largely
responsible for the fact that an organization is effective, although
the structure is plainly inadequate. The reasons for this fact were

examined and the contributions of the informal organization toward communication and cooperation were stressed.

The next important area discussed was the concept of sound organization and ten principles were described. In addition, the importance of the board of directors to many human service agencies was stressed as a communications and public relations vehicle and a way to maintain community-agency relatedness. Exploring problems, developing plans, and formulating recommendations were shown to be functions of both standing and ad-hoc committees.

SUGGESTIONS FOR FURTHER STUDY

As organizations become larger and more complex the simple structures of the past are no longer sufficient. Organization theorists have examined the potentials of new organizational structures, including the "project" structure, free form, and the matrix patterns.[1] The four types of project structures include individual, staff, intermix, and the aggregate project organization.[2] Large companies representing conglomerates and some highly technical areas have chosen to experiment with free-form structures. No one knows for certain which new structures will emerge as possible solutions to structural problems in organizations. In a recent analysis, Drucker reviews the organizational structure issues and notes that: "To tackle the new realities, we have in the past 20 years improvised ad-hoc design solutions to supplement the Fayol and Sloan models," and that we now have five distinct organization structures: in addition to the two traditional ones, Fayol's functional structure, and Sloan's federal decentralization, there are three new "design principles," not commonly recognized: team organization, simulated decentralization, and systems structure.[3] Drucker's stimulating insights should be the basis for further study.

Further study is also recommended in the area of organizational processes, including power, conflict, leadership, motivation, decision making, group interaction, and work group deployment. Organizational and administrative reactions to problems of organizing within an agency need to be studied in order to gain new insights into effective administrative practice.

SUGGESTIONS FOR FURTHER READING

Cleland, David I., and King, William R. *Systems Analysis and Project Management.* New York: McGraw-Hill, 1968.

Crowston, Wallace B. "Models for Project Management." *Sloan Management Review,* Spring 1971: 25–42.

[1] Two textbook discussions of these items may be found in Fred Luthans, *Organizational Behavior* (New York: McGraw-Hill, 1973), Chapter 8; and in Keith Davis, *Human Behavior at Work: Human Relations and Organizational Behavior,* 4th ed. (New York: McGraw-Hill, 1972).

[2] Luthans, *Organizational Behavior,* pp. 169–170.

[3] Peter F. Drucker, "New Templates for Today's Organizations," *Harvard Business Review* (January–February 1974): 45–53.

Davis, Keith. *Human Behavior at Work: Human Relations and Organizational Behavior.* 4th ed. pp. 354–357. New York: McGraw-Hill, 1972.

Davis, Keith. *Organizational Behavior.* 4th ed. New York: McGraw-Hill, 1974.

Drucker, Peter F. "New Templates for Today's Organizations." *Harvard Business Review,* January-February 1974: 45–53.

Galbraith, Jay R. "Matrix Organization Designs," *Business Horizons,* February 1971: 29–40.

Hall, Richard H. *Organizations: Structure and Process.* Englewood Cliffs, N.J.: Prentice-Hall, 1972.

Herzberg, Frederick. *Work and the Nature of Man.* Cleveland: World Publishing, 1966.

Heydebrand, Wolf V. *Hospital Bureaucracy: A Comparative Study of Organizations.* New York: Dunellen, 1973.

Johnson, Richard A.; Kast, Fremont E.; Rosenzweig, James E. *The Theory and Management of Systems.* New York: McGraw-Hill, 1963.

Likert, Rensis. *The Human Organization.* New York: McGraw-Hill, 1967.

Luthans, Fred. *Contemporary Readings in Organizational Behavior,* New York: McGraw-Hill, 1972.

Luthans, Fred. *Organizational Behavior.* New York: McGraw-Hill, 1973. See especially Chapter 8.

Maslow, Abraham H. *Eupsychian Management.* Homewood, Ill.: Irwin-Dorsey, 1965.

Vroom, Victor H. *Work and Motivation.* New York: Wiley, 1964.

Wren, George R. "Can Business Benefit from New Organizational Patterns?" *Atlanta Economic Review,* 21 (January 1971): 14–17.

1. The two essential elements of organization are:

   A. An organizational chart and cooperation.
   B. Process and structure.
   C. Cooperation and structure.
   D. Process and cooperation.

2. *Organizational Structure*

   |
   Board of Directors
   |
   Associate Executives
   |
   Regular Staff Members
   |

   What group(s) of individuals are missing from the above structure of a small private agency?

   A. Executive director.
   B. Committees.
   C. Supervisors.
   D. A and C above.
   E. A, B, and C above.

3. The first major task in creating an organization is to:

   A. Secure personnel.
   B. Define its goals and objectives.
   C. Develop a procedural network.
   D. Establish the structure upon which it will function.

4. Which of the following would not describe the structure of a human service agency or program?

   A. Budget.
   B. Constitution.
   C. By-laws.
   D. Manual of operations.

5. Which of the following would not ordinarily be considered as part of an agency structure?

   A. Board of directors.
   B. Legislative body.
   C. Personnel promotion formulas.
   D. Committees.

6. Which of the following is usually responsible for overseeing the administration of a public agency?

   A. Board of directors.
   B. Legislative body.
   C. Executive committee.

7. It is important for the executive director to keep the two types of organization within an agency consistent with each other.

   A. True.
   B. False.

8. Units of work are established in order to:

    A. Get all the tasks accomplished.
    B. Help employees improve their skills.
    C. Create a division of labor.
    D. Develop a priority scale.
    E. Primarily A and B above.

9. In general, for which of the following is the executive director least responsible?

    A. Developing the agency structure.
    B. Understanding the agency structure.
    C. Identifying the strengths and weaknesses of the agency structure.
    D. Increasing the effectiveness of the agency structure.

10. In order to foster cooperation and improve communication in the agency, the executive should keep the formal and informal organizations within the agency:

    A. Separate from one another.
    B. Consistent with each other.
    C. Under tight control.
    D. In competition with each other.

11. Units of work are based on:

    A. Time/activity sequences.
    B. The organization scheme.
    C. Personnel preferences.
    D. Similarities of tasks.

12. Which of the following are frequently used to help clarify staff and committee members' responsibility and relationships?

    A. Written assignments.
    B. Commissions.
    C. Organizational chart.
    D. A and C above.
    E. A, B, and C above.

13. Which of the following is recognized as a method of clarifying task assignments?

    A. Written assignments.
    B. Commissions to staff.
    C. Organizational chart.
    D. A and B above.
    E. A, B, and C above.

14. In order to insure the effectiveness of written assignments, they should:

    A. Originate from top level management.
    B. Be developed jointly by the originator and the recipient.
    C. Be subject to change.
    D. Reflect concern for the agency's informal structure.

15. An organizational chart is a (an):

    A. System of communications flow.
    B. Hierarchy.
    C. Dependency system.
    D. Autonomous system.

16. All authority in an agency is derived from:

    A. The board of directors or the legislative body.
    B. The agency's articles of incorporation and its constitution.
    C. The executive director.

17. The professional staff members of a private agency are delegated responsibility and authority from the:

    A. Executive director.
    B. Board of directors.
    C. Legislative body.
    D. None of the above.

18. The development of a singleness of purpose is one way to develop:

    A. Esprit de corps.
    B. Coordination of work units and employees.
    C. A parochial attitude among workers.
    D. Resistance to innovation.

19. It has been found, under most conditions, that a manageable and effective span of control for one executive is:

    A. One to three persons.
    B. Six to twelve persons.
    C. Ten to twenty persons.
    D. Four to ten persons.

20. Work schedules, record keeping, and purchasing of supplies are examples of tasks which should be:

    A. Delegated.
    B. Standardized.
    C. Reviewed frequently.
    D. Handled at the discretion of the executive director.

21. The ultimate responsibility for agency performance in a private agency falls upon the:

    A. Board of directors.
    B. Legislative body.
    C. Executive director.
    D. Committee members.

22. Which of the following is not a purpose of a board of directors?

    A. To provide agency funds.
    B. To establish good community rapport.
    C. To administer the agency.
    D. To provide an element of continuity to the agency.

23. Which of the following is not a function of a board of directors?

    A. To validate agency services.
    B. To assist in raising funds.
    C. To direct agency operations.
    D. To establish good community rapport.

24. In performing their function of establishing general policies and services, boards of directors:

    A. Direct the use of capital funds.
    B. Approve policy documents.
    C. Approve public relations plans.
    D. Guide agency services.

25. Which of the following methods does the board utilize in performing its function of supervising the operation of the agency?

    A. Guide the agency's services.
    B. Appoint all agency personnel.
    C. Authorize, approve, and adopt agency budgets.
    D. A and C above.
    E. A, B, and C above.

26. The board of directors performs its function of fund raising by:

    A. Negotiations with funding agencies.
    B. Participating in the work of the agency.
    C. Revising and approving plans.
    D. Appointing executive director and major committees.

27. Which of the following is a standing committee?

    A. Executive committee.
    B. Selection committee.
    C. Reception committee.
    D. B and C above.
    E. A and B above.

28. Which of the following is a function of a special committee?

    A. Public relations.
    B. Liaison function.
    C. Budgeting.
    D. Adjusting function.

29. The committee that acts as a central planning group is called the:

    A. Personnel committee.
    B. Executive committee.
    C. Program committee.
    D. Special committee.

You may now check your answers at the end of this unit.

No. Although the executive director is delegated the responsibility for over-all agency administration, including all eight administrative functions, that is, POSDCORBE, he does not have the ultimate responsibility for agency performance. Return to Q1 and select the correct answer.   **A1**

Reread answer A in Q2, then see if you still think B is the correct answer. Answer Q2 correctly before going to M2.   **A2**

Exactly. The board of directors retains the ultimate responsibility for assuring that an agency performs its functions effectively, although it delegates day-to-day administrative responsibility to the executive director.   **A3**

Continue with Q2

The two purposes of the board you have chosen are correct. The two remaining purposes of the board include improving public relations between the agency and the community and providing continuity to the work of the agency.   **A4**

Continue with M2

Numbers 1, 2, 3, and 5 are all methods used by boards when performing the function of establishing agency policies and services. Although, as you will learn, appointing the executive director and guiding agency services are methods used by boards to oversee the operation of an agency, they are not related to the establishment of agency policies and services.   **A5**

Continue with Q8

Since only two of the five choices in this answer are correct, we would recommend that you return to M2 and review the methods used by boards to perform their functions before answering Q13 again.   **A6**

You have chosen the correct answer. The facilitation of effective public relations is one of the primary functions of the board. The public relations function includes, 1. interpretation of the work of the agency to community leaders, and 2. interpretation of community attitudes and problems to agency personnel.   **A7**

Continue with Q5

To be sure, board members do this, but it is not their primary method of securing or raising funds. Read M2 again, then select the correct answer to Q10.   **A8**

No, the selection of all agency personnel is not one of the tasks of the board of directors. The board selects only the executive director. In most cases, the board also approves the selection of associate executives. Return to M2 for a review before attempting to answer Q8 again.   **A9**

Fund raising is not one of the ways boards improve public relations. However, it is one of the functions of boards. Read M2 again, then select the correct answer for Q4.   **A10**

Although by lending their personal prestige to an agency as they   A11
participate in the work of the agency and commend the agency to
community leaders, board members may be indirectly helping to
raise funds, but this is not the specific function they perform. Return
to Q11 and select the more precise answer.

This answer is two-thirds correct, but one of the methods is not   A12
serving as a disciplinary body. Read M2 again, then answer Q9
correctly.

The five major board functions include: A13

1. *Establishing agency policies and services.*
2. *Overseeing the operation of the agency.*
3. *Helping to secure or raise funds.*
4. *Validating agency services.*
5. *Improving public relations.*

If you could not name all of these functions, review them again
before continuing with Q7.

Board members do not oversee the operation of an agency by   A14
lending their personal prestige. Return to M2 for a review before
attempting to answer Q11 correctly.

Although guiding the services of the agency is one of the activities   A15
of the board in overseeing agency operations, this is only part of the
answer. If you feel you need a review, return to M2 before answering
Q8 correctly. If not, return now to Q8 and make another selection.

Well done. You have correctly matched the three functions with   A16
their respective methods.

Continue with Q14

One of the primary functions of the board is to establish general   A17
policies. Return to M2 and review the other four primary functions of
a board before attempting to answer Q3 again.

Interpreting community attitudes and problems to agency personnel   A18
is only one of the ways boards improve agency public relations. Read
M2 again, then select the correct answer for Q4.

You have confused the use of one method, namely, authorizing   A19
agency budgets. This is not used to help secure or raise funds but to
oversee agency operations. The other functions and methods have
been correctly matched. Return to Q13 and select the correct answer.

Very good. Usually it is not the function of the board to provide   A20
funds but merely to secure or raise them.

Continue with Q4

This answer is two-thirds correct. The board does guide agency   A21
services as well as authorize, approve, and adopt agency budgets.
However, the board does not appoint all agency personnel, only the

executive director and major committees. Return to M2 for a review   **A21**
of the methods used by boards when performing their function of   **cont.**
overseeing agency operations before answering Q8 correctly.

This is correct. Boards do fulfill their public relations function   **A22**
through personal contacts and through the public relations plans they
approve.

Continue with Q13

Read M2 again. You should then be able to select the correct   **A23**
answer to Q7.

Right! Three other methods used by boards to perform the function   **A24**
of overseeing the operation of an agency include:

1. Appointing the executive director and major committees.
2. Approving the appointment of associate executives.
3. Investing and safeguarding capital funds.

Continue with Q10

Correct. Board members represent their agencies in negotiations   **A25**
with funding agencies in order to secure agency funding. Some boards
participate in fund raising drives to help raise needed funds for their
agencies.

Continue with Q11

This is only partially correct. The board does authorize agency   **A26**
budgets, and invest and safeguard the capital assets of the agency.
However, the board also performs other tasks related to the function
of overseeing agency operations. Return to M2 if you feel you need
a review. If not, return to Q8 now and select the correct answer.

Excellent! In fulfilling its function of overseeing agency operations,   **A27**
the board uses such methods as guiding agency services, and author-
izing, approving, and adopting agency budgets and other important
plans.

Continue with Q9

This answer includes one of the methods: investing and safeguard-   **A28**
ing capital funds. Read M2 again and then answer Q9 correctly.

Good. Board members validate agency services by lending their   **A29**
personal prestige as they participate in the work of the agency and
commend the agency to community leaders.

Continue with Q12

Approving basic policy documents is a function of boards, not a   **A30**
method of performing the function of improving agency public re-
lations. Read M1 again then select the correct answer to Q12.

Two final board functions and the methods used to fulfill them   **A31**
include: 1. validation of agency services as board members lend their

personal prestige to the agency; and 2. the public relations functions **A31**
as board members interact with their personal contacts, as well as **cont.**
when they approve public relations plans. If you were able to state
these two functions along with their proper methods of accomplish-
ment, continue with M3. If you had any trouble giving them, return
to M2 for a review before continuing with M3.

No. Interpreting the work of the agency to the community is one **A32**
of the primary responsibilities of the board—this is part of the public
relations function. Return to M2 and review the other four functions
of the board before answering Q3 correctly.

Initiating fund raising activities is not a method used by a board **A33**
in performing its function of improving agency public relations. Read
M1 again then select the correct answer to Q12.

You should have circled all of the letters in Q5. If you did not, **A34**
review M2 before going to Q6.

Read M2 again. You should then be able to select the correct **A35**
answer to Q7.

No. In most cases the chairman of the agency's finance committee **A36**
negotiates with the funding agency. Although the agency executive
will be present and may well be called upon to answer numerous
questions. Read M2 again, then select the correct answer to Q10.

If this was the only program committee in the agency, then this **A37**
feasibility study would be assigned to this committee. However, there
is a better answer. Return to Q19 and select the answer that seems
more likely to be true.

Correct! The three functions performed by a public relations com- **A38**
mittee include: 1. exploring problems related to agency-community
relations; 2. developing public relations plans; and 3. formulating
recommendations related to agency-community relations.

Continue with Q19

Right you are. The executive committee, composed of agency **A39**
executives and the chairmen of other major committees, acts as a cen-
tral planning group. It also functions for the board between board
meetings.

Continue with Q18

Yes, that's correct. If a standing adult program committee has been **A40**
appointed by the board or executive director of the agency, then a
feasibility study related to marital counseling would be properly as-
signed to this committee. The committee would be expected to formu-
late recommendations concerning the feasibility of creating such a
service in this agency. If the board or the director decided that such a
service was needed and the agency could handle such a responsibility,
then the responsibility for developing a plan to implement such a

program would probably also be assigned to the adult program com-   **A40**
mittee. Continue with M5 for a presentation of the four major functions   **cont.**
of special committees.

A program committee explores problems, develops plans, and/or   **A41**
formulates recommendations related to a specific agency service or
program. It does not act as a central planning group. Return to M4
for a review before attempting to answer Q17 again.

The answer you have chosen includes only one of the three func-   **A42**
tions of the public relations committee. Review M4, then select the
correct answer for Q18.

The two types of committees are, 1. standing, and 2. special.   **A43**

Continue with Q16

The three major functions that may be performed by a committee   **A44**
include:

A. Exploring problems.
B. Developing plans.
C. Formulating recommendations.

Continue with M4

No. A feasibility study related to marital counseling would not be   **A45**
within the realm of a public relations committee. The members of the
committee would have to wonder about your competence if you assigned them such a task. Return to M4 for a review before answering
Q19 correctly.

No. The personnel committee explores problems, develops plans,   **A46**
or formulates recommendations related to agency employees. It is not
the central planning group. Return to M4 for a review before attempting to answer Q17 again.

The answer you have chosen includes only two of the three func-   **A47**
tions of the public relations committee. Review M4, then select the
correct answer for Q18.

Standing committees do not deal with terminal assignments nor do   **A48**
special committees deal with continuous assignments—the reverse is
actually true. Standing committees derive their name from the fact
that they deal with long-term problems and activities. Special committees are formed to deal with short-term problems and activities and
then disband. Return to Q20 and select the correct answer.

The answers are as follows: **A49**

A. Special—Nominating function.
B. Standing—Executive committee.
C. Standing—Personnel committee.
D. Standing—Program committee.
E. Standing—Financial committee.
F. Special—Ad-hoc (special committee).

You have now reached the end of Unit IV. If you had any trouble with this lesson, review the necessary material before continuing with the review questions at the end of this unit. Also be sure to note our summary and suggestions for further study at the end of the unit.

A49 cont.

Correct! Standing committees derive their name from the fact that they deal with long-term, continuous problems and activities. Special committees are appointed to deal with short-term or terminal problems and activities. Once the problem is solved or the activity is completed, the special committee is dissolved.

A50

Continue with Q21

**ANSWERS TO
REVIEW QUESTIONS**

The following are correct responses to questions for Unit IV.

Questions	Answers	Questions	Answers
1	B	16	B
2	E	17	A
3	D	18	B
4	A	19	B
5	C	20	B
6	B	21	A
7	A	22	A
8	E	23	C
9	A	24	B
10	B	25	D
11	D	26	A
12	E	27	A
13	E	28	D
14	B	29	B
15	A		

If you answered 24 or more of these questions correctly, you have successfully completed this unit and may now proceed to Unit V. However, if you answered less than 24 questions correctly you should review those areas that gave you trouble before proceeding to Unit V.

UNIT V
STAFFING

LESSON 1
Personnel Selection

UNIT V OBJECTIVE—STAFFING

Following this unit, given a situation requiring decision making skills related to hiring and maintaining a competent staff, you will be able to demonstrate your skills in this area by making competent decisions.

Specific Objective

Given a description of an agency and a situation requiring the selection of a new employee, you will be able to explain an efficient procedure for hiring any employee including the individual(s) responsible for the hiring.

Enabling Objective 1
You will be able to explain why a qualified staff is of special importance in human service agencies.

Enabling Objective 2
Given a description of an agency structure and the need to hire a new staff member, you will be able to identify the title of the individual(s) responsible for selecting the new employee to fill the position.

Enabling Objective 3
Given the need to hire a staff member, you will be able to explain the procedures involved in hiring an individual to fill the position.

Continue with M1

IMPORTANCE OF A QUALIFIED STAFF

It is the staff members of a human service agency or program who do **M1** the actual work of the agency, from operations to client services. The quality of their performances combine to make up the total output of any agency. Staff personnel are, therefore, a key determining factor in effective and efficient agencies or programs.

The term *staff* is often used to refer to personnel hired to assist the executive as planners, evaluators, consultants, accountants, and the like. The term *line* is used for the worker who produces the product or renders the service. In this unit, however, we are simply following the usual practice of designating all workers below the executive as staff.

RESPONSIBILITY FOR SELECTING STAFF

As you learned in Unit I, Lesson Two, the executive director is given the over-all responsibility for running the agency. However, he must delegate many responsibilities since no one individual is able to perform all the functions of any agency.

One of the responsibilities that the executive director usually delegates is the selection of staff members below the level of department head or middle management. The persons usually delegated to hire staff members include: 1. the assistant director; 2. the personnel supervisor; or 3. department heads. In a small agency the assistant director may well be the person responsible for hiring staff members if there is no personnel department. Occasionally the assistant director delegates this responsibility to the department heads.

In larger agencies there is usually a personnel department, in which case the personnel director would have the responsibility for selecting all staff members.

Continue with Q1

A qualified staff is important to a human service agency or pro- **Q1** gram since it is the staff that:

A. Performs the actual work and delivers the services A3
B. Accomplishes all the menial tasks required in an agency . . A6
C. Directs the operation of the agency A1

In a small agency, the responsibility for selecting staff members **Q2** may be delegated by the executive director to the _____ _____, while in large agencies, the _____ _____ would handle this responsibility.

In order of appearance:

A. Assistant director; personnel director A7
B. Personnel director; assistant director A5

In a small agency, who would be responsible for hiring a clerk **Q3** typist:

A. Assistant director A8
B. Clerical department head A4

SELECTION PROCEDURES

Human services agencies usually have a personnel policy and pro-   **M2**
cedure document that outlines the basis for selection and the procedure to be used in selecting new staff members. These policies
and procedures should be adhered to as closely as possible by the
executive responsible for hiring.

A typical selection procedure to follow in human services agencies
should include at least the following steps:

1. Obtain a job analysis for the position in question or else write one
   that will be based on an analysis of the duties required and the
   qualifications needed.
2. Consult an existing job description or write one, if necessary.
3. Obtain the names of available, qualified candidates.
4. Obtain relevant information on these candidates.
5. Select the most desirable applicant.
   (The next two steps are obvious, yet sometimes the details are
   overlooked.)
6. Inform the applicant that he has been selected, clearly explaining
   all important considerations including salary, duties, responsibilities,
   and relationships with reference to a written job description and
   the agency's personnel policies.
7. If the first applicant chosen takes the job, inform all other candidates that the job has been filled. If the first applicant chosen
   rejects the job, go on to the second choice and so forth until the
   job has been filled.

Further clarification of the first two steps is important if we are to
understand the personnel selection process. The first step is the need
for obtaining or developing a job analysis. Such an analysis should
describe the duties of the job and analyze the qualifications needed
by the applicant to fulfill the job. Such a job analysis should include:

1. *What* the worker does.
2. *How* he does it.
3. *Why* he does it.
4. The *skill* involved in doing it.[1]

The second step is to obtain or write a job description.[2] After a
job analysis, a job description can be written to include the work
to be done and the abilities and skills involved in its performance. Job
descriptions in human service agencies or programs should include:

1. A description of the position: what the position is and to whom
   the person is responsible.
2. Duties and responsibilities.
3. Qualifications.
4. Relationships.[3]

Continue with Q4

Circle the letter(s) corresponding to the component(s) of a job   **Q4**
analysis. Check your answer by turning to A2.

A. What the worker is expected to do.
B. When the worker is expected to accomplish a given task.

[1] Ray Johns, *Executive Responsibility* (New York: Association, 1966), p. 80.
[2] For examples of three human service job descriptions, see Ibid., pp. 244–246.
[3] Ibid., p. 80.

C. How the job is to be performed.

D. The reasons for performing the job.

E. Where the job is to be performed.

F. The persons to whom the worker will be responsible.

G. The necessary skills required to perform the job.

Q4
cont.

The elements of both a job analysis and a job description are listed below. Circle the letters corresponding to the elements in a job description. Check your answer by turning to A15.

Q5

A. The worker's duties and responsibilities.

B. How the worker performs his tasks.

C. The necessary skills involved in performing the job.

D. The worker's relationships with his fellow employees.

E. A description of the position.

F. What the worker does when performing his job.

G. The reasons for performing his job.

H. The necessary qualifications of the worker.

I. The persons to whom the worker is responsible.

The third step in the process of staff selection is to obtain the names of available, qualified candidates. This may be accomplished through media advertising in national, state, or local professional journals, through contacts at professional schools, through employment offices, and through personal contacts or the "grapevine."

M3

The fourth step in the selection process is to obtain all relevant information on each of the available candidates so as to facilitate the selection of the candidate best qualified to fill the position. This may best be accomplished by securing the following information using the tools suggested:

1. Application form for essential personal data.

2. Personal interview for in-depth supplemental information to help evaluate the applicant's knowledge and experience as well as personal and emotional characteristics.

3. References from previous employers to better appraise skills.

4. School records and pre-employment examinations to check intellectual qualifications, if necessary.

5. Medical examination to secure health information.[4]

Continue with Q6

If a new professional social worker is needed in an agency, what would be the best source for securing applicants?

Q6

A. Employment office *A13*

B. Professional   schools *A17*

From the list of tools presented below, select those that may be used to get the different types of information required for selection. Write the letter(s) corresponding to the tool(s) in the spaces pro-

Q7

[4] Maxine Bishop, *Dynamic Supervision Problems and Opportunities* (New York: American Management Association, 1969).

vided beside each of the different types of information that may be   **Q7**
secured by that tool.   **cont.**

Check your answer by turning to A11.

Selection Tools

A. Application form.
B. Medical examination.
C. Personal interview.
D. School records.
E. Pre-employment examination.
F. References.

Types of Information

1. Appraisal of skills _____.
2. Essential personal data _____.
3. Intellectual qualifications _____.
4. Health information _____.
5. In-depth evaluation of relevant knowledge, experience, and personal and emotional characteristics _____
   _____.

The fifth step in the selection process is the actual selection of the   **M4**
most desirable applicant. This is accomplished by comparing the job
analysis and job description with the applicant's qualifications obtained
in step four. In this manner, the best fit may be found between applicant and job.

The final two steps need no further clarification. Once the position
is filled, all other applicants should be notified. One important point
should be repeated here. When the applicant is notified that he has
been chosen to fill the position, he should be sent all the important
information concerning the job so that he is able to make his decision
with as much knowledge as possible regarding his new position. Such
information would include salary, duties, responsibilities, and relationships, as well as a written job description and the agency's personnel policy.

Continue with Q8

If you are hiring a psychologist for a mental health agency and   **Q8**
are about to make the actual selection from among five different
applicants, upon what basis would you make your decision?

A. Choose the applicant with the best school record *A9*
B. Choose the applicant with the most experience and the best references *A16*
C. Choose the applicant whose over-all qualifications fit best with
   the qualifications required in the job analysis and the job description *A12*

After you have selected the most qualified applicant, you should: **Q9**

A. Inform all other applicants that the job has been filled . . *A14*
B. Contact the applicant chosen and inform him of all the important
   considerations regarding the position *A10*

Hopefully, you now have an understanding of the tasks and necessary skills required by a personnel director regarding the staffing of an agency.   M5

You have now completed Lesson One of Unit V. If you have any questions please review before proceeding to the next lesson that deals with effective ways of utilizing agency manpower.

No. Directing the operation of an agency or program is accomplished   **A1**
by the agency executive. It is not the responsibility of the staff. Return
to Q1 and select the correct answer.

A job analysis would include A, C, D, and G, or the what, how, and   **A2**
why of the job, and the skills involved in job performance.

Continue with Q5

Yes, it is important to have a competent staff since they perform the   **A3**
actual work with the clients and they are the ones who deliver the
services to the agency's clients. An incompetent staff will, therefore,
lead to a very ineffectual agency.

Continue with Q2

Exactly. In a small agency, the assistant director would probably   **A4**
delegate this responsibility to the clerical department head.

Continue with M2

A small agency rarely has the funds to set up a personnel depart-   **A5**
ment nor would it need such a department. Therefore, in a small
agency the assistant director is delegated the responsibility for staff
selection while in a large agency a personnel department is usually
required and the director would receive this delegation. Return to Q2
and select the correct answer.

Although the staff does have to perform many of the menial but   **A6**
necessary tasks in an agency, this is not the primary reason for having
a competent staff. Return to Q1 and select the correct answer.

Yes, in a small agency, the assistant director is usually delegated the   **A7**
responsibility for hiring staff members while in a large agency, the
personnel director would have this responsibility.

Continue with Q3

In a small agency, the assistant director would probably delegate   **A8**
the responsibility for hiring a clerk typist to the head of the clerical
department. Return to Q3 and select the correct answer.

No, the applicant with the best school record may not have the   **A9**
other qualifications necessary for the job. This is only one of the
qualifications to be considered when selecting the most desirable
applicant. Return to Q8 and select another answer.

Excellent! After selecting the most desirable applicant he should   **A10**
be informed of this and given all the important considerations con-
cerning the job. It is only after he has accepted the position that the
other applicants should be informed that the position has been filled,
not before.

Continue with M5

Types of information best derived from each tool is as follows: **A11**

1. F—references from previous employers.
2. A—the application form.

3. D—school records and/or E—pre-employment exams.   **A11**
4. B—medical examination.   **cont.**
5. C—a personal interview.

If you were able to select the correct tools for each type of informa-tion, continue with M4. If not, review M2 and M3 before continuing with M4.

Good! If you chose this answer, you would most likely have selected   **A12**
the most qualified applicant.

Continue with Q9

No, employment offices would be a good source for nonprofessional   **A13**
employees but not for professionals. Return to Q6 and answer the
question correctly.

It would be unwise to inform any other applicants that a position   **A14**
is no longer open until the applicant chosen has accepted the job. If
the first applicant, after considering all the important aspects of the
position, decided to turn down the offer, you would have to find other
applicants. It is probable that these new applicants would be less
qualified than those you incorrectly informed. Return to M4 for a
review before answering Q9 correctly.

The elements included in job descriptions include A, D, E, H, and   **A15**
I. The remaining elements listed correspond to job analysis.

Continue with M3

Although this applicant may appear to be the most desirable, if his   **A16**
over-all qualifications are not fitted to the qualifications of the job as
described in the job analysis and the job description, he may not be as
desirable as some other applicant. Return to Q8 and select another
answer.

Yes, professional schools as well as professional journals would be   **A17**
the best sources for locating qualified available professional human
service workers, while ads in newspapers and employment offices
would be the best sources for nonprofessional employees.

Continue with Q7

UNIT V
STAFFING

LESSON 2
Manpower
Utilization

Specific Objective[1]   Given a task statement, you will be able to identify any missing components and explain why the missing component is necessary to make the statement operationally useful to managers, supervisors, personnel officers, and educators or trainers.

Specific Objective[2]   You will be able to describe the process involved in writing an operationally useful job description that will be helpful in improving the utilization of human service manpower.

Enabling Objective 1
You will be able to briefly describe the meaning of job factoring.

Enabling Objective 2
You will be able to briefly describe the developmental approach to the formulation of job activities.

Enabling Objective 3
Given a description of a characteristic, you will be able to identify it as a characteristic of job factoring or the developmental approach.

Enabling Objective 4
You will be able to state the primary and secondary focus of all work activities in a human service agency when the developmental approach is utilized.

Enabling Objective 5
You will be able to explain the value of the generalist in human service agencies as compared to the specialist.

Enabling Objective 6
Given the titles of different jobs, and/or a description of the tasks performed on a job, you will be able to identify those requiring a generalist.

Enabling Objective 7
You will be able to explain what is meant by "role" and "job" as they are defined when using the developmental approach to job formulation.

Enabling Objective 8
Given the name of a role and descriptions of different objectives, you will be able to identify the objective to be reached if the role is successfully performed.

Enabling Objective 9
Given the name of one of the four major levels of work, you will be able to state the amount of education needed by a person performing at the given level.

Enabling Objective 10
You will be able to describe the three major steps involved in formulating human service jobs.

Enabling Objective 11
You will be able to state the four major questions that must be answered by an operationally useful task statement according to the functional job analysis method.

Enabling Objective 12
Given a task statement, you will be able to identify any missing components in the statement that would reduce its effectiveness operationally.

Continue with M1

UTILIZING MANPOWER

The objective of this lesson is to introduce you to possible ways in which agencies can more effectively utilize human services workers who are trained at less than the graduate level, since the overwhelming majority of workers in agencies hold a bachelor's degree or less.   **M1**

The major problem in the area of manpower utilization, then, is that human service planners, "are faced with the dilemma of trying to provide a wider range of services to an increasing population while having to draw upon a cadre of trained workers which diminishes proportionately each year."[1]

---

[1] Robert J. Teare and Harold L. McPheeters, *Manpower Utilization in Social Welfare* (Atlanta: Southern Regional Education Board, 1970), p. 2.

Among the many approaches to solving the manpower problem, three have been given the most consideration. First, attempts have been made to reduce or redesign the spectrum of services available to the public. Second, attempts have been made to increase the number of workers in the human service field or to accelerate the educational process. The third approach focuses on the tasks carried out by a human service worker.

This third approach appears to be most appropriate for our discussion of manpower utilization and will therefore be emphasized in this lesson. The basic concern in focusing on the tasks carried out by the human service worker has been in the reformulation and reallocation of existing tasks and the creation and development of new tasks and functions to be included as part of the purview of human service activities.[2]

M1 cont.

FORMULATING JOB FUNCTIONS

It has been stated that there are basically two conceptual frameworks for formulating and configuring job activities; both have their origins in the way that careers emerge more or less naturally in the world of work.[3] These two frameworks have been referred to as job factoring and the developmental approach.

The developmental approach begins with an analysis of the needs of the public and then proceeds to the definition of tasks designed to meet these needs.

Since the job factoring approach starts with tasks that are currently being carried out by workers on the job, new tasks rarely if ever emerge as part of the new job definitions. This strategy, then, is best for creating or stimulating more jobs rather than new jobs—new in that the tasks involved have never been performed previously. Therefore, if client's needs are not being met by the existing system, the jobs constructed by job factoring will not meet the needs of the client and may even reduce the likelihood that the needs of the client will be met.

Continue with Q1

Formulating job activities by first analyzing the needs of the public and then defining tasks to meet these needs is called:　　**Q1**

A. The developmental approach *A4*
B. Job factoring *A1*

When the traditional job factoring approach to formulating or reformulating job roles and functions is applied, (more/new) jobs are created which usually (are/are not) more in line with the needs of the clients being served.　　**Q2**

Underline the correct answers in the parentheses, then check your answers by turning to A2.

---

[2] Ibid., p. 3.
[3] Sidney A. Fine, *Guidelines for the Design of New Careers* (Washington, D.C.: W. E. Upjohn Institute for Employment Research, 1967).

The developmental approach assumes that each task or cluster of   M2
tasks derive their meaning from some goal or purpose. From the start,
then, this approach focuses on needs or problems and not on jobs.
Since this approach focuses separately on client and agency needs,
discriminations can be made between those activities that originated
in order to aid the agency (system oriented objectives).

After the tasks related to both clients and the system have been
defined, a rationale for grouping the activities into jobs may be implemented. The rationale for grouping activities used in the developmental approach is based upon clearly defined client needs, the skills
of all levels of workers, and the objectives and purposes of the agency.
Based on this much wider range of criteria, the old activities and the
new ones are clustered into programs and jobs.[4]

Continue with Q3

Discriminations between client oriented objectives and system   Q3
oriented objectives can be made if which of the following approaches
are utilized in the formulating or reformulating of jobs?

A. Developmental approach *A6*
B. Job factoring approach *A5*

CHANGING THE FOCUS OF JOB FORMULATION

Since the major focus of all work activities in a human service agency   M3
should be the needs of the client, family, or neighborhood, a major
shift must occur in agencies regarding job formulation. Traditionally,
agencies have used one of three focuses for grouping work activities
when using the job factoring approach: 1. the task or activity; 2. the
characteristics of the worker; and 3. the logistics of the work setting.
All three of these focuses are most sensitive to the bureaucratic needs
of the agencies or the professions and least sensitive to the needs of
the client.

The highest priority for focusing the activities of human service
workers should be the target person or group (that is, the client,
family, or neighborhood).

Continue with Q4

Which of the following should have the highest priority as a focus   Q4
of jobs in the area of human services?

A. Agency needs *A10*
B. The needs of the target person or group *A8*
C. The needs of the professions, that is, social work, psychology,
   psychiatry *A12*

The client needs the help of a single person whom he can trust and   M4
through whom he can relate to other specialists or agencies. This
could be a generalist who would have a wide background and the
focus of his tasks would be client oriented. Such a focus should,
whenever possible, be built into worker jobs and assignments.

[4] Teare and McPheeters, *Manpower Utilization in Social Welfare*, p. 8.

Therefore, the highest priority for focusing the activities of human **M4** service workers should be helping the target person or group meet all **cont.** their needs. In order to help apply this principle in an agency, it would be ideal if each worker was a generalist working as a personal agent for each client or client group. However, in most agencies, it may not be possible to assign workers to single clients to meet all their needs. In these cases, it is best to focus on service objectives, in which case the worker does only those activities that lead to accomplishing the assigned objectives. These objectives would be aimed at meeting client needs.

Continue with Q5

In order to reduce the client's confusion and apprehension and **Q5** increase his ability to relate to human service workers and agencies, a new type of worker must emerge. This worker would be a:

A. Generalist *A13*
B. Specialist *A9*

A model of the generalist would be the: **Q6**

A. Psychiatrist *A11*
B. Receptionist *A3*
C. Probation or parole worker *A7*

In order to accomplish the major service objectives, worker roles **M5** must be defined. A role is conceived as a cluster of alternative activities that are performed toward a common objective.[5] Jobs for individual workers would then be some combination or blend of these roles. (The specific roles are discussed in M6.)

Continue with Q7

Since it is often impossible, in most agencies, to have one worker **Q7** serve as a personal agent for each client in order to meet all his needs, it is often necessary for workers to be assigned service objectives. A worker could also become a generalist under these conditions if he were assigned a combination of roles. A role, in this context, is seen as:

A. Any assumed function *A14*
B. A cluster of activities aimed at accomplishing a common objective *A16*

Therefore, while a role is seen as a (single activity/cluster of **Q8** activities) leading to the accomplishment of a common objective, a job is conceived as a (single role/cluster of roles).
Underline the correct words in the parentheses, then check your answer before turning to A15.

SPECIFIC ROLES AND Twelve major roles of human service personnel and their objectives **M6**
THEIR OBJECTIVES have been identified.[6] These could be expanded further, although

[5] Ibid., p. 34.
[6] Ibid., pp. 34–35.

they cover the major objectives which, if accomplished, will fulfill the needs of most human service clients. These roles and their objectives are as follows:

M6 cont.

1. Outreach—actively reaching out into the community to detect people with problems and help them find help.
2. Brokerage—a linkage role that involves the joining of a person or family with the services they need and assuring that they get to the proper agencies and are served effectively.
3. Advocacy—includes two major elements:
   a. Pleading or fighting for services for a client whom the system would otherwise reject.
   b. Pleading or fighting for changes in laws, rules, regulations, policies, and so on, for all clients who would otherwise be rejected.
4. Evaluating—involves getting information, assessing client or community problems, weighing alternatives and priorities, and making decisions for action.
5. Teaching—all types of instruction from teaching clients to plan a meal, to teaching staff in an in-service training program.
6. Behavior changing—precise ways of changing people's behavior, such as, coaching, counseling, behavior modification, and psyhotherapy.
7. Mobilizing—working to develop new facilities, resources, and programs, and/or making them available to those not being served.
8. Consulting—helping other persons or agencies increase their skills and their ability to solve their clients' problems.
9. Community planning—helping community groups and agencies as well as community or government agents develop community programs to meet the human service needs of the community.
10. Care giving—giving supportive services to those who are unable to fully resolve their problems and meet their own needs, for example, supportive counseling, fiscal support, protective services, and day care.
11. Data managing—gathering, tabulating, analyzing, and synthesizing data such as case records, process recordings, mileage reports, and the like, for making decisions and taking action.
12. Administering—includes all the activities directed toward planning and carrying out a program (POSDCORBE).

Continue with Q9

Beside each of the roles listed below write the letter corresponding to the objective to be reached by the person who assumes the role, then check your answer by turning to A18.

Q9

Objectives

A. Linkage.
B. Fighting for services for rejected clients.
C. Assessing problems and making decisions for action.
D. Detecting people with problems and helping them find needed help.

Roles

Brokerage _____

Outreach _____

Advocacy _____   **Q9**
Evaluating _____   **cont.**

Another role that is not common to all human service personnel   **Q10**
but requires a great deal of expertise is the role of mobilizing. From
the objectives listed below, select the one that fits for the mobilizing
role:

A. Assist neighborhood groups, agencies, and others in planning the
   development of community programs *A19*
B. Work to develop new facilities, resources, and programs . *A17*
C. Work with other persons or agencies to help them in solving their
   clients' problems *A20*

RATIONALE FOR FORMULATING JOBS USING THE DEVELOPMENTAL APPROACH

As was stated earlier, a job should be composed of a blend or cluster   **M7**
of roles. If a job includes only one role, it is much too specialized.

The rationale for formulating or reformulating jobs using the developmental approach depends on two major elements: 1. client needs,
and 2. agency goals. Therefore, if an agency is concerned with services
to individual clients (for example, a mental health agency or an adoption agency), the majority of jobs should reflect primarily those roles
having to do with individuals, including brokerage, advocacy, teaching, and behavior changing. An agency servicing a community (for
instance, a neighborhood organization) should reflect jobs with roles
related primarily to communities such as mobilizing, community
planning, administrating, data managing, and the like.

LEVELS OF WORKERS

After the major roles of human service workers are identified, it is
necessary to identify the major levels of work that ought to reflect the
unique competencies of workers at each level. The major difference
from one level to another is the unique clustering of roles performed.
As the worker proceeds from one level to the next, he acquires more
roles and, therefore, increased competency.

The four major levels of human service workers are as follows:[7]

Level I—Entry aide, or new careerist—high school or less with a
    short period of in-service training in the field.
Level II—Technical assistant, apprentice—one or two years of formal
    education at vocational school or community college.
Level III—Technological associate, journeyman—baccalaureate de-
    gree; this level is also regarded as "professional" for those persons
    who have completed a specialized university human service pro-
    gram.
Level IV—Professional, specialist, master—graduate degree programs
    usually prepare a person for this level of work.

Although no method has yet been found for identifying levels other
than in terms of education, these educational levels should be viewed
as floors and not as ceilings where a person may be blocked from
further advancement.

[7] Ibid., p. 38.

**FORMULATING
HUMAN SERVICE
JOBS**

We now arrive at the actual task of formulating human service jobs. This consists of the following three steps:

1. Describing the tasks within the major roles to be assigned.
2. Assigning the tasks and activities within any particular role to the four levels of work.
3. Developing the cluster or blend of activities that will comprise each job from several roles and possibly from more than one level.

**M7
cont.**

Continue with Q11

The roles assigned to a technical assistant or apprentice level worker should be (dissimilar/similar) to those assigned to a technological associate or journeyman level worker. The major difference between levels (is/is not) the unique clustering of roles.

Underline the correct answers in the parentheses, then check your answers by turning to A21.

Q11

Before jobs can be formulated, that is, composed of many tasks from different roles, the tasks themselves must be accurately and precisely described in behavioral terms. Task statements must, therefore, be written in such a manner as to be operationally useful and provide clear and consistent guidelines for managers, supervisors, personnel officers, and trainers.

A very useful tool to help write operationally useful task statements is the method known as functional job analysis (FJA).[8] FJA uses explicit action verbs, for example, "asks," "listens to," and "writes," rather than process words such as "interviewing" or "counseling," to describe worker behavior. In addition, FJA makes an effort to distinguish between worker behavior (what the worker does) and the outcome of his behavior (the results expected from the worker's action). In this way, most of the confusion resulting from the traditional method (process naming) of job description is eliminated and the focus may be placed more on the needs of the clients rather than on those of the agency or profession.

M8

Continue with Q12

FJA or functional job analysis is, in essence, a method for setting up guidelines for writing accurate and precise task statements. In order to write such statements, it is necessary to use (process names/action verbs) to describe worker behavior.

Underline the proper term in the parentheses, then check your answer by turning to A25.

Q12

**Components of
Operationally Useful
Task Statements**

There are essentially four components of a task statement. These are presented in the form of questions that are used to determine whether a task statement contains all the information needed and whether it can be consistently interpreted by managers, supervisors, personnel officers, and trainers.

M9

[8] For a complete description of this method see Sidney A. Fine and Wretha W. Wiley, *An Introduction to Functional Job Analysis* (Kalamazoo, Mich.: The Upjohn Institute for Employment Research, 1971).

The subject of any task statement is always assumed to be the worker. So the four questions to be answered by the task statement are:[9]

M9 cont.

1. The worker performs what action? An action verb must be used to state what is to be performed.
2. To accomplish what immediate result? The purpose of the action must be explicit so that its relation to the objective is clear and performance standards for the worker can be set.
3. With what tools, equipment, or work aids, if any?
4. Upon what instructions? The statement should indicate what in the task is prescribed by a superior and what is left to the worker's discretion or choice.

Continue with Q13

Identify the missing component in the following task statement: asks client questions, listens to responses, and writes answers on standard intake form, exercising leeway as to sequence of questions.

Q13

A. Performs what action? **A24**
B. Accomplishes what result? **A23**
C. With what tools? **A26**
D. Upon what instructions? **A22**

FJA can be utilized to help describe tasks for each of the four levels of workers within each of the twelve roles identified earlier.[10] After the tasks have been operationalized, the last step in the formulation of human service jobs is to decide which roles and which specific tasks within these roles should make up each job. Any individual job, as stated earlier, may be made up of some blend of several roles and could even include roles performed at more than one level. The final job description will depend upon the needs of the clients served by the agency and the goals of the agency.

M10

In sum, then, the problem of formulating or reformulating human service jobs to make them operationally useful to managers, supervisors, personnel officers, and educators is a difficult task. It is important to make sure that jobs focus on the needs of the clients instead of on the bureaucratic needs of agencies and the professions. However, a start has been made and should be implemented and improved by administrators in all human service areas.

If these new concepts and principles (such as the developmental approach, FJA, and the generalist) are applied in practice, several benefits should result. First, the clients, families, and communities will be provided with services aimed at fulfilling their needs and not necessarily the needs of the human service bureaucracy. The workers will benefit since they will gain a higher level of satisfaction by assuming a variety of roles. Agencies should function more smoothly and will be better able to justify their financial needs by showing the results of past performances and future possibilities.

It is not difficult to visualize the value of this system for other groups, especially personnel officers, educators at all levels, and the

[9] Ibid., pp. 10–11.
[10] See Teare and McPheeters, *Manpower Utilization in Social Welfare*, pp. 42–51, for task statements related to each role.

human service professions themselves. These groups will have at their disposal clearly specified behavioral objectives that must be reached by their students and members before they will be allowed to graduate or assume a new position. The prestige of the professions should be enhanced greatly when their contributions to society are clearly delineated.

You have now reached the end of Lesson Two. The final lesson in Unit V will describe methods of staff development. Turn now to Lesson Three and complete this unit.

M10 cont.

No. Job factoring starts with the existing tasks currently performed **A1**
on the job, not with an analysis of client needs, and then regroups
these tasks into more homogeneous clusters of activities. Return to
M1 and review the material on formulating job functions before attempting to answer Q1 again.

You should have underlined more and are not. Traditional job **A2**
factoring creates more similar jobs, but these regrouped jobs rarely
improve services to clients in terms of their needs.

Continue with M2

No. A receptionist, although (s)he could become a generalist, is **A3**
in many agencies a technician who performs mainly system oriented
tasks aimed at helping the agency. Return to Q6 and select another
answer.

This is correct. The developmental approach starts with an analysis **A4**
of needs and then tasks are defined in such a way as to meet these
needs. Job factoring, on the other hand, starts with the tasks themselves as they are currently carried out in various jobs. These tasks
are then broken down and regrouped into more homogeneous clusters
of activities.

Continue with Q2

This is incorrect. The job factoring approach makes little or no **A5**
discrimination between client oriented and system oriented goals when
defining job tasks. It concentrates solely on the characteristics of the
task itself. Return to Q3 and select the correct answer.

Right! An additional advantage of the developmental approach over **A6**
the job factoring approach is that it allows for discriminations between
client oriented and system oriented goals.

Continue with M3

Yes. The parole or probation worker is an example of a generalist. **A7**
It is his job to help his clients function in the outside world. He assumes many roles in performing this major function. He relates directly
to his client and attempts to use as many services as possible to help
him adjust to the environment outside prison.

Continue with M5

Exactly. In the human service field, the major focus of job formu- **A8**
lation should be aimed at meeting client needs.

Continue with M4

The specialist in the human service field has found it difficult to **A9**
relate to the wide range of client needs. The client needs help in
meeting his needs—not numerous referrals. Return to M4 for a review
before answering Q5 correctly.

No. This has been the case in the past. The major focus of jobs has **A10**
been on the bureaucratic needs of the agencies, to the detriment of

the delivery of needed services to clients. Return to M3 and review the material presented there before selecting another answer for Q4.

The psychiatrist is an excellent example of the specialist who relates only to specialized client needs. Return to Q6 and select another answer. **A11**

Although this is often the case, the needs of the professions should not be the major focus of job formulation. When the needs of the professions are the major focus, the needs of the clients are often neglected or overlooked. Return to M3 for a review before answering Q4 correctly. **A12**

Yes. More generalists with a client oriented focus must emerge if the needs of human service clients are to be served. **A13**

Continue with Q6

No. This is the dictionary definition of role, but it is too restricted for use in this context. Return to M5 for a brief review before answering Q7 again. **A14**

Cluster of activities *and* cluster of roles *should have been underlined. Rarely, if ever, is a role made up of a single task, and jobs, likewise, should not be made up of a single role.* **A15**

Continue with M6

Yes. This is the way the concept of role is conceived in the context of the developmental approach to job formulation. **A16**

Continue with Q8

This is correct. The mobilizing role involves working to develop new facilities, resources, and programs and to make them available to persons not being served. **A17**

Continue with M7

Roles that correspond to the objective to be reached are: **A18**

Brokerage—A
Outreach—D
Advocacy—B
Evaluating—C

As you may have noted these four roles are common to much of the work done by human service agencies.

Continue with Q10

No. Community planning is involved in assisting neighborhood groups and agencies as well as community agents in the development of community programs. Return to M6 for a review of the roles of human service workers before selecting another answer for Q10. **A19**

No. The objective of the consulting role is to work with other persons or agencies to help them increase their skills and solve their **A20** *clients' problems more effectively. Return to M6 for a review of the* **A20** *different roles of human service workers before selecting another* **cont.** *answer for Q10.*

You should have underlined dissimilar *and* is. *The journeyman is* **A21** *Level III and he should be able to perform different roles than the apprentice worker who is Level II, although there may be some overlaps.*

Continue with M8

Although this answer is incorrect, it is difficult to identify the **A22** *phrase in the statement that explains the instructions. However, the phrase is included, namely, "exercising leeway as to sequence of questions." This phrase is really saying that the worker is free from external authority as to how (s)he will go about asking the questions that are necessary to accomplish the objective. Return to Q13 and select another answer.*

Exactly! This statement does not explain the result of the worker's **A23** *actions. Why is the worker to perform the task? A phrase such as "in order to record basic identifying information" could be added to the statement to clarify the reason for accomplishing this task.*

Continue with M10

No. The action to be performed is well specified; namely, asks **A24** *client questions, listens to responses, and writes answers. It is not written in traditional process terms but in action terms. Return to Q13 and identify the proper missing element.*

Action verbs must be used to write accurate task statements to **A25** *describe worker behavior.*

Continue with M9

This task statement includes a description of the necessary tools **A26** *to be used in performing the task, namely, "standard intake forms." Items such as pencils or pens are assumed and not considered to be other tools or equipment needed to perform this specific task. Return to Q13 and select another answer.*

UNIT V
STAFFING

LESSON 3
Developing Staff

Specific Objective

Given a description of an agency with a problem situation that requires improving the staff development program of the agency, you will be able to explain the method(s) that could be used to improve the program.

Enabling Objective 1
You will be able to explain the major purposes of staff development.

Enabling Objective 2
You will be able to cite the six major purposes of staff development.

Enabling Objective 3
Given the name of one of the methods used in staff development in agencies, you will be able to explain how this method may help improve staff development.

Enabling Objective 4
Given a description of a problem situation related to staff development, you will be able to explain a method that may be used to eliminate it.

Continue with M1

As you learned in Lesson Two of Unit I, an agency develops a **M1** competent staff through a variety of in-service training programs.

However, staff development also depends to a considerable degree upon skillful personnel recruitment, sound organization, and the establishment of effective personnel and administrative procedures.[1]

This lesson will deal with the purposes of staff development, the components of staff development programs, and the specific training methods and programs most useful in developing human service staff.

The development of a competent human service staff is a continuous process. Staff development is one of the responsibilities of the executive director. However, in most cases, this responsibility is then delegated to the assistant director, if it is a small agency, or to the director of in-service training in a very large agency. Often, it is a responsibility that no one person is able to fulfill alone. It is an agency responsibility and involves every employee.

In-service training does not mean training some of the staff, some of the time. It requires planning programs to help develop all of the staff, all of the time. Training on the job, in sum, seeks the continuous improvement of the performance of every staff member.

M1
cont.

PURPOSES AND COMPONENTS OF A STAFF DEVELOPMENT PROGRAM

Two major interrelated and interdependent purposes of staff development are: 1. to responsibly and effectively accomplish the work of the agency; and 2. to enhance the growth and development of all agency employees.[2] According to Alice Taylor, staff development consists of the following six components:[3]

1. Introduction or orientation.
2. Supervision.
3. Participation of staff in policy formulation.
4. Plans and policies regarding educational leave.
5. Adequate and up-to-date equipment with which to work.
6. Full use of resources within the agency and the community.

In the following sections, each of these components of staff development will be explained briefly and various methods and programs that may be used by agencies to operationalize each component will be presented.

INDUCTION OR ORIENTATION

The induction or orientation process actually begins during the personal interview as the applicant learns about the agency and its work and the tasks and responsibilities assumed if the position is accepted.

After accepting the position, the employee's superior(s) must begin to acquaint him/her with the agency, his fellow workers, the community, and the specific responsibilities within the agency. This orientation phase is a crucial period for the employee as well as the agency,

---

[1] Ray Johns, *Executive Responsibility* (New York: Association, 1954). See Chapter Eight, "Developing an Able Staff," for further discussion on this important area.

[2] Ibid., p. 95.

[3] Alice L. Taylor, "Agency Responsibility for Staff Development," *Selected Papers in Group Work and Community Organization* (Columbus, Ohio: National Conference of Social Work, 1952), p. 91, as quoted in Johns, *Executive Responsibility*, pp. 95–96.

since the first few weeks can be critical determining factors in a   **M1**
worker's effectiveness.   **cont.**

In order to properly orient the new employee with the agency, the
community, fellow workers, and job responsibilities, many methods may
be utilized. Some of these methods are:

1. Interviews by executives and supervisors.
2. Introductions and conferences with other staff members and board
   members.
3. Observation of work in progress in the agency.
4. Visits to other agencies in the community.
5. Examination of agency documents and materials.[4]

Continue with Q1

A staff development program should: **Q1**

A. Enhance the growth and development of all agency employees *A14*
B. Concentrate on the growth and development of the professional
   staff members only *A3*

In order to orient new workers to a local welfare agency, it has   **Q2**
been customary to give them a copy of the agency's manual of operations and other documents and materials pertaining to the agency and
to let them read these materials during the first week. The employee
is then expected to begin work. Is this an effective orientation process?

Yes *A4*
No *A9*

One objective of the orientation period should be to allow the new   **Q3**
worker to meet and start establishing working relationships with coworkers and superiors. Circle the letters before the statements that
represent the primary methods by which this objective could be
achieved within the agency. Check your answer by turning to A8.

A. Interviews by executives and supervisors.
B. Observation of work in progress.
C. Introductions and conferences.
D. Visits to other agencies.
E. Orientation courses.
F. Examination of agency documents and other materials.

In addition to reading agency documents, other methods could be   **Q4**
used to help new professional or paraprofessional employees learn
about agency operations. Circle the letters in front of the statements
that represent the primary methods that could be used to achieve
this objective. Check your answer by turning to A13.

A. Observation of work in progress.
B. Visits to other agencies.
C. Orientation courses.

---

[4] For a more comprehensive explanation of the specific information that
should be imparted to the new employee during the orientation process,
consult Johns, *Executive Responsibility*, pp. 96–97.

A third major objective of the orientation period is to help the   Q5
new employee become acquainted with the community. Circle the
letters before the statements that represent the primary methods that
could be used to achieve this objective. Check your answer by turning to A1.

A. Visits to other agencies.
B. Observation of secretarial procedures.
C. Orientation courses.
D. Interviews with staff.

SUPERVISION

M2

The second component of staff development is supervision. Supervision or the person-to-person teaching process is one of the most
important and most potentially effective methods of staff development.[5] Both executives and supervisors employ supervision in their
relationships with employees and both the supervisor and employee
profit from the supervisory process as long as it is based on a mutual
sharing of problems.

Although supervision may occur through many different processes
such as by telephone, letters, reports, and records, the major supervisory methods are: 1. the individual interview; 2. supervisory observation; 3. supervisory group conferences; and 4. periodic evaluations
of workers.[6]

SUPERVISORY GROUP CONFERENCES

This method is used as a supplement to individual interviews or conferences. During group conferences, information about policies and
plans may be imparted, common issues may be discussed, and plans
may be formulated. Such conferences may also be useful in strengthening a sense of common purpose and unity of effort.[7]

PERIODIC EVALUATIONS OF WORKERS

Appraisal of a worker's performance may be used to provide a basis
for 1. planning ways of increasing the worker's competence, 2. discussion during supervisory interviews, and 3. effecting transfers, promotions, and resignations.[8] Basic personnel records should be kept
up to date and progress reports written by supervisors should be discussed with the workers. All such reports should be used in a con-
fidential manner.

To summarize, it is the rare individual who is capable of objectively
appraising his/her own competence on a job. Workers need feedback
from others, especially from the supervisor. Periodic evaluations or
appraisals are essential in helping workers to obtain a clearer understanding of their strengths and weaknesses and to plan ways to increase their competence, as well as helping them grasp the reason for
a transfer, promotion, or even their resignation, if this is found to be
a logical course to follow in light of the evaluation.

[5] Ibid., p. 97.
[6] Ibid., p. 99.
[7] Ibid., p. 79.
[8] Ibid., p. 100.

THE INDIVIDUAL INTERVIEW

Through this method, a mutually helpful relationship may be established between worker and supervisor. Each worker's specific needs can be discussed frankly and confidentially. Therefore, the individual interview is often considered the most useful supervisory method.[9]

M2 cont.

SUPERVISORY OBSERVATION

This method is used mainly in group work and community organization situations and gives the supervisor first-hand information about a situation. In addition, this method may help furnish a realistic basis for supervisory interviews and coaching.[10]

Continue with Q6

Assume a supervisor or worker wishes to discuss a specific problem that is adversely affecting a worker's performance. Which method should be used?

Q6

A. Individual interview *A15*
B. Supervisory observation *A7*

If the supervisor wishes to obtain insight concerning a worker's performance so as to improve it, which method should be used:

Q7

A. Individual interview *A2*
B. Supervisory observation *A5*

One supervisory method often considered to be the most useful in delivering casework services is for the supervisor to gain supplemental information about the worker through:

Q8

A. Supervisory observation *A6*
B. Individual interviews *A16*
C. Group supervisory conferences *A12*

Circle the letters below that correspond to the uses of supervisory group conferences. Check your answer by turning to A17.

Q9

A. Formulate plans.
B. Discuss worker's specific problems.
C. Disseminate information about plans and policies.
D. Foster or strengthen a sense of common purpose.
E. Allow the supervisor to obtain a first-hand observation of the situation.

You have now been introduced to two of the six major components of staff development—induction or orientation and supervision. Circle the letter(s) corresponding to the remaining components. Check your answer by turning to A10.

Q10

A. Encouraging staff to participate in policy formulation.
B. Plans and policies regarding educational leave.
C. Plans and policies regarding sick leave.
D. Utilization of modern equipment.
E. Full utilization of agency and community resources.
F. All of the above.

[9] Ibid., p. 99.
[10] Ibid.

PARTICIPATION OF STAFF IN POLICY FORMULATION

In order to foster their growth and development and involvement in the agency, staff members should be given the opportunity to voice their opinions and recommendations concerning ongoing agency policy formulation, especially when such policies affect them directly. **M3**

Two methods of fostering such participation are:

1. Scheduling regular staff meetings or conferences during which new and old agency policies and procedures can be discussed. All staff members should be encouraged to participate in such discussions.
2. Forming staff committees and delegating the responsibility for tasks such as studying and planning new agency policies and procedures. Staff members should be free to join these committees and to become involved in solving agency problems, thereby establishing a feeling of unity with other agency employees and with the entire agency.

Continue with Q11

Assume that you are an agency executive and you want your staff to become more involved in the agency by participating in policy formulation. Circle the letter(s) that correspond to the possible method(s) listed below you could use to achieve this objective. Check your answer by turning to A11. **Q11**

A. Set up regular staff meetings.
B. Set up supervisory conferences.
C. Appoint staff committees.
D. Discussions during individual interviews.

EDUCATIONAL LEAVE PLANS AND POLICIES

Plans and policies for educational leave is the fourth major component of staff development. Policies should be formulated and plans made for any staff member who wishes to improve himself/herself through educational opportunities outside the agency. Staff members should be encouraged to keep up to date and improve their performance through attendance at colleges, universities, workshops, or any other similar study facility whenever they feel they are ready for such activities. Such attendance could be full time or a combination part-time study and part-time work. In addition, refresher courses could be taken, possibly through continuing education programs, to help employees keep up with current practices. **M4**

Education is a lifelong process and agency executives should encourage all staff members to constantly seek out educational opportunities.

ADEQUATE AND UP-TO-DATE EQUIPMENT

The value of adequate and up-to-date equipment with which to work is self-explanatory. It is one of the major ways in which executives of an agency are able to directly improve working conditions and thereby facilitate effective performance by the staff. Without such equipment, agency staff are constantly hampered in their growth and development.

In addition to such equipment as modern typewriters for the clerical staff and other staff members, calculators for the budgeting staff, comfortable office furniture for all staff members, and the like, there

are other types of modern equipment that may be overlooked but **M4**
that would also be very useful. Such equipment may include audio **cont.**
and videotape recorders, movie projectors, and computers. Used
creatively, this modern technology could be used to play a decisive
role in staff development and in improved services to clients. The
human service field is far behind in this area. You, as future executives, hopefully will play a large role in developing many innovative
improvements in human service agencies.

The following examples illustrate ways in which modern equipment can be used to improve the quality of human services:

1. Taping an interview with a client and then using it to study ways
   to improve the worker's performance.
2. Taping staff meetings or conferences and group therapy sessions
   and then discussing ways of improving such meetings or sessions
   in the future as well as showing group members how they appear
   to others in real-life situations.
3. The use of programmed instruction, or its computerized equivalent,
   Computer Assistent Instruction (CAI), for in-service training in
   every agency, especially in those remote areas where staff do not
   have ready access to study facilities. Television could also be used
   to bring in-service training to those in remote areas. Improvement
   services and the teaching of these new methods could be programmed and sent instantaneously to all areas of the country
   equipped with computer terminals (for CAI) or television sets
   with cassette receivers.

Future possibilities are hampered only by our imagination and by
our tendency to fight the new and unfamiliar while holding tenaciously
to the old but familiar.

FULL USE OF RESOURCES

The last component of staff development is the full utilization of
resources within the agency and the community. Some of the methods
that could be used to help staff members make full use of such
resources are:

1. *Monthly or Bimonthly Training Conferences:*
   During such conferences, ongoing experimental projects as well
   as previously assigned study materials and resources can be discussed and evaluated. New projects can be assigned and new
   resources can be distributed.

2. *State, Area and National Conferences:*
   Wider conferences that include workers from many different communities can be valuable for stimulating thinking and widening
   staff members' perspectives.

3. *Personal Reading and Observation:*
   Professional staff members should be encouraged to begin or expand their own personal library of resources pertaining to their work
   and to the work of the agency. They should also be encouraged to
   visit and observe the operation of other agencies in their own community or in the communities in order to obtain new ideas, and
   possibly to report on these experiences at training conferences.

4. *Membership in Appropriate Professional Societies:*   **M4**
Executives should encourage all their professional staff members   **cont.**
to become members of professional societies to keep them alert to
new developments.

In addition to the preceding suggestions, executives of agencies
who discover that professional employees are locked into outdated
professional practices that are reducing their effectiveness, might take
one or more of the following actions to remedy the situation:

1. Encouraging visits to other agencies by allowing time off and possibly by setting up a program with other agencies whereby professional staff members would be exchanged for a few hours or a
full day to observe and even participate in the work of the agency.
2. Bringing in outside resource persons to staff meetings. This is a
good way of sharing new techniques and practices.
3. Encouraging professional staff participation in outside activities
such as planning, developing, and implementing community programs.

You have now completed Unit V. After reading the Unit Summary
and Suggestions for Further Reading found at the end of this unit,
turn to the Review Questions and test yourself on how well you have
learned this material.

SUMMARY

In this unit on staffing, we have emphasized several aspects of
the personnel process. We have discussed the recruitment of
qualified personnel and the managerial functions of a personnel
director. In addition, we have discussed the major components
of any personnel process, including job analysis, job description,
recruitment, and selection. Special emphasis was given to the
problems of staffing human service programs. In particular, we
highlighted the importance of job analysis and the difference
between job factoring and the developmental approach. Special
attention was also given to the difference between generalists and
specialists, along with the emerging role assumed by generalists
in human service agencies. The degree to which work is carefully described in any human service organization requires the
development of special skills in constructing task statements
related to over-all work performance.

The importance of developing staff was also emphasized in
this unit, noting the special benefits to both the agency and
the worker. The classic process of inducting new workers through
orientation programs was cited alongside the importance of the
supervisor as trainer and evaluator of workers. The staff development function in any agency also opens up unique opportunities
to participate in policy formulations related to the future directions of the agency. In addition to in-service training activities, it
was also emphasized that educational leave programs and professional conferences provide another opportunity for workers
to expand their knowledge and practice skills.

SUGGESTIONS FOR FURTHER STUDY

This unit provided merely an introduction to the entire personnel process in any human service organization. Further study ought to include an analysis of those central personnel agency functions that are classically found in civil service agencies in contrast to the operating personnel functions that are usually found in the human service agency itself. Further analysis and study ought to be directed toward the issue of personnel functions which relate primarily to senior staff and over-all administrative policy as distinct from line personnel functions, which relate to day-to-day operations of a program for human service facilities.

Further study would also be necessary in order to understand the process of job classifications and the relationship to training and experience requirements along with the problems of merit increases and pay grade determinations. Future human service administrators will be called upon in their daily administrative activities to demonstrate their working knowledge of the entire personnel process including job preparation, recruitment, screening, job preparation and staff development, job deployment, and job evaluation. The issues of job evaluation are particularly complicated as they require a careful assessment of the work performed in order to provide meaningful employee performance evaluation standards by which both supervisors and workers can judge employee productivity. In a similar fashion, increased attention needs to be focused on the process of staff development and the manner in which new knowledge developed in research settings as well as in agencies is transmitted, in an effective fashion, back to the line worker in order to improve services to clients. This process has been called "knowledge transfer" and will require considerable attention by those individuals who assume administrative positions with primary responsibility for staff development.

SUGGESTIONS FOR FURTHER READING

Budget Division, Community Fund of Chicago. *A Personnel Management Program Guide.* Chicago, Ill.: Community Fund of Chicago, 1971.

Clegg, Reed W. *The Administrator in Public Welfare.* Springfield, Ill.: C. C. Thomas, 1966.

Fine, Jean S., ed. *Working Papers #1: National Study of Social Welfare and Rehabilitation Workers, Work, and Organizational Contexts.* Washington, D.C.: U.S. Government Printing Office, 1971.

Flippo, Edwin B. *Principles of Personnel Management.* New York: McGraw-Hill, 1971.

Havelock, Ronald G. *Planning for Innovation through Dissemination and Utilization of Knowledge.* Ann Arbor: University of Michigan Institute for Social Research, 1971.

Katzell, Raymond A.; Korman, Abraham K.; and Levine, Edward L. *Research Report No. 1: Overview Study of the Dynamics of Worker Job Mobility.* Washington, D.C.: Department of Health, Education, and Welfare, Social and Rehabilitation Service, 1971.

Moe, John F. ed. *Personnel Handbook.* New York: Ronald, 1952.

Mosher, William E.; Kingsten, T. Donald; and Stahl, O. Glenn. *Public Personnel Administration.* New York: Harper & Row, 1950.

Pigors, Paul, and Myers, Charles A. *Personnel Administration.* New York: McGraw-Hill, 1965.

Powell, Norman John. *Personnel Administration in Government.* Englewood Cliffs, N.J.: Prentice-Hall, 1956.

Stahl, O. Glenn. *Public Personnel Administration.* New York: Harper & Row, 1971.

Torpey, William G. *Public Personnel Management.* New York: Van Nostrand Reinhold, 1953.

U.S. Civil Service Commission. *Classification Principles and Policies.* Washington, D.C.: U.S. Government Printing Office, 1963.

U.S. Department of Labor. *Job Descriptions and Organizational Analysis for Hospitals and Related Health Services.* Washington, D.C.: U.S. Government Printing Office, 1970.

U.S. Department of Labor. *Handbook for Analyzing Jobs.* Washington, D.C.: U.S. Government Printing Office, 1972.

1. The primary function of the members of the regular staff of an agency (excluding the executives) is to:

   A. Perform the actual work and delivery of services.
   B. Make the required decisions in the agency.
   C. Direct the operation of the agency.
   D. Help raise the necessary funds for agency operations.

2. In a small agency, who would be responsible for hiring a clerk typist?

   A. Assistant director.
   B. Clerical department head.
   C. Personnel director.
   D. Training director.

3. The first step in the procedure for selecting a staff member is to obtain or write:

   A. The names of available candidates.
   B. The relevant information about the candidate.
   C. A job analysis.
   D. A job description.

4. Job descriptions in human service agencies include:

   A. Duties.
   B. The necessary qualifications for the job.
   C. Relationships with other employees.
   D. A and B above.
   E. A, B, and C above.

5. Which of the following would be the best source of possible available applicants for the position of professional social worker in an agency?

   A. Employment office.
   B. Professional schools.
   C. Other agencies.

6. Once the most qualified applicant has been selected, the executive in charge of hiring should:

   A. Inform all other applicants of the choice.
   B. Contact the applicant and inform him of all considerations regarding the position.
   C. Inform the other applicants that the job is filled and recommend other agencies that they may contact.
   D. Contact the chosen applicant and establish the date for him to begin work.

7. The traditional method used by agencies to formulate job activities is called:

   A. The developmental approach.
   B. Job factoring.
   C. The systems approach.
   D. Job autonomy.

8. The method for formulating job activities which begins with an analysis of the needs of the public and the professions and then proceeds to define the tasks needed to meet these needs is:

   A. The developmental approach.
   B. Job factoring.
   C. Job autonomy.
   D. The delineation approach.

9. If job factoring is used only to formulate jobs by factoring out the tasks to be performed, jobs will:

   A. Change to more effectively meet the needs of clients.
   B. Change to more effectively meet the needs of the workers.
   C. Remain substantially the same.
   D. A and B above.

10. When the developmental approach is used, the highest priority for the focusing of jobs in the human services is given to:

    A. The task or activity.
    B. Worker characteristics.
    C. The needs of the target person or group.
    D. The needs of the professions.

11. This individual focuses mainly on the needs of the agency and the professions (system oriented).

    A. Specialist.
    B. Generalist.

12. A generalist focuses on:

    A. The bureaucratic needs of the agency.
    B. The needs of the client.
    C. The needs of the profession.
    D. The needs of the executive director.

13. Within the context of the developmental approach, a job is viewed as:

    A. A cluster of activities.
    B. A combination or blend of roles.
    C. Any assumed function.
    D. A single role.

14. The objective of this role is to help develop new facilities, resources, and programs, and to make them available to those not being served.

    A. Outreach worker.
    B. Advocate.
    C. Broker.
    D. Mobilizer.

15. The person who is helping other persons or agencies increase their skills and their ability to solve their clients' problems is acting as a:

    A. Mobilizer.
    B. Consultant.

C. Care giver.

D. Community planner.

16. Within the context of the developmental approach to job formulation, the roles assumed by workers on different levels may be similar but the activities performed in fulfilling each role are more:

A. Complex.

B. Flexible.

C. System oriented.

D. Relevant.

17. A very useful tool that facilitates the writing of operationally useful task statements is the method known as:

A. Job factoring.

B. Systems analysis.

C. Job ordering.

D. Functional job analysis.

18. Which of the following questions must be answered in order to develop an operationally useful task statement?

A. The action that the worker must perform.

B. The result of the action.

C. The tools, work aids, and so on, to be used.

D. A and C above.

E. A, B, and C above.

19. The following is an example of a task description:

The worker will ask each new client the questions on the intake form and write his answers in the appropriate spaces. Any other questions needed to help clarify certain hazy answers should be asked at the discretion of the intake worker.

What component is missing from this task description that makes it incomplete as an operationally useful description?

A. What action?

B. What tools, work aids, and so on?

C. Upon what instructions?

D. What result?

20. A staff development program should be aimed primarily at:

A. Enhancing the growth and development of all agency employees.

B. Enhancing the growth and development of the professional staff members.

C. Reducing cost of supplies.

D. Reducing cost of in-service training.

21. Staff meetings, committees, agency training conferences, area conferences, and formal study are:

A. Supervisory development tools.

B. Supervisory training methods.

C. Training and staff development methods.

D. Orientation and supervision techniques.

22. The orientation process for new workers begins with:

A. An explanation of the philosophy, structure, and objectives of the agency program.

B. The personal interview during the candidate's application procedures.

C. The applicant's introduction to board members and the executive staff.

D. An examination of agency documents and materials.

23. All staff of a social service agency should have:
    A. At least a high school education.
    B. Been trained in the social services.
    C. An opportunity for continued growth and development of the job.
    D. Access to board hearings.

24. Of the methods listed below, indicate the two by which a new worker can meet and start establishing working relationships with his coworkers and superiors.

    1. Interviews by executives and superiors.
    2. Observation of work in progress.
    3. Introductions and conferences.
    4. Visits to other agencies.
    5. Orientation courses.
    6. Examination of agency documents.

    Select your answer from those listed below:

    A. 2 and 4
    B. 1 and 3
    C. 4 and 6
    D. 5 and 2

25. Identify below the two best methods by which new employees learn about agency operations.

    1. Interviews.
    2. Introduction and conferences.
    3. Observation of work in progress.
    4. Visits to other agencies.
    5. Orientation courses.

    Select your answer from those listed below:

    A. 1 and 4
    B. 2 and 3
    C. 3 and 5
    D. 2 and 4
    E. 3 and 4

26. To discuss a specific problem that is adversely affecting a worker's performance, which method would be best for the supervisor to select?

    A. Individual interview.
    B. Supervisory observation.
    C. Staff conference.
    D. Orientation course.

Turn to the last page of this unit for the answers.

The new employee could become acquainted with the community **A1**
through:

A. *Visits to other agencies in the community.*
C. *Orientation courses.*
D. *Interviews with staff.*

Continue with M2

The individual interview is not the best method for obtaining **A2**
needed insights into a worker's performance. Such performance must
be observed. Return to M2 for a review and then select a more appro-
priate answer for Q7.

Although the growth and development of the professional staff **A3**
members is very important, a staff development program should not
concentrate on this aspect alone. Such a program should be aimed
at the growth and development of all agency employees. Return to Q1
and select the correct answer.

You have stated that by merely reading relevant agency material **A4**
the employee will be sufficiently oriented to the agency. Although
this is what many agencies refer to as their orientation process, it is
ineffective in orienting any employee if it is the only method used.
In addition to reading about the agency, every employee should be
acclimated to the surroundings by meeting coworkers and superiors,
observing the ongoing work of the agency, and, for new professional
workers, by visiting other agencies and learning about the community.
Return to Q2 and select the correct answer.

Right! Supervisory observation may be used to help gain objective **A5**
insight into a worker's performance.

Continue with Q8

No. Supervisory observation is often used to help furnish realistic **A6**
bases for supervisory interviews. It is rarely, if ever, regarded as the
most useful supervisory method. Return to Q8 and select a more
appropriate answer.

Supervisory observation would not, of course, be used to discuss **A7**
a specific problem with a worker, although it may be a way to obtain
objective insight into the problem. Return to M2 for a review before
answering Q6 correctly.

You should have circled A and C. The new employee should meet **A8**
coworkers and agency executives during the orientation period through:

A. *Interviews by executives and supervisors.*
C. *Introductions and conferences.*

Continue with Q4

Right! Loading new employees down with reading material is a **A9**
sure way to turn them off. Although some reading is necessary, it
should be combined with many other orientation methods in order to

properly acclimate the employee with the job, the agency, and the **A9**
community. **cont.**

Continue with Q3

Correct, if you circled A, B, D, and E. In addition to induction or **A10**
orientation and supervision, the components of staff development in-
clude:

A. *Participation of staff in policy formulation.*
B. *Plans and policies regarding educational leave.*
D. *Adequate and up-to-date equipment with which to work.*
E. *Full use of resources within the agency and the community.*

Continue with M3

You should have circled letters A and C. You can set up regular **A11**
staff meetings or conferences or appoint staff committees to deal with
agency policies and/or procedures.

Continue with M4

No. The group supervisory conference is often supplemental to the **A12**
individual conference and is rarely, if ever, considered to be the most
useful supervisory method. Return to Q8 and select a more appropriate
answer.

You should have checked A and C. In addition to reading agency **A13**
materials, the new employee could learn about the agency through:

A. *Observation of work in progress.*
C. *Orientation courses.*

Continue with Q5

Yes. In order to enhance the growth and development of all agency **A14**
employees, thereby facilitating the effective accomplishment of the
work of the agency, an executive should establish a staff development
program.

Continue with Q2

Yes. The individual interview may best be used to frankly and **A15**
confidentially discuss the problems and needs of individual workers.

Continue with Q7

Exactly. The individual interview or conference is often considered **A16**
to be the most useful supervisory method available.

Continue with Q9

The correct letters are A, C, and D. In addition to these three uses, **A17**
group conferences also afford an opportunity to discuss common issues.

Continue with Q10

**ANSWERS TO
REVIEW QUESTIONS**

The following are the correct responses to questions for Unit V.

Question	Answer	Question	Answer
1	A	14	D
2	B	15	B
3	C	16	A
4	E	17	D
5	B	18	E
6	B	19	D
7	B	20	A
8	A	21	C
9	C	22	B
10	C	23	C
11	A	24	B
12	B	25	C
13	B	26	A

How well did you do? If you answered 24 or more questions correctly, go right on to Unit VI. If you had less than 24 correct responses, review those areas that gave you trouble and then go to Unit VI.

UNIT VI
DIRECTING

LESSON 1
Identifying Leadership Potential

UNIT VI OBJECTIVE—DIRECTING (LEADERSHIP)

Following completion of this unit, and given a problem case, you will be able to demonstrate your skills in leadership by making competent decisions.

Specific Objective

Given a situation with descriptions of different kinds of behavior, you will be able to point out those individuals who are evidencing qualities of leadership.

Enabling Objective 1
You will be able to explain why agency employees need direction.

Enabling Objective 2
You will be able to define, in your own words, the meaning of leadership.

Enabling Objective 3
Given a list of characteristics, you will be able to identify those necessary for leadership.

Enabling Objective 4
Given brief descriptions of various characteristics, you will be able to distinguish between those that depict leadership ability and those that do not.

Continue with M1

THE EXECUTIVE AS A LEADER

As has been stated previously, if an agency is to be effective in ful- **M1**
filling its purposes, all agency employees must know what they are
expected to accomplish, their responsibilities and specific tasks, the
process by which they are expected to accomplish assigned tasks and
responsibilities, and why these are important. If employees are to
make a contribution to an agency and not just drift along "doing their
own thing," they must have direction. Such direction must come from
agency executives who are the primary leaders of the agency.

WHAT IS LEADERSHIP?

Most authorities are in agreement concerning the meaning of leadership as is evident in the following definitions. Trecker states that
"leadership can be defined as the ability one has to inspire people to
work together in the achievement of a common objective."[1] According
to Pigors and Cabot, "leadership is a process of mutual stimulation
which, by the successful interplay of relevant individual differences,
controls human energy in the pursuit of a common cause."[2]

The two major aspects of leadership, therefore, seem to be 1.
inspiring others to work together, and 2. working toward achieving
a common, mutually agreeable goal or objective.

Continue with Q1

If any agency is to be effective in dispensing its services and ful- **Q1**
filling its other purposes, the employees must be:

A. Left alone to do their own thing *A9*
B. Given direction *A3*

To be effective the agency executive must have the capability of **Q2**
motivating agency employees to work together to achieve:

A. The goals of the agency *A17*
B. Their own personal goals *A6*

WHAT ARE THE CHARACTERISTICS OF A LEADER?

Although there is common agreement concerning the importance of **M2**
leadership, it is difficult to obtain any consensus concerning the specific
qualities or characteristics that a leader should possess. We know that
leadership, including executive leadership, is usually earned, not
bestowed by position. The executive, to become a leader, must possess
certain qualities and act in such a manner as to demonstrate leadership
ability.

From our previous discussion concerning the meaning of leadership, the two characteristics that every leader seemingly must possess
include 1. dedication to the achievement of the goals and objectives
of the organization, and 2. ability to motivate others to work toward
achieving the goals and objectives of the organization. Although dedication to agency goals and ability to motivate others are two important

[1] Harleigh Trecker, *Social Work Administration, Principles and Practices* (New
York: Association, 1971), p. 44.
[2] Paul Pigors and Richard Cabot, *Leadership or Domination* (Boston: Houghton
Mifflin, 1935), p. 16.

qualities needed by an executive leader, there are additional char-   **M2**
acteristics and abilities that the leader must possess. One of the most   **cont.**
important of these characteristics is the ability to effectively delegate
responsibility and authority. Since this skill is of utmost importance,
it will be discussed separately in the next lesson.

Seven other necessary qualities of leadership have been identified
by Johns.[3] They are:

1. A mature social philosophy including a belief in the dignity of
   human personality and responsibility for the common good.
2. Intellectual capacity, imagination, creativeness, the ability to deal
   with complicated problems, to master one's field of service, to
   understand social and economic forces that determine the environment in which he or she operates, and to think in an orderly, consistent manner.
3. Ability to get people of different background and abilities to work
   together effectively.
4. Willingness and ability to carry complex responsibilities simultaneously and to make decisions based on available facts, under
   pressures of time.
5. Insight into human behavior and potentialities for growth.
6. Emotional poise, maturity, and security.
7. Ethical sensitivity and personal integrity.

This list represents one of many approaches to defining leadership
characteristics.[4]

Continue with Q3

Bill A., an executive of a small agency, feels that all his employees   **Q3**
are mature individuals and should be left alone in the performance
of their jobs unless they are performing poorly. Do you think Bill is
an effective leader?

A. Yes *A1*
B. No *A10*

Let us review now the seven basic characteristics identified by Johns   **M3**
as "likely to prove useful in most situations."[5]

The first characteristic mentioned is a mature social philosophy.
Human service administrators, to be effective leaders, should have
high ethical and moral standards that motivate their conduct as well
as a mature conception and acceptance of professional ethics and
values.

Continue with Q4

---

[3] Ray Johns, *Executive Responsibility* (New York: Association, 1954), p. 43.
[4] For other presentations of important characteristics of leaders, see the following: Donald K. Davis, quoted by Myles L. Mace in *The Growth and Development of Executives* (Boston: Harvard Graduate School of Business Administration, 1950), p. 190; and Ordway Tead, *The Art of Leadership* (New York:
McGraw-Hill, 1935). The reader is referred to this classic which is still relevant to the modern scene.
[5] Johns, *Executive Responsibility*, p. 43.

Circle the letter(s) corresponding to the behavior(s) described **Q4** below that depict a mature social philosophy. Check your answer by turning to A2.

A. Fostering client and citizen participation in problem-solving.
B. Developing agency programs and formulating agency policies with the help of staff members, allowing little, if any citizen participation.
C. Allowing client records to be open to any interested party.
D. Maintaining high ethical and moral standards with respect to clients.

The second important characteristic of executive leadership is **M4** intellectual capacity, imagination, and creativeness. Intellectual capacity involves, among other things, mastery of required knowledge to operate effectively in one's chosen field of service. In the human service area, this also includes a substantial knowledge of the social and economic forces that impinge on the agency's program. Lastly, intellectual capacity also involves the ability to think through problems in an orderly and consistent way.

Leadership then involves an intellectual component coupled with the ability to look at things with imagination and creativeness. An executive without these qualities would probably not be a very effective or dynamic leader.

Continue with Q5

. The second important quality of an effective leader is intellectual **Q5** capacity, imagination, creativeness, and the ability to deal creatively with complicated problems. Circle the letter(s) corresponding to the behavior(s) listed below that depict some aspects of this important ability. Check your answer by turning to A4.

A. Allowing for little, if any, variability in agency policy once it is established.
B. Clearly and effectively presenting all possible policy alternatives to the board of directors.
C. Reacting defensively whenever questioned by the board or citizens about agency expenditures or accomplishments.
D. Obtaining diversified viewpoints from staff, board, and community members on agency problems.
E. Guiding subordinates in obtaining solutions to their problems.

The third characteristic mentioned by Johns is the ability to get **M5** people of different backgrounds and abilities to work together. Basically, this skill relates to the task of coordination. Leadership here is not unlike the function performed by the conductor of a symphony orchestra: to bring harmony out of a variety of sounds made by different instruments. Those who play the strings, brasses, woodwinds, or percussion instruments certainly vary both in temperment and in the type of sound produced. The essence of leadership, on the conductor's part, is the ability to get the musicians to work together— to coordinate their various abilities to provide the over-all harmony.[6]

[6] See Tead, *Art of Leadership*, p. 118.

It seems unnecessary to elaborate on the need for this coordinating **M5**
skill on the part of a leader.   **cont.**

Continue with Q6

In order to get people to work together, even though they represent   **Q6**
different backgrounds and skills, you, as the executive, should:

A. Point out to them the importance of working together for the good
   of the agency *A11*
B. Ask them to coordinate their efforts so working together will be
   possible and harmony will be achieved *A14*
C. Lead them to working together by making the best use of each
   person's individual skills and blending these skills into one coordinated whole *A16*
D. Try to hire people who are agreeable and with the same backgrounds in order to minimize differences of opinion . . . *A12*

Regarding the fourth characteristic of leadership—the ability to   **Q7**
carry complex responsibility and make decisions under pressure—
assume you are the executive director of a large agency. You are being
harassed by a subordinate with a family problem that is affecting his
work, by a citizen committee concerning a community-agency problem, and by your board of directors concerning a budget imbalance,
among other problems and decisions needing your attention. What
would you do if you were the executive of this agency?

A. Delegate each problem to a subordinate *A8*
B. Set up priorities and schedule time needed for each problem   *A18*
C. Begin the task of solving each problem immediately and when one
   problem is finished, go on to another *A5*

The fifth important leadership characteristic is insight into human   **Q8**
behavior and potentialities for growth. Underline the proper word
or words in the parentheses in the paragraph below. Check your
answer by turning to A13.
   If you were the executive director of an agency and you felt that
it was not part of your job to keep abreast of such mundane events
as the birthdays and wedding anniversaries of your key personnel,
you (would/would not) be showing insight into human behavior.

Recognizing the strengths as well as the weaknesses of subordinates   **Q9**
and taking them into consideration (is/is not) an important aspect
of leadership. Underline the proper answer, then check your answer
by turning to A7.

The sixth set of characteristics are especially important for leaders   **Q10**
in human services. They are, emotional poise, maturity, and a personal
sense of security. In a brief example below we portray how these
characteristics may be involved in a simulated office situation. After
reading the case, circle the letter(s) corresponding to the individuals
described who seem to be exhibiting the characteristics of poise,
maturity, and security.
   Charles, Harry, and Betty all work in the same vocational rehabilitation office along with Hugh and Phyllis. Although they are all

counselors with the same ratings, Hugh and Phyllis are unable to work
together in the same office without the "sparks flying" as the saying
goes. Each one appears to be trying to dominate the other. Charles
has come to Hugh's support, blaming Phyllis for a domineering attitude. Betty blames Hugh and claims that, "He asks for it. He's
simply not very competent!" Harry has taken the position that laying
blame will not solve the problem and that since the whole department
appears to be emotionally involved in the problem, it would be better
if some outside party were asked to resolve the dispute. He suggested
that a well-qualified counselor from another section, whom they all
respected, might be the proper person. To check your answer turn to
A15.

Q10
cont.

A. Charles
B. Harry
C. Betty
D. Hugh
E. Phyllis

The last of the seven important characteristics of a leader relate to
1. ethical sensitivity and 2. personal integrity. The first of these represents the need for the leader to live up to a high moral code of
honesty and ethical standards that properly reflect a profession.
Employees respond to leadership by example. Subordinates interested
in moving up the career ladder will take their behavior cues from
the person above them. They expect superiors to demonstrate the
qualities and standards of leadership that will bring honor and credit
to human services. Although they may put up with lower standards of
ethical sensitivity because they need to retain their jobs, they are not
inspired by or moved to greater productivity by the unethical or the
insensitive leader.

M6

The second aspect of personal integrity is closely akin to the first
item mentioned above but appears to be a personality trait as well.
Integrity relates to trust, and subordinates need to be able to trust
their leaders. Honesty and reliability are important aspects also, in
that subordinates need and want a person who will be honest with
them and who keeps promises. Making and keeping promises are
part of the personal integrity required of effective leaders.

Continue with Q11

In the space on p. 205, write out, in your own words, what you believe
to be the characteristics that are most important for successful leadership in the human services area. To check your answer, turn to A19.

Q11

ANSWERS

Leadership involves motivating employees through positive reinforcement (encouraging, congratulating, and other such positive measures). We would have to conclude that Bill is probably a poor leader. Return to Q3 and select the correct answer.

A1

Letters A and D should have been circled. A mature social philosophy is evidenced by fostering client and citizen participation in problem-solving, agency program development, and policy formation, and maintaining high ethical and moral standards in respect to clients (confidentiality of records, client's rights as a person).

A2

Continue with M4

This is correct. Directing the employees of an agency to work alone and with others toward the achievement of common goals and objectives is a necessity if the agency is to be effective. The directing function must be assumed by the agency executives and it can only be fulfilled if the executives are effective leaders.

A3

Continue with Q2

If you circled the letters B, D, and E, you have correctly identified some of the components of leadership behavior related to dealing creatively with complicated agency problems.

A4

Continue with M5

Although this would be an acceptable answer if you had few problems to solve or few important decisions to make, it is not recommended for harried executives with multiple problems and decisions. When the executives fail to organize their work and plan their time, they soon will find themselves hopelessly behind. Return to Q7 and select a more appropriate answer.

A5

Not likely. Once again, if agency employees are busy pursuing their own personal objectives, the probability of achieving the goals of the agency are indeed slim unless all the employees' personal goals and all the goals of the agency coincide, and this would certainly be a rare situation.

A6

If one of the goals of an employee is similar to an agency goal then the competent leader will recognize this and use it to enhance the employee's motivation. However, whether the employees' personal goals are similar or different than those of the agency, they should never be ignored by the executive. The competent leader is able to recognize an employee's personal goals and consider them as he helps motivate the employee to achieve the goals of the agency. Return to Q2 and select the correct answer.

Recognizing and taking into consideration the strengths and weaknesses of subordinates definitely is a very important aspect of competent leadership, especially in regard to fostering the growth and development of each subordinate.

A7

Continue with Q10

Although this would be a possibility if all your subordinates were competent to assume your problems, but in many cases it would be

A8

an unwise choice since there are some responsibilities you must not **A8**
delegate as you will discover in Lesson Two. Return to Q7 and select **cont.**
a better answer.

If members of a group or agency are allowed to drift along on **A9**
their own, there is little, if any chance that the goals of the group
will ever be realized. A purposive group or organization must have
direction. Return to M1 and review the materials presented there
before answering Q1 correctly.

This is a better answer. A sign of good leadership is the ability **A10**
to give subordinates credit, encouragement, and recognition.

Continue with M3

Sometimes exhortation works, especially if you have enough cha- **A11**
risma, or, shall we say, charm, but most often just telling people to
work together is ineffectual. Return to Q6 and select a better response.

Sorry, but you would find this not to be a very workable solution. **A12**
Hiring practices have changed drastically in recent years. Hiring only
one ethnic group member or only blue-eyed blonds is no longer
possible. Return to Q6 and select another response.

You should have underlined the words would not *since it is im-* **A13**
portant for you, as an executive, to keep abreast of the important
events in the lives of your key subordinates. By remembering these
events, you are showing them that you care about them. This is one
of the ways that they feel needed and appreciated by you.

Continue with Q9

Asking your employees to coordinate their efforts would probably **A14**
be a useless exercise. Employees need to be shown how to coordinate
their efforts. This can be accomplished through leadership. Return to
Q6 and select a better response.

Although Hugh shows some poise and maturity, Harry shows the **A15**
most poise, maturity, and security by observing the entire situation
and not letting himself get as involved as the others and then by
making an objective, constructive suggestion that may lead to a
solution.

Continue with M6

Yes, we would agree with you. Leading employees into coordinating **A16**
their efforts by means of using their different skills is a better answer
than exhortation.

Continue with Q7

Yes. The effective agency leader should be agency goal oriented **A17**
and inspire all agency employees to work toward the accomplishment
of these goals.

Continue with M2

Right! The competent leader, faced with many problems to solve   **A18**
*and decisions to make, must take time to organize the work load by
setting priorities and deciding how much time should be delegated to
the accomplishment of each task.*

Continue with Q8

Although stated in your own words we hope you included some or   **A19**
*all of the seven characteristics important for leadership in the human
services area.*
    To review, they are:

1. *A mature social philosophy including a belief in the basic dignity
   of the human being regardless of race, creed, or color.*
2. *Intellectual capacity, imagination, and the willingness to deal with
   complicated problems that involve organizations and the persons
   in them.*
3. *Ability to get people of different backgrounds and abilities to work
   together effectively.*
4. *Willingness to carry out complex responsibilities simultaneously
   and to make decisions based on available facts, under pressures
   of time.*
5. *Insight into human behavior and sensitivity to their growth as
   persons and as professionals.*
6. *Emotional poise, maturity, and security.*
7. *Ethical sensitivity and personal integrity.*

    *After you have reviewed your own answer you have completed
Lesson One on leadership.*

UNIT VI
DIRECTING

LESSON 2
Effective
Delegation
of Responsibility

Specific Objective

Given a list of tasks and responsibilities, and a list of employees with a description of their respective titles and abilities, you will be able to:

1. Identify the tasks that should be delegated.
2. Match the employees with the task to be delegated and explain the reason for each choice.
3. Explain how the three major areas of authority, resources, and conditions for feedback are important for successful delegation.

Enabling Objective 1
You will be able to explain what is meant by delegating duties and/or responsibilities.

Enabling Objective 2
Given a description of ineffective delegation, you will be able to identify the reasons why the recipient was unable to carry out the delegated tasks.

Enabling Objective 3
Given a situation where the need for delegation is indicated but avoided, you will be able to explain the reasons why the delegation was avoided.

Enabling Objective 4
Given a list of different tasks and duties, you will be able to distinguish between those the executive must perform personally and those that should be delegated to different employee groups.

Enabling Objective 5
You will be able to understand and apply four major criteria by which an executive evaluates an employee's ability to assume delegation.

Enabling Objective 6
You will be able to identify the reasons why authority, resources, and conditions for feedback must be specified at the time a task is delegated.

Enabling Objective 7
Given a description of a delegation, you will be able to describe six methods that the executive may use to retain control of the delegation.

Continue with M1

DELEGATION—ITS MEANING AND VALUE

Inherent in any democratic administrative approach is the wide distribution of responsibility and authority that helps foster the growth and development of all employees in an agency. Wider distribution of responsibility as well as participation in making and carrying out service plans have been the basic components of a human service philosophy for many years, especially in dealing with clients. It is equally as important to apply this philosophy to agency employees. In order to allow for this wide distribution of responsibility and authority, executives must be able to freely delegate many of their responsibilities. Executives unable or unwilling to delegate responsibilities generally become ineffective leaders. Delegation refers to the act of assigning to another individual or group of individuals the responsibility as well as the requisite authority needed for the accomplishment of a task.

Continue with Q1

M1

Jack A. has been given the responsibility for setting up a new in-service training program, but he has been given no specific authority over those who will work with him on the project. Is it correct to assume that he should have little trouble accomplishing this task?

A. Yes *A25*
B. No *A6*

Q1

PREREQUISITES FOR EFFECTIVE DELEGATION

If delegation is to be effective in any agency, it must be preceded by a fairly high degree of work organization It requires the following prerequisites:

M2

1. Goal setting.
2. Policy formulation.
3. Program planning.
4. Employee training and evaluation.
5. Effective communication.
6. Performance control and review.[1]

It is rarely sufficient to merely tell employees to do something and expect them to perform it effectively. They must have a clear conception of what is to be accomplished and why it is important. Organizing the work of an agency includes the identification of worker tasks necessary to development of effective and efficient services.

For delegation to be effective, the agency must be well organized with the recipients of any delegation clearly informed of the tasks for which they are responsible. Furthermore, recipients of delegation should always be given the necessary authority to carry out these tasks if they do not already possess this authority.

Continue with Q2

Dolores C., the head of the social services department of a mental health clinic, has been told by Dave S., the executive director, that her department is not very efficient and that he expects her to improve the situation. Dolores will probably be unable to accomplish this task because: **Q2**

A. She does not understand what it is that the director wants her to do *A3*
B. She has not been given any reasons why her department "is not very efficient" *A16*
C. She has been given no authority to accomplish the task . . *A28*

Since this mental health clinic is a fairly new agency, the director **Q3** has explained the goals of the agency to each of the department heads and asked them to set up programs and formulate policies and procedures for their own departments. Although other department heads have been able to make attempts at accomplishing this task, Dolores, who directs the social services department, has been totally occupied with the actual delivery of services to clients and supervising her staff. She has been reluctant to tell the director of her problems since she fears he will fire her.

Circle below the letter(s) corresponding to those areas of organization that are probably causing the inefficiency in the services department. Check your answer by turning to A23.

A. The lack of well-formulated policy.
B. The establishment of goals.
C. Effective agency-wide program planning.
D. The training and evaluation of employees.
E. Faulty communication.
F. Performance control and review.

[1] Joseph D. Cooper, *How to Get More Done in Less Time* (Garden City, N.Y.: Doubleday, 1962), p. 116.

BARRIERS TO EFFECTIVE DELEGATION

The barriers to effective delegation are created mainly by the person who should be doing the delegating. You should be aware of the possible barriers and attempt to avoid them. Although many barriers may be psychological and, therefore, hidden from view, others are readily apparent and include the following: **M3**

1. A work overload leads to no time to explain things to others. This is a cyclical barrier where overload is increased by the lack of time to delegate tasks.
2. Insecure feelings about the abilities of your subordinates to whom you should delegate tasks.
3. A lack of personal knowledge about the tasks you should delegate so you are unable to explain them to others.
4. Fear of one's ability to maintain control over the tasks once they are delegated.
5. One's superior(s) may not permit delegation of specific tasks.
6. A person may feel he can do it faster (short-term view) and so he overlooks the long-term view or the gains from investing a little time in developing greater capabilities in his subordinates.
7. Fear of lessening one's own power and strengthening the power of possible rivals.
8. A person may simply not know how to plan his work and supervise its execution through others.[2]

Continue with Q4

Circle the letters corresponding to the situations presented below in which the executive is evidencing leadership behavior resulting from the ability to delegate effectively. Check your answer by turning to A29.   **Q4**

A. Allan A. feels threatened by his subordinates and prefers to complete most tasks himself.
B. Barbara B. usually finds time to plan ahead.
C. Carl C. finds himself letting one task slip in order to take on another.
D. Delores D. is usually able to find a subordinate who is able to relieve her when she is under pressure or must go out of town.
E. Edward E. has time for public relations and professional engagements since his work at the office takes less time than other executives in the same position.
F. Freda F. works long hours and still brings work home with her.
G. George G. explains his plans to his entire staff and sets the majority of his assignments down in writing.

WHAT TO DELEGATE

Although there are some tasks and responsibilities that you, as an executive, cannot properly delegate, there are a surprising number of tasks you can delegate. The decision to delegate depends upon the nature of the item to be delegated. The following list of eight major   **M4**

---

[2] See Ibid., pp. 119–120, for a more comprehensive presentation of the barriers to delegation.

types of transferrable duties might be useful as a check list to help you think through the decision of whether or not to delegate.

1. Tasks related to fact finding and analysis prior to review and decisions.
2. Tasks related to the formulation of goals, policies, programs, plans, and projects on which you, the executive, must make personal decision—making the final decisions are, of course, your responsibility.
3. Tasks related to the execution of the plans, programs, or projects after you have made your decision.
4. The preparation of first drafts.
5. The performance of routines and carrying out of details and supporting activities.
6. Tasks others can do better, sooner, or at less cost to the organization.
7. Tasks such as representing you at meetings and conferences, where your point of view can be presented.
8. Tasks that will help develop your subordinates through exposure to new problems.[3]

Continue with Q5

Circle the letter corresponding to the duties that you could properly delegate, then check your answer by turning to A35.

A. Approval of a new project.
B. The implementation of a new program.
C. Representing you at all meetings and conferences.
D. Fact finding tasks.
E. Tasks related to the formation of policies.
F. Final determination of goals.
G. Preparation of the first draft of a report.

**WHAT NOT TO
DELEGATE**

There are some duties that you, as an executive, cannot properly delegate. You should, in most cases, reserve for yourself duties such as the following:

1. Making those critical decisions that commit substantial resources or are important to the success of the enterprise as a whole, including the determination of goals or policies and the approval of programs, plans, and projects.
2. Personal representation at meetings, conferences, and the like, where your own presence is very important because of its implications for your agency's public relations, or because of the effects on the morale of those who need and desire your presence.
3. The execution of tasks where the goals or policies are unclear or where the policies are so new that intimate contact is required during a trial period and the execution of new programs or projects where the commitments of resources and the risks are very great.
4. The hiring, disciplining, and firing of your immediate staff.
5. Tasks that must be accomplished under great pressure without time for feedback.

[3] Ibid., pp. 122–123.

6. Emergency, short-term tasks when there is little, if any, time to explain or train. **M5 cont.**

7. Unique tasks that have little probability of coming up again.

8. Tasks that must be kept secret.[4]

Continue with Q6

You are the assistant director of a human service agency. You have **Q6** been under heavy pressure and were given a task that must be accomplished within a short period of time. You should:

A. Delegate this task to a competent subordinate A22
B. Do the task yourself A37

If you, as an executive, have a task that you feel none of your sub- **Q7** ordinates can accomplish without your supervision, you should:

A. Delegate the task and make time for supervision A32
B. Perform the task yourself to save time A18

You have just received an important new task that must be ac- **Q8** complished immediately. The goals and policies are unclear and you are pressed for time by other commitments. You should:

A. Perform the task yourself A26
B. Delegate the task to a competent subordinate A2

Circle the letters corresponding to the types of tasks listed below **Q9** that you, as an executive, can properly delegate and underline the letters of those you must perform yourself. Check your answer by turning to A7.

A. Performing routine tasks.
B. Hiring an employee on your immediate staff.
C. Performing a task that will never come up again.
D. Carrying out details and supporting activities.
E. Accepting a task in your area of specialization.
F. Executing a new project entailing large resources.
G. Executing a program with no heavy expenditures or risks.

POSSIBLE RECIPIENTS OF DELEGATION

In most well-organized agencies there are certain logical recipients **M6** of delegation. However, since the objective of all delegation is to get the job accomplished, the executive may, at times, depart from this logical pattern. In such cases, the executive should have an overriding reason and should be able to explain the need to "go around" someone to all concerned. The logical recipients of delegation, as noted by Cooper, include the following groups of employees:

1. Those in line of responsibility (those who report directly to you).
2. Functional employees who are task or technique specialists.
3. Specially qualified or knowledgeable employees.
4. Those designated as trouble-shooters to handle emergencies that must be handled outside of the normal workload.

[4] Ibid., pp. 123–124.

5. Those with seniority who feel entitled to certain favorite assign- **M6**
   ments.[5]   **cont.**

Cooper has also noted the following tasks that could be delegated
to specific individuals:

1. *Employees in Line of Responsibility:*
   These individuals could be delegated any of the ten major types of
   duties mentioned earlier as long as they did not require special
   knowledge or qualifications not possessed by these employees.

2. *Functional Specialists:*
   These individuals are not usually on your immediate staff and should
   be called in to be delegated specific tasks that require the specific
   techniques they possess. The specialists would, therefore, be delegated tasks they could accomplish better, sooner, or at less cost
   than you or any of those who report directly to you.

3. *Specially Qualified or Knowledgeable Employees:*
   These persons may or may not be on your immediate staff and
   should be delegated those tasks they could accomplish better,
   sooner, or at less cost than you or other members of your staff due
   to their background of prior experience in the area of responsibility
   to be delegated. Such tasks could include those related to fact
   finding and analysis, those related to the formulation and/or execution of policies, plans, and the like, the preparation of first drafts
   or reports.

4. *Trouble-Shooters:*
   These individuals should only be called in and delegated tasks that
   do not fall within the realm of the normal work load. These are
   usually problem oriented tasks that you and your staff would be
   unable to solve without the help of an outside source.

5. *Employees with Seniority:*
   These persons should receive choice tasks such as representing you
   at meetings or conferences; tasks you have been doing, and whose
   delegation would reduce your tendency to be overloaded.

Continue with Q10

The performance of routine and supporting activities should be   **Q10**
delegated to:

A. Subordinates reporting directly to the executive *A13*
B. Subordinates with seniority *A5*
C. A functional specialist . . . . . . : *A9*

Making the final decision concerning approval of a large project   **Q11**
could be delegated to:

A. A subordinate with seniority *A19*
B. A specially qualified subordinate *A34*
C. No one *A36*

[5] Ibid., p. 125.

The executive should try to send _____ Q12
_____ to represent him at a technical
meeting where his point of view can be expressed without him being
there. (Insert either phrase A or B.)

A. A specially qualified subordinate *A12*
B. Any subordinate reporting directly to him *A31*

**EVALUATING
DELEGATED
RESPONSIBILITY**

After the executive has decided which group of employees should be   **M7**
the logical recipients of a delegation, he must then make a decision
concerning the specific individual from the group who will receive the
delegation. The following criteria are presented in order to help you
make a knowledgeable decision concerning the proper recipient of
any delegation.[6]

1. The recipient's ability to develop a work program with a minimum
   of direct supervision and the ability to carry it out on his own
   responsibility.
2. The recipient's temperamental suitability for the assignment.
3. The recipient's acceptability to others with whom he must work or
   who have a major interest in the conduct of the work.
4. The recipient's ability to absorb additional work loads.
5. The availability of unused skills and initiative in the recipient.

Continue with Q13

You have a task that you want to delegate to one of your immediate   **Q13**
subordinates. Circle the letters corresponding to the criteria that you
would use as aids in making the decision as to who would be the
specific recipient of the delegation. Check your answer by turning
to A4.

A. The person who has the ability to get the work done with a
   minimum of supervision.
B. The person who is eager for more responsibility.
C. The person with the most suitable temperament for the task.
D. The person who is most able to get along with all agency
   employees.
E. The person who is most accepted by those with whom he must
   work to accomplish the task.
F. The person with the most ability to dominate his subordinates.
G. The person who has the most positive relationship with you.
H. The person whose potentials have not been fully realized in the
   interest of the agency.

HOW TO DELEGATE

After the executive has decided whether or not to delegate a task   **M8**
and has identified the group of possible recipients and the actual
person within that group who will receive the delegation, the next
step is to actually delegate the task. Delegation has the best chance
of being effective if the recipient clearly understands what is expected

[6] Ibid., p. 125.

of him/her and is capable of performing the tasks involved. When delegating, the executive must make sure that the recipient clearly understands the following: **M8 cont.**

1. The amount of authority the recipient will have to enable him to carry out the tasks. He should understand his rights and powers including what decisions he can make on his own and what decisions must be left to the executive.
2. The resources that will be available and the limitations on their use in terms of money, personnel, physical facilities, and time.
3. The conditions for checkback and feedback with the executive or other predesignated parties. This includes such things as the points at which the recipient should check back to obtain a go-ahead for the next phases and the points when he should merely send in progress reports—without interrupting his activity.[7]

The amount of clarification and guidance needed during this initial stage depends mainly upon the background of the recipient. Everything possible should be done to start him off adequately prepared and confident. The recipient, therefore, must be satisfied that he has sufficient authority to accomplish the task as effectively and efficiently as possible. The recipient must also clearly understand the resources available for this task and the limitations on their use in terms of money, personnel, and physical facilities, as well as the conditions for checking feedback with the executive or other parties that will facilitate control of the delegated task.

Continue with Q14

Barbara B. is an extremely busy executive. She has delegated a large task to John C., one of her subordinates who, she feels, is very competent. Barbara explains the task to John and tells him when she wants the task completed. Barbara feels she has no time for further explanation and believes that John needs no more help. If you were John, what would you do?   **Q14**

A. Start to work on the task *A17*
B. Ask Barbara for further clarification on several items that she did not mention *A10*
C. Tell Barbara to find someone else to do the job since you have other tasks to complete first *A20*

Which of the following questions would be most appropriate for you to ask if you were John?   **Q15**

A. What types of decisions am I authorized to make on my own?   *A8*
B. What resources are available to me and what are the limitations on their use? *A30*
C. When should I submit reports and at what points should I check back with you for a go-ahead? *A11*
D. All of the above *A1*

HOW TO CONTROL DELEGATION

Since the executive is responsible for the accomplishment of delegated tasks, control must be retained over the tasks no matter how much   **M9**

[7] Ibid., p 126.

confidence one has in the ability of the recipient to complete the task. **M9**
The controls used should be neither too restrictive nor too permissive. **cont.**
A few methods that can be used by the executive to retain control of
delegated tasks include:

1. Establishing the minimum number of feedback requirements at
   the beginning of the assignment.
2. Setting up controls, including guidance or review by another party
   without having to report.
3. Establishing a check list of achievement points or sensitive points
   of performance that should be observed.
4. Using routine methods of checking through staff meetings and
   progress reports.
5. Being reasonably accessible for conferences.
6. Using indirect reminders such as noting on related memorandum
   sent to the recipient an interest in progress to date.[8]

Assume that Barbara B., of our previous example, in delegating the **Q16**
task to John C., had set March 1 as a deadline for a progress report. It
is now March 3, and she has not received a report. What action should
she take to obtain the report from John C.?

A. Go to his department and ask him for his report **A21**
B. Send him a related memorandum and attach an inquiry about
   progress **A24**
C. Remind him publicly at a staff meeting that his report is late and
   wanted as soon as possible **A33**

Assume you are in charge of a project in an agency and you must **Q17**
submit a progress report every four months. Your task is to prepare
a first draft for each report. Answer the following questions by cir-
cling the letters beside the appropriate answers. Check your answers
by turning to A15.

1. Would you delegate this task?
   A. Yes.
   B. No.
2. If you answered yes to question one, from what groups would you
   choose a recipient for this delegation?
   A. Functional specialists.
   B. Specially qualified subordinates.
   C. Subordinates in line of responsibility.
   D. Trouble-shooters.
3. Who would you choose as the actual recipient of this delegation?
   A. The individual with the best personality.
   B. The individual who could carry out the job with a minimum of
      direct supervision.
   C. The individual who has the best relationship with other members
      of your staff.
   D. The individual who has the heaviest work load.

Referring to the situation presented in Q17, what would you include **Q18**
in your explanation of the task to the recipient? Check your answer by
turning to A14.

[8] Ibid., pp. 127–128.

A. His responsibilities and authority.   **Q18**

B. Communication requirements, such as provisions for checking   **cont.**
and feedback.

C. Both of the above.

D. Both of the above plus another important element. If you choose
this answer, explain the missing element in the space below.

In the space below, and still referring to the situation in Q17, list   **Q19**
at least four methods by which you could control this delegation.
Check your answer by turning to A27.

A.

B.

C.

D.

SUMMARY

In this unit, special attention was given to the issues related to
directing staff in any human service organization. The concept
of leadership was identified along with the rationale for the need
for effective leadership that included the ability to inspire staff
and to work toward a careful and continuous effort to make clear
to staff the over-all goals of any human service organization. The
leadership qualities required for effective management in human
services include dedication, an ability to motivate staff, and skills
needed to effectively delegate authority and responsibility to
subordinate staff. Considerable emphasis was given to the process
of delegation, stressing the concept of responsibility and authority. The process of delegation includes a clear understanding of
the prerequisites necessary to delegate responsibilities and an
understanding of the potential barriers to effective delegation.
Human service administrators are also required to have the
ability to assess the capabilities of employees to receive delegated responsibilities and authority and to follow up on all delegated responsibilities. The process of self-assessment is also
crucial to effective delegation, and administrators must also
periodically assess their own successes and failures in the delegation process. Special emphasis was given in this unit to the
problems of executive performance.

**SUGGESTIONS FOR
FURTHER STUDY**

Further study will be needed to fully understand the process of
effective leadership, including the dynamics of leadership and
communication, leadership requirements for creating organizational change, leadership characteristics related to creating community change, and the leadership qualities required for effective
work with groups of people.

Additional study will also be needed in the area of effective delegation and decision making. Such study will lead to a further analysis of authority patterns in organizations, assessing organizational loyalties and identification, selecting criteria for evaluating efficiency and effectiveness, and the concept of power in an organization. The expanding literature on decision making and policy formulation should prove to be valuable.

Further study will also be needed in the area of executive performance. Studies in this area will provide the future human service administrator with an opportunity to assess how effectively time is utilized during the work day, how others are involved in team work, how talent is recognized and promoted, how priorities are set, and how one refines and expands decision making skills. Areas of particular concern to effective administrative performance include issues related to staff relations, board of director relations, labor relations, client relations, and community and interagency relations.

SUGGESTIONS FOR FURTHER READING

Bass, B. *Leadership: Psychology and Organizational Behavior.* New York: Harper & Row, 1960.

Bennis, Warren G. "Leadership Theory and Administrative Behavior." *Administrative Science Quarterly* 4. no. 3 (1959).

Barnard, C. J. *The Function of the Executive.* Cambridge, Mass.: Harvard University Press, 1948.

Cartwright, D. and Zander, A. F., eds. *Group Dynamics: Research and Theory.* New York: Harper & Row, 1953.

Coch, L. and French, J., Jr. "Overcoming Resistances to Change." *Human Relations* 1 (1948).

Drucker, Peter F. *Management: Tasks, Responsibilities, Practices.* New York: Harper & Row, 1974.

Dyer, Frederick C. *Executive's Guide to Handling People,* Englewood Cliffs, N. J.: Prentice-Hall, 1958.

Gibb, Cecil A. "Ledership," in Gardner Lindzey, ed. *Handbook of Social Psychology.* Vol. II. Reading, Mass.: Addison-Wesley, 1954.

Ginsberg, Eli. *What Makes an Executive?* New York: Columbia University Press, 1955.

Henry, W. E. "Executive Personality and Job Success." *American Management Association, Personnel Series,* no. 120 (1948).

Jenkins, W. O. "A Review of Leadership Studies with Particular Reference to Military Problems." *Psychological Bulletin* ILIV (1947).

Katz, Daniel and Kahn, Robert L. *The Social Psychology of Organizations.* New York: Wiley, 1966.

Lassey, William R., ed. *Leadership and Social Change.* Iowa City, Iowa: University Associates Press, 1971.

Likert, R. *New Patterns of Management.* New York: McGraw-Hill, 1961.

Pelz, D. C. "Leadership Within a Hierarchical Organization." *Journal of Social Issues* VII (1951).

Schatz, Harry A., ed. *A Casebook in Social Work Administration.* New York: Council on Social Work Education, 1970.

Selznick, Philip. *Leadership in Administration.* New York: Harper & Row, 1957.

Simon, Herbert A. *Administrative Behavior*. New York: Free Press, 1957.

Stogdill, R. M. "Personal Factors Associated with Leadership: A Survey of the Literature." *Journal of Psychology* XXV (1948).

Tannenbaum, R. and Schmidt, W. H. "How to Choose a Leadership Pattern." *Harvard Business Review* XXXVI (1958).

Tead, O. *The Art of Leadership*. New York: McGraw-Hill, 1935.

Wald, R. M. and Doty, R. A. "The Top Executive: A Firsthand Profile." *Harvard Business Review* XXXII (1954).

1. Employees of an agency need direction in order to :

    A. Effectively fulfill their own goals.
    B. Effectively fulfill the goals of the agency.
    C. Get along with each other.
    D. Reduce the work load for each employee.

2. Leadership is:

    A. A process by which human energy is controlled through mutual stimulation in the pursuit of a common cause or goal.
    B. An inborn characteristic that cannot be learned.
    C. The use of power of position to effect the goals of a group or organization.
    D. A process by which the efforts of individuals are controlled by another individual in order to fulfill his own goals.

3. A competent agency leader possesses which of the following characteristics?

    A. Competitiveness.
    B. Imagination.
    C. Creativeness.
    D. B and C above.
    E. A, B, and C above.

4. Which of the following is (are) qualities that the competent agency leader should possess?

    A. Personal integrity.
    B. Insight into human behavior.
    C. Emotional poise and maturity.
    D. A and B above.
    E. A, B, and C above.

5. When an agency executive allows clients' records to be open to the public, he is lacking which leadership quality?

    A. Maturity and security.
    B. Insight into human behavior.
    C. Ability to carry complex responsibilities.
    D. A mature social philosophy.

6. When the executive director of a private agency shows a willingness to compromise with the board of directors, he is demonstrating:

    A. Weakness.
    B. The ability to deal with complicated problems in a mature manner.
    C. A mature philosophy.
    D. Ethical sensitivity and personal integrity.

7. An executive who makes sure that there is little variability in agency policy once it is established is demonstrating:

    A. A lack of leadership ability.
    B. The ability to deal creatively with complicated problems.
    C. Emotional poise, maturity, and security.
    D. Personal integrity.

8. The act of delegation includes:

   A. Assigning responsibility to another individual or group.
   B. Assigning authority to an individual or group.
   C. Assigning the responsibilty for performing a task along with the authority needed to perform the task.

9. If you expect a delegated task to be performed effectively, you should:

   A. Tell the recipient to perform the task.
   B. Explain the task to the recipient.
   C. Explain the reason(s) for performing the task.
   D. A and B above.
   E. A, B, and C above.

10. Most of the barriers to effective delegation are created by:

    A. The person receiving the delegation (the recipient).
    B. The person making the delegation.
    C. The method used to delegate.

11. Mack is capable but insecure in his job as assistant director of an agency. He believes some of his subordinates are trying to take over his position. What may be leading to Mack's reluctance to delegate his responsibilities?

    A. His superiors are not permitting him to delegate most of his responsibilities.
    B. He probably lacks personal knowledge about the tasks he should delegate so he is unable to explain them to others.
    C. He probably fears the lessening of his own power and the strengthening of the power of his rivals.
    D. He is probably insecure about the abilities of his subordinates to whom he should be delegating tasks.

12. Joe is a well-qualified executive and is always trying to make a good impression in everything he does. Joe probably has trouble delegating responsibility because:

    A. He has a work overload, and has no time to explain the delegated tasks to the recipient.
    B. He is afraid of losing control over the delegated tasks.
    C. He is unable to plan his work.
    D. He has a fear of lessening his own power and strengthening the power of his rivals.

13. If you were the executive of an agency, which of the following tasks or duties would you consider transferrable?

    A. Tasks related to fact finding and analysis.
    B. Final approval of a new project.
    C. Final determination of goals.
    D. A and C above.
    E. A, B, and C above.

14. If you are given a unique task to accomplish that has little probability of appearing again soon, you should:

    A. Delegate it.
    B. Accomplish it yourself.

C. Have your secretary complete it if it is an easy task.

D. Hire new staff.

15. As an executive, which of the following tasks should you accomplish yourself?

    A. Emergency, short-term tasks.

    B. Hiring your immediate staff.

    C. All tasks related to the execution of plans, programs, and projects, no matter how heavy the expenditures or risks.

    D. A and B above.

    E. A, B, and C above.

16. If you are overloaded with work and you have a meeting to attend, you should:

    A. Send a representative if your presence is required.

    B. Skip the meeting.

    C. Attend the meeting no matter what the circumstances.

    D. Send a representative if your point of view can be expressed without your being there.

17. Which of the following groups of individuals should be considered for delegation of responsibility?

    A. Functional specialists.

    B. Trouble-shooters.

    C. Employees with seniority.

    C. A and B above.

    E. A, B, and C above.

18. A choice task should be delegated to:

    A. A trouble-shooter.

    B. A specially qualified employee.

    C. A functional specialist.

    D. An employee with seniority.

19. Which of the following criteria should you use when deciding who should receive a delegation?

    A. The recipient's temperament.

    B. The recipient's ability to get along with everyone.

    C. The availability of unused skills of the recipient.

    D. A and B above.

    E. A and C above.

20. If a recipient of delegation has proven his ability to handle the development of a work program and carry it out on his own responsibility, his ability to absorb additional work loads:

    A. Becomes an unimportant consideration.

    B. Is another important consideration.

    C. Is the only other major consideration.

    D. None of the above.

21. Which of the following is *not* an important consideration when deciding who should receive a delegation?

    A. The recipient's ability to get along with those with whom he will be working when accomplishing this task.

    B. The recipient who has the most positive relationship with you,
the person making the delegation.

    C. The person whose potentials have not been fully realized.

    D. The person with the most suitable temperament for the task.

22. Harold, the executive director of a small agency, has delegated a
task to Heather, his assistant director. What questions must be
answered if Heather is to be able to carry out this delegation in a
competent manner?

    A. The amount of authority she will have.

    B. The resources available.

    C. The conditions for checkback and feedback.

    D. All of the above.

23. Assume that you wish to retain control of a delegation. Which of
the following actions could you take?

    A. Establish the checkback and feedback requirements.

    B. Be accessible for conferences.

    C. Use indirect reminders.

    D. A and C above.

    E. A, B, and C above.

Turn to the last page of this unit to check your answers.

ANSWERS

Exactly! All three questions covering the three major aspects of all delegations must be answered by the executive to the satisfaction of the recipient. **A1**

Continue with M9

Even if you are pressed for time on other tasks or problems, it would be unwise to delegate this new task since it would take longer for you to explain the task to your subordinate and, if necessary, give him the training that may be required to accomplish the task than if you accomplished it yourself. Return to Q8 and select the more appropriate answer. **A2**

This is probably true and is the major reason she will be unable to improve the situation. What does the director mean by improving efficiency? What specific reasons does he have for saying her department is not efficient? These and other questions pertaining to this topic must be answered if Dolores is expected to handle the situation. She has been given no reasons for accomplishing the task, but she is certainly able to infer them, and, being head of the department, she already has the authority to take over this responsibility. Inefficiency in this department may be the result of a low degree of work organization throughout the agency and this must be improved before departmental efficiency is improved. **A3**

Continue with Q3

The criteria that you should use to aid you in your decision include A, B, C, E, and H. Concerning the other criteria, there is no necessity for the recipient to get along with the whole agency staff since he/she will not be working with the whole staff. Also, there is little reason to believe that a dominating person will be able to accomplish a task more capably than one who uses persuasion and cooperation. **A4**

Finally, you should attempt to remain as objective as possible when making a delegation decision. The person who is able to relate well with you may not be the person who is able to get this specific task accomplished effectively. This is not a wise criterion to use in making such a decision, although it is difficult to avoid using it subconsciously.

Continue with M8

No, the subordinate with seniority has usually had a great many such tasks to perform and may become annoyed that a less experienced colleague was not given this task. Return to Q10 and select a more appropriate answer. **A5**

Of course not—no one should ever be given the responsibility for accomplishing an assignment without also being given the proper authority. Delegation, then, includes the transfer of both responsibility and authority. **A6**

Continue with M2

You should have circled letters A, D, E, and G, and should have underlined B, C, and F. If you had any trouble with these, return to M4 and M5 for a brief review before going on to M6. If you feel you have a competent grasp on the types of tasks that can and cannot be delegated, continue with M6. **A7**

Although this is one of the questions that must be answered, there **A8**
are others. This is certainly one of the questions that busy people
should be able to answer to your satisfaction. You, as the recipient of
the delegation, should clearly understand the amount of authority you
have and you should be sure it is sufficient to effectively and efficiently
accomplish the task. Return to Q15 and select a more complete
answer.

No, routine tasks are not within the realm of the functional special- **A9**
ist. The services of a specialist are not required to perform routine
tasks. Return to Q10 and select a more appropriate answer.

Right. No matter how busy the executive happens to be, if a del- **A10**
egation is made, the executive must take time to clarify the important
aspects of the delegation to the recipient.

Continue with Q15

When to submit progress reports and when to check back with the **A11**
executive or others is a very important aspect in the performance of
all tasks. Without this important element, the executive would prob-
ably lose control of the delegation and this is one of the responsibilities
he/she must retain. However, this is only one of the important ques-
tions that must be clearly answered by the executive. There are also
other equally important topics that must be clarified. Return to Q15
and select a more appropriate answer.

A specially qualified subordinate should represent the executive at **A12**
a technical meeting. Well done.

Continue with M7

Yes, this would be the wise choice for such a delegation. **A13**

Continue with Q11

The answer is D and the important element that is missing includes, **A14**
"the resources to be made available as well as the limitations on their
use."

Continue with Q19

The answers are as follows: **A15**

1. *A—If you answered B. or no, then you should review the section on*
   delegation.
2. *C—A person in subordinate status can be helped to develop by*
   such an assignment.
3. *B—A person who can carry out an assignment with a minimum of*
   direct supervision is usually the better choice.

Continue with Q18

Although Dolores has been given no specific criteria for improving **A16**
efficiency, she does already have the authority to examine work or-
ganization in her own department and to ask the necessary questions
of her staff to evaluate work efficiency. Return to Q2 and select a
more appropriate answer.

This would be unwise since you have been given no information   **A17**
concerning how you are to accomplish the task, the necessary authority,
or the resources. You do not know if she wants written reports and,
if she does, when they are due. There are other unanswered questions.
You will soon become frustrated if these aspects are not clarified and
valuable time will be wasted unnecessarily. Return to Q14 and select
a more appropriate course of action.

This would not be wise, in most cases. If your subordinates are   **A18**
allowed to perform new tasks and solve new problems, their growth
and development will be severely hindered and they will soon feel
that you have little confidence in their abilities. Part of your responsi-
bility as an executive is to assist in the development of your sub-
ordinates, and you should try to carry out this responsibility whenever
possible. Return to Q7 and select the correct answer.

Final decisions concerning policies, plans, and programs, especially   **A19**
when substantial resources or risks are involved, should only be made
by the executive. This responsibility should never be delegated. Return
to Q11 and select a more appropriate answer.

This is usually unwise. If Barbara B., as the executive, feels this   **A20**
task is important enough, she will expect you to give it precedence
over other tasks that you may now be doing. You are then back where
you started, although now the executive may have become upset be-
cause you have tried to reject her request. Return to Q14 and select a
more appropriate answer.

No, this may be considered a very threatening and upsetting action   **A21**
by John C. In addition, it would make him appear irresponsible to
any of his staff members who are present. Return to Q16 and select a
more appropriate answer.

No, if a task is to be accomplished under heavy pressure, it should   **A22**
not be delegated even to a competent subordinate since there will be
little time for the requisite feedback necessary for successful accom-
plishment of such a task. Return to Q6, and select the correct al-
ternative.

You should have circled letters A, C, E, and F. Department heads   **A23**
are generally not expected to formulate policies and plan programs on
their own. Such activities are usually carried out with top administra-
tion. Communication is also ineffective, due possibly to an unreceptive
attitude by the director or to insecurity on the part of Dolores. The
supervision of her staff, including controlling, reviewing, and evaluating
their performance, as well as training them, when necessary, is all
she can be expected to handle effectively and she seems to be doing
this.

Continue with M3

Yes, this is certainly one way to meet this problem. It is a very   **A24**
unthreatening method of reminding John C. and it usually produces

results. However, a direct memo may also be just as productive since John was advised of the time element when delegated the task.

Continue with Q17

You have said that Jack should have little trouble setting up a new program even though he has been given no specific authority. However, no delegation should be made without the necessary amount of authority required to complete the assignment. Responsibility without authority is like a sailboad without wind! Very few, if any, assignments are accomplished if there is a lack of authority to carry them out. Return to Q1 and answer the question correctly.

In this case, you are correct. Emergency, short-term, and new tasks should be accomplished by you since there is usually little time to explain them to a subordinate, and, if necessary, give them the training needed to accomplish the task. With new tasks, policies may also be unclear. Efficiency is the key here and it would be more efficient for you, the executive, to accomplish these tasks.

Continue with Q9

The six methods previously discussed by which you can control this or any delegation include:

A. *Establish checkback and feedback requirements when the delegation is made.*
B. *Set up lateral controls.*
C. *Give the recipient a check list setting forth the criteria of achievement or the sensitive points of performance that he should observe. If possible, a model of performance could be suggested as a tangible basis of comparison.*
D. *Use routine checking methods such as periodic meetings, progress reports, and the like.*
E. *Be reasonably accessible for conferences with the recipient.*
F. *Use indirect reminders.*

If you had any trouble listing at least four out of six methods, return and review M9, otherwise you have now completed this lesson and this unit. Test yourself by doing the review questions at the end of this unit. Also, be sure to read the summary and suggestions for further reading before going on to Unit VII.

This is untrue—as head of the department, Dolores would usually possess all the authority necessary for performing the task of improving efficiency. What might be the reason for her inability to accomplish the task? Return to Q2 and select the correct answer.

You should have circled B, D, E, and G. These executives were all evidencing leadership behavior which was a result of being able to delegate responsibility. The other three executives were evidencing behavior that depicts their inability to delegate responsibility. The executive should be able to plan the work load and effectively delegate those tasks that subordinates should be able to accomplish, with or without supervision.

Continue with M4

A24
cont.

A25

A26

A27

A28

A29

This is but one of the important questions that must be answered   **A30**
to your satisfaction by the executive. It is certainly important for you,
the recipient, to clearly understand the resources that will be available
to you and the limitations on their use in terms of money, personnel,
and the like. Without this information, you can easily get into frus-
trating, time wasting arguments with other employees working on other
tasks. Return to Q15 and select a more appropriate answer.

No, the executive should attempt to send a specially qualified sub-   **A31**
ordinate since social skills may be called upon in a technical meeting.
Return to Q12 and select the correct answer.

In most cases, this would be the best choice. Your objective here   **A32**
would be to help develop your subordinates. If you do not allow them
to take on new tasks and problems, their growth and development will
be greatly hindered and they may begin to feel you have little confidence in their ability to learn.

Continue with Q8

This would be an unwise course of action that could be very em-   **A33**
barrassing. Requests of this nature should be by memo or in private.
It may well be that John C. has a legitimate reason for being late,
although we would hope that the reason had been communicated to
the executive before the deadline. Return to Q16 and select a more
appropriate course of action.

No, the final decisions concerning goal and policy determination   **A34**
and program plan or project approval, especially when substantial
resources are to be allocated, should be made by the executive. This
responsibility should never be delegated. Return to Q11 and select the
correct answer.

You should have circled B, D, E, and G. The final approval of   **A35**
programs, plans, and projects, as well as the final determination of
goals and policies should be handled by the executive himself, not
delegated. Regarding C, representing you at all meetings and conferences, the wise executive should not make it a policy to allow a
subordinate to represent him at all meetings. Some meetings require
the executive's presence, some do not. The effective executive is able
to make this important distinction.

Continue with M5

Excellent! No one but the executive should make the final decisions   **A36**
concerning goal and policy determination, program, plans, or project
approval, especially when substantial resources are to be allocated.

Continue with Q12

Right! A task that must be accomplished under heavy pressure,   **A37**
be it time or any other variable, should not be delegated since the
requisite feedback would be difficult, if not impossible, to obtain.

Continue with Q7

ANSWERS TO REVIEW QUESTIONS

The following are the correct responses to questions for Unit VI.

Question	Answer	Question	Answer
1	B	13	A
2	A	14	B
3	D	15	D
4	E	16	D
5	D	17	E
6	B	18	D
7	A	19	E
8	C	20	B
9	E	21	B
10	B	22	D
11	C	23	E
12	B		

Did you answer 18 or more correctly? If so, move right on to Unit VII. If not, review your trouble spots and then go on to Unit VII.

UNIT VII
COORDINATING

LESSON 1
The Coordination Process

**UNIT VII OBJECTIVE—
COORDINATING**

Upon completion of this unit, given a decision making situation requiring the ability to coordinate the efforts of agency personnel, you will be able to make those decisions necessary for the effective coordination of the agency's services.

Specific Objective

Given a description of an agency with problems in coordination, you will be able to identify the causes and explain how these are leading to inefficient or ineffective service delivery.

Enabling Objective 1
You will be able to explain what is meant by coordination.

Enabling Objective 2
You will be able to explain the meaning of the coordination of jobs.

Enabling Objective 3
You will be able to explain why jobs must be coordinated before the individuals performing the jobs can be coordinated.

Enabling Objective 4
You will be able to explain the meaning of vertical and horizontal coordination.

Enabling Objective 5
Given a description of either vertical or horizontal coordination, you will be able to identify the type of coordination, describe how

233

the given form is operationalized, and explain how a lack of coordination can lead to ineffective and inefficient delivery of services by the agency.

Continue with M1

COORDINATION

You were introduced to this concept in Lesson Two, Unit I, where it was referred to as that all important duty of interrelating the various parts of the work of an agency so that it functions as a whole. However, a more explicit definition has been stated by Walton as follows:

M1

> Coordination is referred to as the activity that allocates and directs various persons, functions, specialties, and spaces with a view to their reciprocal relations in such a way that they contribute maximally to the accomplishment of an organization's purposes.[1]

It is evident from this definition that coordination is a fundamental and vital process within any organization. However, it should never be viewed as an end in itself. The accomplishment of agency purposes is the goal of all agency functions, including coordination. If an agency is highly coordinated but fails to accomplish its purposes, then the effort expended in the coordinating process was wasted.

COORDINATION OF JOBS AND COORDINATION OF THE HUMAN EFFORT

From Walton's definition of coordination it is evident that there are two major aspects to be coordinated—jobs and personnel effort. The coordination of the human effort necessary for effectively accomplishing the purposes of the agency always presupposes the jobs to be coordinated. According to Mooney, "The job as such is therefore antecedent to the man on the job, and the sound coordination of these jobs, considered simply as jobs, must be the first and necessary condition in the effective coordination of the human factor."[2]

Every job and every function must be clearly defined in its relation to all other jobs and functions and these must all be tied either directly or indirectly to the purposes of the agency.

Assume that you are a consultant hired by a human services agency to help discover the causes of inefficient service delivery in the agency. You begin by questioning some of the employees concerning their jobs and the jobs of their fellow employees. You find that there are many discrepancies in their descriptions of what they should be doing and what their fellow employees think they should be doing. There is very little, if any, coordination of effort and a great deal of duplication of effort.

Coordination is the continuous process of allocating and directing resources aimed at:

Q1

[1] John Walton, *Administration and Policy Making in Education* (Baltimore, Md.: Johns Hopkins Press, 1959), p. 86.
[2] James D. Mooney, "The Principles of Organization," in Luther Gulick and L. Urwick, eds., *Papers on the Science of Administration* (New York: Institute of Public Administration, 1937), p. 92.

A. Providing maximum efficiency of agency personnel . . . *A1* **Q1**
B. Providing for maximum effectiveness in the performance of agency **cont.**
tasks *A6*
C. Accomplishing agency purposes with maximum efficiency and
effectiveness *A18*

What would you suspect as being the cause of the following dis- **Q2**
crepancies?

A. The employees are incapable of performing their jobs and functioning competently *A10*
B. The jobs and functions have not been clearly defined, especially in
relation to other jobs *A4*
C. The employees are too self-centered and are unwilling to work together toward the accomplishment of the agency's purposes *A2*

STRUCTURAL PRINCIPLES OF ORGANIZATION REQUIRED FOR COORDINATION

After defining the exact functional definitions of all agency jobs and **M2**
explaining these to every employee as he or she begins to perform on
the job, the executive's task is to make sure that the efforts of all the
individuals performing the jobs are coordinated. Coordination in any
organization has primarily two forms: perpendicular or vertical coordination and horizontal coordination.

PERPENDICULAR COORDINATION

Perpendicular coordination (coordination from top executives to the
line worker) is effected through the competent delegation of responsibility and the corresponding authority for the performance of
every act from the largest to the smallest.

According to Mooney, the sound application of the delegating
principle is absolutely necessary to an orderly and efficient organization.[3] As you learned in an earlier lesson, the one to whom a task or
any assignment is delegated becomes responsible for doing that job,
but the superior (leader) who delegates this responsibility remains
responsible for getting the job done. The chain of responsibility and
authority which Mooney calls "the scalar chain," extends from the top
to the bottom of the entire organization but always emanates from
the top leadership, which is responsible for the whole.[4]

Continue with Q3

Perpendicular coordination is characterized by: **Q3**

A. Total responsibility delegated from top to bottom of the organization *A7*
B. Total authority delegated from top to bottom of the system . *A3*
C. Responsibility with corresponding authority delegated from top to
bottom of the system *A11*

[3] Ibid., p. 93.
[4] Ibid., pp. 93, 94.

Walter B., an executive in a local agency, has put John R. in charge   **Q4**
of a feasibility study concerning the establishment of a new agency
service.

Choose from the following statements those that adequately describe the degree of responsibility in this situation:

A. Walter is no longer responsible for seeing that the study is
   accomplished.
B. John is responsible for completing the study.
C. Walter is responsible for completing the study.
D. Walter is responsible for seeing that the study is completed.

Statements A and C are correct *A8*
Statements B and D are correct *A5*
Statements A and B are correct *A13*
Statements C and D are correct *A17*

HORIZONTAL COORDINATION

According to Mooney, the second and equally important form of co-   **M3**
ordination is horizontal coordination. Horizontal coordination like perpendicular coordination, may very well also begin at the top but reflects
more of a two-way flow of information.

It is not the leader alone who has things to make known to his subordinates through the usual channels of staff service. These subordinates
may likewise have something important to tell the leader; things that he
should know in the exercise of his leadership. They may also have important
things to tell each other, and this mutuality of things to be made known
extends upwards, downwards, and sideways, from the very top to the bottom of the organized structure.[5]

There must be coordination of this flow of information so that
everyone in the agency is informed about those facts, ideas, and
opinions that need to be known in order to do the job. In addition,
those in positions requiring decision making must be supplied with
the advice and counsel needed to make the proper decisions.

Continue with Q5

Circle the appropriate words in parentheses in order to correctly   **Q5**
complete the following sentence.

Authority and the scalar chain of command are characteristics of
_____ coordination and a two-way flow of information is characteristic of _____ coordination.
If you selected:

A. (perpendicular/perpendicular) *A12*
B. (horizontal/horizontal) *A9*
C. (perpendicular/horizontal) *A14*
D. (horizontal/perpendicular) *A19*

[5] Ibid., p. 96. Since Mooney's classical statement, there have been many attempts to find satisfactory solutions to horizontal coordination. For example,
interdependent departments and peer groups of like status have been found
to voluntarily coordinate their efforts. For further reading see: Peter M. Blau
and W. Richard Scott, *Formal Organizations* (San Francisco: Chandler, 1962),
pp. 183–185. See also: Victor A. Thompson, *Modern Organizations* (New York:
Knopf, 1961), pp. 180–188.

Assume that you are the director of programs and services of a   **Q6**
newly created welfare agency. During the first few months of operation, you have discovered that some of the programs and services of
the agency are beginning to function smoothly while others are being
ineffectively or inefficiently operated. Your inquiries of your own staff
members as well as of your superiors and fellow employees of equal
status have revealed some interesting findings.

Although your superiors seem to be making themselves clear concerning what they want accomplished, you are receiving very little
feedback from your subordinates. They seem to be unclear as to what
is expected of them. Other agency executives are also finding this to
be true of their staff members. It is also becoming clear that, when
asked for their advice regarding possible program changes or changes
in the delivery of services, your staff seems to be reluctant to share
their ideas and opinions.

Which of the following may be causing the disharmony in this
agency?

A. Lack of perpendicular coordination *A16*
B. Lack of horizontal coordination *A20*
C. Lack of coordination of jobs *A15*
D. Both B and C above *A22*
E. All of the above *A21*

**COORDINATION
BY OBJECTIVE**

The preceding material emphasized the role of the executive in terms   **M4**
of reconciling differences, talking with people, getting feedback, and
making decisions as these relate to coordination.

In addition, we need to understand that modern management leans
heavily on another concept, that is, coordination by reason of the fact
that the entire staff understood and accepted the organization's goals
and objectives. Coordination of purpose and function results from the
managerial use of "management by objectives and results" (MOR).
Coordination is most effective when individuals see how their jobs
contribute to the dominant goals of the enterprise.[6]

We conclude then, that one of the best ways to coordinate an
enterprise would come through a thorough knowledge of that part of
the management system known as management by objectives.[7]

Continue with Q7

Earlier we said that coordination may be achieved through co-   **Q7**
ordination of jobs (for example, through technology-computerization
or assembly line) or through coordination of the human effort.

Complete the following statement: then check your response by
turning to A23.

Management by objectives would achieve coordination through:

---

[6] See Harold Koontz and Cyril O'Donnell, *Principles of Management* (New
York: McGraw-Hill, 1964), p. 41.
[7] See George L. Morrisey, *Management by Objectives and Results* (Reading,
Mass.: Addison-Wesley, 1970).

Although this is an important aspect of coordination, providing for **A1**
maximum efficiency of personnel alone is not the major goal of co-
ordination. Coordination should never be viewed as an end in itself.
Return to M1 for a brief review and then answer Q1 correctly.

This is a far-out conclusion! We wouldn't say it could never hap- **A2**
pen, but the real causes usually run deeper than blaming it all on the
employees. The great majority of workers, especially in human
services agencies, are willing to perform their jobs in cooperation with
others. Lack of cooperation and coordination of effort usually results
from ignorance of what exactly is expected of each employee. The
worker then attempts to define his own job and the jobs of others and
then imposes this view on his fellow workers resulting in friction and
lack of coordinated effort. Return to M1 for a review and then answer
Q2.

The individual who delegates a task does not transfer his total **A3**
authority. Return to M2 for a review, then return and answer Q3
correctly.

Excellent! The administrators of this agency have failed to clearly **A4**
define the tasks, functions, and responsibilities of each employee or
else these definitions have never been explained to each employee,
especially in their relation to the duties of their fellow employees and
in their relation to the purposes of the agency, thereby causing friction
and lack of coordination of effort.

Continue with M2

Exactly right. John's responsibility is to complete the feasibility **A5**
study, while it is Walter's responsibility to see that the study is com-
pleted.

Continue with M3

The effective performance of agency tasks is an important aspect **A6**
of coordination, but it is not the major goal—only a means to that
goal. Coordination should never be viewed as an end in itself. Return
to M1 for a brief review, then answer Q1 correctly.

No. The individual who delegates a task does not transfer his total **A7**
responsibility for getting that task accomplished. Return to M1 for
a review and then answer Q3 correctly.

If you selected A and C, you were asleep! These two statements **A8**
are incompatible. Return to Q4 and select another answer.

Your answer was a horizontal coordination for both examples. This **A9**
is not entirely correct. Return to M3 for a brief review before answer-
ing Q5 correctly.

To an inexperienced consultant, this may appear, at first glance, **A10**
to be the cause of the inefficiency. However, the more experienced
person would be able to discern between incompetence on a job and
ignorance of what is expected in the performance of the job. Return
to M1 for a review and then answer Q2 correctly.

This is correct. Perpendicular coordination is characterized by the delegation of responsibility and corresponding authority.   **A11**

Continue with Q4

Your selection was that both examples represent a perpendicular coordination. This is not entirely correct. Please return to M3 for a brief review before answering Q5 correctly.   **A12**

You have selected statements A and B as representing the degree of responsibility. However, this is not entirely correct. Return to Q4 and select another answer.   **A13**

Good! You selected perpendicular for the scalar chain of command and horizontal coordination for the two-way flow of information. That is correct.   **A14**

Continue with Q6

This is correct as a generalization, but it is not the only answer. Although there is evidence pointing to the fact that most staff members are confused concerning their duties, there is also evidence that another form of coordination is lacking in this agency that is adding to the inefficient functioning of programs and delivery of services. Return to Q6 and make another selection.   **A15**

This seems to be the only form of coordination that is functioning in this agency, albeit in a shaky fashion. Perpendicular coordination is not completely lacking. The scalar chain of authority emanating from the top executives to the beginning workers appears to be functioning, at least in some respects, since some of the work of the agency is being accomplished and the top executives are making their desires known to their subordinates. However, even this coordination could use improvement. Return to Q6 and select another answer.   **A16**

You have selected statements C and D as adequately representing the degree of responsibility in the situation. However, this is not entirely correct. Return to Q4 and select another answer.   **A17**

Exactly. The major overriding goal of coordination is to effectively and efficiently accomplish the purposes of the organization (agency). Even if agency personnel are working efficiently and agency tasks are being performed effectively, the purposes of the agency may be lost in the coordination effort. The agency's purposes must be clearly understood by all agency personnel and the tasks being performed must be tied directly to agency purposes.   **A18**

Continue with Q2

The answer you indicated is horizontal for the scalar chain of command and perpendicular for the flow of information. This is not entirely correct. Please return to M3 for a brief review and then answer Q5 correctly.   **A19**

Yes. *There is a lack of horizontal coordination in this agency. Necessary feedback information and knowledge is not being disseminated among the employees. However, there is also evidence of another type of coordination that is lacking and this is contributing greatly to the lack of harmony in this agency. Return to Q6 and choose another answer.*   A20

Although this may seem to be the case since both horizontal coordination and coordination of jobs appear to be lacking, there is not a complete lack of perpendicular coordination. The scalar chain of authority emanating from the top executives appears to be functioning, although it could be greatly improved. Return to Q6 and choose another answer.   A21

Excellent! You have arrived at the most desirable response. Not only has there been a lack of coordination of jobs as evidenced by the confused responses of most of the staff members concerning their duties, but there is also a lack of horizontal coordination evidenced by the lack of feedback and the reluctance of many agency employees to express their ideas and opinions to their superiors and, in some cases, even to their equals. The necessary information and knowledge is not being disseminated throughout the agency, and, as a result, the employees are not obtaining a sense of common purpose in the pursuit of the agency's objectives.   A22

Continue with M4

Your response should have included something like the following: Human effort to understand the goals and objectives of an organization leads to coordination by reason of the fact that the persons involved have arrived at an understanding, at least, of direction and purpose.   A23

You have now completed Lesson One. Continue with the next lesson which discusses steps and methods that an agency's executive should use to establish effective coordination of agency personnel.

UNIT VII
COORDINATING

LESSON 2
Essential
Steps and Methods
for Coordination

Specific Objective

Given a description of a problem in coordination within an agency, you will be able to describe an effective method by which coordination may be established.

Enabling Objective 1
Given a brief description of different responsibilities of an agency executive, you will be able to identify those that are directly related to the function of coordination.

Enabling Objective 2
You will be able to explain five essential steps required to achieve effective coordination of personnel in an agency.

Enabling Objective 3
Given a description of a situation in which the agency executive has neglected a coordinating responsibility, you will be able to identify the unfulfilled responsibility and explain the consequences resulting from this neglect.

Enabling Objective 4
Given a list of methods, you will be able to identify those that are most often used by agency executives to maintain the coordination of personnel.

241

Enabling Objective 5
Given a situation requiring the need for improving coordination in an agency, you will be able to explain a method that could be used in the situation.

Continue with M1

COORDINATION OF STAFF EFFORT

Coordination of staff effort is an executive responsibility. Cooperation is the key to effective coordination. This includes cooperative thinking, planning, and action. The major executive responsibilities related to coordination of agency personnel include the following: **M1**

1. Make provisions for direct, face-to-face contacts among the agency staff members.
2. Make sure that mutual agreement is obtained concerning plans of action and that the plans are carried out at the earliest possible time.
3. Create an atmosphere within the agency for mutual response wherein each staff member feels free to respond to new ideas and suggestions as they arise, as well as make their own ideas and suggestions known to fellow employees, subordinates and superiors alike.
4. Provide for continuity of working relationships and avoid, as much as possible, constant movement of employees from one department to another.[1]

With these essential responsibilities it is important to note the basic steps necessary to apply them in a coordinating situation.[2]

Continue with Q1

Which of the responsibilities described below is *not* related to coordination of agency personnel?   **Q1**

A. Maintain effective community-agency relationships.
B. Foster an atmosphere wherein all agency employees feel free to respond in an open manner.
C. Provide for salary increases based on merit.
D. Set up situations that will require face-to-face contacts among agency employees.
E. Provide for continuity of relationships.
F. Provide for full use of agency resources.

Select your answer from those presented below:

1. A, E, and F *A1*
2. E and F *A5*
3. A, C, and F *A9*

In order to carry out the executive responsibility related to the effective coordination of agency personnel, it is necessary to take account of at least the following essential steps of coordination: **M2**

[1] Ray Johns, *Executive Responsibility* (New York: Association, 1954), p. 83.
[2] Ordway Tead, *The Art of Administration* (New York: McGraw-Hill, 1951).

1. Assembling an adequate body of relevant fact and informed opinion   **M2**
   and requiring presentation of these facts by those who are knowl-   **cont.**
   edgeable.
2. Providing clear definitions of who has responsibility for all specific
   operating duties.
3. Assuring that those who are responsible for each assignment are
   knowledgeable about the duties required, have the requisite ability
   to perform these duties, and agree to carry out the assignment.
4. Providing for review and continuing appraisal of results.[3]

A fifth factor or step in the coordination process is the conscious
drive to create unity in a program through the development of a sense
of collective responsibility among participants.[4]

Continue with Q2

Assembling an adequate body of relevant fact and informed opinion   **Q2**
is the first major step in coordination. Which of the following describes
how this step is to be accomplished in an agency?

A. The presentation of relevant facts and informed opinions by the
   executive director *A2*
B. The presentation of relevant facts and informed opinions by an
   employee who may have them *A6*
C. The presentation to the board of directors or the legislative body
   of the relevant facts and informed opinions *A13*

The director of a local mental health agency assembled a small but   **Q3**
competent group of employees and announced that they were to
establish a marriage counseling program as soon as possible. The
director explained that the community and the board of directors had
exerted pressure on the agency for such a service. It was then explained that these staff members had been called together since they
were highly competent in the area of marriage counseling. Hurriedly
departing for another meeting, the director's final comment was, "You
are free to set up the program as you see fit."

Circle the letter(s) of the coordinating step(s) that the director
omitted and then select your answer below.

A. Presentation of some facts and informed opinions.
B. A description of the responsibilities of the group members.
C. Relevant knowledge concerning the content of the program, shared
   by those assigned the responsibility to carry out the assignment.
D. Necessary abilities to carry out the assignment.
E. Agreement by group members to carry out the assignment.

1. A, C, and D *A3*
2. B, C, and D *A7*
3. A, B, and C *A14*
4. B, C, and E *A18*

[3] Ibid., p. 182.
[4] See Victor A. Thompson, *Modern Organization* (New York: Knopf, 1961),
Chapter 9, on cooperation and collective responsibility as an important element in coordinating the efforts of personnel.

Assume that you are the executive director of an agency. Your   **Q4**
board of directors has made a request for the creation of a new service
to replace one that, in their view, is no longer needed. Which of the
following actions would you take first in order to help assure that a
coordinated effort will result?

A. Make sure that you assign competent employees to establish the
   methods for delivering the new service *A4*
B. Survey the agency employees and collect information concerning
   the need for and feasibility of the service *A8*
C. Define which employee will be responsible for what specific duties
   and tasks *A10*

If the necessary facts and opinions from all informed staff members   **Q5**
and outside parties are favorable, you as the director would make the
decision to implement the new service. Your next step would then be
to:

A. Select those individuals who will be responsible for implementing
   the new service, and define the responsibility for the specific
   operating duties *A11*
B. Clearly explain the new service to those employees whom you
   feel are competent in the service area and obtain their commitment
   to work on the project *A15*
C. Foster a sense of collective responsibility by agency employees for
   the accomplishment of the task *A21*

Facts and opinions concerning the feasibility of implementing a   **Q6**
marriage counseling service have been gathered by you, the director.
You have also made the decision to carry out the project, and selected
competent staff members to carry out the project. The next step in the
coordination of effort is to:

A. Review and appraise results in order to insure accomplishment
   of goals *A22*
B. Make sure that those chosen to accomplish the task have been
   made aware of their responsibilities and agree to carry out the
   assignment *A16*
C. Create a sense of unity or collective responsibility among all agency
   employees in order to accomplish this project *A20*

The final step that must be taken by the executive director is to   **Q7**
make sure that provisions are made for:

A. Continuous monitoring of employees to insure the completion of
   assigned tasks *A12*
B. Periodic review and appraisal of results *A17*

METHODS USED TO   As you have learned in earlier lessons, there are two major methods   **M3**
MAINTAIN   most often used by agency executives to maintain coordination of
COORDINATION OF   agency personnel. These two methods meet the criteria of providing
AGENCY PERSONNEL   a. direct, face-to-face contacts, and b. the opportunity for early action

on assignments, mutual response, and continuity of working relation-   **M3**
ships.[5] These two methods are: **cont.**

1. Committees.
2. Conferences.

Through these two major methods executives maintain effective channels of communication with their entire staff. Coordination among staff positions and among departments is achieved primarily through effective channels of communication.

Continue with Q8

If you were an executive, which of the following could you use to   **Q8**
help facilitate the creation of effective channels of communication?

A. Set up and make effective use of committees *A19*
B. Schedule regular staff conferences as well as conferences with
   department and branch heads *A23*
C. Both of the above *A24*

SUMMARY

This unit addressed the question of coordination in the management process. Special attention was given to highlighting the importance of coordination functions unique to an organization and then coordinating the people working for that organization. The concept of horizontal coordination among staff at similar levels in the hierarchy of the organization as well as vertical coordination between the top management of an agency and the line staff, are two crucial concepts in the process of coordination. The methods of building coordination in an organization are also extremely important as well as complex. In this unit, we outlined the various steps needed to carry out effective coordination and the process by which administrators build a cooperative environment in an agency. Special attention was given to committees and conferences as two major mechanisms for building effective coordination in any organization.

SUGGESTIONS FOR FURTHER STUDY

The concept of coordination can be further understood through the analysis of systems theory concepts. New innovations from the organization that put a man on the moon, the National Aeronautics Space Administration, provide important lessons for new approaches to the concept of coordination. The NASA experience helps to identify such issues as systems integration, tolerance for more than one boss, performance review, activities, using intermediaries to improve coordination (such as translators), and the difficult process of fixing responsibility for coordination as demonstrated by such new job titles as project manager and lead planner.

[5] See H. Koontz and C. O'Donnell, *Principles of Management* (New York: McGraw-Hill, 1964), pp. 41–43, in which they quote Mary Parker Follett on coordination.

Additional attention is needed in the area of committee process. Future human service administrators will need specialized knowledge of committee process and how people are coordinated in order to fulfill the over-all objectives of the organization. Effective use of coordination by administrators also provides a mechanism for control. When the functions of an organization are coordinated, the staff can thereby also assist administrators by identifying new opportunities for organizational change and growth. Through coordination, administrators will be able to draw upon the expertise of their staff as well as the new insights derived from people working together and sharing their views of current organizational needs and future priorities.

The further study of the strengths and weaknesses of the committee process will help to clarify how committees serve to integrate group judgment, promote coordination, secure cooperation, and train the members.

SUGGESTIONS FOR FURTHER READING

Buckley, Walter. *Sociology and Modern Systems Theory.* Englewood Cliffs, N. J. Prentice-Hall, 1967.

Houle, Cyril. *The Effective Board.* New York: Association, 1970.

Kaufman, Herbert. *Administrative Feedback: Monitoring Subordinates Behavior.* Washington, D. C.: Brookings Institute, 1973.

King, Clarence. *Your Committee in Community Action.* New York: Harper & Row, 1952.

Litterer, Joseph A. *Organizations: Systems, Control and Adaption.* New York: Wiley, 1969.

Lohmann, Melvin R. *Top Management Committees, Their Functions and Authority.* New York: American Management Association, 1961.

Newman, William H. *Administrative Action: The Techniques of Organization and Management.* Englewood Cliffs, N.J.: Prentice-Hall, 1951.

Sayles, Leonard R., and Chandler, Margaret K. *Managing Large Systems: Organizations for the Future.* New York: Harper & Row, 1971.

Trecker, Audrey, and Trecker, Harleigh B. *Committee Common Sense.* New York: Whiteside, 1954.

1. Coordination is the activity that allocates and directs various agency resources aimed at:

   A. Providing for maximum effectiveness in the performance of agency tasks.
   B. Accomplishing the purposes of an agency with maximum efficiency and effectiveness.
   C. Reducing the costs of the delivery of agency services.
   D. Developing agency personnel.

2. The coordination of jobs refers to:

   A. Coordination of the human factor.
   B. Clearly defining every job and every function in relation to all other jobs and functions all tied to agency purposes.
   C. Clearly defining job functions.
   D. Coordination of the human effort necessary for effectively accomplishing agency purposes.

3. Line authority refers to:

   A. Functional coordination.
   B. Horizontal coordination.
   C. Perpendicular coordination.
   D. Systematic coordination.

4. Staff service is referred to by Mooney as:

   A. Horizontal coordination.
   B. Functional coordination.
   C. Systematic coordination.
   D. Perpendicular coordination.

5. Which type of coordination is related to the competent delegation of responsibility and authority for the performance of every act?

   A. Functional coordination.
   B. Systematic coordination.
   C. Perpendicular coordination.
   D. Horizontal coordination.

6. The person who receives a delegation is responsible for:

   A. Getting the assignment accomplished.
   B. Actually performing the assignment.
   C. Finding someone to accomplish the assignment.
   D. None of the above.

7. Which type of coordination operates through the dissemination of knowledge and requires the coordination of staff positions?

   A. Perpendicular coordination.
   B. Horizontal coordination.
   C. Systematic coordination.
   D. Functional coordination.

8. Horizontal coordination extends:

   A. Upward.
   B. Downward.
   C. Sideways.

D. A and B above.

E. A, B, and C above.

9. Which type of coordination operates through the scalar chain of command?

   A. Functional coordination.
   B. Horizontal coordination.
   C. Systematic coordination.
   D. Perpendicular coordination.

10. Which of the following structural principles must be established and maintained if there is to be a harmonious coordination of effort by agency employees so as to effectively accomplish agency purposes?

   A. Horizontal coordination.
   B. Perpendicular coordination.
   C. Coordination of jobs as jobs.
   D. A and B above.
   E. A, B, and C above.

11. The key to effective coordination in any agency is:

   A. A sound organizational plan.
   B. Cooperation.
   C. A well-trained staff.
   D. Competent executives.

12. A list of executive responsibilities are presented below. Which is (are) directly related to coordination of agency personnel?

   A. Provide for continuity of working relationship.
   B. A sound organizational plan.
   C. Create an atmosphere for mutual response.
   D. A and C above.
   E. A, B, and C above.

13. When the executive of an agency obtains mutual agreement among employees regarding a plan of action, he is:

   A. Facilitating coordination of personnel.
   B. Inhibiting coordination of personnel.
   C. Avoiding future problems.
   D. Employing a bureaucratic principle.

14. When an executive schedules staff conferences, meetings, and so on, he is:

   A. Providing for continuity of working relationships.
   B. Making provisions for direct, face-to-face contacts among agency employees.
   C. Interfering with the delivery of agency services.
   D. Providing for full use of agency personnel.

15. Committees and conferences are:

   A. Decision making groups used to facilitate communication in an agency.
   B. Methods used to effect coordination in agencies.
   C. Small and discussion is closed-group.
   D. A and B above.
   E. A, B, and C above.

The responsibilities not related to the coordination of agency person- **A1**
nel were to be selected. You selected one, E, that is related. Return
to Q1 and select another answer.

The executive director does not have a monopoly on the relevant **A2**
information. Return to Q2 and select another answer.

Statements A, C, and D do not all represent an ommission by the **A3**
director of the local agency. Return to Q3, reread the case, review
the answers, and then make the proper choice.

Although staff assignment is an important task, it is not the first **A4**
step to take in assuring a coordinated effort. Return to Q4 and choose
another answer.

The responsibilities not related to the coordination of agency per- **A5**
sonnel were to be selected. You selected one, E, that is related. Return
to Q1 and make another selection.

This is the correct answer since the more information and opinions **A6**
received, the greater are the chances of a coordinated, unified effort
aimed at accomplishing agency goals.

Continue with Q3

You selected B, C, and D as omissions by the director of the agency. **A7**
This answer is partially correct. However, another answer is more
representative of the situation. Turn back to Q3, review the case, and
select another set of statements.

Exactly! This should always be your first step if coordination of **A8**
effort toward the achievement of your objectives is desired. No one
is able to work in a vacuum without the relevant facts and opinions,
especially pertaining to the need and feasibility of the task.

Continue with Q5

The responsibilities not related to the coordination of agency per- **A9**
sonnel were to be selected. Your choice of A, C, and F was correct.

Continue with M2

The determination of specific duties is an important step in coordina- **A10**
tion. It is not, however, the first step in assuring coordination. Return
to Q4 and choose another answer.

Excellent! After collecting the relevant facts and opinions needed **A11**
to decide whether the program should be implemented, the executive
director must select those employees whom he feels capable of im-
plementing the new service.

Continue with Q6

If the other steps in coordination have been well executed, con- **A12**
tinuous monitoring of agency staff should not be necessary. Return to
Q7 and select the correct answer.

The board of directors or the legislative body may provide valuable information. However, this is not the kind of material that is apt to help in coordinating the work of the agency staff. Return to Q2 and select another answer.   **A13**

You selected statements A, B, and C as omissions by the director in establishing a marriage counseling service. Although partially correct, this is not the best answer. Return to Q3, review the case, and select another set of statements.   **A14**

Although it is difficult to say which action should come next, it is usually best if the executive director, after deciding to implement the project based on the facts and opinions obtained in step one, selects those persons thought to be most capable of carrying out the project and outlines their duties before asking them to make a more realistic assessment of what will be expected of them and whether or not they will be able to handle this new assignment, especially if it is to be conducted in conjunction with their other duties, which is often the case. Return to Q5 and make another selection.   **A15**

Precisely. After selection of competent staff, then knowledge of the assignment and commitment to its completion is the third major step in coordination in order to carry out the responsibility of the director.   **A16**

Continue with Q7

The final step by the executive director is to make sure that provisions are made for review and appraisal (evaluation) of results. You have now finished reviewing the executive's responsibilities pertaining to coordination as well as the essential steps in the coordination process.   **A17**

Continue with M3

You selected statements B, C, and E. This is the best answer for the described situation.   **A18**

Continue with Q4

Although this is one widely used method to help facilitate effective communication in an agency, there is another method that is often used. Return to Q8 and select the more complete answer.   **A19**

No. Since this is an intangible aspect of coordination it is not to be confused with the specific essential steps in coordination. It is an indispensable element that must be fostered by the executive director from start to finish of the project. Return to Q6 and choose another answer.   **A20**

The fostering of a sense of collective responsibility is a very important aspect of coordination, but it is somewhat intangible and is not the second step in coordination as we have presented it. Return to Q5 and select another answer.   **A21**

Although review and appraisal of results are important, they are   **A22**
not the next step in coordination. Turn to Q6 and select another
answer.

This is partly correct. You could use conferences to help facilitate   **A23**
communication among agency staff members. However, there is another
widely used method as well. Return to Q8 and select the more com-
plete answer.

Exactly! As an agency executive, you will want to use both com-   **A24**
mittees and conferences to help facilitate communication among staff
and departments of the agency.
*   You have now finished this lesson on coordination. Be sure to read*
the summary, the suggestions for further study, and then complete the
review questions at the end of this unit.

**ANSWERS TO
REVIEW QUESTIONS**

The following are the correct responses to questions for Unit VII.

Questions	Answers	Questions	Answers
1	B	9	D
2	B	10	E
3	C	11	B
4	A	12	D
5	C	13	A
6	B	14	B
7	B	15	D
8	E		

How did you do? You have mastered this Unit if you answered 10 or more questions correctly. You should now tackle Unit VIII. If you had less than 10 correct answers, review those areas that gave you trouble before proceeding to Unit VIII.

UNIT VIII
REPORTING

LESSON 1
The Reporting Function

UNIT VIII OBJECTIVE—REPORTING

Following this unit, you will be able to demonstrate your reporting skills by responding to decision making situations in a competent manner.

Specific Objective

Given a situation requiring a report, you will be able to: 1. name the groups or individuals to whom the report should be addressed; 2. name the type of report that should be made; and 3. identify the essential elements of the report.

Enabling Objective 1
You will be able to explain three major purposes of reporting.

Enabling Objective 2
You will be able to cite the three activities that must be carried out in order to help the executive fulfill the reporting function.

Enabling Objective 3
Given the name of one of the groups of individuals to whom the executive must report, you will be able to cite at least two major types of reports that are made to the stated group.

Enabling Objective 4
Given a description of an agency and the name of a report, you will be able to identify the individual(s) and/or group(s) to whom the report should be sent.

253

Enabling Objective 5
You will be able to identify the important elements of a report, given the name of the report and a list of different elements.

Continue with M1

This unit is concerned with the important function of reporting. **M1**
The first lesson will focus on the types of agency reports and the methods used in human services agencies by executives to facilitate the reporting function. The second lesson will deal with the essential steps used to prepare a report as well as the most efficient manner in which to arrange reports. The third lesson will focus on the public relations aspects of reporting.

PURPOSES OF REPORTS

Reports, based on accurate records, inspection, and research, are an indispensable part of sound organization. Reports are necessary for three major reasons:

1. To identify personnel, program, project, financial, and over-all agency strengths and weaknesses.
2. To measure personnel, program, project, and over-all agency progress.
3. To furnish a basis for planning.[1]

It should be noted here for your future reference that suggestions for the necessary record forms and procedures have been developed by most of the national voluntary organizations as well as federal and state governmental agencies to which local human service agencies are related. They should be used, if available, and adapted to local conditions.

Continue with Q1

In addition to describing agency progress, reports are necessary as **Q1**
a basis for:

A. Planning future agency activities.
B. Informing the public of available services.
C. Measuring agency progress.

Select your answer from these combinations:

1. A and B *A5*
2. A and C *A11*
3. B and C *A20*

WHO RECEIVES AGENCY REPORTS?

Reporting is essentially another method used for internal agency com- **M2**
munication as well as for communication between an agency and outside organizations such as the funding agency, other agencies working on similar projects, or programs and community organizations.

---

[1] Ray Johns, *Executive Responsibility* (New York: Association, 1954), p. 62.

Different types of reports must be made to help keep the executive   **M2**
director, the associate executives and supervisors informed concern-   **cont.**
ing personnel, finances and programs. In this way, executives can keep
up-to-date on agency progress and, in turn, obtain the necessary
reports required of them concerning the agency. These reports are
submitted to agency boards or legislative bodies and to outside organizations.

Continue with Q2

To which of the following persons and/or groups are agency re-   **Q2**
ports submitted?

A. Executive director *A4*
B. Governing bodies *A14*
C. Other related organizations *A12*
D. All of the above *A2*

There are different ways in which reports may be classified, and   **M3**
the following are the most common types:

1. Subject matter—finance, personnel, program, project, research.
2. Time interval—daily, weekly, monthly, semiannually, annually.
3. Interim reports—memorandums, letters.
4. Miscellaneous—progress, recommendation, improvement.[2]

Continue with Q3

Match the following types of reports used by agencies with their   **Q3**
proper classifications by placing the number corresponding to each
type in the space provided beside the classification, then check your
answer by turning to A21.

1. Daily, weekly, monthly, semiannually, annually.
2. Finance, personnel, program, project, research.
3. Progress, recommendations, improvement.
4. Memorandum, letter.

Classification:

Subject matter _____
Time interval _____
Interim _____
Miscellaneous _____

REPORTS TO
ADMINISTRATIVE
STAFF

Different types of reports from all four classifications listed above are   **M4**
written within an agency to help keep the executive director and
his associate executives and supervisors up to date on agency activities.

We shall consider only a few of the many examples starting with
the first report classification.

    I. Subject Matter Reports
        A. Client services reports—those working with clients in any
           capacity must make reports to their supervisors regarding each
           client or client group.

[2] From Raymond V. Lesikar, *Report Writing for Business* (Homewood, Ill. R. D.
Irwin, 1969), pp. 9–13.

B. Program, project, or research reports—the director of these **M4**
activities must make periodic (daily, weekly, and/or monthly) **cont.**
reports to the executive director concerning progress toward
goals.
C. Personnel reports—associate executives and supervisors must
make periodic reports to the personnel director or the assistant
director, if he or she is in charge of personnel, concerning
the progress or lack of progress being made by their employees.
D. Financial reports—periodic (usually semiannually or annual)
budget reports must be made to the executive director by program, project, and research directors and by the agency's
finance executive.

II. *Time Interval Reports*
Many subject matter reports (financial, program, project, research, and others) are submitted on a pre-set time interval. In
addition, a pre-set time interval for progress reports is found in
most well-managed agencies, for example, a six-month report or
an annual report.

III. *Interim and Miscellaneous Reports*
Memorandums are used frequently within an agency to help keep
staff and executives informed of agency activities and as reminders. Such memos are often used in place of other more complete reports for disseminating information on short-time intervals
(daily, weekly, and sometimes monthly).
Miscellaneous reports include:
A. Progress reports—such reports are made by directors of programs and projects to keep the executive director up to date
on how these activities are progressing.
B. Improvement reports—these could be made by program and
project directors concerning their programs or they could be
used to report employee progress.
C. Recommendation reports—these reports are usually made to
the executive director by committees formed by the director.
Such reports may also be expected from conferences.

Continue with Q4

Decisions must be made concerning promotions of agency staff. **Q4**
Upon what type of report would such decisions primarily be made.

A. Financial reports *A3*
B. Personnel reports *A9*
C. Client service reports *A13*

Circle the letters corresponding to the types of reports listed be- **Q5**
low that are usually also classified as time interval reports, then check
your answers by turning to A6.

A. Financial.
B. Memo.
C. Program.
D. Project
E. Letters.

F. Personnel.

G. Improvement.

H. Recommendation.

Q5 cont.

Program or project activities directors may be called upon to submit the following reports to executives:

Q6

A. Progress reports and improvement reports *A7*

B. Improvement reports and recommendation reports . . .   *A10*

C. Recommendation reports and progress reports *A15*

**REPORTS SUBMITTED
TO THE BOARD OF
DIRECTORS OR THE
LEGISLATIVE BODY**

The executive director must submit reports to the agency board of
directors or legislative body. Reports to these groups from the executive director are usually financial reports (annual budget report),
and/or progress reports (periodic over-all agency reports). Other
types of reports received by members of a board or legislative body
include:

M5

1. Letters from the executive director on specific problems needing
their attention.

2. Recommendation reports from those committees formed by the
board or legislative body.

Continue with Q7

The board of directors or the legislative body primarily receive
reports from which of the following classifications? Circle the letters
corresponding to the proper classifications and check your answer
by turning to A8.

Q7

A. Subject matter.

B. Time interval.

C. Interim report.

D. Miscellaneous.

**AGENCY REPORTS
RECEIVED BY
OUTSIDE AGENCIES**

In order to create and maintain favorable agency-community relations,
agency reports are indispensable. All influential community organizations and any community organization that has shown an interest
in the agency should receive periodic (at least annual) progress reports on agency activities. These organizations should be kept informed, through written reports and, if possible, through oral reports,
regarding all agency programs and services. They should be informed
of any new programs and services that are being created or old ones
that are being phased out. Favorable agency-community relations are
an essential ingredient of the effective delivery of services to the members of the community.

M6

Continue with Q8

Circle the letter(s) corresponding to the primary report(s) that
funding agencies should receive from those agencies they are supporting, then check your answer by turning to A16.

Q8

A. Annual financial report.
B. Agency progress reports.
C. Special project and research reports.
D. Memorandums.
E. Improvement reports.
F. Recommendation reports.

Q8
cont.

An indispensable element in creating and maintaining favorable agency-community relations is:

Q9

A. Making all agency reports available to the public A19
B. Dissemination of agency progress reports to community groups A17
C. Regular submission of memos to the agency board . . . A22

ESSENTIAL ELEMENTS OF AGENCY REPORTS

There are five essential elements that should be included in any report that will be sent to individuals or groups outside of the agency (such as the board of directors, legislative body, community organizations, funding agency). These elements are:

M7

1. The dates of the period covered by the report.
2. The address of the agency.
3. The names of the officers, board, or legislative body members, committee members, and executive and supervisory staff members.
4. A concise statement of the agency's character, purposes, and aims.
5. The report itself (a suggested outline of the components of the report as well as a suggested sequence are presented in Lesson Two of this unit).[3]

For reports that will be for use within the agency only, the essential elements would include:

1. The dates covered by the report.
2. The names of the individuals involved in preparing the report.
3. A statement of the purposes and aims of the activity being reported.
4. The report itself.

Continue with Q10

Circle the letters below corresponding to the essential elements that should appear in all types of reports, then check your answers by turning to A18.

Q10

A. The address of the agency.
B. The dates covered by the report.
C. The names of the officers, board, or legislative body members, committee members, and executive and supervisory staff members.
D. The report itself.
E. The agency's purposes and aims.

Assume you are writing an annual report that will be distributed to several community organizations. Circle five elements from the

Q11

[3] Mary S. Routzahn, ed., *Annual Reports and How to Improve Them* (New York: Social Work Publicity Council, 1941) p. 2.

list below that should be included in the report, then check your answer by turning to A1.

Q11 cont.

A. The dates of the period covered by the report.
B. Purpose, aims, and character of the agency.
C. Past history of the agency.
D. Names of officers, board, or legislative body members, committee, executive, and supervisory staff members.
E. Agency title and address.
F. Body of the report.
G. Annual budget report.

The essential report elements in an annual report to community orga- **A1**
nizations are: A, B, D, E, and F. Past history may be obtained by
reading prior reports; and the annual budget report is a financial
report to the agency board.

You have now completed the first lesson on reporting and should
have a clearer conception of the three major purposes of reports, the
four main types of reports, as well as a basic knowledge of the essential elements of agency reports.

If you are satisfied with your understanding of these objectives,
go on to Lesson Two. However, if you are at all unsure of yourself
regarding these topics, return to M1 and review this lesson.

Excellent. There are three major groups of individuals who must **A2**
receive agency reports to keep up to date on agency progress and
activities. These include:

1. Executive director, associate executives, and supervisors.
2. Board of directors or legislative body.
3. Organizations outside the agency, that is, funding agencies, community organizations, and others.

Continue with M3

Financial reports are only indirectly related to decisions concerning **A3**
employee promotion, that is, enough finances to pay for a raise. The
actual decision on promotion would usually be made on the basis of
another type of report. Return to Q4 and select the correct answer.

This is only one of the answers. Executive directors need reports **A4**
from their staff in order to keep up to date on agency progress so that
they will be able to make the reports required of them. Return to M2
for review, then select the correct answer.

You selected statements A and B as a basis for reports. This answer **A5**
is only partially correct. Return to Q1 and choose another answer.

The letters A, C, D, and F should have been circled. Subject matter **A6**
reports are usually also classified as time interval reports, that is,
monthly research reports, annual budget reports, and others. Also
there are weekly, monthly, and annual progress reports on programs,
projects, research, as well as over-all agency progress reports made
to the board of directors or legislative body.

Continue with Q6

Exactly correct! Project or program directors submit progress and **A7**
improvement reports generally to executive directors.

Continue with M5

You should have circled all four classifications since the board and **A8**
the legislative body may receive budget reports, which are subject
matter reports; periodic (time interval) progress reports on the over-
all progress of agency activities; letters that represent a type of interim
report; and recommendation reports, which are miscellaneous reports.
If you failed to answer this question correctly, you may need a review
of the report classifications and the types of reports within each found
on M3. If you answered correctly, continue with M6.

Exactly. Decisions concerning employee promotions are usually **A9**
based on personnel reports, although financial considerations would
also be involved since money must be available to cover salary in-
crements.

Continue with Q5

Your answer was improvement reports and recommendation re- **A10**
ports. However, this is not entirely correct. Return to Q6 and select
another answer.

Correct! Reports are necessary for planning future agency activities **A11**
and measuring (evaluating) agency progress.

Continue with M2

This is only partially correct. Agency reports are used to help create **A12**
and maintain favorable agency-community relations as well as to keep
outside agencies and community organizations up to date on agency
activities. Return to M2 for a brief review before answering Q2 cor-
rectly.

Only if the quality of client service was being considered would **A13**
such reports be involved in a promotion decision. Client service re-
ports may be involved only indirectly in decisions concerning pro-
motion. The primary purpose of such reports is to aid in improving
services to clients. Return to Q4 and select the correct answer.

Yes, the board of directors or legislative body receives reports from **A14**
the executive director. However, this is only part of the answer. Re-
turn to M2 for a brief review and then select another answer from Q2.

Recommendation reports and progress reports are the two types that **A15**
you selected. Usually committee chairmen, however, and not pro-
gram or project directors would submit recommendation reports.
Return to Q6 and choose another answer.

The reports that must be sent to funding agencies include A (annual **A16**
financial reports), and B (agency progress reports). Some funding
agencies may also request other reports such as special project and
research reports, but these reports are usually summarized in the
over-all annual agency progress report. Memos are only for interagency
use and improvement and recommendation reports are rarely sent
outside the agency unless a specific request is made by an outside
agency.

Continue with Q9

Correct. One essential element of agency-community relations is **A17**
the dissemination of periodic over-all agency progress reports to
community organizations. Personal contact is, of course, also essential.

Continue with M7

You should have circled letters B (dates covered by the report) and **A18**
D (the report itself). Letters A, C, and E correspond to elements that

are not necessary to include in intraagency reports, although they would be included in reports sent outside the agency.

A18 cont.

Continue with Q11

Making all agency reports available to the public will not necessarily improve public relations, since a "direct link" between the agency and representatives of the public has not been established. Return to Q9 and choose another answer.

A19

Your answer was B and C. This answer is only partially correct. Return to Q1 and select another answer.

A20

Subject matter   2   *(finance, personnel, program)*
Time interval   1   *(daily, weekly, monthly)*
Interim   4   *(memo, letter)*
Miscellaneous   3   *(progress, recommendation, improvement)*

A21

Continue with M4

Regular submission of memos does not inform public representatives of agency accomplishments. Return to Q9 and select another answer.

A22

UNIT VIII
REPORTING

LESSON 2
Effective Agency-Community Relationships Through Reporting

Specific Objective

Given a description of a situation requiring a report, you will be able to cite the ten essential steps that must be taken in preparing the report, and set up an outline that you would use to write the report.

Enabling Objective 1
You will be able to name the three steps referred to by the letters "SDSP," as well as the step numbers.

Enabling Objective 2
You will be able to state the steps and the step numbers corresponding to the letters "CAI."

Enabling Objective 3
You will be able to identify the process of directing a written report to a specific audience.

Enabling Objective 4
Given outlines for writing reports, you will be able to identify the best arrangement.

Enabling Objective 5
Given the headings included in an outline, you will be able to arrange these headings in a manner most suitable for writing an agency report.

Enabling Objective 6
Given the various essential steps in writing a report, you will be able to arrange the given steps in proper sequence.

Enabling Objective 7
Given a situation requiring repetitive reports, you will be able to give the remaining essential steps for preparing the report.

Continue with M1

TEN VITAL STEPS IN PREPARING A REPORT

In Lesson One you learned about the types of reports made in agencies and the people who should receive these reports. In this lesson you will be exposed to the essential steps in preparing a report. Any report must be prepared one step at a time. Such preparation takes time, thought, skill, and hard work. There is no easy way to prepare a report since each report is a new creative effort. According to Gallagher there are basically ten steps involved in preparing a report.[1] They are:

1. Stating the problem.
2. Defining the scope of the problem.
3. Planning the research.
4. Collecting the information.
5. Analyzing the information.
6. Forming the conclusion(s).
7. Organizing the report.
8. Preparing the first draft.
9. Editing the draft.
10. Publishing the report.

M1

We shall begin with the first three steps of SDSP—Stating and then Defining the Scope of the problem and Planning the methods used for research or for obtaining relevant information. The problem is stated first in very general terms, and then it is analyzed to bring it into closer focus. It is during the second step that the limits are placed on the scope of the problem and these limits need to be clearly defined. During the third step, methods are developd to obtain or retain relevant information to be used in the report. If it is a research project report, then the methods to be used in the project are noted in this step in the process. Since the subjects of most reports prepared by human service agencies are repetitive (for example, annual reports, progress reports, financial reports, reports from committees), these first three steps may only require brief updating from prior annual reports.

The fouth and fifth steps in the reporting process are CAI,

4. Collecting and
5. Analyzing the Information.

With the fourth step the reporting process would usually begin for the repetitive types of reports such as weekly, monthly, or annual budget reports, as well as personnel, project, and program reports. The problem, its scope, and the methods for collecting and retaining rele-

[1] William J. Gallagher, *Report Writing for Management* (Reading, Mass.: Addison-Wesley, 1969), p. 14.

vant data are usually determined and stated in earlier reports. The **M1** person(s) responsible for such repetitive reports begins by collecting **cont.** the data for the current report and analyzing this data.

Although the above sequential arrangement may appear to be overly rigid, the writer of any report may start at some other step in the process. Where you begin is determined by:

1. The type of report to be prepared.
2. The requirements the report must satisfy.
3. The extent of your involvement in the total effort.

Continue with Q1

If you were preparing a year-end progress report for a project and **Q1** only had the collected data in front of you, which of the following steps in the process of report preparation would you take next?

A. Analyzing the information A2
B. Forming the conclusions A9
C. Stating the problem and defining its scope A4

In which of the following steps would you focus on the specific **Q2** aspects of a problem or task that will be included in a report?

A. Stating the problem A1
B. Defining the scope of the problem A5
C. Planning the research or the methods used, to obtain and/or retain relevant information A10

If you were writing a report other than a first annual budget re- **Q3** port, which step would follow the steps of stating and defining the problem?

A. Third step—planning data collection methods A3
B. Fourth step—collecting the data A6
C. Fifth step—analyzing the data A11

The sixth step, forming the conclusions, is the final phase of agency **M2** report writing but is not placed at the end of the report. If you have prepared term papers or research papers where the conclusions come at the end of the paper, this approach to agency report making may seem out of place. In an agency report the conclusions should be presented first. This allows the reader to get to the important aspects of a report without wasting time reading the details that are less important to him (for example, methods of data collection, data analysis). If the reader has time or needs further information to understand the conclusions and recommendations, then the body of the report can be reviewed.

Continue with Q4

Which of the following is presented first in any agency report? **Q4**

A. Organization of the report A7
B. Statement of conclusions A12
C. Data analysis A13

After forming the conclusions, you should organize the report (step **M3**
7) and then prepare the first draft (step 8). In performing the
seventh step—organizing the report—you should always keep the
needs of the intended reader(s) in mind. Although it is impossible
to assume that one arrangement will satisfy every reader, the following arrangement has proved to be suitable to the needs of a wide
variety of readers.[2]

1. Summary.
   a. Purpose and Scope.
   b. Conclusion(s).
   c. Recommendation(s).
2. Introduction.
3. Body.
4. Appendix.

The benefit to the reader should be obvious in this arrangement.
You have quickly stated the conclusions reached. People want to find
out what you have concluded. They are not interested in your travail
in gathering the facts nor do they want to be bothered by scholarly
erudition. This outline then meets the needs of the reader.

Continue with Q5

Does the following arrangement of an agency's annual report take **Q5**
into account the needs of the reader?

1. Introduction.
2. Body.
3. Conclusion(s).
4. Recommendation(s).

A. Yes *A14*
B. No *A8*

The final two steps (step 9 and 10) in the reporting process include: **M4**

9. Editing the first draft.
10. Publishing the report.

The first draft should be edited, revised, and rewritten until it is
in an acceptable form for publication and dissemination.

Continue with Q6

You have now reached the end of Lesson Two. However, before **Q6**
you leave this lesson, answer the following questions.

I. Which steps do the following letters stand for in the reporting
   process—SDSP?

[2] Ibid., p. 52.

II. How about CAI—What do they stand for?

Q6 cont.

III. Arrange the following in proper order when preparing an agency report by placing the proper number from 6 through 10 in the spaces provided. Check your answer by turning to A15.

_____ Preparing the first draft.
_____ Editing.
_____ Organizing the report.
_____ Publishing the report.
_____ Forming the conclusions.

Although it is necessary to first state the problem in general terms, it is not during this step that you focus on the specific aspects of a problem, that is, delimiting the problem. Return to Q2 and select the correct answer. A1

Possibly, but this step usually comes later in the process of writing up the report. Return to Q1 and select the correct answer. A2

This step may already have been completed in a prior report such as an annual budget and can be skipped thereafter. Return to M1 for a brief review before answering Q3 correctly. A3

This is correct. Although the data has been collected, it is necessary to first state the nature and scope of the problem. A4

Continue with Q2

Exactly! When you define the scope of the problem, you have, by definition, delimited the problem. A5

Continue with Q3

Precisely—an anual report is, of course, repetitive and, except for the first such report, the first three steps in the reporting process are also repetitive. Therefore, the place to begin would be step 4, collecting the data for the report. A6

Continue with M2

You selected A or organization of the report. This answer is not correct. Turn back to Q4 and select another answer. A7

Correct. This arrangement is typical of term papers and research papers, but it is not recommended for agency report writing. A8

Continue with M4

No, this step comes later in the process of writing up the report. Return to Q1 and select the correct answer. A9

No, this is the third step in the process of report preparation. You should delineate the problem before you begin planning the research methods or obtain relevant information pertaining to the problem. Return to Q2 and select the correct answer. A10

No. Sorry! You need to collect the data before you can analyze it. Return to Q3 and select the correct answer. A11

The answer, statement of conclusion, is indeed correct since it should be presented first in an agency report. A12

Continue with M3

Data analysis is not the first item in an agency report. Return to Q4 and select another answer. A13

No, this arrangement is more beneficial to the writer than to the   A14
reader. Turn to Q5 and select the correct answer.

The steps in report preparation are as follows: A15

   I.   1. *Stating the problem.*
          2. *Defining the scope of the problem.*
          3. *Planning the data collection or research methods.*
  II.   4. *Collecting the information.*
          5. *Analyzing the information.*
 III.   6. *Forming the conclusions.*
          7. *Organizing the report.*
          8. *Preparing the first draft.*
          9. *Editing.*
        10. *Publishing the report.*

You have just completed Lesson Two. If you had any trouble ar-
ranging the above steps in proper order, review M3 and M4 before
proceeding to the final lesson in this unit.

UNIT VIII REPORTING

LESSON 3
The Public Relations Function

Specific Objective

Given a description of an agency program or service that will involve the organization of a public relations campaign, you will be able to define the steps necessary in planning the campaign, write communications for the news media, and determine the type of public relations that will be used.

Enabling Objective 1
You will be able to define public relations and identify five types of communications used in a human service agency.

Enabling Objective 2
You will be able to list the four major steps that should be taken in solving public relations problems.

Enabling Objective 3
You will be able to define news and identify the guidelines that should be followed in writing a press release.

Enabling Objective 4
Given an agency situation requiring a press release, you will be able to name three important aspects that should be remembered in sending a press release to the news media.

Enabling Objective 5
You will be able to describe two ways of involving the local community in a public relations campaign.

Continue with M1

INTRODUCTION

Every year large sums of the taxpayers' money are spent by federal and   M1
state governments in an attempt to provide adequate human services.
Since the existence of the human service agencies depends on the
consent of the public, it is essential that the public be informed about
the activities of these agencies. The responsibility for gaining the
support of the public lies in the public relations function of the human
service administrator, who must recognize that every administrative
decision has public relations implications since every such decision
ultimately affects service to the public.[1]

Although public relations is a factor in fulfilling all of the administrative activities noted in this text, it is most distinguishable as a
functon in reporting. The human service administrator has a dual
responsibility in reporting. These responsibilities include: 1. reports
of agency activities and policies must be given regularly to agency
staff and other officials associated with the agency; and 2. agency
programs and services must be explained to the entire range of interested publics, including prospective clients, legislators, other agencies,
and the taxpaying public who support the programs of the agency.

This lesson will introduce you to some basic public relations concepts.

A DEFINITION OF
PUBLIC RELATIONS

Public relations is viewed by many as an integral part of an organization reflecting a continuous and planned activity. A common definition of public relations emphasizes the three elements, research, action,
and communication, which are the essential activities in public relations. This definition states that, "public relations is the management
function which evaluates public attitudes, identifies the policies and
procedures of an organization with the public interest, and executes
a program of action [and communication] to reach public understanding and acceptance."[2]

Public relations is usually equated with activities such as advertising, publicity, propaganda, or lobbying, but these activities should
be viewed primarily as the tools of public relations. Such activities
are only part of the public relations function needed to manage human
services.

Continue with Q1

Which of the following is the most accurate definition of public   Q1
relations?

A. Public relations is the art of persuasive communication that emphasizes the use of advertising, good press relations, and lobbying
to gain public understanding and acceptance A5
B. Public relations is the management function that evaluates public
attitudes, identifies the policies and procedures of an organization
with the public interest, and uses action and communication to
influence public understanding and acceptance A8

[1] Gordon E. Brown, "The Public Relations Function of the Administrator," in
Frances Schmidt and Harold Weiner, eds., *Public Relations in Health and
Welfare* (New York: Columbia University Press, 1966), pp. 47–48.
[2] John E. Marston, *The Nature of Public Relations* (New York: McGraw-Hill,
1963), p. 5.

C. Public relations is a transitory activity of management that is used   Q1
to interpret the policies and procedures of an organization to   cont.
the public . . . . *All*

THE TOOLS OF PUBLIC RELATIONS IN HUMAN SERVICE ORGANIZATIONS

The tools of public relations used in human service organizations may   M2
be classified as internal or external.[3] Internal media are used to inform
those already closely connected with the organization, such as employees or community leaders. External media are used to inform
the general public or special groups such as legislators or educational
institutions.

The principal media of internal communication used in a human
service organization are:

1. Public relations handbooks: These are prepared by national public relations staffs for guidance of local units in planning and carrying out effective community relations programs. Human service
administrators can call upon agencies like the National Public Relations Council of Health and Welfare Services for assistance.
2. Public relations reports: To inform other administrators and staff
members about public relations accomplishments, annual and
special public relations reports can be published by the agency.
3. Organization magazines or newspapers: These may range from a
single mimeograped sheet to a large, elaborate magazine. These
publications are generally aimed at audiences closely connected
with the organization.
4. Bulletin boards and posters: These offer a good place to confirm
information that circulates through interdepartmental correspond-
ence. It is important that the boards be kept current and interesting.
5. Memorandums and bulletins: Memorandums, individually written
and addressed, are a direct and inexpensive way of establishing
speedy communication with specific publics within the organization.

Continue with Q2

Place a check in the appropriate blank and then turn to A3 and   Q2
check your answer. In a human service organization, internal media
of communication are used primarily to inform:

———— A. The general public or special groups such as legislators.
———— B. The potential clients of the agency.
———— C. Those already closely connected with the organization.

The principal media of external communication used in a human   M3
service organization are:

1. *Media Press Publicity:*
Publicity in newspapers, magazines, radio, and television are the
major media used by human service public relations programs.

2. *Periodicals and Brochures:*
Human service organizations frequently publish periodicals and
brochures to inform the public about their current programs and
services.

[3] See Bertrand R. Canfield, *Public Relations* (Homewood, Ill.: Irwin, 1968), pp.
316–321. See also: Scott M. Cutlip and Allen H. Center, *Effective Public Relations* (Englewood Cliffs, N.J.: Prentice-Hall, 1964), chapter 11.

3. *Public Speaking:*
Speeches by officials of human service organizations are another important technique for communicating with the general public.

4. *Conferences:*
Conferences on both the national and local levels may be used to inform staff about the program of an organization and to inform the general public, and can thus be used as both internal and external means of communication.

5. *The Telephone:*
The telephone is a major medium of communication with the general public and the staff of the organization. It, too, is used as both an internal and external means of communication.

6. *Special Events:*
Special events such as open houses or agency tours can be used to inform the public about the services of an organization.

The human service administrator must be familiar with these and the many other communication media that are available. It is important to note that many communication media can be used both internally and externally. The examples used in this lesson are designed to show how these media are most frequently used. The determination of which method(s) of communication should be used will depend on a careful application of the R-A-C-E formula which is described in the next section.

Continue with Q3

Classify each of the following media of communication as primarily internal (place an I in the blank) or primarily external (place an E in the blank), and then turn to A7 and check your answers.

_____ A. Bulletin boards and posters.
_____ B. Open houses and agency tours.
_____ C. Press publicity.
_____ D. Public relations handbooks.
_____ E. Public speaking.
_____ F. Memorandums and bulletins.

A FORMULA FOR SUCCESSFUL PUBLIC RELATIONS

Like any other administrative activity, effective public relations requires careful research, planning, and evaluation. In public relations a formula has been developed to aid the practitioner in solving public relations problems. This formula uses the letters R-A-C-E, which stand for, Research, Action, Communication, and Evaluation.[4]

1. *Research:*
The first step in planning a public relations program is research, which should seek answers to questions such as: What are the organization's goals? What are its resources? What are the existing opinions or attitudes of the groups to whom communication will be directed? How can the opinions of these groups be measured?

[4] Marston, *Nature of Public Relations*, pp. 161–168.

M3 cont.

Q3

M4

2. *Action:*

After the existing situation has been fully studied, the second step in the formula is action. Action may take the form of changing a situation, or of expressing externally an abstract quality of the organization. For example, how can a human service agency demonstrate its extensive counseling services for dependent children? Action may also take the form of an organization showing how it is responsive to the public.

3. *Communication:*

This step requires a knowledge of the media of communication and their uses, acquaintance with the experts in the field, and skill in writing for the media. It also includes the ability to approach the public in a way that will command their attention and obtain their interest and agreement. Thus, this step involves facility in spreading information and understanding how it is received.

4. *Evaluation:*

The final step of the formula is evaluation, which involves determining the results of a public relations effort. When actions have been taken and messages sent out, what happened to people's opinion? Who listened? What effect did it have on their attitudes? Their actions? The answers to these questions will measure the impact of a program and will provide the basis for any further efforts.

M4 cont.

Continue with Q4

The formula for successful public relations is R-A-C-E, which stands for _____, _____, _____, and _____. Fill in the blanks and turn to A1.

Q4

One of the nation's largest state human service agencies is in Bigcity, Florida. For years this agency has been trying to expand its program of services to the elderly, however, each time the bill is brought before the state legislature, it is voted down. The agency is now trying to develop a public relations program that will seek better public understanding and support. The administrator in charge of this program has decided to apply the R-A-C-E formula. See if you can match, by placing the proper letters in the blanks, each set of questions with the corresponding step in the formula and then check your answer by turning to A9.

Q5

_____ 1. *Research*

A. How can the citizens of the state be told about the need for this program? By tours of the homes for the elderly? By advertising?

_____ 2. *Action*

B. How can the agency demonstrate the need the elderly have for this program? How can the agency show how limited present services are?

_____ 3. *Communication*

C. What are present public attitudes toward the agency? The

	elderly? What resources does	Q5
	the agency have?	cont.
_____ 4. *Evaluation*	D. Has public opinion changed to	
	support this program? Has the	
	legislature passed a bill pro-	
	viding funds for the program?	

HOW TO WRITE A PRESS RELEASE

The ability to write a clear, accurate, and informative press release **M5**
is one of the basic skills required of anyone involved in public relations. However, before a decision is made to issue a press release, the
administrator must be able to determine whether the content of the
release will be considered "news" by those receiving it. News is an
account of a current event, idea, or problem that interests people. An
administrator must examine a release for the following five elements.

1. *Timeliness:*
   When did the event occur? Since even one hour can change the
   value of a story, the time of disclosure of a release must be carefully planned.

2. *Nearness:*
   The release should be written to interest editors and their readers.
   Thus, where the event occurred in relation to the potential audience
   is important.

3. *Size:*
   What makes this story big? Who makes this story big? Size may
   also be measured in terms of oddity or conflict. Is there anything
   rare or unusual in the story? Is there any conflict?

4. *Importance:*
   How or why did this event occur? What caused it?

5. *Personal Benefit:*
   How will this story benefit the reader and the agency? What is the
   breadth of appeal of the release? Frequently what is relevant to
   one audience will be irrelevant to another.

If even one of these elements is missing, the item may not be considered newsworthy.[5]

News is an account of an event, _____ _____, or problem that **Q6**
_____ people. Fill in the blanks and check your answers by
turning to A2.

There are five elements that are important in all news stories. These **Q7**
are:

A. Timeliness, size, cost, personal benefit, and importance . . *A4*
B. Size, nearness, style, personal benefit, and timeliness . . . *A6*
C. Importance, personal benefit, size, timeliness, and nearness . *A10*

[5] Laurence R. Campbell and Roland E. Wolsely, *How To Report and Write the
News* (Englewood Cliffs, N.J.: Prentice-Hall, 1961), pp. 8–16. See also: Harold
P. Levy, *Public Relations for Social Agencies* (New York: Harper & Row,
1956), pp. 105–106.

The key to writing a press release is brevity and using the correct **M6** format. The following is a list of five practical guidelines that should be followed:[6]

1. The top left-hand corner of the first page should contain the following information relating to the person submitting the release:
   a. Name and title.
   b. Address.
   c. Office and home phone numbers.
   d. Specification of release time, such as FOR IMMEDIATE RELEASE.
   e. Date of the release.
2. The release should be typewritten in a double or triple-space format, leaving extra space in the margins of all pages for editorial corrections.
3. All spelling, punctuation, and capitalization should be correct, especially the spelling of proper names of individuals and places.
4. Provide full names and essential identification for all persons who are not well known (that is, position, title, agency).
5. Always write the release in the third person, except when using a direct quotation.
6. Do not send a press release if it is not for immediate release.

Continue with Q8

The following information is at the top left-hand corner of a press **Q8** release:

John Smith, Information Director
School of Social Welfare
Hillside University
307 East 23rd Street, Bigcity, Florida
599-4820 (office), 222-9841 (home)

FOR IMMEDIATE RELEASE

Based on what you have learned about the first page of a press release, is the above information complete? Check answering by turning to A14.

A. Yes
B. No

Additional practical guidelines for a press release include the fol- **M7** lowing:

1. The first sentence of the release should answer who, what, when, where, and why. After the lead introduction, the remainder of the news release should be developed as an inverted pyramid, where each succeeding paragraph should be less important than the one preceding it. This allows an editor to cut the release to fit his space requirements without losing an important fact.

[6] See Richard W. Darrow, Dan J. Forrestal, and Aubrey O. Cookman, *The Dartnell Public Relations Handbook* (Chicago: The Dartnell Corporation, 1967), pp. 545–547; John E. Marston, *The Nature of Public Relations* (New York: McGraw-Hill, 1963).

2. The word *more* should appear at the bottom of the first page if the story is continued, and should be repeated at the bottom of any other page preceding continuations. **M7 cont.**

3. Second and subsequent pages should be numbered in the upper right-hand corners, and should also be identified by a slug line based on the essence of the news, such as "Askew's Speech."

4. The end of the story should be identified by a crosshatch (#) or some other indication of conclusion.

5. Avoid dividing words between two lines and complete a paragraph on a page rather than continuing it on the next. Remember that short sentences make the release more acceptable.

Continue with Q9

The following two paragraphs are on the first page of a two-page press release. You may assume that the heading and other information in the top left-hand corner are complete. **Q9**

Graduate students in Hillside University's Social Administration Program are spending this week learning how to be good reporters. "It's part of a growing need to have administrators in public agencies better able to work with the media." explained Dr. Fred M. Jones, director of the new social administration program. "These students will soon be in administrative positions in public agencies," continued Jones, "and the public is entitled to know as much as possible about any agency supported by their tax dollars."

Topics for the week will include learning to write press releases, instructional public relations, and how the media get the news to the public. The special seminars are designed to bring about better working relationships between administrators and newsmen. The guest lecturer is Mr. Allan Madden.

As the first page of a two page press release, do these two paragraphs meet all the practical guidelines recommended for a press release?

A. These two paragraphs meet all the mechanical requirements *A12*

B. The word *more* should be at the bottom of the page, and more information should be given on Mr. Allan Madden . . . *A15*

C. A crosshatch (#) should be at the end of the second paragraph *A17*

The following paragraph is on the second page of the press release begun in Q9. **Q10**

page 2

Mr. Madden told the group of future administrators that, ". . . the very survival of social administration as a profession will depend on public acceptance. It is up to them to inform the public regarding their services. The new administrator cannot afford to neglect his contact with the community, and working with media is a vital part of service delivery." The seminars will provide students with an opportunity to ask questions and present problems in public relations that they expect to encounter.#

As the second page of a two page press release, does this paragraph meet all the practical guidelines recommended for a press release? Check your answer by turning to A13.

Q10 cont.

A. Yes

B. No

HOW TO GET THE MOST FROM A PRESS RELEASE

In addition to using the correct format in a press release, the administrator must also learn, "the technique of sending the release to the proper media."[7] Local stories rarely present a problem in this regard. For national stories, the United Press (UP) or Associated Press (AP) will handle any newsworthy story of national importance. Occasionally, however, the administrator needs to send a story to editors in another state. Here we recommend the use of a reference such as the N. W. Ayer and Sons' Directory of Newspapers and Periodicals, which is revised annually.[8] It is also suggested that you place your address and phone number on the upper left-hand corner of the release so that the responsible persons in the news media can call you for further information, if necessary.

Even under the best situations, news items are printed with incorrect facts due to an editor's or printer's error. We recommend that you "keep your cool" and realize that the mistake was not made on purpose and that the editor is probably as anxious as you are to "get the facts straight." A correction printed in an early edition or an announcement if it is on radio or TV may resolve the situation. Sometimes, a letter in the "Letters to the Editor" section of the newspaper can also be used to make a correction.

M8

Continue with Q11

Place a check mark in the appropriate blanks(s) and then turn to A16 to check your answers. In addition to using correct format in a press release, it is also important that:

Q11

_____ A. The release is sent to the proper media.

_____ B. Any problems regarding printing errors be directed to the editor of the publication.

_____ C. A cover letter accompanies the release.

_____ D. Any problems regarding printing errors be directed to the individual reporter who received the release.

ORGANIZING A PUBLIC RELATIONS CAMPAIGN

Since many human service organizations have limited budgets and shortages of manpower, they are unable to invest a great deal of time in developing individualized approaches to all the special publics they would like to reach.[9] Thus, in organizing a public relations campaign, the administrator will frequently draw upon the resources that are already available in the organization. For example, speeches by staff members might be used as a basis for a brochure; bulletin boards

M9

[7] Darrow, Forrestal, and Cookman, *Dartnell Public Relations Handbook*, p. 548.
[8] Ibid., p. 549.
[9] Levy, *Public Relations for Social Agencies*, p. 66.

and newsletters can be used very effectively as internal media of
communication; local universities and public schools can be used as
sources for speakers and advisers on specialized subjects; and press
releases can be sent to the proper media.

In addition to the other methods described in this lesson, one
very effective method of reaching the general public is through citizen
groups and organizations. Even though some of these groups may
not be primarily involved in the human services, they will often
have sufficient interest to be involved with the agency. Finally, the
agency may create special organizations of citizens who will help
them in their cause. For example, citizen committees might be formed
to assist in publicizing and evaluating a day care program administered
by a human service agency. No matter how an organization decides
to organize a public relations campaign, it is important to remember
that the effectiveness of the effort will be determined by how carefully the R-A-C-E formula is applied.

Continue with Q12

In addition to utilizing the internal and external media of communication in organizing a public relations campaign, the administrator may involve the community by creating _____
_____ or by seeking the support of citizen
groups that are already organized. Check your answer by turning to
A18.

Since many human service agencies do not employ a public relations specialist, this function will frequently become part of the
administrator's responsibility. Thus, the effective administrator must
recognize the importance of establishing public relations principles
and functions and have some proficiency in public relations techniques.[10]

The basic principles outlined in this lesson highlight the public
relations function. Effective public relations must also be based on
systematic research, action, communication, and evaluation in order
to meet the public's demand for accountability.

This concludes the material for this unit. Test yourself by doing
the review questions at the end of the unit. Then read the summary
with its suggestions for further study. You should find this helpful in
going beyond the introductory material presented here.

SUMMARY

This unit on reporting has outlined the importance of communicating both within the agency and between the agency and the community. The reporting function is an extremely important part of the
management of an organization, whether one is reporting on the
progress of past activities or reporting on future planning for
serving clients. Various types of reports have been described in
this unit, including subject matter reporting, time oriented reports, and various other types of agency reports. In addition, the
importance of reporting to special organizations such as legislative

[10] Brown, "Public Relations Function of the Administrator," p. 63.

bodies and boards of director was also noted. The essential elements of report writing were described, including the various steps utilized in preparing a report.

The public relations aspect of administration was also stressed in this unit. Particular emphasis was placed on the research, action, communication, and evaluation phases of public relations. Internal agency public relations activities include bulletins and organizational newspapers. External public relations activities include press releases, magazine articles, and public speeches. All managers of human service agencies will be required to convey their agency activities in a form the public can understand. In this regard, special attention was addressed to the writing of press releases and to the organizing of public relations campaigns.

SUGGESTIONS FOR FURTHER STUDY

Further study in the area of reporting would include the analysis of fund raising activities utilized by a wide variety of public and private organizations. An analysis of fund raising activities provides the future human service administrators with another perspective on public relations and the art of communicating the mission of an agency for the purposes of securing public and private funds. Such further study would also lead to an analysis of agency survival in both the public and private sectors and the politics of gaining public support through carefully planned and executed public relations campaigns. In addition to the issue of agency survival, it will become increasingly important for administrators to communicate with and receive input from client groups. Again, skillful relations with this special "public" will require skills in consumer analysis and a study of citizen participation. One approach to assessing the impact of an agency on the community as a whole would be to evaluate current agency activities in the light of the following selected public relations standards developed by the National Health Council and the National Social Welfare Assembly (1964):

I. The agency is accountable to its supporters and the general public.
   A. The agency publishes an annual report which is distributed to all interested parties and is also available to all who request it.
   B. The annual report is a clear and understandable account of activities. It also includes names of board members and chief administrative personnel, as well as a financial statement showing income, expenditures, assets and liabilities, and designated funds.
   C. *Standards of Accounting and Financial Reporting for Voluntary Health and Welfare Organizations* form the basis for financial reporting.
   D. Inquiries regarding the agency are answered accurately, frankly, and promptly.
II. Integrity, candor, and accuracy are maintained in all public relations activities.

A. Full and accurate reporting is required. Facts are presented so as not to be misleading.

B. The interpretation of services is realistic and is based on records, statistics, and actual performance.

C. The dignity of the individual is preserved. For example, public information concerning blind persons and the field of blindness reflects a positive and constructive viewpoint. In the case of minors, the parents or guardians are required to give written permission. The principles of confidentiality are observed.

III. The agency maintains effective communications within the agency.

A. Methods to insure sound relations and the easy and swift flow of communications within the agency are established.

B. All staff members, board members, and other volunteers are continually informed of the reasons for and substance of pertinent policies and program developments.

C. Effective communication is maintained with all persons served by the agency, such as workshop employees, trainees, and clients, concerning pertinent policies and program developments.

IV. The agency seeks the opinions of key individuals and groups in the community.

A. The agency establishes methods to enable staff members, board members, and other volunteers to assess the community's reaction to the policies and program of the agency. These agency representatives are encouraged to report back on favorable and unfavorable public opinion, misunderstandings, etc., that they encounter.

B. The agency's policy makers and program planners give due consideration to the information gained under (A) in the formulation of policies and programs.

C. The agency provides opportunities for developing relationships with specific groups such as the client and his family, contributors, government bodies, and related agencies.

V. The agency develops and maintains effective communications with related agencies.

A. The governing body and staff cooperate and participate in activities of community planning bodies and other agencies having interests in common.

B. Representatives of community agencies are invited to participate in activities of mutual interest.

C. Appropriate publications such as annual reports, brochures, magazines, and pamphlets, are exchanged with related agencies.

VI. Primarily in voluntary agencies the governing body is responsible for initiating and maintaining the public relations program.

A. The governing body establishes and appoints a standing committee concerned with public relations.

B. A member of the governing body serves as chairman of this committee.

C. The governing body provides for an adequate budget for

the public relations program to insure an effective program.

D. In cooperation with the public relations committee and agency administrator, the governing body establishes public relations policies and goals.

E. The governing body provides for a review and evaluation of the public relations program at least annually.

SUGGESTIONS FOR FURTHER READING

Bloomenthal, Howard. *Promoting Your Cause.* New York: Funk and Wagnalls, 1971.

Bortner, Doyle. *Public Relations for Teachers.* New York: Simmons-Boardman, 1959.

Canfield, Bertrand R. *Public Relations: Principles, Cases and Problems.* Homewood, Ill.: R. D. Irwin, 1973.

Center, Allen H. *Public Relations Ideas in Action.* New York: McGraw-Hill, 1957.

Church, David M. *The Public Relations Committee.* New York: National Publicity Council for Health and Welfare Services, 1949.

Coffey, Alan; Eldefonso, Edward; and Hartinger, Walter. *Police-Community Relations.* Englewood Cliffs, N.J.: Prentice-Hall, 1971.

Curlip, Scott M., and Center, Allen H. *Effective Public Relations.* Englewood Cliffs, N.J.: Prentice-Hall, 1971.

Dapper, Gloria. *Public Relations for Educators.* New York: Macmillan, 1964.

Dawe, Jessamon, and Lord, William J. *Functional Business Communication.* Englewood Cliffs, N.J.: Prentice-Hall, 1968.

Leibert, Edwin R. *Handbook of Special Events for Nonprofit Organizations: Tested Ideas for Fund Raising and Public Relations.* New York: Association, 1972.

Lesly, Philip, ed. *Lesly's Public Relations Handbook.* Englewood Cliffs, N.J.: Prentice-Hall, 1971.

Levine, Howard, and Levine, Carol. *Effective Public Relations for Community Groups.* New York: Association, 1969.

McCloskey, Gordon E. *Education and Public Understanding.* New York: Harper & Row, 1967.

National Recreation Association. *Communications and Public Relations.* New York: National Recreation Association, 1959.

Robinson, Edward J. *Public Relations and Survey Research: Achieving Organizational Goals in a Communication Context.* New York: Appleton-Century-Crofts, 1969.

Schmidt, Frances and Weiner, Harold N. eds. *Public Relations in Health and Welfare.* New York: Columbia University Press, 1966.

Schoenfeld, Clarence A. *Publicity Media and Methods: Their Role in Modern Public Relations.* New York: Macmillan, 1963.

Siegel, Arthur I.; Felderman, Philip J.; and Schultz, Douglas G. *Professional Police—Human Relations Training.* Springfield, Ill.: C. C Thomas, 1963.

Stein, Herman D. *Measuring Your Public Relations: A Guide to Research Problems, Methods and Findings.* New York: National Publicity Council for Health and Welfare Services, 1952.

Stephenson, Howard, ed. *Handbook of Public Relations.* New York: McGraw-Hill, 1971.

1. The purpose of agency reporting is to:

    A. Help measure the progress of agency personnel, programs, projects, etc.
    B. Help reduce costs of agency personnel, programs, projects, etc.
    C. Furnish a basis for planning.
    D. A and B above.
    E. A and C above.

2. Which of the following activities must be performed in an agency in order to help the executive fulfill his reporting function?

    A. Research.
    B. Inspections.
    C. Record keeping.
    D. B and C above.
    E. A, B, and C above.

3. Agency reports are seldom, if ever, submitted to:

    A. Community organizations.
    B. The executive director and his associates.
    C. The board of directors or legislative body.
    D. None of the above.

4. Finance, personnel, program ,and project reports are:

    A. Functional reports.
    B. Miscellaneous reports.
    C. Subject matter reports.
    D. Formality reports.

5. Recommendation reports are submitted to:

    A. The executive director.
    B. The board of directors or the legislative body.
    C. Community organizations.
    D. A and B above.
    E. A, B, and C above.

6. The annual over-all agency progress report should be submitted to:

    A. Influential community organizations.
    B. The funding agency.
    C. The board of directors or legislative body.
    D. B and C above.
    E. A, B, and C above.

7. Favorable agency-community relations may be created and maintained through:

    A. Well-written reports.
    B. Positive personal contacts.
    C. Improved services.
    D. A and B above.
    E. A and C above.

8. Periodic program progress reports submitted to the executive director of a private agency should include primarily:

A. The dates of the period covered by the report.
B. The address of the agency.
C. The names of agency officers and the names of board members.
D. A and B above.
E. A, B, and C above.

9. Any report sent to a community organization from a public agency should include:

A. The address of the agency.
B. A concise statement of the agency's character, purposes, and aims.
C. The names of agency officers and legislative body members.
D. A and C above.
E. A, B, and C above.

10. Every agency report should include:

A. The dates covered by the report.
B. The names of the officers and board or legislative body members.
C. The agency's purpose and aims.
D. A and B above.
E. A, B, and C above.

11. A concise statement of the agency's character, purposes, and aims should be included in:

A. Every report.
B. Only those reports to be disseminated outside the agency.
C. Only those reports to be disseminated within the agency.
D. Only those reports sent to community organizations.

12. In a research project, the report writer must make decisions concerning the research methods to be used. What step(s) must have been accomplished before this step in the report preparation process is begun?

A. Selecting and analyzing the information.
B. Stating the problem.
C. Defining the scope of the problem.
D. B and C above.
E. A, B, and C above.

13. If you were in charge of writing the third annual progress report of an agency, at which step in the reporting process would you begin?

A. Planning the methods for obtaining and/or retaining relevant data.
B. Defining the scope of the problem.
C. Collecting the information.
D. Analyzing the information.

14. In report preparation, which of the following steps would come first?

A. Forming the conclusion(s).
B. Preparing the first draft.
C. Organizing the report.

15. When writing a report, the needs of _____ _____ should be of utmost importance.

   A. The writer.
   B. The reader.
   C. The executive director.
   D. Your immediate superior.

16. The final two steps in the report preparation process are:

   A. Preparing the first draft and then publishing the report.
   B. Preparing the first draft and then editing it.
   C. Editing and then publishing the report.
   D. Publishing and then disseminating the report.

17. Public relations is a management function that:

   A. Identifies the policies of an organization with the public interest.
   B. Evaluates public attitudes.
   C. Executes a program of communication to earn public acceptance.
   D. A and C above.
   E. A, B, and C above.

18. Press publicity, public speaking, and open houses are primarily:

   A. Internal media of communication.
   B. Used to inform the staff of a human service organization.
   C. External media of communication.
   D. Steps in solving public relations problems.

19. Which of the following activities should be performed by the agency executive in fulfilling the public relations function?

   A. Action, research, discussion, and evaluation.
   B. Communication, research, action, and evaluation.
   C. Evaluation, record keeping, communication, and research.
   D. Action, evaluation, reports, and communication.

20. The key to writing a press release is:

   A. Brevity.
   B. Sending the release to the proper media.
   C. Using the correct format.
   D. A and C above.
   E. A, B, and C above.

21. Which of the following reflects an accurate definition of "news"?

   A. News is an account of an event, idea, or problem.
   B. News is an account of an event, idea, or problem of interest to a reporter.
   C. News is an account of an event, idea, or problem that interests people.
   D. News is an unbiased personal account of a public event.

22. Every press release should include:

   A. The date of the release.
   B. A slug line on second and subsequent pages.
   C. Answers to who, what, when, where, and why.

D. B and C above.

E. A, B, and C above.

23. In organizing a public relations campaign, the executive may involve the community by:

A. Seeking the support of organized citizen groups.

B. Creating special organizations of citizens.

C. Keeping bulletin boards updated in the organization.

D. A, B, and C above.

E. A and B above.

Turn to the last page of this unit to check your answers.

ANSWERS

You should have answered: research, action, communication, and **A1**
evaluation. If you answered incorrectly, review the discussion in M4
and then continue with Q5.

You should have answered: idea and interests. If you answered **A2**
incorrectly, review the definition in M5 and then continue with Q7.

You should have checked C—those already closely connected with **A3**
the organization. If you answered incorrectly, review M2 before
continuing with M3.

This is incorrect. Cost is not an element that is important in news **A4**
stories. Review the five elements in M5 before you answer Q7
correctly.

This is incorrect. This definition does not include the three elements **A5**
of research, action, and communication. In addition it does not state
that public relations is a function of management. Return to Q1 and
answer the question correctly.

No, style is not one of the elements that is important in news stories. **A6**
Review the five elements discussed in M5 before you answer Q7
correctly.

You should have answered: **A7**

1. I—Bulletin boards and posters.
2. E—Open houses and agency tours.
3. E—Press publicity.
4. I—Public relations handbooks.
5. E—Public speaking.
6. I—Memorandums and bulletins.

Continue with M4

Excellent! This definition includes the three elements of research, **A8**
action, and communication, and identifies public relations as a func-
tion of management.

Continue with M2

You should have answered: **A9**

1. C—Research.
2. B—Action.
3. A—Communication.
4. D—Evaluation.

If you answered any incorrectly, you need a careful review of M4
before proceeding to M5.

Right! The five elements that are important in all news stories are: **A10**
importance, personal benefit, size, timeliness, and nearness.

Continue with M6

You have missed the point. Remember that public relations is a con- **A11**
tinuous activity of management—it is not transitory. Also remember

287

that an accurate definition of public relations will include the three **A11** elements of research, action, and communication. Review the definition **cont.** of public relations presented in M1 before you answer Q1 correctly.

This is incorrect. Remember that the word *more* should appear at **A12** the bottom of the page if there is more than one page of the release. In addition, more essential information should be given about Mr. Allan Madden: What is his position? With what organization? Return to Q9 and answer the question correctly.

You should have answered no. Second and subsequent pages of a **A13** press release should be identified by a slug line at the top right-hand corner of the page. In this instance, an appropriate slug line would be: *Future Administrators.*

Continue with M8

Hope you answered no! What is the date of the release? Without **A14** this information, this release could end up in the wastebasket. Continue now with M7 for additional press release guidelines.

Excellent! Since this is the first page of a two page release, *more* **A15** information should also be given to identify Mr. Allan Madden. What is his position? With what organization? *More* should be at the bottom of the page.

Continue with Q10

You should have checked A and B. A—the release is sent to the **A16** proper media, and B—any problems regarding garbled stories are directed to the editor. If you answered this question incorrectly, you need to review M8 before going on to M9. If you chose the correct answer, continue with M9.

No, a crosshatch is placed at the end of the release. Since this is **A17** the first page of a two page release, a crosshatch would not be placed at the end of the second paragraph. Review M7 before you try Q9 again.

You should have answered, by creating special organizations of **A18** citizens. If you missed this answer, you need to review M9 before proceeding to M10. If you answered this correctly, continue with M10.

**ANSWERS TO
REVIEW QUESTIONS**

The following are the correct responses to questions for Unit VIII.

Questions	Answers	Questions	Answers
1	E	13	C
2	E	14	A
3	D	15	B
4	C	16	C
5	D	17	E
6	E	18	C
7	D	19	B
8	A	20	E
9	E	21	C
10	A	22	E
11	B	23	E
12	D		

If you answered 17 or more of these questions correctly, you have successfully completed this unit and may now proceed to Unit IX. However, if you answered less than 17 questions correctly, you should review those areas that gave you trouble before proceeding to Unit IX.

UNIT IX
BUDGETING

LESSON 1
Identifying
Crucial Budget
Components

**UNIT IX OBJECTIVE—
BUDGETING**

Given a problem requiring the application of budgeting process skills, you will be able to demonstrate your skills by making decisions that will lead to an acceptable budget.

Specific Objective

Given a description of an agency and a budget for the agency, you will be able to:

1. Identify the major steps in the budgeting process.
2. Evaluate the chances of the budget's acceptance by the funding body depending on whether or not the budget meets the criteria for possible acceptance.

Enabling Objective 1
Given a description of an agency's budget process, you will be able to determine whether or not the process was completed.

Enabling Objective 2
Given a completed budget you will be able to determine if all the fiscal components have been accounted for.

Enabling Objective 3
Given a completed budget, you will be able to analyze the chart of accounts and determine its relevance for the agency.

Enabling Objective 4
Given a completed budget, you will be able to identify whether or not it is a sound budget, ready to go through the next step—the adoption process.

Continue with M1

THE AGENCY BUDGET

The chief executive is responsible for the development of a workable budget. He may delegate portions of the task to his financial officer and to his department heads, but, in the end, the executive must take the responsibility for the finished product.   **M1**

A budget, whether for an agency or a program, is a financial plan and is the final product of a planning effort. The initial step in the process may be somewhat different for an older established program or agency than for a new agency or program, but it always involves developing a statement of goals and objectives. Goals may be general and long range in nature, for example, an agency's goal may be to educate people regarding mental illness. Objectives must be specific and quantifiable, such as to enroll one million new members in the agency, or to publicize the attributes of a mentally healthier person in a one page ad in ten national magazines every month for the next year.

The first component of a budget (the goals and objectives) is most often overlooked, or worse yet, not seen as a vital element of the budget process. However, without a clearly stated goal and a set of objectives, budget making is limited to asking for "more of the same," a "ten percent increase over last year," or some other nonspecific request unrelated to goals and objectives. In order for a budget to be well designed, the executive, the staff, and the board of directors need to analyze their total needs and problems in terms of services to be rendered and the costs for such services.[1]

Continue with Q1

The chief executive is: **Q1**

A. Totally responsible for the budget *A3*
B. Only partially responsible for the budget if he delegated the work to someone else *A7*

The first component of a workable budget is: **Q2**

A. A financial plan or program for the agency *A1*
B. A statement of purpose *A4*
C. A statement of goals and objectives *A8*

Budgets should be designed with due consideration for the basic service needs by: **Q3**

A. Requesting salary increases of ten percent *A9*
B. Analyzing the total needs and problems *A2*
C. Just reviewing last year's budget *A5*

[1] Note that this type of planning is a necessary aspect of the Planning-Programming Budgeting System (PPBS) approach. See Lesson Four of this unit for more specifics.

Getting ready to set up goals and objectives involves a review of the situation in which the agency finds itself, and a thorough-going analysis. The kinds of questions that need answers are A. What is the felt need? B. Can (or should) this need be met with the existing program or by the agency? C. If a new program or agency is needed, who will inaugurate the service (or meet the need)? D. Is the need or problem imbedded in other needs and problems (so that the real need or problem is not clear)? E. If the problem or need can be agreed upon, can it be separated into its component parts for a more complete analysis? F. Can a service or program be devised that will have a reasonable chance of solving the problem (or meeting the need)? G. Can a way of evaluating what is being done be designed so everyone involved will know if their goals and objectives are being met? H. How much money will it take to meet these goals and objectives?   **M2**

Assuming that the preliminary questions have been answered and that goals and objectives have been agreed upon, the next step is to write a plan of action. This written plan then becomes the rationale for the budget that will be submitted to a financing source. Persons familiar with grant proposal writing will recognize the format. The plan answers the questions: Why certain action is recommended, what action is recommended, how the action is to be carried out and by whom, and a timetable that details in a Gantt chart the phasing of the work load for the next twelve months or longer.[2]

Continue with Q4

It should be clear that: **Q4**

A. The question—How much money? does not need any preliminary analysis *A6*
B At least seven or eight questions need to be answered before deciding on—How much money *A10*

After goals and objectives have been agreed upon: **Q5**

A. A money goal is the next step *A11*
B. An executive then has the responsibility to set up a plan . *A14*
C. A written plan should be devised that answers who, what, where, when, and how *A17*

The discussion thus far has been about the two basic components of a budget: 1. the goals and objectives; and 2. the plan or rationale for the budget. The next component, the chart of accounts, is a practical necessity without which one could not devise a workable budget. It is basically a list of all of the items, both income and expenses, to be accounted for. This chart may be extremely simple, or, as in government budgeting, it may be quite complex.   **M3**

The basic idea behind the chart of accounts is that every expenditure falls into a specified category. All potential income or expense items are usually assigned to predetermined, numbered categories.

---

[2] Developed by Henry L. Gantt in 1917, the Gantt chart is in use around the world as a method of presenting facts regarding the work load in relation to a time span. See: Wallace Clark, *The Gantt Chart* (New York: Ronald, 1922); also see: Henry W. Albert, *Organized Executive Action* (New York: Wiley, 1963 edition), pp. 406–408.

This method makes it possible for everyone to understand, without question, where a certain item belongs. For example, if the personnel category is #2000 and professional salaries are numbered #2100, then secretarial salaries may be assigned #2400 and maintenance salaries #2500. Some such numbering scheme should clearly, quickly, and easily identify each division of personnel, and the amount of money being spent for each. In a similar fashion, all other accounts are also given a basic number that is used in developing budget figures and later in approving expenditures.

M3 cont.

Continue with Q6

Which of the following statements is correct?

Q6

A. A chart of accounts is used to identify the goals and objectives *A12*

B. A chart of accounts may be numbered or unnumbered but is a practical necessity *A18*

C. The basic reason for having a chart of accounts is that it provides a rationale for the budget *A15*

We have just illustrated a budgeting system that numbers every item and classifies by functions, that is, expenditures for personnel of various types, operating expenses for rent, fuel, water, light, and so on.

M4

There are other methods of grouping expenditures. A system borrowed from private industry and developed by the federal government, known as Planning-Programming-Budgeting System (PPBS), calls for appropriations and cost figures to be related clearly to services both in respect to performance and volume. Briefly, this system involves classifying expenditures based on an analysis of objectives and resources and relates this data to the over-all budget.[3] Another method used to classify income and expenses is to group items according to departments. The similarity to program budgeting is, of course, quite close. This type of budgeting makes it possible for the executive to quickly compare costs and income for each department. In all systems, though, a chart of accounts is still a necessity whether presented as program or departmental budgeting.

Continue with Q7

Which of the following is (are) correct?

Q7

A. Accounts may be classified numerically according to specific areas of expense or income *A13*

B. Accounts may be classified numerically and according to program units *A23*

C. Accounts may be classified numerically and according to departments *A19*

D. All of the above *A22*

E. Only A above *A16*

[3] See: Arthur Smithies, "Conceptual Framework for the Program Budget," in David Novick, *Program Budgeting*, 2d ed. (New York: Holt, Rinehart & Winston, 1969), p. 24. Smithies says, "Planning, programming, and budgeting constitute the process by which objectives and resources, and the interrelations among them, are taken into account to achieve a coherent and comprehensive program of action . . ."

You now have some background in preparing a budget, going **M5** through the process of setting goals and objectives, developing a plan of action, and finally setting up a chart of accounts. You are also aware that a budget is one device used by an executive and a board of directors to control expenditures. A budget also can release an executive from day-to-day decision making. If every expenditure had to be approved by the executive every day of the year, this would be an unnecessary time and energy drain. By agreeing on a set of spending rules ahead of time (the budget), certain expenditures can be approved far down the line, thus improving the efficiency of the chief executive.

We have discussed a number of the components making for a sound budget which deal with factors other than money, although eventually, actual figures must be attached to all budget items. The figures that an executive finally decides on should tell the story as accurately and as precisely as possible. This is the ideal. In practice, decisions must often by made with inadequate data resulting in a budget item request that is "watered," bloated, inflated, or otherwise inaccurate. This inaccuracy may even be purposeful. Executives often use such bloated items as a way of balancing out in the event of a strain elsewhere on the budget sometime during the year.

Continue with Q8

A budget may be used for the following purposes: **Q8**

A. To set up the goals and objectives of the agency *A20*
B. To control the expenditures *A26*
C. To release the executive from day-to-day budget decisions . *A24*
D. A and B above *A28*
E. B and C above *A31*

Which of the following statements is correct? **Q9**

A. All budgets are precise instruments used to allocate funds . *A25*
B. Budgets are often a mixture of fairly precise items and a number of items that may be educated guesses *A21*

We conclude this introductory material on Identifying a Sound **Q10** Budget with a quick test review of the major points covered.

The board of directors must take final responsibility for the budget since they administer it.

True *A27*
False *A32*

The executive is responsible only for that part of the budget that he **Q11** or she developed.

True *A29*
False *A33*

A budget is the final product of a planning effort. **Q12**

True *A37*
False *A34*

The first component of a sound budgeting process is a set of financial **Q13**
figures.

True *A36*
False *A30*

A budget should be designed only after a complete analysis of total **Q14**
needs and projected costs for services.

True *A35*
False *A38*

In developing a budget the executive needs to know the answer to **Q15**
only one basic question—how much money do I need?

True *A41*
False *A44*

A plan of action should include the answers to why, what, how, **Q16**
and by whom the action is to be carried out.

True *A46*
False *A40*

A chart of accounts is a good idea but most often is not necessary. **Q17**

True *A42*
False *A45*

Accounts can always be classified according to departments or **Q18**
programs, thus eliminating the need for a chart of accounts.

True *A39*
False *A47*

An important function of the budget is to make it possible for per- **Q19**
sons other than the chief executive to approve expenditures.

True *A43*
False *A50*

Budgets should always be seen as precise statements of income and **Q20**
expenditures.

True *A48*
False *A49*

ANSWERS

You said a financial plan is the first component. Sorry, but this is not **A1** correct. There is an important area that must first be covered. Return to M1, read the material, then select the right answer to Q2.

Right! First make an analysis of the problem to determine the needs. **A2**

Continue with M2

Right! The executive is always totally responsible regardless of the **A3** fact that portions of the job are delegated to others.

Continue with Q2

A statement of purpose is a good idea, but it is not the first com- **A4** ponent. Return to M1 and read the material presented there, then select another answer to Q2.

Just reviewing last year's budget was your answer and it is not a **A5** complete answer. You may also wish to review last year's budget, but that is not what needs to be done first. Return to M1 and read the material there, then select the right response to Q3.

How much money? is a later question preceded by preliminary **A6** analysis. Return to Q4 and select the other answer.

Sorry. The executive is always totally responsible even though **A7** portions of the budgeting job are delegated. Return to Q1 and select the other answer.

Right you are! A statement of goals and objectives is the first and **A8** basic component of a budget.

Continue with Q3

Sorry. You need to do more than design a budget based on a ten **A9** percent increase in salaries. Return to M2 and read the material pre-sented there before selecting the correct answer to Q3.

Right you are! There are at least seven or eight questions that must **A10** be answered first.

Continue with Q5

A money goal is not the next step. It comes later. Return to M2 for **A11** a review, then select the correct answer to Q5.

This is not correct. A chart of accounts is not used to identify goals **A12** and objectives. Return to M3, and, after reading it, carefully select the proper answer to Q6.

You have overlooked another answer that is more complete. Return **A13** to Q7 and select a more complete answer.

Sorry. The executive does have the responsibility of setting up a **A14** plan, but you neglected that part of the plan that answers the questions why, what, how, and by whom. Return to Q5 and select the correct answer.

Not at all. A chart of accounts is a numbering system for accounts, not a rationale. Return to Q6 and select another answer.   **A15**

Accounts may be classified numerically and according to departments, but you neglected a more complete answer. Return to Q7 and select another answer.   **A16**

A written plan should be devised answering the questions what, where, when, how, and by whom. Right you are.   **A17**

Continue with M3

Now you have it! A chart of accounts is a practical necessity.   **A18**

Continue with M4

Sorry, but you have overlooked the fact that more than one method is possible. Return to Q7 and select the correct answer.   **A19**

Not really. A budget is not used to set up the goals and objectives. Return to M5 and read the material presented there before answering Q8 correctly.   **A20**

Yes. This was probably an easy question for you. Obviously a budget must be a mixture of precise items and educated guesses.   **A21**

Continue with Q10

Right you are! All the answers are correct. There is more than one way to set up a chart of accounts.   **A22**

Continue with M5

Sorry, but you have overlooked another answer that is more complete. Return to Q7 and select that answer.   **A23**

Not enough. To release the executive from day-to-day budget decisions, is only a partial answer. Return to Q8 and select another more complete answer.   **A24**

No. All budgets are far from precise instruments and most often contain a mixture of fact and fiction. Review M5, then select the proper response to Q9.   **A25**

To control expenditures is only a partial answer. Return to Q8 and select a more complete answer.   **A26**

Sorry, but the board of directors does not administer the budget. This is the job of the executive director. Return to Q10 and select the other answer.   **A27**

To set up the goals is not the correct response. The other part, to control expenditures, is correct. Return to Q8 and select the correct answer.   **A28**

No, sorry. The executive is responsible for the entire budget even though the job of development was shared with others. Return to Q11 and select the other answer.   **A29**

You are correct in calling this a false statement. Nothing could be further from the truth. Sound planning involves setting goals and objectives first, then a plan of action, and finally a set of figures.   **A30**

Continue with Q14

Absolutely! B and C are correct: to control expenditures and to release the executive from day-to-day budget decisions.   **A31**

Continue with Q9

You said it is false and you are correct. Well done! The chief executive must take final responsibility for administering the budget.   **A32**

Continue with Q9

Excellent! You said that the statement was false and you are correct. The executive is always responsible even though he may delegate a job to be done to someone lower down in the organization.   **A33**

Continue with Q12

You said a budget is not the final product of a planning effort. This does not square with the facts that seem to indicate that the best budgets are the end product of a planning effort. Return to Q12 and select the proper answer.   **A34**

Correct. The best budgets are always the result of such analysis and projection of costs for services.   **A35**

Continue with Q15

This is incorrect. The finances are worked out after goals and objectives are agreed upon and a plan of action is devised. Return to Q13 and select the other answer.   **A36**

Well done! A budget is the product of a planning effort. And we might add that the better the planning, the better the budget.   **A37**

Continue with Q13

Sorry! The correct answer should be true. It does take a complete analysis of total needs and projected costs for services to design a budget. Return to Q14 and select the other answer.   **A38**

Sorry, but even though accounts are set up by departments or programs, a chart of accounts is still needed. Return to Q18 and select the other answer.   **A39**

This is incorrect. We do need the answers to the questions why, what, how, and by whom. Please return to Q16 and select the other answer.   **A40**

Sorry, but we cannot buy true as the answer. The executive needs to know about goals and objectives and how to achieve them, as well as how much money should be budgeted. Please return to Q15 and select the other answer. **A41**

A chart of accounts is always necessary. Regardless of whether you classify accounts by function, by department, or by programs, you need a specified chart of accounts. Return to Q17 and select the other answer. **A42**

Well done! Allowing persons other than the chief executive to approve budgeted expenditures improves efficiency and reduces the day-to-day load on the chief executive. **A43**

Continue with Q20

False is the correct answer in this case. There are many other questions that must be answered before the money question. Good for you. **A44**

Continue with Q16

You are absolutely correct! A chart of accounts is always necessary. **A45**

Continue with Q18

Right you are! We need answers to the questions why, what, how, and by whom. **A46**

Continue with Q17

False is correct. Keep up the good work. **A47**

Continue with Q19

No. Most often they are not precise statements of income and expenses. Return to Q20 and select the other answer. **A48**

Yes, you are quite right. Precise statements cannot always be made and budgets, therefore, are only "guidelines" to income and expense. You have now successfully completed Lesson One. Continue right on to the next lesson, which focuses on some important ideas to consider when preparing a budget. **A49**

This is a poor answer. Properly utilized, the budget allows the chief executive to delegate decision making down the line. Return to Q19 and select the other answer. **A50**

UNIT IX
BUDGETING

LESSON 2
Budget Preparation Considerations

Specific Objective

Given a description of the problems faced by an executive in preparing a budget for adoption, you will be able to identify those related to personnel and to describe possible remedies.

Enabling Objective 1
Given a problem involving coordination, you will be able to identity the conditions needed to secure participation.

Enabling Objective 2
Given examples of problem personalities, you will be able to delineate how and what is needed to secure a working relationship with each type.

Continue with M1

COORDINATION OF REQUESTS

In Lesson One we discussed the preliminary steps necessary and vital to the budgeting process. Possibly you considered the preliminary steps too involved or too lengthy. Unfortunately, there is no easy way to make up a budget and no easy way to get one approved or adopted under most of our private agency or governmental systems.

In Lesson One it was noted that there must be good communication and a high degree of agreement regarding agency goals and objectives. If there is good morale and unanimity among the staff, this agreement may take place rather quickly. If the agency is in the throes of changes due to outside or inside pressures, then the process may be lengthy and complicated.

M1

301

Assuming, however, that agreement has been reached and that all the preliminaries have been cared for, the next step is to coordinate the various departmental or divisional requests. This effort requires the executive to work closely with the department or division executives in order to obtain their interest in devising workable budgets and to motivate them to consider the good of the entire agency. This requires all the skills of leadership. Some departments may be feuding with each other. The skill of a peacemaker or negotiator may be required to resolve differences. Department heads may need to be motivated to get moving, to consider innovative ideas for other departments as well as their own, thus considering the needs of the total agency.

M1 cont.

Continue with Q1

Which statement(s) below is (are) correct?   **Q1**

A. The executive motivates the department heads to devise workable budgets A3

B. The executive motivates the department heads to consider the welfare of the entire agency A5

C. The executive may ask the department heads to consider creative, innovative approaches A6

D. The skilled executive also acts as a negotiator to resolve differences A4

E. All of the above A7

COORDINATION THROUGH PARTICIPATION

Coordination has its "people side." There are a number of human factors that must be taken into account. The need to get people to work together—to coordinate their efforts—is a major responsibility for the executive. The key word in achieving such staff cooperation is *participation*. People want to be involved, to be a part of the process rather than just being told to do something. This basic fact should be known by the executive who seeks not only involvement but a high level of participation from department heads.

M2

The degree or depth of involvement goes back to the question of setting goals and objectives. If serious consideration is given to various viewpoints at this first stage, then it is easier to get good participation in the give and take of finally pulling together a workable budget. What happens, of course, is that people who are heavily involved become invested in the proposed budget and, therefore, committed to its success. This commitment is the goal toward which the executive should work.

Although there are many department heads who work together easily, there are usually some problem types. The most prevalent are the overanxious, the uninterested, and the prima donnas.

The overanxious are usually the activists in the agency. They are often excessively and, in some cases, obsessively concerned with details and appear to want reassurance that what they are doing is "right." They may also be fearful, hostile, or just anxious. They may plague the executive with minor details and want to assure themselves that all eventualities have been accounted for and that they will not

be held responsible in the event of any failure. The executive needs
patience and an ability to keep the overanxious actively involved
while, at the same time, limiting and controlling their demands.

Continue with Q2

M2
cont.

In respect to coordination, which of the following must be taken
into account if we are to get people to "work together:"

Q2

A. The need to be told what to do *A9*
B. The need to participate or become actively involved in the process
    from the beginning *A10*
C. Neither of the above *A12*

From the three responses below, circle the one answer that is true.
Check your answer by turning to A16.

Q3

A. Becoming invested in a proposed budget is more likely to lead to
    commitment to its success.
B. Giving serious consideration to various viewpoints is not a concern
    of the executive when getting a budget adopted.
C. A workable budget is the product of the executive alone.

The executive, in coordinating the work of a number of department
heads during the budgeting process, will often discover that there
are the following problem types. Fill in the blanks, then check your
answer by turning to A8.

Q4

A. _____
B. _____
C. _____

Fill in the blanks in the following sentence.

The executive, working with the overanxious type, will need to
exhibit patience while, at the same time, keeping the person _____
_____ involved while _____ and _____
their demands.

Q5

Turn to A11 and check your answers.

THE UNINTERESTED

The second problem type, the uninterested, presents a real challenge
to the agency executive. Most often people do not openly reveal a
lack of interest, for to do so would label them. Only occasionally will
someone admit that "I never did like working with figures," or "I came
into this agency to work with people—not to muck around with a
bunch of figures," or some similar type of comment that reveals inner
feelings. The outward behavior of this problem type may be reflected
in lethargic responses to requests for data, or lack of interest in staff
discussions regarding budget needs, or hostility directed toward the
executive. Naturally not everyone exhibits all three of the above
responses.

The inexperienced executive may be bewildered when first en-
countering such behavior. Employees are expected to be interested

M3

in all aspects of their jobs. When they aren't, laying blame, although possibly ego satisfying, is no solution.

M3
cont.

Some executives confronting this problem see firing the person as a solution to their problem. They appear to be operating under one of McGregor's assumptions in Theory X—that people work only when forced to do so. From this they extrapolate a wrong conclusion—that firing or the threat of firing will motivate people to work.

In reality, however, every executive must consider how to get people to work for the organization, to cooperate rather than just how to get rid of the uninterested or uncooperative employee. After considering the total skills and abilities of an employee, one may find that firing the person is neither possible nor desirable. The executive may then find that instigating nonthreatening discussions with the employee to get at the root of the problem may be a much more satisfying solution.

Continue with Q6

Which of the following courses of action would seem most appropriate when dealing with the uninterested individuals described in M3?

Q6

A. Tell them that they must get interested in the budget process or you will fire them *A13*
B. Tell them that you don't care about their personal problems with figures, that they must cooperate *A2*
C. Sit down with them in a relaxed nonthreatening manner and discuss their fears regarding the budget process *A1*

THE PRIMA DONNA

The third type, the prima donna may be male or female. These are the people who, like pampered children, always want their own way. Any agency that attempts to make the budget an open one will have one or more prima donnas. Such people, although qualified, think very highly of themselves and their abilities and are convinced that they are right. Here the problem for the executive is not one of motivation but of controlling through a process of selective constraints. This involves: 1. requesting additional data to support claims; 2. setting meetings with other department heads who have been encouraged to present points of view that the "prima" is unwilling to look at or is overlooking; and 3. emphasizing the tentative nature of budget making at this stage, since final approval is the responsibility of the board of directors or the legislature.

M4

Getting the budget adopted, as we have seen, involves more than simple acquiescence on the part of one's coworkers or department heads. But, assuming that we have this aspect of the problem under control, we are still a long way from getting the budget adopted. Two more hurdles stand in our way: 1. the policy approval and acceptance of the board of directors (private agency), and the approval and acceptance of possibly the governor or the mayor, the cabinet officers or the commissioners (for public agencies); and 2. the funding source for private agencies, which would either be a united fund or some charitable foundation, and for public agencies, the commissioners or the legislature.

Continue with Q7

Which of the following methods would be most effective when   **Q7**
dealing with prima donnas?

A. In order to reduce conflict, the prima donna should always be
    given his own way *A17*
B. Conflict is to be expected, but the prima donna who cannot con-
    form should be fired *A19*
C. Conflict is to be expected, but the prima donna can be controlled
    through selective constraints *A15*

Assuming that all the preliminary steps have been completed, goals   **Q8**
and objectives agreed to, a written plan devised, the budget discussed with department heads who have helped formulate it, there
are still two steps that must be taken. Fill in the blanks, then check
your answers by turning to A14.

A. For a private agency the _____ must first
    approve the budget.
B. For a public agency, the _____ or the
    _____ must first approve the budget.

Even though the budget has been approved internally and ex-   **Q9**
ternally, funding requires further approval and agreement to fund. Fill
in the blanks, then check your answers by turning to A18.

A. For a private agency the _____ (or some other
    funding source) must not only approve the budget but also agree
    to fund it.
B. For a public agency, the _____ or, _____
    _____ will probably be the body that approves and
    agrees to fund the agency.

Yes! You said to sit down and in a relaxed nonthreatening manner dis- **A1**
cuss their fears regarding budgeting. This takes time, but it is worth-
while in the long run.

Continue with M4

This course of action would prove negative and not result in de- **A2**
veloping an employee's ability. Return to M3, reread the material, and
then select another response to Q6.

You said the executive motivates the department heads to devise **A3**
workable budgets. This is true, but much more needs to be done. Re-
turn to Q1 and select another response.

You said the skilled executive also acts as a negotiator, however **A4**
much more is needed. Return to Q1 and select another answer.

You said the executive motivates the department heads to consider **A5**
the welfare of the entire agency. This is true, but more is required.
Return to Q1 and select another response.

You said the executive may ask the department heads to consider **A6**
creative innovative approaches. Yes, but much more is required. Re-
turn to Q1 and select another response.

You said all of the above, which is absolutely correct. Good for you! **A7**

Continue with M2

The three problem types are: 1. the overanxious, 2. the uninterested, **A8**
and 3. the prima donnas. Did you get all these correct? Good!

Continue with Q5

Being told what to do will rarely, if ever, lead to cooperation. Re- **A9**
turn to M2, reread the material, and select another response to Q2.

You said the quality of participation and this is correct. People **A10**
must be actively involved in any project if cooperative efforts are to
result.

Continue with Q3

You should have filled in the words, actively, limiting, and con- **A11**
trolling. You did? Well, great!

Continue with M3

Your answer is only partly correct. Being told what to do will not **A12**
facilitate cooperation, but active participation is vital to such co-
operation. Return to M2, reread the material, and select another
response to Q2.

This course of action allows you to get rid of your anger and **A13**
frustration but doesn't help the employee or get your budget problem
solved. Go back to M3, reread the material, then select another response
to Q6.

You should have filled in the words, A. board of directors, B. gover-   **A14**
nor (or mayor) or the commissioners (or cabinet).

Continue with Q9

Yes, the use of selective constraints is a method of keeping the   **A15**
prima donna under control.

Continue with Q8

The first response, A, appears to be true in most cases. Becoming   **A16**
invested in a proposed budget is more likely to lead to its success.

Continue with Q4

Giving prima donnas their own way may be the only thing you   **A17**
can do in some instances, but it is not recommended as a consistent
course of action, especially when their actions are not in harmony
with, or will create conflict with, other departments. Return to Q7 and
select another answer.

You should have filled in the words, A. united fund* B. the legisla-   **A18**
ture, or city or county commissioners.
You have now completed Lesson Two. Lesson Three discusses
specific ways of making a presentation to those groups mentioned in
this lesson.

You said that the prima donna who cannot conform should be fired.   **A19**
This may be necessary, but conformity alone should not be the criteria
for firing. Very often prima donnas are creative people who will not
conform to the usual standards but are still kept in an organization
because of their innovative ideas. Please return to Q7 and select
another answer.

* The board of directors, in addition to their policy function, may also be responsible for funding.

UNIT IX
BUDGETING

LESSON 3
How to Make
a Budget
Presentation

Specific Objective

Given the task of making an agency budget presentation to a funding source, you will be able to specify the factors involved that are likely to lead to budget acceptance.

Enabling Objective 1
Given the problem of preparing for a budget presentation, you will be able to ascertain and specify whether all of the necessary preliminary steps have been taken.

Enabling Objective 2
Given a description of the funding source, you will be able to devise a game plan detailing the factors in the system that need to be recognized and dealt with in making the presentation.

Continue with M1

PRELIMINARY STEPS

Three specific factors need to be examined in order to ascertain whether the budget is ready for presentation to a funding body. **M1**

First, have the goals and objectives been firmly agreed upon? Have any changes occurred since they were agreed upon? If changes were made, what effect if any will they have on your budget? Other questions of this order may reveal inconsistencies that must be clarified prior to the budget presentation. The executive who comes to a budget hearing and, under the stress of questioning, indicates unclear or divergent goals and objectives, rapidly loses credibility.

Second, the executive needs to ascertain whether any negative in-   **M1**
terpersonal staff relations exist, and whether there is any resultant   **cont.**
anger, frustration, or hostility that will adversely affect the budget
presentation. This second item requires insight into group dynamics,
sensitivity to individuals, knowledge of how they react, and, possibly,
some contact with the organizational grapevine. Awareness of feelings
that exist and preparing oneself to deal with them constructively is
essential.

Third, regarding the question—Do I have all of the facts I need
to make a presentation?—the answer must be yes, at least to the extent
that they are available. Predictions about possible client load, numbers
of new clients, and similar information enter into the budget presentation only as projections from known facts that are used to project
or predict some possible future numbers.

Continue with Q1

Indicate which combination of conditions should be met prior to the   **Q1**
budget presentation:

A. All the facts possible should be known; the executive needs to make
    friends with the staff, and think positively *A3*
B. Facts should be known so that adequate predictions can be made;
    interpersonal relations will be settled without conflict; and the
    goals would be agreed upon *A2*
C. The executive will be aware of interpersonal conflicts and sensi-
    tized to any implications for the budget; the facts will have been
    gathered and budget projections made on known data; the goals
    and objectives will be clear and known to the executive, the staff,
    and the board *A5*
D. The goals would have been accepted, although substantial dis-
    agreement existed; some but not all of the facts were used in
    making up the budget; staff that had been in disagreement were
    now quiet and apparently accepting *A1*

ESSENTIAL   We have dealt with the personality factors that may influence ac-   **M2**
HOME WORK   ceptance of a budget. We now turn to other data the executive must
have readily available. This is what is often called the hard data of
facts and figures. It would seem obvious that no one should go into
a budget hearing without hard data to support the budget request.
Sadly, however, all too often agency executives are ill prepared to
answer many questions asked of them. Inability to answer factual
questions with confidence tends to undermine the total validity of the
request, even though every item may be justifiable and correct.

Continue with Q2

We are aware that the executive must be sensitive to personality   **Q2**
factors that may influence acceptance of the budget. What additional
data does the executive need? Write your answer in the space below,
then check by turning to A4.

The executive needs _____.

**ANSWERS ARE
IMPORTANT**

Having the answers to all the questions that might be asked may be   **M3**
difficult, and, in some complex budgets, impossible. Nevertheless,
answers must be sought for questions dealing with 1. personnel, 2.
other expenses, and 3. budget analysis.

Personnel questions for which we need answers are:

A. Who (who is employed in the agency or program? Professionals,
paraprofessionals, clerical, and so on).
B. What (what do they do?).
C. Why (why do they do what they do?).
D. Salaries (this year, last year, projected).
E. Fringe benefits (insurance, social security, health plans, other).
F. Increases or decreases in salaries along with reasons.

Continue with Q3

In preparing a budget for agency personnel, the following informa-   **Q3**
tion is needed (choose one correct answer):

A. The number of persons, what they do, and how they get paid   *A7*
B. Why people do certain jobs, who they are, and what they do   *A9*
C. Who, what, why, salaries for this year, last year, and projected
for next year *A8*
D. Salaries (this year, last year, and projected), fringe benefits, rea-
sons for salary increases or decreases *A10*
E. None of the above *A14*
F. All of the above *A12*

Other items will involve all direct and indirect expenses other than   **M4**
personnel. Such a list might look like this:

A. Direct costs (listed below are typical examples of such costs).
  1. Materials or merchandise purchased.
  2. Transportation (travel, car upkeep for staff).
  3. Utilities (heat, light, oil, water).
  4. Telephone (usually listed separately).
  5. Insurance (especially for private agencies).
  6. Miscellaneous.
  7. Office equipment expenses (for typewriters, adding machines,
     dictaphones, and so on).
  8. Office supplies (paper, typewriter ribbons).
  9. All other supplies (nonoffice such as brooms, soap, mops).
  10. Services purchased by the agency.
B. Indirect costs (expenses that cannot be directly charged to a
department).
  1. Overhead charges (accounting expenses, central administration,
     and so on).
  2. Fringe benefits.
  3. Taxes.
  4. Advertising, cost of publications, printed reports.
  5. Depreciation (on equipment serving all departments).
  6. Rent.

It is important to note that the above division of direct and indirect
costs is not necessarily the way your agency may divide these items.
The decision in your agency may be to prorate items such as insurance,

utilities, depreciation, and rent to each of several departments. Rent **M4**
is often charged to departments on the basis of square footage of **cont.**
space occupied. Often these decisions are arbitrary and can cause
dissention when a department considers itself overcharged by this
bookkeeping practice. In so-called program budgeting, the criteria for
charging overhead items to a program may become a matter of deli-
cate negotiation.

Continue with Q4

Although it may be a bookkeeping fiction, all items called "other **Q4**
expenses" may be divided into two categories.
What are the two categories? Answer in the space below then
check your answer by turning to A6.

You probably did very well on the last question. Right? OK, now **Q5**
list as many items as you can under each of the two categories. Check
your answers by turning to A11.

Direct Costs   *Indirect Costs*

_____   _____
_____   _____
_____   _____
_____   _____
_____   _____
_____   _____
_____   _____

The third item, budget analysis, is the most difficult for persons not **M5**
familiar with the language of bookkeeping. Persons in human service
administration rarely hear, much less need to use, various common
terms used in business budget analysis, such as stock-sales ratios,
variable expenses, inventory ratios, profit and loss, and similar terms.
However, agency executives must, at least, become familiar with the
meaning and proper usage of the following terms: 1. ratios, 2. comparisons, 3. trends, and 4. projections.
The use of ratios in budget analysis is a simple way of showing
the relationship of two items to each other. Cost of clients served in
relation to income received would be one ratio. Costs of specific
services may also be expressed in ratios, for example, counseling costs
in relation to total professional personnel, administration costs in
relation to total costs. If, for example, administrative costs have regularly been 1 to 10 (one dollar administration cost to ten dollars of
total cost or 10 percent), and this year administrative costs have
jumped to 1:5 (or one dollar administration costs for every five dollars
of total cost or 20 percent), this fact clues the executive to be prepared to answer questions posed by funding bodies regarding the
reasons for the 100 percent increase.

Comparisons, in contrast to ratios, simply compare numbers of **M5** dollars for an item this year as against the same item last year or **cont.** even over the last few years. This kind of analysis, although a must for every executive, does not necessarily indicate trouble spots such as might show up with a good ratio analysis. A simple illustration, although overexaggerated, would be a case where administrative costs for the last five years have remained the same but the client load has decreased, or the services to one entire segment of the client population have been eliminated. Comparisons, therefore, while an important element in budget analysis, should not be relied upon as the only method of making an analysis of budget needs or problems. In a case as obvious as the one above, the executive would presumably be aware of the fact that administrative costs have remained high in comparison with services and would be prepared to answer questions about this imbalance. However, many less obvious comparisons may be better dealt with using the ratio method of analysis.

The trend factor in budget analysis should always receive the attention of the executive. Gradually rising costs as well as greatly increased costs should be plotted on a graph along with other significant or related expenses. Trends can then be recognized that may otherwise go unnoticed. Budget analysis frequently makes use of trend charts that show both income and expenditure trends over a period of months or years.

Projections may be desired from trends using figures of past years performance or, in the case of new items, the executive may have to project (or, in a sense, predict) income or expense for a year or more into the future. Projection analysis frequently needs to be examined for the following three factors: the highest or most optimistic expectations; the lowest or most pessimistic expectations; and, lastly, a middle of the road kind of expectation. The conservative budgetmaker evaluates both extremes and then balances them off by choosing a middle path that is defensible. Conversely, an executive who is an optimistic type person may tend to overestimate income and underestimate expenses. These projections, if built on false hopes or promises, may lead the entire budgeting process into trouble.

Another use for projections is to set up a contingency or variable budget. Such budgets are designed to fit all three cases mentioned above—the high, low, and middle figures. The executive then watches income and tries to match budgeted expenses to the authorized funding.

Continue with Q6

For a brief review of the overall game plan, what three items would **Q6** you consider must be included in your budget presentation? Please write them in the space below. To check your answer, turn to A13.

A. _____
B. _____
C. _____

A ratio analysis: **Q7**

A. Compares last years cost with this years *A15*
B. Contrasts one sum of money against another *A17*
C. Shows the relationship of two items to each other *A19*

Another important element in budget analysis is the trend factor. **Q8**
Which of the following best describes the use of the trend factor?

A. Trend lines are examined to determine which expenses need
curbing *A16*
B. Trend lines are examined in order to analyze the direction of flow
(whether of expenses or income) *A18*
C. Trend lines are examined by the executive in order to determine
whether to spend more money or increase income *A21*

How would you use comparisons? **Q9**

A. To compare numbers of dollars for an item this year as against the
same item last year *A20*
B. To compare client ratio this year against dollars last year . *A23*
C. To compare dollars in one category against dollars in another
category but in two succeeding years *A25*

Projections are useful. They can predict: **Q10**

A. How much to charge the client for services rendered . . . *A22*
B. Income or expense for a year or more ahead *A26*
C. Income only but not expenses for the year ahead *A24*

VARIABLE BUDGETING

Most budgets submitted to funding agencies are of the static type: so **M6**
many dollars of income and so many dollars of expense in relation to
a twelve month period. There is nothing wrong with this budget concept except that the knowledgeable executive will have prepared
additional figures based on what is called a variable budget and sometimes also known as a moveable budget. This latter type of budget is
designed on a series of projections. The projections for both income and
expense are graphed for each of the twelve months ahead. A set of
projections can be made for anticipated expenses related to client
services. The projections would be based on potential high levels and
low levels of service, thus projecting a high or higher than normal
expense level and similarly a low or lower level of services with con-
comitant lowering of expenses. If income is received from client fees,
then this figure must also be projected on a high, normal, and low
basis.

From the above type of analysis the executive ends up with a second
kind of budget that can be used as an administrative tool. The value
of this type of budgeting is that the figures are ready and the executive, even if under considerable stress to make a quick decision, can
do so with some assurance of a factual base.

CONTINGENCY BUDGETS

Many human service administrators do not perceive of the variable
budget as being a useful tool even though it can be, especially in
times of rapid change. But these same administrators often do set up
contingency budgets that are more static in nature but do contain
some aspects of the variable budget. The contingency budget is again
a separate budget based on presumed sources of income that are as-

sumed might be available if certain requirements are met. An example   **M6**
would be government funds that are available to agencies upon sub-   **cont.**
mission of a proposal, which, if approved, will allow the money to be
released. In cases of this sort no executive can operate on a budget
with the assumption of money arriving later. Instead, two budgets
are required: 1. a budget based on known sources of income and
expense, and 2. a speculative budget (the contingency budget) based
on the possibility of receiving additional funds, or reduced funding.

Continue with Q11

The variable budget may best be described as: **Q11**

A. Providing the executive with a series of possible choices related
   to increases or decreases *A31*
B. Providing the executive with projections of possible income and
   expense so that better budget decisions may be made . . . *A29*
C. Providing the executive with comparisons of past income and
   expense *A27*

The contingency budget is a second, additional budget often   **Q12**
used to:

A. Project expenses for new programs *A28*
B. Eliminate the uncertainty of a more stable or static budget . *A30*
C. Project potential income and therefore expense related to a new
   or reduced income *A32*

Sorry, but this would not be an acceptable combination of conditions. **A1**
The executive would be going into a budget presentation meeting
with too many unknown factors. Return to Q1 and select another
answer.

You said, "facts should be known so that adequate predictions can **A2**
be made." This is close to being correct but is not as complete as it
could be. Return to Q1 and select the more complete answer.

Sorry, but this would not be a sufficient combination of conditions **A3**
to insure the success of the presentation. Making friends with the
staff and being positive are not bad ideas but would not be necessary
steps in getting budget acceptance. Return to Q1 and select another
answer.

The executive needs the hard data of facts and figures. Did you **A4**
get the right answer?

Continue with M3

Yes—you have it right! The executive may not be able to resolve **A5**
conflicts regarding the budget prior to a presentation, but must be
sensitive and aware of the issues involved and be able to deal with
them.

Continue with M2

You should have answered, direct and indirect. You did? Fine, then **A6**
continue with Q5.

You selected answer A, which is only a partial response to the in- **A7**
formation needed in respect to the budget for personnel. Return to
M3 and reread the section on personnel, then return to Q3 and select
another response.

You selected answer C, which is only a partial answer. More in- **A8**
formation is needed. Reread M3, the section on personnel, then return
to Q3 and select another response.

You selected answer B, which is a partial answer. More information **A9**
is needed. Reread M3, then return to Q3 and select the proper answer
that will give all the needed data.

You selected answer D, which is a partial answer. More informa- **A10**
tion is needed. Reread M3, then return to Q3 and select the proper
answer that will give all the needed data.

You should have listed the following items as typically under Direct **A11**
costs:

Materials, merchandise purchased.
Transportation.
Utilities.
Telephone.
Insurance.

Office equipment.
Office supplies.
All other supplies.

All
cont.

Under Indirect costs, the following are typical:

Overhead charges, such as accounting services, central administration, and so on.

Fringe benefits.
Taxes.
Advertising.
Depreciation.
Rent.

Important! Remember, you were cautioned that your agency may divide up indirect and direct costs in a different way. There is no hard and fast rule on some items; for example, rent may be divided up on a prorata basis; fringe benefits may be added to personnel costs and charged as direct costs. These decisions are sometimes locally based, at other times it may be the policy set by a national office to charge an item one way or another. You are hereby forewarned!

Continue with M5

Right you are! You really need all of the data you can get! Congratulations!

A12

Continue with M4

Your budget presentation game plan would require you to have adequate answers on: 1. personnel, 2. other expenses, and 3. budget analysis. Did you get all three correct? If not, return to M3 for a review, otherwise continue with Q7.

A13

You must be joking! (we were!) But, just in case you are serious, we suggest you go back over the material in M3 before trying to again answer Q3.

A14

You said a ratio analysis compares last year's cost with this year's. Sorry, but this is not correct. Ratios show a relationship. Return to Q7 and select the proper answer.

A15

No. Sorry! Trend lines are not examined to determine expenses that need curbing. Review M5, on trends, before trying again to answer Q8.

A16

Sorry! You said ratios contrast one sum of money against another. This is not correct. Ratios show a relationship. Return to Q7 and select the right answer.

A17

Right! Trends help us determine the direction of flow, whether of income or expense.

A18

Continue with Q9

Yes—you've got it! A ratio analysis shows the relationship of two items to each other. Good!

A19

Continue with Q8

Right you are! Comparisons are used very simply to compare numbers of dollars for an item this year as against numbers of dollars for any number of past years.   A20

Continue with Q10

Well . . . not exactly. The executive may decide not to spend more money or increase income but makes this decision more on the basis of analyzing the direction of flow. Return to Q8 and select the right answer.   A21

No, sorry. How much to charge the client cannot be determined simply by a projection, even though projections may be used in making the final decision. Return to Q10 and select another answer.   A22

No, I'm afaid this answer is too confused to be useful. Please return to M5 and reread the section on comparisons and ratios before returning and answering Q9.   A23

You said, "Income only but not expenses . . ." Sorry, but this would not be useful at all. Please return to M5 and reread the material on projections before returning and answering Q10.   A24

No, I'm afraid not. Comparisons must be made of two identical categories in order to have any validity. Please return to M5 and reread the material on comparisons before returning and answering Q9.   A25

Right you are! Income or expense may be predicted for a year or more ahead.   A26

Continue with M6

You said the variable budget may best be described as, "providing the executive with comparisons of past income and expense." This is incorrect. Return to M5 and reread this material before returning and answering Q11.   A27

No. A contingency budget is not just used to "project expenses for new programs." Although it may very well include money for new programs, it is in effect a completely new or separate budget. Reread M6 before returning and answering Q12 correctly.   A28

Right! The variable budget can provide the executive with income and expense projections on a variable basis, thereby making possible better budget decisions.   A29

Continue with Q12

Sorry, but the contingency budget is not used to eliminate uncertainty but instead sets up a plan to utilize new or reduced income and related expense. If you have any question about the difference between variable and contingency budgeting please return to M6 and reread the material before returning and answering Q12.   A30

Not really. The variable budget sets up a series of projections; it   **A31**
does not provide the executive with ready made choices. Reread the
material in M5, then return to Q11 and answer it correctly.

Good for you! The contingency budget is a second (or additional   **A32**
budget) that reflects income and related expense for some proposed
new program for which extra funding, as well as reduced funding,
may be available. It is often used in anticipation of funding to be
received if a program proposal is found acceptable.

You have just completed Lesson Three. Go on now to the last lesson
in this unit which focuses on PPBS, or the Planning Programming
Budgeting Systems approach to budgeting.

UNIT IX BUDGETING

LESSON 4
The PPBS
Approach
to Budgeting

Specific Objective

At the conclusion of this lesson, you will be able to demonstrate your skill by solving a variety of given problems in PPBS budgeting.

Enabling Objective 1
Given the task of developing a program budget, you will be able to specify and describe all four of the basic elements of the PPBS concept.

Enabling Objective 2
Given the task of developing a program budget, you will be able to specify and describe all ten of the crucial operational phases included in planning, programming, and budgeting.

Enabling Objective 3
Given the task of distinguishing between traditional line-item budgeting practice and systems approach of planning programming budgeting (PPBS), you will be able to distinguish between the two and delineate the strengths and weakness of both approaches.

Continue with M1

BRIEF REVIEW

In the first three lessons of this unit we emphasized the issues related primarily to the preparation phase of the budgeting process. Although **M1**

we will not elaborate on this topic, it is important to note that there are two more phases to the budgeting process, namely, approval and execution, for a total of three: 1. preparation, 2. approval, and 3. execution.

M1 cont.

In the budget approval phase, administrators of human service programs must present their budgets and justifications to their funding source. For private agencies, this means the United Fund and/or foundations. For public agencies, this means city councils, county commissioners, state legislatures, or the U.S. Congress. Gaining budget approval is still very much of an art. It is a political process of give and take in which the effective administrator utilizes public relations skills to sell the funding source on the merits of the value and purpose of the agency and its budget. This process involves the careful justification of items in the budget as well as graphic representations, charts, expert witnesses, and service consumers to underscore the merits of the request. We shall not elaborate further on this phase since other references can be consulted.[1] A commonly overlooked "reference" is actual observation. Observing the approval phase of budgeting is an education in itself. Budget review committees of the United Fund are usually open to the public and similar review activities are always open to the public in the case of local, state, and federal governmental bodies.

The traditional aspects of this third budgetary process, execution, include the basic principles of financial administration and accounting. Standard texts in accounting related to vouchers, journals, and general ledgers should be consulted.[2] In order to understand agency financial management it is important to sit down with the business manager or fiscal officer in order to gain first-hand knowledge of the basic accounting components of the budget execution process. As an administrator, you will need a working knowledge of this process, but it is important to remember that you are not an accountant. A knowledge of terminology and a general background in accounting makes it possible for the administrator to delegate the operating responsibilities of the budget execution process to fiscal personnel. A reminder, however: The ultimate responsibility for making or revising budgetary allocations still resides with the administrator.

Continue with Q1

The three major components of the budgeting process include:

Q1

A. Preparation.
B. Allocation.
C. Execution.

True *A2*
False *A9*

---

[1] Aaron Wildavsky, *The Politics of the Budgetary Process* (Boston: Little, Brown, 1964).

[2] For an excellent self-instructional text at an introductory level, see A. B. Turnbull, *Governmental Budgeting and PPBS: A Programmed Introduction* (Reading, Mass.: Addison-Wesley, 1970). For more advanced study of accounting procedures, a standard text in accounting should be consulted.

Public relations skills are the primary skills in the third phase of   Q2
the budgetary process related to budget execution.

True *A1*
False *A8*

SYSTEMS APPROACH TO BUDGETING

In one sense planning, programming, and budgeting is nothing new.   M2
Good administration has always been responsible for keeping goals and
objectives clearly in mind, for updating them from time to time, for
"planning ahead" rather than just meeting emergencies on an ad-hoc
basis, and, finally, for considering various alternatives, given the fact
that these are seldom enough.

PPBS has, however, introduced a systematic analysis concept which,
when followed in a scientific manner, allows for a rigorous and rational
approach to budgeting. It is this kind of mandatory, rigorous, and
rational thinking made explicit that is dealt with in this lesson.

First, planning, programming, and budgeting should be visualized
as a tool that can be used by management to help focus on the main
goals of the agency. This tool contrasts with the traditional approach
of line-item budgeting where administrators simply itemized their
budgetary needs for the year in such categories as personnel, rent,
supplies, travel, and the like. Too often those using the line-item
approach developed budgets that were incremental (simply added
to each year) and that avoided looking at the over-all goals of the
agency and the specific benefits derived from the costs of running the
agency.

PPBS budgeting forces the use of broader conceptualization and
comprises four basic programming elements: 1. system, 2. planning,
3. programming, and 4. budgeting.

The entire package of PPBS must be seen as a system and also a
systematic approach to the problems of budgeting. It appears wise,
therefore, to emphasize that the basis of the PPBS concept is imbedded in systems theory, that is, looking at the interrelatedness of
programs and activities, at means and ends (goals and objectives),
all in relation to the crucial question of cost-effectiveness.

Continue with Q3

PPBS is basically a: Q3

A. Way of budgeting for programs and functions *A4*
B. Systematic way of dealing with line items *A13*
C. Method that involves analyzing the many complex elements that
make up an agency budget, ascertaining interrelatedness and interdependence of the various factors and the cost-effectiveness of
programs *A5*

PPBS includes: Q4

A. Planning and budgeting *A3*
B. Programming and systems *A10*
C. All of the above *A12*
D. None of the above *A7*

PLANNING FOR BUDGETING

We have emphasized the concept of system as the approach in which the entire concept of PPBS is imbedded. The systems approach then is basic to understanding what PPBS is all about. The important and crucial element of planning will now be examined.   M3

One approach is to view planning from the widest spectrum possible by analyzing all the vital elements of planning. Dror identifies seven such elements, "planning is the process, of preparing, a set, of decisions for action, in the future, directed at achieving goals, by optimal means."[3]

Planning, in the context of developing guidelines for a budgeting system, has also been identified as five interrelated and interdependent elements: 1. definition of goals, 2. determination of a course of action to achieve the goals, 3. laying out or detailing the course of action, 4. development and use of needed information, and 5. specification of time period.[4]

Finally, in addition to these wide spectrum views, the planning process must be viewed in terms of its three major operational phases: 1. development of budgetary guidelines, 2. identification and definition of goals, and 3. development of needed information. The budgetary guidelines phase includes assumptions about the current conditions that affect your agency, constraints related to existing or projected conditions that will affect your agency, priorities that reflect the program areas perceived as most important for your agency, and priorities that reflect the program areas perceived as most important for your agency in the coming year.[5]

The second operational phase of goal identification includes the long-range concerns of the agency that are reviewed and revised annually, as well as statements of program objectives for each major service element of the agency. The third operational phase of the planning process includes the systematic development of needed information. Information regarding the size and characteristics of the target population receiving services and the approximate costs required to serve such a population provide the basis for delineating needs and planning priorities.[6]

Continue with Q5

Which one or more of the following statements is (are) correct? Planning in the context of PPBS is a process: Q5

A. Directed at achieving goals by optimal means.
B. Designed to prepare a set of decisions for action in the future.
C. Aimed at cost reduction over time.

Circle your answer(s) and then turn to A6.

[3] Yehezkel Dror, "The Planning Process: A Facet Design," in Fremont J. Lyden and Ernest G. Miller, eds., *Planning Programming Budgeting: A Systems Approach to Management* (Chicago: Markham, 1969), p. 99. Dror's definition includes seven different elements. For further explication we refer you to his article.
[4] See: United Way of America, *A "PPBS" Approach to Budgeting Human Service Programs for United Ways* (Alexandria, Va.: United Way of America, 1972).
[5] Ibid., p. 18.
[6] Ibid.

The planning process can be divided into three phases related to   **Q6**
the development of budgetary A. _____, identification
and definition of program B. _____, and the development of needed C. _____. Fill in the blanks and check
your answers by turning to A14.

**PROGRAM
COMPONENT**

The program component of PPBS includes the three operational   **M4**
phases of 1. examining current programs, 2. analyzing feasible alternatives, and 3. defining desired program changes. The essence of this
component is the process of self-study whereby an agency assesses
its interest and ability to deliver the best services in the community
by either complementing the programs of other agencies or seeking
to avoid duplication of other agency programs.

By examining current agency programs, it is possible to note 1.
the major activities, 2. staff used to implement programs, 3. characteristics of the client population and time span used to serve clients, 4.
the facilities, equipment, and total costs required to operate the programs, and 5. the actual results achieved with current programming.

The second phase of the programming component relates to analyzing feasible alternatives by determining the advantages and disadvantages of different approaches to programming for the needs of
the agency's target population. Such analysis should include documenting both the accepted and rejected alternatives. The criteria for
analyzing alternatives will be easier to remember if you use the
acronym FETLEBEACO.

1. *F*easibility: Is the alternative economically, socially, and/or politically feasible at this time?
2. *T*iming: Is this the "right time" for this type of program?
3. *L*egality: Are there legal barriers?
4. *B*enefits: What benefits would the potential recipients of the services
receive?
5. *E*ffectiveness and Efficiency: How effective is the alternative in
achieving the desired impact and how efficient is the use of resources?
6. *A*ppropriate Manpower Availability: Can current agency staff handle the alternatives, will they need special training, and are the
necessary types of personnel in the agency not currently available?
7. *C*apital and Operating Costs: How does the alternative program(s)
compare in terms of initial and continuing financial requirements?
8. *O*ther Funding Possibilities: Is the alternative likely to produce
partial funding from other sources (public and/or private)?[7]

These criteria lead to the third operating phase of programming
where desired program changes are reviewed. In this phase the agency
identifies the programs it desires to add, eliminate, or modify. In this
case, the advantages and disadvantages for every change must be
fully documented in order to assist with final decision making. This
phase is the true test of the agency self-study, in which agency goals
(what is to be accomplished?) are linked directly with objectives (by

[7] Ibid., p. 21.

means of what programs?) leading to different ways (in relation- **M4**
ship to which alternatives?) of achieving the desired objectives. **cont.**

Continue with Q7

By way of review, the budgetary guidelines phase in the planning **Q7**
process include:

A. Assumptions about current conditions that affect your
   agency *A16*
B. Contradictions related to existing conditions *A11*
C. Priorities reflecting most important program areas . . . *A22*
D. All of the above *A19*
E. Only A and C *A15*

Indicate whether the statement below is true or false. **Q8**
Programming in PPBS means defining desired program changes,
examining current programs, and analyzing feasible alternatives.
Check your answer by turning to A17.

————— A. True.
————— B. False.

FETLEBEACO is an acronym (check one answer): **Q9**

————— A. Criteria used for examining current programs.
————— B. Criteria used for analyzing feasible alternatives.
————— C. Criteria used for defining desired program changes.

Check your answer by turning to A20.

BUDGETING COMPONENT

This final budgeting component of PPBS includes four operational **M5**
phases:

1. Specifying desired financial support.
2. Reviewing budget requests.
3. Modifying the budget.
4. Allocating funds.

The first phase simply spells out the amount of money needed to
accomplish the previously determined goals and objectives. Broad
categories of financial requests for one or more programs might be
developed for such usually large items as personnel and facilities. This
does not mean, however, that you simply place a line-item budget
inside a budget developed through PPBS. Broad categories refer to
only a few selected and strategic subtotals of the total budget.

The second phase of reviewing budget requests from within the
agency refers to an assessment by the administrator of the relationship between program goals and program costs. The range of review
can include everything from checking the computations to reviewing
the sufficiency of the money requested and the clarity of the program
objectives.

The third operational phase of the budgeting component relates
to budget modifications. Four possible options are usually considered
in modifying the budget:

1. Eliminating all or part of a program.
2. Reducing the level of service planned under one or more programs.
3. Attempting to operate the planned program more efficiently by making certain shifts and adjustments in the use of its resources.
4. Attempting to make up the difference in allocation by additions from sources other than the primary funding sources.[8]

The fourth operational phase is concerned with the actual allocation of funds after the budget request has been reviewed and acted upon by the funding source. If the allocation by the funding source is either less than requested or more than requested, additional planning is required in order to modify the budget before the funds can be expended. The confusion and time pressures that often accompanies this allocation phase can be partly averted if contingency planning has been completed prior to budget submission. In this case contingency planning involves the development of alternative expenditure plans should the budget request be modified by the funding source.

Continue with Q10

By way of review, the third operating phase, in which desired program changes are reviewed, recommends three options when reviewing programs; these are:

A. _____   _____
B. _____   _____
C. _____   _____

Check your answers by turning to A18.

Which one of the following items does not appear in the four operational phases of the budgeting component of PPBS? Check your answer by turning to A21.

A. Allocating funds.
B. Development of budgetary guidelines.
C. Modifying the budget.
D. Specifying desired financial support.
E. Reviewing budget requests.

THE PROS AND CONS

The advantages of PPBS surface dramatically when viewed in relationship to traditional approaches to budgeting. Rarely have agencies been forced to clearly identify their goals and objectives and specify alternative ways of meeting them. Minimal budget planning has led to partial costing of programs, limited time spans for budget review and decision, and, usually, no consideration of the implication of this year's decisions on future years. The traditional line-item budget emphasizes inputs (expenditures). PPBS, however, focuses on outputs (that is, measurable performance on results that can be tagged with dollar signs). In so doing, the PPBS approach involves concern with the total agency, analyzes programs, identifies objectives, allocates finances

[8] Ibid., p. 24.

according to some scheme based on values, priorities, results, and finally, measures and evaluates the outcomes.

These values of PPBS have been stated succinctly by Tudor and follow from his clear statement of the basic objectives of PPBS:

a. To define jurisdictional objectives clearly and to relate them to defined needs and goals;

b. To stimulate the in-depth analysis of all existing and proposed new programs in terms of their costs and benefits;

c. To link the planning and budgeting process through the annual review of multiple year plans;

d. To measure actual and planned performance; and

e. To provide a systematic way of integrating all of these elements in order to arrive at a more effective system for the allocation and management of resources.[9]

Novick in a recent publication, expands the major features of program budgeting to ten items, but, in discussing the primary reason for program budgeting, he narrows it down to the fact that, "it provides a formal, systematic method to improve decisions concerning the allocation of resources."[10] Whether stated as a purpose, a reason, or a value, such a statement certainly emphasizes the basic reason that PPBS is a valuable addition to organization theory and practice.

On the negative side, we might first call attention to the fact that the critics of the PPB system see it as a great big bueaucratic, paper shuffling boondoggle. That PPBS is difficult and complex must be admitted. There is no easy way in a large organization to involve scores of middle management and upper echelon personnel in the difficult task of analysis, problem solving, setting of objectives, and painful fiscal decisions.

Another criticism leveled at PPBS is that it is a process that involves countless hours of discussion and negotiation. Involving lower echelon personnel as part of their job enrichment means allowing inputs at lower levels of the organization. This, in turn, means lengthy step-by-step processes that often become irksome or tiresome to some of the personnel.

Lastly, although PPBS has been around for more than twenty-five years, human service agencies are just now beginning to look at the possibilities it offers. Experience, therefore, is limited and can be seen as a negative factor by administrators who might otherwise feel that they should try the PPBS approach.

You have now completed the material for Unit IX. But before leaving this unit, read the summary and suggestions for further study; then complete the unit review questions located at the end of the unit.

SUMMARY

In this unit we have discussed the basic budgetary processes of which everyone in the human services must be aware. Admittedly, budgetary skills can only be really learned by doing. Practice in

[9] Dean Tudor, *Planning-Programming-Budgeting Systems* (A Bibliography) (Monticello, Ill.: Council of Planning Librarians, 1970). (*Exchange bibliography #121 and #183.*)

[10] David Novick, ed., *Current Practice in Program Budgeting (PPBS)* (New York: Crane, Russak, 1973), pp. 5–6, 10–12. Note: Novick's items include, "recognition of what costs are," and that PPBS provides "a basis of choosing between available and feasible alternatives . . ."

writing budgets and presenting them to a simulated "legislative body" or United Fund would help ingrain the concepts presented in this unit.

In brief, we have dealt with the major steps in the budgeting process, analyzed what is necessary to gain budget acceptance, described the traditional line-item budget, and talked about some newer concepts that involve program results, cost analysis, variable budgeting, and finally, we took a brief look at the planning, programming, budget system concept.

It would have to be taken for granted, as stated above, that budget skills cannot just be learned from reading one unit nor can they be learned from only one text. We have therefore suggested the possibility of setting up practice sessions that are simulations of reality. Secondly, we are recommending some selected readings that will add depth to your basic understandings gained from reading this text.

SUGGESTIONS FOR FURTHER STUDY

Although we are still in the early stages of grasping some of the new, more comprehensive program budgeting concepts, the outlines are known and clear. For one thing, we are moving toward greater accountability. No longer can agency executives, hiding under the cloak of righteousness, think they will be immune from investigation into what they are doing with the money allocated. "Doing good" and "helping people" may have been satisfactory answers in the past; they no longer suffice.

Roderick Macleod, in discussing the questions he raised as a board member of a small (100 professionals) mental health agency, said, "The principal conceptual innovation in program budgeting is disciplined thinking about what it is that an institution is producing. It follows logically that it is useful to budget the costs associated with those products and to evaluate the social benefits realized in relation to costs and alternative uses of funds and other resources."[1]

Macleod's use of the expression "disciplined thinking" is an excellent choice since this appears to be the second requirement for the future—that, in addition to accountability, we are going to be required to do some disciplined thinking about the social service programs sponsored by human service agencies. This kind of thinking involves much more than simply allocating dollars, balancing the budget, and then staying within that balanced budget. It involves asking the hard questions related to the values and social utility of the programs sponsored.

Obviously, some of the newer concepts of management by objectives (MBO) or management by objectives and results (MOR) will need to be understood by new generations of executives coming up in the human services.[2] This is especially so since, although the concepts are not really all that new, the techniques for utiliza-

[1] Roderick K. Macleod, "Program Budgeting Works in Nonprofit Institutions," *Harvard Business Review*, September–October 1971, p. 49.
[2] See, George L. Morrisey, *Management by Objectives and Results*, (Reading, Mass.: Addison-Wesley, 1970).

tion are of more recent origin. It may take some more time, therefore, for people to understand the relationship of concepts like MBO and MOR to the basic budgeting process. Once these concepts are understood, then it becomes clear that program objectives, developed from a thorough analysis of values, needs, and results, form the basis for a modern program budget.

Whether or not PPBS as a total concept will remain on the management scene or whether it will fade away is not our concern here, nor do we need to enter into that controversy. Certainly, however, it appears that PPBS has caused enough management people to ask themselves whether there aren't better ways of planning, programming, and budgeting. The end product of this type of critical analysis has resulted in articles that can help human services executives think through the step-by-step processes involved in setting up a modern budget based on systems thinking.[3]

SUGGESTIONS FOR FURTHER READING

Balls, H. R. "The Budget and Its Function." *Cost and Management,* October 1967: 25–28.

Crihfield, Brerard, and Bell, George A. "Budgeting for State and Local Government Services." *Annals of the American Academy of Political and Social Sciences,* September 1968: 31–38.

Davis, Otto; Dempster, M. A. H.; and Wildavsky, Aaron. "A Theory of the Budgeting Process." *American Political Science Review,* September 1966: 323–341.

Elkin, Robert. "Applying PPBS to Public Welfare." *Management Controls* 26 (November 1967): 237–242.

Gabis, Stanley T. *Mental Health and Financial Management: Some Dilemmas of Program Budgeting.* East Lansing, Mich.: Michigan State University, 1960.

Held, Virginia. "PPBS Comes to Washington." *Public Interest,* Summer 1966: 102–115.

Hinrichs, Harley H., and Taylor, Graeme M. *Program Budgeting and Benefit-Cost Analysis: Cases, Text and Readings.* Pacific Palisades, Calif.: Goodyear Publishing, 1969.

Levine, Abraham S. "Cost-Benefit Analysis and Social Welfare." *Welfare in Review,* February 1966: 1–11.

———. "Cost-Benefit Analysis of the Work Experience Program." *Welfare in Review,* August–September 1966: 1–9.

———. "Cost-Benefit Analysis and Social Welfare Program Evaluation." *The Social Service Review* 42, no. 2 (June 1968): 173–183.

Lyden, Fremont J., and Miller, Ernest G. eds. *Planning Programming Budgeting: A Systems Approach to Management.* Chicago: Markham, 1969.

[3] Although the reader is also referred to the bibliography at the end of this unit, we call special attention to the article previously mentioned by Roderick Macleod, as well as the following: William Gorham, "Allocating Federal Resources among competing Social Needs," *Health, Education and Welfare Indicators,* August 1966, pp. 1–13; Abraham S. Levine, "Cost-Benefit Analysis and Social Welfare," *Welfare in Review* 4 (February 1966): 1–11; Helen O. Nicol, "Guaranteed Income Maintenance, a Public Welfare Systems Model," *Welfare in Review* 4 (November 1966): 1–12.

Macleod, Roderick K. "Program Budgeting Works in Nonprofit Institutions." *Harvard Business Review,* September–October 1971: 46–56.

Murphy, Joseph S. "Planning, Programming and Budgeting: The Quiet Revolution in Government Planning Techniques." *Management Review,* April 1968: 4–11.

Novick, David, ed. *Progam Budgeting: Program Analysis and the Federal Budget.* Cambridge, Mass.: Harvard University Press, 1965.

———. *Current Practice in Program Budgeting (PPBS): Analysis and Case Studies Covering Government and Business.* New York: Crane, Russak, 1973.

Novick, David. "The Origin and History of Program Budgeting." *California Management Review* 11 (Fall 1968): 7–12.

———. "Long-range Planning Through Program Budgeting." *Business Horizons* 12 (February 1969): 59–65.

"PPBS: Its Scope and Its Limits." *The Public Interest,* 8 (Summer 1967). Elizabeth Drew, William Gorham, Aaron Wildavsky et al.)

"PPBS Reexamined: Development, Analysis, and Criticism." *Public Administration Review,* March–April 1969: 111–202.

Schultze, Charles L., *The Politics and Economics of Public Spending.* Washington, D.C.: The Brookings Institution, 1968.

Seidman, David R. "PPB in HEW: Some Management Issues." *Journal of the American Institute of Planners* 36 (May 1970): 168–178.

Tudor, Dean, *Planning-Programming Budgeting Systems (A Bibliography).* Monticello, Ill.: Council of Planning Librarians, 1970. (Exchange bibliography #121 and #183.)

U.S. Congress, Joint Economic Committee, Subcommittee on Economy in Government. *Innovations in Planning, Programming, and Budgeting in State and Local Governments: A Compendium of Papers.* Washington, D.C.: Government Printing Office, 1969.

Wildavsky, Aaron B. *The Politics of the Budgetary Process.* Boston: Little, Brown, 1964.

———. "Rescuing Policy Analysis from PPBS." *Public Administration Review,* March–April 1969: 189–202.

Young, Helen. "Performance and Program Budgeting: An Annotated Bibliography." *A.L.A. Bulletin,* January 1967: 63–67.

Zwick, Charles J. "Budgeting for Federal Responsibilities." *Annals of the American Academy of Political and Social Science,* September 1968: 13–21.

1. Regarding the agency budget, the chief executive is responsible for:

    A. Only the executive aspects of the budget.
    B. All of the administrative budget items.
    C. Only various parts of the total budget.
    D. All of the budget.
    E. Only that part of the budget that reflects the new figures for the ensuing year.

2. A budget should be designed only after which of the following has been accomplished?

    A. The executive has made a decision regarding the goals and objectives.
    B. The cost of living increases have been established and can be added to last year's budget.
    C. The decision to increase the budget has been approved by all of the administrative staff down to the supervisory level.
    D. Last year's budget has been analyzed.
    E. The total needs and problems of the agency have been analyzed, program goals and objectives, and financial needs identified.

3. After reaching agreement on goals and objectives the next step is:

    A. To devise a written plan or rationale that answers the questions who, what, where, when, and how.
    B. To decide on a money goal.
    C. To organize all the facts needed to convince people of the correctness of the budget.
    D. To minimize opposition to the plans that have been made.

4. A chart of accounts:

    A. Is like a graph.
    B. Is made up a list of all items in the budget on the expense side only.
    C. Is made up of items in both expense and income categories.
    D. Is necessary not so much for the executive but to keep the accountant happy.

5. The main reason an agency needs a budget is:

    A. To provide the United Way, United Fund, or the budget authority with the facts so they can raise more money.
    B. So the staff (personnel) can be paid.
    C. To make possible a system of control and to release the executive from day-to-day budget decisions.
    D. To keep all income and expense items in a chart of accounts so the accountant can produce the monthly balance sheet.

6. The skilled executive motivates personnel to devise workable budgets:

    A. Thereby making the tool of negotiation unnecessary.
    B. Thereby obtaining their assistance.
    C. But, may still need to be not only peacemaker but negotiator to resolve differences.
    D. But, in the process, will need to be authoritarian and demanding or the job will not be completed.

7. The executive must often work with the "overanxious" department head who exhibits behavior that is or may appear to be:

   A. Excessively or obsessively concerned with details.
   B. Fearful, hostile, needing reassurance.
   C. Meek but also defiant.
   D. Both A and B above.
   E. Both A and C above.

8. If a department head appears to be uninterested in working on a budget, you should:

   A. Fire him.
   B. Point out why it should be interesting.
   C. Discuss the problem in a relaxed, nonthreatening manner.
   D. Find out who is to blame for the problem.
   E. Shrug your shoulders and not worry about trying to solve the problem.

9. Which of the following behavior types needs controlling through a process of selective constraints?

   A. The uninitiated.
   B. The uninterested.
   C. The prima donna.
   D. The overanxious.

10. In a private agency, which of the following must approve the budget if they agree also to fund it?

    A. The executive and staff.
    B. The local board of commissioners.
    C. The United Way (or United Fund).
    D. The board of directors.
    E. The accounting firm that handles the books.

11. Prior to a budget presentation, which of the following is of utmost importance to the executive making the presentation:

    A. All conflict must have been resolved prior to the presentation.
    B. All issues must be resolved.
    C. The executive must be aware of any interpersonal conflicts and sensitized to any implications for the budget.
    D. The executive must know who the dissenters and troublemakers are so they can be dealt with sternly.

12. Which of the following are factors that may adversely affect acceptance of an agency budget?

    A. An executive's insensitivity to personality factors.
    B. An executive's knowledge of the facts and figures related to the budget.
    C. An executive's confidence in the agency's program.
    D. An executive's ability to adequately deal with questions of facts and figures.
    E. Both A and D.
    F. Both B and C.

13. If you are to really understand your agency budget, for which of the following items will you need answers?

A. A definition of agency function and goals.
B. Personnel (Who, what, why, and so on).
C. Objectives (of the agency).
D. Other expense items.
E. Budget analysis.
F. Items A, C, and E.
G. Items B, D, and E.

14. We use ratios in budget analysis as a way of showing:

A. Why one item is more important than another.
B. The relationship of cause and effect.
C. Why some items are being increased.
D. The relationship of two items to each other.
E. The comparison of last year to this year.

15. The essence of a variable budget is a series of:

A. Computations documenting all expenses.
B. Graphs that indicate highs and lows.
C. Projections based on low, medium, and high income and expense.
D. Projections based on levels of service.
E. Projections based on levels of service (or product) and related to high, medium, and low income and expense.

16. The concept-planning, programming, budget systems or (PPBS) is:

A. Applicable only to bureaucratic organizations.
B. Too complicated for private agencies.
C. A way of budgeting for programs and functions.
D. A method that involves analyzing complex items, interrelatedness, and interdependence of items and cost effectiveness.
E. A method of analyzing cost effectiveness for every single line item in the program.

17. Which of the following have been identified as the three major operational phases of the planning process?

A. Information and goals.
B. Optimal timing of budgetary decisions.
C. A designated plan for cost reductions.
D. Guidelines.
E. Both A and C.
F. Both B and C.
G. Both A and D.

18. In respect to the budgetary guidelines phase in the planning process, which two items are linked?

A. Priorities reflecting most important program areas.
B. Assumptions about current conditions that affect your agency.
C. Contradictions related to existing conditions.
D. All of the above.
E. None of the above.
F. Only A and B.

19. Which of the following have not been identified as budgeting components included under the four operational phases of the budgeting process?

    A. Development of budgetary guidelines.
    B. Modification of the timing component.
    C. Specifying desired financial support.
    D. Allocating funds.
    E. Both A and B.
    F. Both C and D.
    G. All of the above.

20. The traditional budgeting approach emphasizes controlling expenditures. The PPBS approach emphasizes:

    A. Quantity of programming.
    B. A process for getting budget approval.
    C. Measuring performance.
    D. Developing a process instead of a plan.

ANSWERS

No. The primary skills related to budget execution are derived from **A1**
the fields of accounting and financial management. Return to M1 and review the three phases of the budgeting process.

Not quite! You missed one word: approval. The three major com- **A2**
ponents of the budgeting process include preparation, approval, and execution. Return to M1 and review the three components of the budgeting process before continuing with Q1.

Almost! Planning and budgeting are only some of the components **A3**
of PPBS. Return to Q4 and select another answer.

Almost! A more complete definition is needed for planning, pro- **A4**
graming, budgeting. Return to Q3, and select another answer.

Right. The analytic aspects of PPBS represent the uniqueness of **A5**
this budgeting approach.

Continue with Q4

You should have circled A and B. While item C may be a con- **A6**
sideration in the overall approach to PPBS, it is not a key element in the planning process of PPBS. If you missed this item, return to M3 for a review. Otherwise, continue with Q6.

You goofed this time! Return to M2 for a careful review, then **A7**
answer Q4 correctly.

Right again! Public relations skills are crucial to the second phase **A8**
of the budgeting process (budget approval), not the third phase.

Continue with M2

Right you are! The second major component of the budgeting **A9**
process is approval, not allocation.

Continue with Q2

Almost! Programming and systems analysis are only some of the **A10**
components of PPBS. Return to Q4 and select another answer.

This is incorrect. Return to M3 for a review, then answer Q7 **A11**
correctly.

Correct! Yes, PPBS includes all of the components listed. **A12**

Continue with M3

Not at all. PPBS represents a considerable departure from line-item **A13**
budgeting. Return to M2 for a review, then answer Q3 correctly.

Your answer to the question on the phases of planning should have **A14**
included A. guidelines, B. goals, and C. information. If you missed any of these return to M3 for a review. Otherwise, continue with M4.

Excellent! The answer includes A and C. Continue with Q8 for **A15**
questions related to the program aspects of PPBS.

Not bad, but a more complete answer is necessary. Return to Q7.   **A16**

Your answer should be True! These are the essential components of the programming phase. If you missed this question, return to M4 for a review. Otherwise, continue with Q9.   **A17**

Your answers should include the options of A. adding programs, B. eliminating programs, C. modifying programs. If you missed any one of these items, return to M4. Otherwise, continue with Q11.   **A18**

This answer includes one incorrect item. Return to M3 and reread the material, then try Q7 again.   **A19**

FETLEBEACO refers to the criteria of feasibility, timing, legality, benefits, effectiveness and efficiency, appropriate manpower availability, capital and operating costs, and other funding possibilities which criteria are used in B, "analyzing feasible alternatives." If you missed this question, return to M4. Otherwise, continue with M5.   **A20**

You should have checked B since the development of budgetary guidelines is not a part of the budgeting component of PPBS. If you missed this item, return to M5 for review. Otherwise, continue with M6.   **A21**

Close, but not quite! A more complete answer is needed so return to Q7 and select the more complete answer.   **A22**

The following are the correct responses to questions for Unit IX.

Question	Answer	Question	Answer
1	D	11	C
2	E	12	E
3	A	13	A
4	C	14	D
5	C	15	E
6	C	16	D
7	D	17	C
8	C	18	E
9	C	19	A
10	C	20	C

If you answered less than 17 questions correctly, you need a brief review of those areas that gave you trouble before proceeding to Unit X. If you answered 17 or more correctly, congratulations, you are now ready for Unit X.

UNIT X
EVALUATING

LESSON 1
An Introduction
to Evaluation

UNIT X OBJECTIVE—EVALUATING

Upon completion of this unit, you will be able to demonstrate your evaluation skills by making the required decisions in a competent manner for a given situation.

Specific Objective

Given a description of a human service agency or program requiring evaluation, you will be able to name the criteria for evaluation, identify the type of evaluation study that should be used to help make the evaluation, and explain the reasons for making such an evaluation.

Enabling Objective 1
You will be able to define evaluation as it applies to a human service agency or program, and will be able to distinguish efficiency from effectiveness.

Enabling Objective 2
You will be able to give at least four reasons for evaluating human service agencies and programs.

Enabling Objective 3
You will be able to define two types of evaluation studies used to assess efficiency and two types of evaluation studies used to assess effectiveness in a human service agency.

337

Enabling Objective 4
You will be able to define two methods used to evaluate the effectiveness of a human service program.

Enabling Objective 5
You will be able to list, define, and measure the variables in each method of evaluation.

Enabling Objective 6
Given a situation in which an executive must make an evaluation of an entire agency or program, you will be able to describe how such an evaluation should be made, including a list of the criteria that should be included in the evaluation.

Continue with M1

INTRODUCTION

One of the most difficult problems facing administrators of human service agencies is determining if their agency is accomplishing what it set out to do. Since human service agencies are frequently placed in the situation of requesting continued support for their programs, those responsible for the agency must evaluate the results of said programs. This unit will focus on this process of evaluation showing that competent evaluation can provide administrators with objective information relating to the effects of past and present programs, and can assist in the efficient planning of future programs or the redesign of the present programs.[1]

M1

Lesson One will introduce the concept of evaluation and will focus on the different types of such studies available. In this lesson, you will learn the important distinction between measures of effectiveness.

Lesson Two will introduce you to a specialized method of evaluation—operations research—which is primarily used to evaluate the efficiency of the total system or organization. Lesson Three describes the program evaluation review technique (PERT) for use in monitoring services and programs. Lesson Four will show you how each of the administrative functions you have studied in the previous units (planning, organizing, staffing, directing, coordinating, reporting, and budgeting) is closely tied to evaluation.

When you complete this unit you will have a basic familiarity with the scientific methods used in evaluation. In addition, you should be able to use evaluation in all aspects of the administrative process.

AN OPERATIONAL DEFINITION OF EVALUATION

Wholey points out that evaluation has several distinguishing characteristics relating to focus, methodology, and function. The following operational definition clarifies these characteristics.

Evaluation

1. Assesses the effectiveness of an on-going program in achieving its objectives.

[1] Joseph S. Wholey et al., *Federal Evaluation Policy* (Washington, D.C.: The Urban Institute, June 1970), chapter 2.

2. Relies on the principles of research design to distinguish a program's effects from those of other forces working in a situation.

3. Aims at program improvement through a modification of current operations.[2]

Thus the function of evaluation is to provide feedback from results to decisions. It is the activity that links program operations to planning and programming, and its findings can be used to modify current operations and to plan future programs and policies.[3]

Since the provision of effective services is the central reason for the existence of human service agencies, it is necessary that some attempt be made to determine the effectiveness of these services.[4] Evaluation therefore becomes a central tool in the decision making process of an agency.

M1
cont.

REASONS FOR EVALUATION

In discussing the reasons for evaluation, it is important to remember that evaluation is a continuous process—it goes on all the time in all parts of the organization.

The key reasons for evaluation are as follows:[5]

1. Evaluation is essential to ascertain the extent to which the objectives of the agency are being achieved.
2. Critical evaluation is an objective and systematic means of improving a service.
3. Evaluation insures the flexibility essential to the continuous re-orientation of a service to the changing needs of persons in a changing social setting.
4. Evaluation is a form of social accountability required by all funding sources and the taxpayer or contributor at large.

TYPES OF EVALUATION

Evaluation studies can usually be differentiated on the basis of measures of efficiency or effectiveness. Evaluations of effectiveness refer to the ultimate influence of a program upon a target population (that is, whether or not the program is fulfilling its goals).[6]

Measures of efficiency are concerned with evaluating alternative methods in terms of costs—in money, time, personnel, and public convenience. Evaluations of efficiency answer questions such as, "Is there any better way to attain the same results?"[7] Generally, evaluations of a human service agency will include both measures, efficiency and effectiveness.

Continue with Q1

---

[2] Ibid., p. 23.
[3] Ibid., p. 19.
[4] Ray Johns, *Executive Responsibility* (New York: Association, 1966), p. 105.
[5] Ibid., p. 108.
[6] Ibid., p. 108–109.
[7] Edward A. Suchman, *Evaluative Research* (New York: Russell-Sage Foundation, 1967), pp. 60–61, 64.

Evaluation links program operations to planning and programming   **Q1**
by:

A. Aiming at program improvement *A12*
B. Emphasizing research design *A18*
C. Analyzing the progress in meeting program goals *A21*
D. Only A and C *A23*
E. All of the above—A, B, and C *A15*

Comprehensive evaluations of a human service agency will gener-   **Q2**
ally seek answers to questions of:

A. Alternative costs in terms of money, time, personnel, and public
convenience *A13*
B. The ultimate influence of the agency upon its target population
and whether there is any better way to achieve the same
results *A2*
C. Whether the agency is doing anything positive *A8*

Evaluation is an essential part of the administration of an agency   **Q3**
because it:

A. Provides a subjective means of improving a program . . *A1*
B. Determines the extent to which the agency is accomplishing what
it set out to do *A7*
C. Insures that programs will occasionally be reoriented to the changing needs of persons in changing social settings *A10*

**EVALUATING A
HUMAN SERVICE
AGENCY**

There are several specialized types of evaluation that measure the   **M2**
efficiency and effectiveness of a human service agency. Two types of
evaluation studies that measure the efficiency of a human services
agency are: 1. the task analysis, and 2. the time-cost study.[8] The task
analysis approach focuses on an assessment of the tasks a worker
performs to determine how a worker spends his time. The results will
indicate whether there is any need for reassigning tasks so that workers
will be spending most of their time on tasks that have been shown to
be most important. For example, in analyzing tasks, a group of workers
might be asked to indicate how frequently each of their tasks is performed, and whether or not they think that someone else could perform any of them. The workers' supervisors would then also be asked
whether they thought someone else could perform each task listed.
The results of the study would be used to determine the essential tasks
of the worker and would provide a basis for reassigning them.

The second type of evaluation study that measures the efficiency of
a human service agency is the time-cost study. This type of study
relates the time spent on various services and tasks to financial costs.
In other words, a time-cost study determines how closely the costs for
various services and tasks parallel the time spent on them. The results
of these studies can provide a more adequate basis for determining
how agency resources of time and money can be most productively and
efficiently distributed.

[8] Johns, *Executive Responsibility*, pp. 113, 114.

In addition to measures of efficiency, evaluations of a human services agency must also measure effectiveness—what is the ultimate influence of the agency upon its target population? There are at least two types of evaluation studies that measure the effectiveness of a human service agency: 1. the community survey and 2. the agency self-study.

M2 cont.

Community surveys evaluate how agency services are delivered to the community and measure whether there is any need to redesign present methods of service delivery.[9] Generally, these surveys are conducted by a team of visiting consultants in cooperation with the agency or planning staff in the larger agency. In the past, the results of these surveys have been helpful primarily in stimulating self-examination by agencies.

The second type of evaluation study that measures the effectiveness of a human services agency is the agency self-study.[10] This type of study evaluates the agency itself using a number of predetermined criteria or characteristics. Although the self-study is primarily intended to measure the effectiveness of a human service agency, it will generally include both effectiveness and efficiency criteria in order to adequately evaluate the entire agency.

Examples of criteria that might be used to measure effectiveness would include: 1. How representative is the board of directors of the membership? 2. How effective are community relationships with other agencies? 3. How effective are agency public relations? 4. How effective is the volunteer service of the agency?

Continue with Q4

Identify the following evaluation activities as either task analysis or time-cost studies and check your answers by turning to A6.

Q4

TA = Task Analysis
TC = Time Cost

_____ A. Staff members rank job activities in order from most to least time consuming.
_____ B. Annual budget items are keyed to the particular agency services for which they are expenditures.
_____ C. Services of the agency are ranked from most to least costly.

Let's assume that you are the director of a mental health agency and have been asked to assess the over-all effectiveness of your agency. What criteria would you probably use in your evaluation?

Q5

_____ A. Representativeness of board of directors, community relationships, public relations, volunteer service, and criteria of efficiency *A9*
_____ B. Volunteer service, physical facilities, public relations, and personnel *A4*
_____ C. Physical facilities, financial policies, and personnel *A3*

[9] Ibid., p. 113.
[10] Ibid., p. 112.

Match the following and check your answer by turning to A5.   **Q6**

1. Time-cost study.
2. Community survey.
3. Agency self-study.
4. Task analysis study.

_____ A. Essentially an analysis of worker activities measuring efficiency.

_____ B. Provides a more adequate basis for determining how time and money can be most productively distributed.

_____ C. Determines how effectively agency services are meeting the needs of community.

_____ D. Uses criteria of effectiveness and efficiency to evaluate over-all functioning of the entire agency.

EVALUATING A HUMAN SERVICE PROGRAM

Before discussing the types of evaluation used in a human service   **M3** program, a distinction should be made between such a program and a human service project.[11] In this lesson, a human service program is defined as a subdivision of the agency which has administrative direction to accomplish a prescribed set of objectives through the conduct of specified activities. For example, in a welfare agency there would probably be a child welfare program and a food stamp program.

A project is the implementation level of a program—the level where resources are used to produce an end product that directly contributes to the objectives of the program. For example, a project in a child welfare program might be a study of the use of paraprofessionals in child welfare.

There are two specialized types of evaluation that are used to assess the effectiveness of a human service program: 1. program impact evaluation and 2. program strategy evaluation.[12] Program impact evaluation is an assessment of the relative effectiveness of two or more programs in meeting common objectives. The primary purpose of program impact evaluation is to assist administrators in reaching decisions on funding levels or on a possible redirection of program. Program impact evaluation depends on the definition and measurement of appropriate output variables, such as the number of clients reached or the impact the program has on other programs. It also depends on the use of appropriate comparison groups.

Continue with Q7

A human service project is defined as: **Q7**

_____ A. A subdivision of the agency that accomplishes a prescribed set of objectives through the conduct of specified activities *A16*

_____ B. The level where resources are used to produce an end product that directly contributes to the objectives of the agency's program *A14*

_____ C. The implementation level of an agency budget . *A19*

[11] Wholey, et al., *Federal Evaluation Policy*, chapter 2.
[12] Ibid.

Program impact evaluation is a measure of (efficiency/effectiveness) **Q8**
and is an assessment related primarily to (cost/objectives).

Circle the proper words above, then check your answer by turning
to A11.

The second type of evaluation that assesses the effectiveness of a **M4**
human services program is program strategy evaluation. This is an
assessment of the relative effectiveness of different techniques being
used in their program.

Program strategy evaluation depends on the definition and measurement of the following variables:

1. *Environmental Variables:*
   How do community characteristics affect the program? Rural or
   urban? Size of population?

2. *Input Variables:*
   How much professional time is involved? How much citizen time?
   What is the source of funding?

3. *Process Variables:*
   How was the job done? How effective was the staff in delivering
   services? Were clients or other agencies involved?

4. *Output Variables:*
   How many clients received services? What was the impact on other
   agencies? What is the ability of the program to sustain itself?

Continue with Q9

You have just received the results of a study that compares the **Q9**
effectiveness of several different approaches being used by your staff
in rehabilitating juvenile delinquents. What type of evaluation study
is this?

———— A. Program strategy evaluation *A17*
———— B. Program impact evaluation *A20*
———— C. Task analysis *A22*

Place the correct letter (A or B) in front of items 1 and 2 below: **Q10**

———— 1. Program strategy evaluation.
———— 2. Program impact evaluation.

A. Assesses the over-all effectiveness of a program in meeting its
   objectives.
B. Depends on the definition and measurement of appropriate environmental, input, process, and output variables.

Check your answers by turning to A24.

This is incorrect. Evaluation is not a subjective process, but an objective and systematic means of improving a program. Return to M1 and review the reasons listed for evaluation, and then answer Q3 correctly.   A1

Right. Evaluations of a human service agency will include measures   A2
of efficiency and effectiveness.

Continue with Q3

Although physical facilities, financial policies, and personnel are   A3
criteria of efficiency, they are not enough for an agency self-study.
You would also need criteria of effectiveness. Return to M2 and review
the discussion of agency self-study and then answer Q5 correctly.

Although this list includes criteria of both efficiency and effective-   A4
ness, it is not complete. Return to M2 and review the criteria that are
used in an agency self-study before answering Q5 correctly.

The answers to Q6 are as follows: A5

4	A—Task analysis.
1	B—Time cost study.
2	C—Community survey.
3	D—Agency self-study.

Continue with M3

The correct answers are: A—TA; B—TC; C—TC. If you answered   A6
incorrectly, return to M2 and review the text. If you identified the
activities correctly, continue with Q5.

Correct. Evaluation is an objective method of determining the   A7
extent to which agency objectives are being achieved.

Continue with M2

Whether the agency is doing anything positive is only a measure   A8
of effectiveness. Comprehensive evaluations of a human service agency
will require measures of both efficiency and effectiveness. Return to
M1 and review the discussion of efficiency and effectiveness before
answering Q2 correctly.

Correct. An agency self-study would include criteria of both effec-   A9
tiveness and efficiency.

Continue with Q6

This is incorrect. Remember that evaluation is a continuous process.   A10
It goes on all the time in all parts of the organization. Thus, evaluation
insures that programs will continuously be reoriented to the changing
needs of persons in changing social settings. Return to M1, review the
reasons for evaluation, and then answer Q3 correctly.

You should have circled effectiveness and objectives. If you answered   A11
incorrectly, review M3 and then turn to M4.

Partially correct, but there are more components to the operational definition of evaluation. Return to Q1 and select another answer. **A12**

You are partially correct. Evaluations of a human service agency include measures of efficiency, but they also include measures of effectiveness. Return to M1 and review the discussion of efficiency and effectiveness before answering the question. **A13**

Well done! A human services project is the level where resources are used to produce an end product that directly contributes to the objectives of the agency's program. **A14**

Continue with Q8

Correct. All three components are key aspects of the operational definition of evaluation. **A15**

Continue with Q2

This is incorrect. You have confused the definition of a program with a project. Return to M3 for a brief review and then select another answer to Q7. **A16**

Right—this was a program strategy evaluation study which would assess the relative effectiveness of different techniques being used by your staff. **A17**

Continue with Q10

Partially correct, but there are more components to the operational definition of evaluation. Return to Q1 and select another answer. **A18**

A human service project is the implementation level of an agency program, not of a budget. Return to M3 for a brief review and select another answer to Q7. **A19**

Program impact evaluation assesses the over-all effectiveness of an agency program in meeting its objectives. It is not concerned with assessing the effectiveness of different techniques used in a program. This is the function of program strategy evaluation. Return to M4 for a review and then answer Q9 correctly. **A20**

Partially correct, but there are more components to the operational definition of evaluation. Return to Q1 and select another answer. **A21**

This is incorrect. Remember we are assessing effectiveness here, not efficiency. The task analysis assesses how efficiently staff are using their time, and is usually used in evaluating a human service agency and not a program. Return to M4 and review the discussion of program strategy evaluation before correctly answering Q9. **A22**

Partially correct, but there are more components to the operational definition of evaluation. Return to Q1 and select another answer. **A23**

The answer to Q10 is as follows: A24

    B   *1. Program strategy evaluation.*

    A   *2. Program impact evaluation.*

The relative importance and feasibility of evaluation studies that measure efficiency and effectiveness will obviously vary among agencies and programs. In addition, these types of evaluations can vary in the level of detail considered and in the level of decision making affected. However, it is important that you are familiar with the distinctions between these specialized types of evaluation studies, since they will provide you with objective information that will assist you in efficient decision making and planning.

UNIT X
EVALUATING

LESSON 2
Operations Research as a Key Element of Evaluation

Specific Objective

Given a description of a system or organization requiring evaluation, you will be able to explain how operations research could be used to evaluate it.

Enabling Objective 1
You will be able to define operations research and to list and define the six steps in the operations research problem solving process.

Enabling Objective 2
You will be able to list and define at least three problems common to all systems.

Enabling Objective 3
You will be able to list four advantages derived from the use of models in operations research.

Continue with M1

A DEFINITION OF OPERATIONS RESEARCH

Operations research applies scientific methods of analysis to the decision making process of organizations and systems, and seeks to develop guidelines that will make the most productive and efficient use of available resources to meet specified objectives.[1] In operations

M1

[1] Edward A. Suchman, *Evaluative Research* (New York: Russell Sage, 1967), p. 145.

347

research (OR), the term system refers to an association of inter- **M1**
dependent components whose activities are integrated to achieve a **cont.**
common goal—thus OR is applicable to the evaluation of the administrative process in human service agencies.

While the OR method is highly technical, our discussion will emphasize how OR focuses on the total system or organization, and
stresses overall performance, clear definition of goals, and quantitative
solutions.[2] Using all aspects of the administrative process, OR attempts to provide those in control of the system with optimum solutions to situations involving conflicting goals.

Operations research is thus a scientific method of:

1. Analyzing the problems encountered in human organizations and
systems and providing optimum solutions to these problems based
on quantitative analysis.
2. Evaluating and improving the efficiency of the system by continuously evaluating the conditions and optimum procedures necessary to attain the predetermined goals.

Continue with Q1

Operations research: **Q1**

_____ A. Emphasizes over-all performance, clear definition of
goals, and qualitative solutions *A1*
_____ B. Is the application of scientific methods of analysis to
problems involving the operations of a system so as to
provide those in control of the system with optimum
solutions to the problems *A4*
_____ C. Uses scientific methods of analysis to provide optimum
solutions to problems encountered only in the individual components of a system or organization . *A7*

**THE OPERATIONS
RESEARCH
PROBLEM—
SOLVING PROCESS
Define the Problem**

The OR approach to problem solving involves a sequence of six steps. **M2**
The first step has two major components of problem definition:

A. Defining the problem, system-wide. OR diagnosis and treats the
system as a totality. Thus, when a problem is defined in OR, it includes all the components of the system and how they interact.
B. Identifying system goals by developing measurable system criteria
and constraints. In order to define a problem in an organization, one
must know what the organization or system is supposed to achieve
(that is, what its goals are). Thus, this first step of the OR problem
solving process involves identifying the goals of the total organization and its components, and the goals of the persons responsible
for making decisions governing the behavior of the organization.
Since it is necessary that these goals be expressed or interpreted
quantitatively, OR seeks to develop measurable system criteria

[2] Harold P. Halpert et al., *An Administrator's Handbook on the Application of Operations Research to the Management of Mental Health Systems* (Washington, D.C.: National Clearinghouse for Mental Health Information, 1970), pub. #1003, pp. 1, 2.

for the organization (for example, the size of staff, scheduling of **M2**
patients). In addition, the definition of goals must include a con- **cont.**
sideration of such system constraints as budget and physical facilities that must be dealt with in reaching the goals.

Continue with Q2

Each of the following statements defines a problem in terms of **Q2**
goals and constraints. Which statement do you think best demonstrates the OR approach to problem solving?

———— A. The goal is to provide the maximum quality level of care
 to clients on an established budget A2
———— B. The goal is to reduce operation costs while still treating
 the maximum number of patients at a specified quality
 level of care A10
———— C. The goal is to treat the maximum number of patients,
 subject to the two constraints of budget and availability
 of physical facilities for treatment A9

Continue with M3

Construct the Model   When the problem has been identified in terms of the goals and con- **M3**
straints in the system, the next step is to build a model representation
of the subject. This model will show how managerial decisions influence the attainment of system goals, and how system constraints act
to limit the range of these managerial decisions.[3] Constructing the
model also entails developing a list of the pertinent factors both controllable and not controllable. This is known as developing criteria to
measure factors subject to managerial decisions and those not within
managerial control in order to gain insight into how the objective can
be achieved.

Since administrators and supervisory personnel are closest to the
system under study, it is essential that they actively participate in this
analysis of operations. In addition, the OR analyst must be familiar
with all the details pertaining to the system so that he will understand
how the system operates. For example, this could be accomplished by
observing one worker for an entire day—observing his actions and
decisions, and uncovering the constraints that limit these decisions
and actions. The OR analyst would then begin to translate these ob-
servable relationships into a model representation of the subject.

Derive a Tentative   The solution may be numerical or may yield a new relationship of
Solution from the Model importance to the decision maker, and may be derived by several
methods from simple cost calculations to computer simulation.

Test the Model   This is done to evaluate how well it predicts operations. If the model
is validated, it can assist in future planning and problem solving.

[3] Ibid., p. 7.

Implement the Solution

If possible, solutions should be implemented even though this may frequently be difficult, since organizations are often resistant to change.

    M3 cont.

Observe the Effects

The effects of the changes on the actual operation of the system will determine whether the solutions from the model give a correct representation of the system or whether further modifications are necessary.

Continue with Q3

After a tentative solution has been derived from the model, the next step is to test the model. In testing the model, operations research evaluates how well the model predicts (actual operations/implementation of solutions). Underline the words that best complete the sentence and then turn to A5 and check your answer.

    Q3

Match the following six steps of the OR problem solving process with statements A through F below by placing proper letters in the blank spaces.

    Q4

———— Step 1. Define the problem.
———— Step 2. Construct the model.
———— Step 3. Derive a tentative solution from the model.
———— Step 4. Test the model.
———— Step 5. Implement the solution.
———— Step 6. Observe the effects of changes on the operation of the system.

A. This step involves evaluating how well the model predicts operations.
B. This step involves identifying system goals by developing measurable system criteria and constraints.
C. This step can be derived by several methods from simple cost calculations to computer simulation.
D. This step requires developing a list of the pertinent variables, and engaging the active participation of administrative and supervisory personnel.
E. This step will determine whether the solutions from the model give a correct representation of the system.
F. This step involves an attempt to put the solutions into effect in the organizations.

Check your answers by turning to A3.

PROBLEMS COMMON TO ALL SYSTEMS[4]

There are certain general classes of problems that are common to all systems. One advantage of operations research is that it allows these problems to be classified according to their basic elements, regardless of the fields in which they occur. Thus, the application of operations research to problematic situations in one system may yield solutions derived from experience with the same class of problems in another system. The following are some examples of classes of problems that are common to all systems:

    M5

[4] Ibid., pp. ix, 11.

1. Allocation problems that occur when resources are limited.   **M5**
2. Scheduling problems that deal with the arrival of individuals at   **cont.**
   some service facility where they may have to wait for service.
3. Search problems that arise when there are limited resources such as
   time, money, or skills to use in detection. The goal is to maximize
   the probability of detection for any specified amount of resources.
4. Sequencing or routing problems in which the goal is to order a sequence of events so as to maximize the time and/or effort required
   to perform a set of given tasks.

The following diagram gives examples of the four common problem
areas found in human services agencies.

Neighborhood Health Center

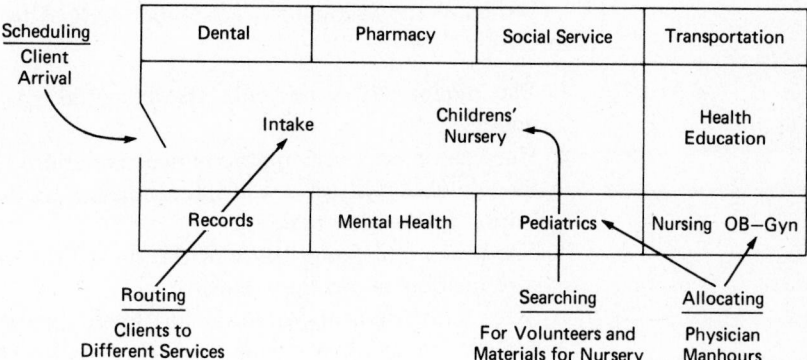

Continue with Q5

Match the following four problems with the examples shown   **Q5**
below:

———— 1. Scheduling problems.
———— 2. Routing problems.
———— 3. Allocation problems.
———— 4. Search problems.

A. A number of patients have arrived at a health facility, and a deci-
    sion must be made on the order in which they should be assigned
    to different services.
B. These problems arise when there are limited resources, such as
    time or skills, to use in detection.
C. These problems occur when there are a number of jobs to be done,
    but not enough resources to carry out the work at the desired level.
D. These problems arise when arrivals at a service facility exceed
    the processing time for service.

Check your answers by turning to A8.

THE ADVANTAGES   The use of analytical models, based on the clear identification of the   **M6**
IN USING MODELS   goals and constraints of the total system, is the necessay prelude to
IN OPERATIONS   problem solving in operations research.[5] The following are four ad-
RESEARCH   vantages derived from the use of analytical models in OR:

[5] Ibid., p. 9.

1. The mere process of going through the steps needed to make a model can furnish insights about the system.

M6 cont.

2. The product of the model building process, the model, shows only the essential elements of the system, thus highlighting those factors at the heart of the operation.
3. It is easier and safer to manipulate a model than a real system, and, although models are no guarantee against disaster, they do provide a test vehicle that should supplement the administrator's intuition in decision making.
4. A model allows comparison with other systems so that insights gained in working with one system can be transferred to other systems.

Continue with Q6

Which of the following are benefits derived from the use of models in OR?

Q6

1. The model will show only the essential elements of the system under study.
2. Since the model uses mathematical equations, it is guaranteed that its solutions will be a valid supplement to the administrator's intuition in decision making.
3. The process of going through the steps in model building will furnish insights about the system.
4. After the system under study has been abstracted to a model, the insights gained in working with this model cannot be transferred to other systems.

Select your answer from those listed below:

———— 1. 1 and 2 only *A6*
———— 2. 3 and 4 only *A11*
———— 3. 1 and 3 only *A12*

This is incorrect. Operations research emphasizes quantitative solu- **A1**
tions, not qualitative solutions. Return to M1 for a review of the
definition of operations research before answering Q1 again.

This statement is a confused mixture of goals and constraints. In **A2**
defining a problem in terms of goals and constraints, the OR analyst
must explicitly specify what the goal is and what constraints operate to
restrict the achievement of that goal. This statement does not clearly
differentiate between the goals and the constraints. Return to Q2 and
answer the question correctly.

You should have answered: **A3**

Step 1. B—Define the problem.
Step 2. D—Construct the model.
Step 3. C—Derive a tentative solution from the model.
Step 4. A—Test the model.
Step 5. F—Implement the solution.
Step 6. E—Observe effects of change.

Continue with M5

Right you are. Operations research is a scientific method of analyz- **A4**
ing the complex problems that develop in the operation of organized
systems. Continue with M2.

You should have underlined actual operations. If you answered **A5**
incorrectly, return to M3 and review steps 3 through 6 of the problem
solving process. If you answered the question correctly, continue with
Q4.

Although 1 is correct, 2 is incorrect. Just because the model uses **A6**
mathematical equations is no guarantee that the resulting solutions
will be a valid supplement to the administrator's intuition in decision
making. Rather, the model provides a test vehicle that should supple-
ment the administrator's intuition in decision making.
Return to M6 and review the benefits derived from the use of
models and then answer Q6 correctly.

You missed the point here. Operations research seeks to provide **A7**
optimum solutions to problems encountered in the total system or
organization. While individual components are obviously included in
an analysis of the system, the focus is on all aspects of the system or
organization.
Return to M1 and review the definition of operations research before
answering Q1 correctly.

You should have answered: **A8**

1. D—Scheduling problems.
2. A—Routing problems.
3. C—Allocation problems.
4. B—Search problems.

If you answered any incorrectly, you need to review the discussion
in M5, otherwise continue with M6.

This statement clearly distinguishes between the goal and the constraints that must be considered in specifying the measureable criteria for the goals of a system.   **A9**

Continue with M3

This is incorrect. The OR analyst would view this statement as a confused mixture of goals and constraints. He would redefine this statement by clearly stating what the goal was and what constraints would have to be dealt with in reaching this goal. For example in this statement, the goal could be viewed as reducing operation costs, or treating the maximum number of patients, or providing a quality level of care. You can see that it is important to specify clearly what the goals are and what the constraints are. Return to Q2 and answer the question correctly.   **A10**

Although 3 is correct, 4 is incorrect. One of the advantages of using analytical models is that insights gained in working with one system can quite often be transferred to other systems. Return to M6 and review the benefits derived from using models in OR, and then answer Q6 correctly.   **A11**

Right! The model will show only the essential elements of the system under study, and the process of going through the steps in model building will furnish insights about the system.   **A12**

From this brief overview of the techniques used in operations research, you can see that it is a valuable means of evaluating and improving the efficiency of human service programs.[6] Its major advantage lies in the fact that it increases the degree of understanding of problems encountered in human service organizations through the use of the scientific method.

You have just completed Lesson Two. Well done! Proceed now to Lesson Three.

[6] Suchman, *Evaluative Research*, p. 66.

UNIT X
EVALUATING

LESSON 3
PERT
for Human Service
Administrators

Specific Objective

Given a description of a human service program, you will be able to explain how the program evaluation and review technique (PERT) can be used to evaluate progress toward stated program goals within over-all time limitations.

Enabling Objective 1
You will be able to define PERT and to list the objectives of the technique.

Enabling Objective 2
You will be able to explain the elements of the PERT network and to describe where they are located in a simplified PERT network.

Enabling Objective 3
You will be able to name the advantages and limitations of PERT.

Continue with M1

THE DEFINITION OF PERT

New management techniques in planning, controlling, and evaluating **M1** have been developed and accepted rapidly in recent years. The program evaluation and review technique (PERT) is closely related to the quantitative decision making techniques of operations research discussed in Lesson Two in that it has a systems orientation. This lesson will present the basic elements of PERT as a planning and control device oriented primarily toward the control of time.

PERT is an acronym for program evaluation and review technique. **M1** Basically PERT is a planning and control technique employing net- **cont.** works and quantitative techniques. The network is a pictorial representation of the activities and events that must be accomplished to reach the program objectives.[1] The network will show not only the many and varied components making up a system, but also the sequence and interrelationships that prevail among these components in such a manner that the end objective is accomplished on time.

Continue with Q1

Which of the following is the best definition of PERT?   **Q1**

——————   A. PERT is a planning and control technique designed primarily to assess program effectiveness *A1*
——————   B. PERT is a managerial tool employing quantitative techniques that do not emphasize sequential relationships among the components *A4*
——————   C. PERT is a management planning and controlling tool employing networks that show the sequence and interrelationships among the activities and events that must be accomplished to achieve the objectives on time . *A8*

PERT is designed to evaluate progress toward the attainment of **M2** program goals, focus attention on potential and actual problems, provide management with frequent, accurate status reports, predict the likelihood of reaching objectives, and determine the shortest time in which a program can be completed.[2]

The simple network below shows "how PERT looks."[3] Further elaboration of the parts of the network will follow later in this lesson.

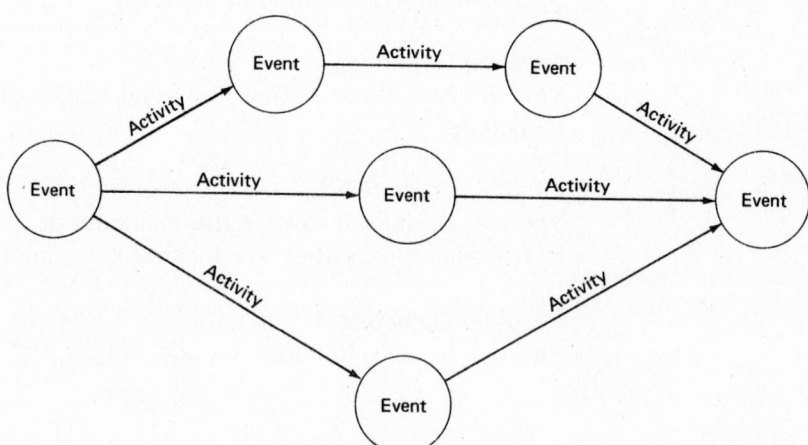

**ELEMENTS OF THE
PERT NETWORK**

The first step in developing a PERT network is to specify the program objective clearly and to visualize all the individual tasks needed to complete the program in a clear manner. You will note that a PERT

[1] Peter P. Schoderbek, *Management Systems* (New York: Wiley, 1968), p. 379.
[2] Harry Evarts, *Introduction to PERT* (Boston: Allyn & Bacon, 1964), p. 2.
[3] Ibid., p. 2.

network is primarily made up of a sequence of events connected by the necessary activities.[4] In all PERT network diagrams, the events are located within the circles, while the activities are indicated by the arrows connecting the circles. An event represents the start or completion of a specified step in a program. It is important to note that since an event is a specific instant of time (start or completion), it cannot consume time. An activity represents the time and resources necessary to progress from one event to the next, therefore, an activity consumes time. A new activity cannot start until all preceding activities have been completed.

M2 cont.

Thus the basic structure of a PERT network consists of a series of events connected by the necessary activities. It is important to note that PERT is an event-oriented technique, and thus interest is focused on the start or completion of events rather than on the activities themselves. Events in a PERT network are typically represented by numbers that are not necessarily in a sequential order. Numbering makes the identification and location of events and activities possible, since each event becomes known by its number and each activity by the numbers of the events at its start and completion.

Continue with Q2

Which of the following objectives is PERT designed to accomplish? **Q2**

A. Predict the likelihood of reaching program objectives.
B. Focus attention primarily on special problems.
C. Determine the shortest time for program completion.
D. Evaluate progress toward the attainment of program goals.
E. Provide management with sporadic status reports.

Select your answer from those listed below:

1. A, C, and D only A2
2. A, D, and E only A6
3. B, C, and E only A9

Based on what you know, is the following diagram a valid example **Q3** of a PERT network? Check your answer by turning to A7.

_____ Yes.
_____ No.

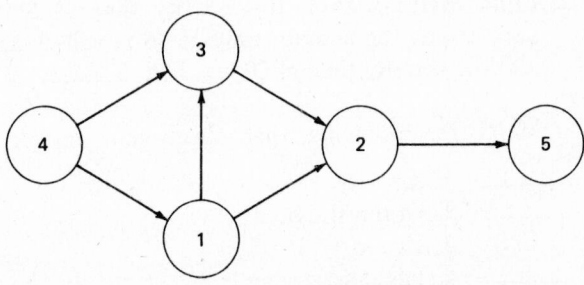

[4] Leonard J. Kazmier, *Principles of Management: A Program for Self Instruction* (New York: McGraw-Hill, 1969).

Since PERT is primarily concerned with control over time, three **M3** estimates for time are assigned to each activity. The three time estimates are required as a measure of the activity's uncertainty and are estimated by people most familiar with the activity involved. The estimates include:[5]

1. Optimistic time: An estimate of the minimum time an activity will take, a result based on the assumption that everything "goes right the first time."
2. Most likely time: An estimate of the normal time an activity will take, a result that would occur most often if the activity could be repeated many times under similar circumstances.
3. Pessimistic time: An estimate of the maximum time an activity will take, a result that can occur only if unusually bad luck is experienced.

The three time estimates are usually written over the arrows that represent the activities in the PERT network, with optimistic being the shortest estimate, pessimistic the longest estimate, and most likely time somewhere between the two.

Continue with Q4

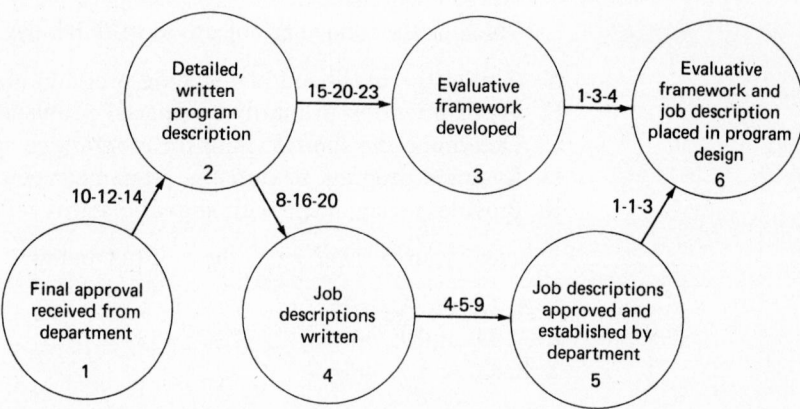

Refer to the above network to answer the following questions, then **Q4** check your answers by turning to A3.

1. The three time estimates which are assigned to each activity are called: _____ time, _____ time, and _____ time.
2. From events 2 to 4, the activity time of 8 is called _____ _____, the activity time of 16 is called _____, and the activity time of 20 is called _____.

Match the following, then check your answer by turning to A10. **Q5**

_____ 1. Activity.
_____ 2. Optimistic time.
_____ 3. Event.
_____ 4. Pessimistic time.
_____ 5. Network.

[5] Robert W. Miller, "How to Plan and Control with PERT," *Harvard Business Review* 40, no. 2 (March, 1962): 93–104.

A. The start or completion of a specified step in a program.
B. A pictorial representation of activities and events.
C. Represents time and resources necessary to progress from one event to the next.
D. Estimate of minimum time an activity will take.
E. The maximum time an activity will take.

Q5 cont.

ADVANTAGES OF PERT

There are many advantages to the PERT technique. Some of the most outstanding are:[6]

M4

1. It creates a realistic, detailed, easy to communicate plan that greatly improves the chances of attaining program objectives.
2. It predicts the time and uncertainties of performance.
3. It focuses attention on those parts of the program most likely to impede or delay its achievement.
4. It provides information about program resources that are not being fully utilized.
5. It provides thorough and frequent program status reports.
6. It can stimulate alternative methods of planning and scheduling.

Continue with Q6

Which of the following are benefits derived from the PERT technique?

Q6

A. It provides thorough and frequent status reports.
B. It predicts the time and uncertainties of performance.
C. It focuses attention on those parts of the program most likely to impede its achievement.
D. It creates a realistic, easy to communicate plan that greatly improves the chances of attaining program objectives.

Select your answer from the following alternatives:

1. A, C, and D only *A11*
2. All of the above *A5*
3. B, C, and D only *A12*

LIMITATIONS OF PERT

Since PERT is a relatively recent development, it has quite naturally been beset with a certain amount of confusion and doubt. Part of this confusion can be alleviated by recognizing the limitations of the technique. Some of these include:[7]

M5

1. PERT does not include the quantity, quality, cost, and manpower distribution information desired in many programs.
2. PERT is not necessarily useful when it is not possible to estimate the occurrence of events.
3. PERT is not necessarily useful on activities and events that are highly repetitive.

[6] Evarts, *Introduction to PERT*, pp. 5–6.
[7] Ivars Avots, "The Management Side of PERT," *California Management Review* 4, no. 2 (Winter 1962): 16–27.

4. When the complexity of the program is large, networking the activ- **M5** ities can become unmanageable, even with the use of computers.   **cont.**

While these are some of the frequently mentioned limitations of the PERT technique, it should be pointed out that more refined techniques for handling these problems are being developed. In addition, PERT is intended to be integrated with other methods of planning and control. Further experimentation will determine how the techniques of PERT can be integrated with methods of manpower distribution and cost.

Continue with Q7

Indicate which of the following are limitations of the PERT   **Q7** technique, then check your answer(s) by turning to A13.

_____ A. PERT cannot predict the time and uncertainties of future performance.

_____ B. PERT does not include the cost and manpower distribution information desired in many programs.

_____ C. PERT is limited in providing program status reports to management.

_____ D. PERT is not necessarily useful on activities that are highly repetitious.

From this brief overview of the program evaluation and review   **M6** technique, you can see the importance of applying it to many of the programs in human service organizations. The technique will be especially valuable in planning and evaluating new programs. At a time when manpower and fiscal resources are limited, application of this technique will give agency administrators the ability to plan and evaluate the best possible use of resources to achieve a given goal within over-all time limitations.

Continue with Lesson Four, which is the last lesson in this text.

You have missed the point completely. Return to M1 and start this **A1**
lesson again.

Correct. PERT is designed to predict the likelihood of reaching **A2**
*program objectives, determine the shortest time for program com-
pletion, and evaluate progress toward the attainment of program goals.*

Continue with Q3

You should have answered: **A3**

1.. *Optimistic, pessimistic, and most likely.*
2.. *The optimistic time is 8, 16 is the most likely time, and 20 is the
pessimistic time.*

*If you answered any questions incorrectly, you need to review M3.
Otherwise, continue with Q5.*

This incorrect. One of the most distinguishing features of PERT **A4**
*is its emphasis on sequential relationships among the components of
the network. In other words, PERT emphasizes the control of time.
Review the definition of PERT in M1 before you answer Q1 again.*

Right! These are all advantages derived from the use of the PERT **A5**
technique.

Continue with M5

Responses A and D are correct, but response E is incorrect. PERT is **A6**
*designed to provide management with frequent and accurate status
reports, not sporadic reports. Return to M2 for a review, then answer
Q2 again.*

You should have answered yes. This diagram illustrates that events **A7**
*are represented by numbers located within the circles, and that these
are not necessarily in a sequential order. If you answered incorrectly,
return to M2. Otherwise, continue with M3.*

Right! PERT is a management planning and controlling tool em- **A8**
*ploying networks that show the sequence and interrelationships among
the activities and events that must be accomplished to achieve the end
objective on time.*

Continue with M2

You have selected only one correct answer—PERT is designed to **A9**
*determine the shortest time for program completion. It is not designed
to focus attention primarily on special problems, rather, it focuses
attention on potential and actual problems. In addition, PERT provides
management with frequent and accurate status reports, not sporadic
reports. Return to M2 and review the discussion before you answer
Q2 again.*

You should have answered: A10

1. C—*Activity.*
2. D—*Optimistic time.*
3. A—*Event.*
4. E—*Pessimistic time.*
5. B—*Network.*

Continue with M4

These are benefits derived from the PERT technique, but you have   A11
overlooked response B which is also a benefit—PERT does predict
the time and uncertainties of performance in the future. Return to M4
for a review, then answer Q6 correctly.

These are benefits derived from the PERT technique, but you have   A12
overlooked response A, which is one of the most important advan-
tages—PERT provides frequent and thorough status reports. Return
to M4 for a review and then answer Q6 correctly.

You should have marked responses B and D. PERT does not include   A13
cost and manpower distribution information, and it is not necessarily
useful on activities that are highly repetitious. If you answered in-
correctly, you need to review the advantages and limitations of PERT,
beginning with M4. If you answered correctly, continue with M6.

UNIT X
EVALUATING

LESSON 4
Evaluation
in All Activities
of Administration

Specific Objective

You will be able to explain the evaluative aspects of each of the eight executive administrative functions discussed in the previous units. Given a situation requiring the use of these executive administrative skills, you will be able to use evaluation in the most appropriate manner.

Enabling Objective 1
You will be able to define each of the executive administrative functions.

Enabling Objective 2
You will be able to explain how evaluation is conducted in each function.

Continue with M1

PLANNING

In the previous units, each of the activities involved in administering an agency or program have been described. These include planning, organizing, staffing, directing, coordinating, reporting, budgeting, and evaluating. Evaluating, the last activity, is closely tied with each of these administrative activities. This lesson will show you how evaluation occurs in each of these administrative activities, and will highlight the special evaluative problems raised with each activity.

You will recall that planning includes the process of determining the purposes, goals, and objectives of the agency, stating the tasks or

M1

activities that must be performed in order to accomplish the purposes, goals, and objectives, and describing the methods to be used in performing the tasks. Evaluation is essential at each one of these steps in the planning process in order to provide a check on the adequacy of the plan and to permit redirection before the plan becomes too fixed.[1] Evaluation conducted at strategic points in the planning process can determine whether a redefinition of objectives is needed and can measure progress toward the long range objective. For example, when determining the objectives of the agency, measurable criteria should be identified. This would allow evaluation of each of these criteria before the next stage of the planning process.

M1 cont.

Continue with Q1

Which of the following statements of possible agency objectives is stated in terms of measurable criteria?

Q1

——— A. The target population of the agency will be expanded *A1*

——— B. Casework services will be expanded in order to double the number of minority group clients currently being served *A5*

——— C. Treatment costs will be reduced and staffing patterns will be changed *A10*

ORGANIZING

Evaluative research is a basic ingredient in organizing, the second executive function. You will recall that organizing refers to the establishment of the formal structure of authority through which components of work are arranged, defined, and coordinated so as to accomplish agency purposes, goals, or objectives. In organizing the structure of agency services, measurable check points must be included in all service areas. These measurable check points will then serve as a basis for evaluating the effectiveness of different organizational structures and modes of operation.[2] In addition, they will serve as a basis for evaluating how effectively the objectives of the agency are being accomplished. One example of establishing measurable check points might be setting up clear lines of authority and providing for regular monthly feedback memos on how responsibilities are being carried out.

M2

STAFFING

The third executive function, staffing, includes the entire personnel function of hiring and training staff as well as maintaining favorable working conditions. Evaluation is an essential activity in all aspects of the staffing function. Evaluative studies can determine how personnel can most effectively be utilized and trained. In addition, evaluation studies can provide data that is helpful in order to establish priorities among programs by determining the best use of the limited

[1] Edward A. Suchman, *Evaluative Research* (New York: Russell Sage, 1967), p. 136.
[2] Ibid., p. 141.

resources of personnel and how they spend their time.[3] In order to build evaluation into this activity, the administrator must identify staff functions in terms of measurable performance criteria against which progress and achievement can be evaluated. For example, in developing agency job descriptions, agency expectations and the range of worker autonomy should be clearly stipulated.

M2 cont.

DIRECTING

The fourth executive function is directing, which means serving as leader of the agency by making decisions and carrying out the tasks necessitated by these decisions or delegating them to subordinates. Evaluative research in this administrative activity can serve the valuable function of assisting the administrator in making effective decisions by assessing the alternative solutions to situations involving conflicting goals. Evaluation studies can also assess how effectively responsibility and authority are being delegated, if the patterns of delegated authority are stated in terms of measurable criteria that assess leadership. For example, one measurable criterion that would assess leadership would be developing a feedback mechanism, such as a suggestion box, for workers to identify service delivery problems and personnel problems.

Continue with Q2

Evaluation is an important activity in directing an agency and can serve the valuable function of:

Q2

_____ A. Assessing how effectively patterns of responsibility and authority are being delegated *A3*
_____ B. Determining whether a redefinition of agency objectives is needed *A6*
_____ C. Evaluating the effectiveness of different organizational structures and modes of operation *A11*

One method of including evaluation in the administrative function of directing is to specify the patterns of delegated authority in terms of _____. Check your answer by turning to A15.

Q3

Match the following by writing the proper letters in the blanks and then check your answer by turning to A2.

Q4

_____ 1. Organizing.
_____ 2. Planning.
_____ 3. Staffing.

A. Client services will be expanded in order to double the number of minority group clients to be served.
B. Should include measurable check points in all service areas.
C. Should include measurable performance criteria against which progress and achievement can be evaluated.

[3] Ibid.

COORDINATING

Coordinating is the fifth administrative activity. You will recall that   M3
this is the function of interrelating the various parts of the work of
an agency so as to reduce or eliminate inter- and intradepartmental
friction. Evaluating coordination helps to increase communication
and information among agency staff in order to improve the coordination of services.[4] Regardless of mechanisms used to establish regular
communication (such as committees, staff meetings, interagency meetings), from an evaluation perspective, it is important that the criteria
for these mechanisms be clearly stated. For example, in developing
specific procedures for case conferencing, statements of the problem
and follow-up plans could be clearly specified on an agency form developed just for such an activity with reporting mechanisms to follow-
up on the effectiveness of coordination.

REPORTING

As you will recall from Unit I, reporting includes the three activities
of record keeping, regular inspections, and research. In all of these
activities, the executive's primary function is to keep all those individuals to whom he is responsible informed concerning agency activities and progress. Evaluation is an important aspect of each of these
activities.

1. *Record Keeping:*
   In this activity evaluation studies can document services by establishing client record forms, memo routing procedures, and periodic
   review procedures. For example, an evaluation study could result in
   the development of a common client record form for use by more
   than one agency. In addition, evaluation studies assess the progress
   of staff members in delivering services to clients on the basis of
   client records.

2. *Regular Inspections:*
   Regular inspections of the agency will help the executive obtain an
   over-all picture of how the agency is functioning. These inspections will also reveal areas that need improvement, resulting in
   evaluation studies to determine how these areas can function more
   efficiently and effectively to meet agency objectives.

3. *Research:*
   This aspect of the reporting function actually means that evaluation
   studies must be continuously conducted to determine how well
   the agency's services are being performed. In addition, evaluative
   research will assess whether or not current services are necessary,
   as well as the need for new services.

Continue with Q5

Evaluation of the coordinating activity in administration requires   Q5
which of the following items as a basic prerequisite?

A. There is adequate communication among agency staff . . *A17*
B. The criteria for communication mechanisms are clearly
   stated *A13*
C. Inter- and intradepartmental friction be eliminated . . .   *A9*

_____
[4] Ibid.

Which of the following reporting activities can use evaluation   **Q6**
studies as a means of developing a common client record form?

_____	A. Regular inspections	_A7_
_____	B. Research	_A12_
_____	C. Record keeping	_A4_

BUDGETING

The seventh administrative function, budgeting, refers to the planning   **M4**
and controlling of agency finances. Evaluation is an essential ingredient
in this function since it can help to determine the most desirable and
effective allocation of monetary resources. In addition, evaluative research can assess the organizational structure from a budgetary standpoint, making sure that this structure clearly defines the basis for
authority and responsibility for making expenditures in all departments. Evaluation of the budgeting procedures can also lead to the
establishment of evaluative mechanisms for program or service area
supervisors to report on changes in financial, physical, and personnel
needs. For example, an evaluation study could result in the development of budget preparation forms for all such areas of the agency
that would require personnel to evaluate their current status and
project future budgetary needs.

Continue with Q7

In the blanks provided check the role of evaluation in the bud-   **Q7**
geting process and then choose your answer from those presented below.

_____ 1. Developing mechanisms for documenting services by
   establishing periodic review procedures.
_____ 2. Increasing communication among agency staff.
_____ 3. Determining the most desirable and effective allocation
   of resources.
_____ 4. Determining how personnel can be most effectively
   trained and utilized.
_____ 5. Assessing the organizational structure to determine the
   most effective delegation of authority for making expenditures.

A. If you selected 1, 2, and 5. . . . . _A14_
B. If you selected 2, 3, and 4. . . . . _A16_
C. If you selected 2 and 4. . . . . _A19_
D. If you selected 3 and 5. . . . . _A8_

Match the following, then check your answer by turning to A18.   **Q8**

_____ 1. Directing.
_____ 2. Budgeting.
_____ 3. Reporting.
_____ 4. Coordinating.

A. Evaluative research in this activity serves the function of increasing communication among staff.
B. Evaluation in this function deals with the activities of record
   keeping, regular inspections, and research.

C. Includes evaluation if the patterns of delegated authority are
stated in terms of measurable criteria that assess leadership.

Q8
cont.

D. Evaluation in this function can result in the establishment of
evaluative mechanisms for program supervisors to report on
changes in financial and personnel needs.

SUMMARY

This unit on evaluation was designed to identify some of the new
aspects of evaluation procedures that have been developed in
recent years to assist human service managers in planning and
evaluating agency programs. Specific attention was given to the
definition of evaluation and to the special meaning of the terms
effectiveness and *efficiency*. Additional techniques were identified
in the form of community surveys and self-studies to assess
organizational effectiveness. In addition, cost-benefit analysis
was also noted as a tool for assessing the value of services
delivered to clients both in terms of client improvement as well
as the cost of individualized services. [We also noted the difference between evaluating the strategy by which a program
was carried out and the impact on a program] One form of evaluation is more process-oriented, while the other form is more goal-
oriented.

The new method of operations research applied to human services was also discussed with a description of how human service
administrators might take a systems view of their organization.
Operations research was shown to have a particular value in
demonstrating a method of model construction in which agencies
would project how they might operate under optimum circumstances. The process of testing a model would include the research and development approach in which agencies would try
new ideas on a small scale. The operations research approach
also assists in identifying common organizational problems including the allocation of manpower, materials, and money, as
well as the problem related to scheduling events such as the
intake of clients for the provision of services. A technique known
as PERT was also defined as a method for scheduling work
activities in an organization. Special attention was given to
the concepts of *activities* and *events*. We also identified some of
the advantages and disadvantages of the PERT method. The unit
was concluded with a discussion of evaluation in terms of all
aspects of the administrative process. In this case we described
how evaluation can be utilized to assess an administrator's approach to planning, organizing, staffing, directing, coordinating,
reporting, budgeting, and evaluation.

SUGGESTIONS FOR FURTHER STUDY

The field of evaluation in the human services is very new and as
a result there are only a limited number of sources available
for further study. However, it will be important for future human
service administrators to study new approaches for forecasting
not only the expenditure of funds for human services but also
the special needs for additional manpower and types of man-

power. Some of the approaches currently under discussion can be found in the literature on Futures. This literature attempts to describe a new methodology of predicting the future in order to plan for the present. One new method that is currently being experimented with involves what is called a "policy delphi." This method attempts to solicit a wide variety of expert opinions in order to reach a general consensus on what future activities and events might be anticipated in the human services and therefore might be planned for during the coming year.

There has also been renewed attention to the whole process of evaluation designs in which researchers are reviewing and assessing the value of traditional designs such as "before and after program comparisons," where program results are assessed before a program has begun and after it is completed. Other designs include comparing the population of clients being served with those not being served. Needless to say, the emerging literature on evaluative research will require further study on the part of future human service administrators in order for them to stay current in their understanding of evaluation as a tool for management.

SUGGESTIONS FOR FURTHER READING

Albrecht, Leong K. *Organization and Management of Information Processing Systems.* New York: Macmillan, 1973.

Bateman, Worth. "Assessing Program Effectiveness." *Welfare in Review,* January–February 1968.

Blumenthal, Sherman C. *Management Information Systems: A Framework for Planning and Development.* Englewood Cliffs, N.J.: Prentice-Hall, 1969.

Brightman, Richard W. *Information Systems for Modern Management.* New York: Macmillan, 1971.

Campbell, Donald T. "Reforms as Experiments." *Urban Affairs Quarterly,* December 1971: 133–170.

Campbell, Donald T., and Stanley, Julian C. *Experimental and Quasi-Experimental Designs for Research.* Skokie, Ill.: Rand McNally, 1966.

Caro, Francis G., ed. *Readings in Evaluation Research,* New York: Russell Sage, 1971.

Head, Robert V. *Manager's Guide to Management Information Systems.* Englewood Cliffs, N.J.: Prentice-Hall, 1972.

Herzog, Elizabeth. *Some Guidelines for Evaluation Research.* Washington, D.C.: U.S. Department of Health, Education, and Welfare Administration, Children's Bureau, 1959.

Kanter, Jerome. *Management-Oriented Management Information Systems.* Englewood Cliffs, N.J.: Prentice-Hall, 1972.

McFarlan, Franklin W.; Nolan, Richard L.; and Norton, David P. *Information Systems Administration.* New York: Holt, Rinehart & Winston, 1973.

Murdick, Robert G., and Ross, Joel E. *Information Systems for Modern Management.* Englewood Cliffs, N.J.: Prentice-Hall, 1971.

Rivlin, Alice M. *Systematic Thinking for Social Action.* Washington, D.C.: Brookings, 1971.

Siemans, Nicolai; Marting, C. H.; and Greenwood, Frank. *Operations*

Research: Planning, Operating and Information Systems. New York: Free Press, 1973.

Suchman, Edward. *Evaluative Research: Principles and Practice in Service and Social Action Programs.* New York: Russell Sage, 1969.

Tripodi, Tony; Fellin, Philip; and Epstein, Irwin. *Social Program Evaluation.* Itasca, Ill.: F. E. Peacock, 1971.

Webb, Kenneth, and Hatry, Harry P. *Obtaining Citizen Feedback.* Washington, D.C.: Urban Institute, 1973.

Weiss, Carol H. *Evaluation Research: Methods of Assessing Program Effectiveness.* Englewood Cliffs, N.J.: Prentice-Hall, 1972.

————. *Evaluating Action Programs: Readings in Social Action and Education.* Boston: Allyn & Bacon, 1972.

Williams, Walter, and Evans, John. "The Politics of Evaluation: The Case of Head Start." *The Annals of the American Academy of Political and Social Sciences* 385 (September, 1969): 118–132.

REVIEW QUESTIONS

1. Evaluation as an activity in human service agencies includes which of the following characteristics?

   A. Assesses effectiveness in achieving stated objectives.
   B. Aims at program improvement.
   C. Emphasizes the principles of research design.
   D. Predicts future costs of agency operations.
   E. A, B, and C above.

2. Evaluation is an essential activity in the administration of an agency because it:

   A. Provides a means of improving a service or program.
   B. Places minor emphasis on achieving agency objectives.
   C. Is a form of social accountability.
   D. A and C above.
   E. A and B above.

3. If you are attempting to determine whether or not a program is fulfilling its goals, you are assessing the _____ of the program.

   A. Positive impact.
   B. Effectiveness.
   C. Cost.
   D. Efficiency.

4. Which of the following evaluation studies measure(s) efficiency in a human service agency?

   A. Task analysis.
   B. Community survey.
   C. Time-cost study.
   D. A and C above.
   E. A, B, and C above.

5. Which of the following evaluation studies measure(s) effectiveness in a human service agency?

   A. Task analysis.
   B. Community survey.
   C. Time-cost study.
   D. A and C above.
   E. A, B, and C above.

6. Program impact evaluation and program _____ evaluation are used to assess the _____ of a human service program.

   A. Planning; efficiency.
   B. Planning; effectiveness.
   C. Strategy; effectiveness.
   D. Strategy; efficiency.

7. Program *impact* evaluation depends on the definition and measurement of appropriate:

   A. Input variables.
   B. Output variables.
   C. Process variables.
   D. Environmental variables.

371

8. Assume you are the director of a service program in an agency and your superior has told you there is reason to believe your staff has been allocating too much time to unimportant tasks. What type of evaluation study would help you in determining whether or not this statement was true?

   A. Task analysis.
   B. Program strategy evaluation study.
   C. Program impact evaluation study.
   D. Agency self-study.

9. Operations research emphasizes:

   A. Over-all performance.
   B. Clear definition of goals.
   C. Only solutions.
   D. A and B above.
   E. B and C above.

10. Defining the problem (step one) in the operations research problem solving process includes definitions of:

    A. Solutions to the problem.
    B. Goals and constraints.
    C. The system problem in terms of system goals and constraints.
    D. The major components of the problem and how they interact.

11. The second step in the operations research problem solving process, namely, constructing the model:

    A. Involves the development of measurable system criteria and constraints.
    B. Requires developing a list of the pertinent variables and engaging the active participation of administrative and supervisory personnel.
    C. Uses computer simulations or analytical and mathematical solutions.
    D. Evaluates how accurately the problem has been stated.

12. How would you classify a situation where an executive has to decide how to order a number of tasks so as to complete them within a certain time period?

    A. Sequencing problem.
    B. Searching problem.
    C. Scheduling problem.
    D. Allocating problem.

13. Which of the following could NOT be called an advantage of the use of models in operations research?

    A. The model will show all elements of the system under study.
    B. The model provides a test vehicle to supplement the administrator's intuition in decision making.
    C. The use of models curtails the transfer of insights from one system to another.
    D. B and C above.
    E. A and C above.

14. PERT is a:

    A. Management planning and controlling tool.
    B. Technique using networks and quantitative methods.
    C. Planning device oriented primarily toward the control of time.
    D. B and C above.
    E. A, B, and C above.

15. PERT is designed to accomplish which of the following objectives?

    A. Focus attention on problems.
    B. Predict the likelihood of reaching program objectives.
    C. Provide management with frequent, accurate status reports.
    D. A and C above.
    E. A, B, and C above.

16. In the PERT network an _____ represents the start or completion of a specified step in a program. An _____ _____ represents time and is shown by the arrows connecting the circles in the network.

    A. Activity; estimate.
    B. Activity; event.
    C. Event; analysis.
    D. Event; activity.

17. Which of the following statements is (are) correct?

    A. Optimistic time is an estimate of the minimum time an activity will take.
    B. Most likely time is an estimate of the maximum time an activity will take.
    C. Expected activity time is an estimate of the average time an activity would take if it were repeated many times.
    D. A and C above.

18. The advantages of using PERT include which of the following?

    A. PERT is useful on activities that are highly repetitious.
    B. PERT provides thorough and frequent status reports.
    C. PERT focuses attention on those parts of the program that are likely to delay achievement.
    D. PERT includes cost and manpower distribution information.
    E. B and C above.

19. The PERT network is:

    A. The fundamental analytical device of the technique.
    B. Limited, since it only shows the varied components making up a system.
    C. Limited, since it does not show the interrelationships in the system.
    D. An effective representation of system limitations.

20. Which of the following statements is correct?

    A. Evaluation is not important in most executive functions.
    B. Some executive functions lend themselves to evaluation while others do not.

C. Evaluation is a necessary activity in all administrative functions.

D. An agency should determine those executive functions in need of evaluation.

21. Evaluation is essential throughout the planning process in order to:

A. Permit redirection before plans become too fixed.
B. Help determine agency goals and objectives.
C. Provide a check on the adequacy of the plans.
D. A and C above.
E. A, B, and C above.

22. Evaluation of the executive organizing function focuses on determining:

A. The effectiveness of different organizational structures and modes of operation.
B. How effectively personnel are being trained.
C. Agency purposes and objectives.
D. The coordination and definition of work subdivisions.

23. In directing an agency, evaluation can serve the function of:

A. Determining the most desirable and effective allocation of resources.
B. Assisting the administrator in making effective decisions and increasing the effectiveness of delegations.
C. Increasing communication among agency staff.
D. Determining the effectiveness of different organizational structures and modes of operation.

24. Establishing evaluative mechanisms for program supervisors to report on changes in financial and personnel needs would improve primarily which one of the following executive functions?

A. Directing.
B. Budgeting.
C. Reporting.
D. Coordinating.

Turn to the last page to check your answers.

ANSWERS

This statement of an agency objective is too ambiguous. Will the **A1**
entire target population of the agency be expanded? Or are there
particular groups or individuals who need to be reached? This objec-
tive would need to be restated in terms of specific measurable criteria.
Return to M1 for a review, then answer Q1 correctly.

You should have answered: **A2**

1. *B—Organizing.*
2. *A—Planning.*
3. *C—Staffing.*

Continue with M3

Correct! In directing an agency, evaluation studies assess how **A3**
effectively patterns of responsibility and authority are being delegated.

Continue with Q3

Correct! Evaluation in record keeping can serve the valuable func- **A4**
tion of developing mechanisms for documenting services by estab-
lishing client record forms, memo routing procedures, and periodic
review procedures.

Continue with M4

Well done! This objective is stated in terms of measurable criteria, **A5**
and would easily lend itself to an evaluation measure.

Continue with M2

This is incorrect. Determining whether a redefinition of agency ob- **A6**
jectives is needed is generally a function of evaluation in the admin-
istrative activity of planning, not directing. Return to M2 and review
the discussion before answering Q2 correctly.

Sorry, but this is not one of the activities using evaluative research **A7**
for developing a common client record form. Review M3 before
you answer Q6 correctly.

Answer D is correct—well done. **A8**

Continue with Q8

You selected answer C, which is actually a function of the coor- **A9**
dinating activity and not a basic prerequisite for evaluating coordi-
nation.
Return to M3 for a review, then select another answer to Q5.

This is incorrect. Will treatment costs be reduced by changing **A10**
staffing patterns? What specific treatment costs need to be reduced
and how is this related to staffing patterns? You can see that this ob-
jective is not stated in terms of measurable criteria.
Return to M1 for a review and then answer Q1 correctly.

Evaluating the effectiveness of different organizational structures and modes of operation is a function of evaluation in the administrative function of organizing, not directing.
Review M2 before answering Q2 again, this time correctly.

A11

This is incorrect. Evaluating the reporting activity in terms of ongoing research does not focus on developing mechanisms for documenting services by establishing client record forms, memo routing procedures, and periodic review procedures. Return to M3 for a review, then answer Q6 correctly.

A12

Correct! A statement of criteria is essential in order for evaluation to take place.

A13

Continue with Q6

A is not correct. Return to M4 for a review, then answer Q7 correctly.

A14

You should have answered, measurable criteria that assess leadership. Continue with Q4.

A15

B is not entirely correct. You may wish to review the material on M4 before answering Q7 again.

A16

You selected answer A, which is a function of evaluation in the coordinating activity but not a basic prerequisite for evaluating coordination. Return to Q5 and select another answer.

A17

You should have answered:

A18

1. *C—Directing.*
2. *D—Budgeting.*
3. *B—Reporting.*
4. *A—Coordinating.*

Any incorrect responses indicate that you need to review these four administrative functions. Evaluation is thus an essential aspect of the entire process of agency and program administration. Evaluation provides the administrator with an objective means of assessing all of the activities involved in administration. Competent evaluation requires the administrator to state his objectives in explicit, measurable terms. Thus, if evaluation is a continuous activity in all parts of the administrative process, it will become an invaluable tool in effective and efficient administration.

You have now completed this lesson and the programmed materials in this text. For a final check up on how you have progressed, see the summary section and review questions at the end of this unit. Best wishes to you from the three of us. We hope you have found this book worthwhile.

Statements 2 and 4 are not correct. You may wish to review the material on M4 before answering Q7 again.

A19

**ANSWERS TO
REVIEW QUESTIONS**

The following are the correct responses to questions for Unit X.

Question	Answer	Question	Answer
1	E	13	E
2	D	14	E
3	B	15	E
4	D	16	D
5	D	17	D
6	C	18	E
7	B	19	A
8	A	20	C
9	D	21	D
10	C	22	A
11	B	23	B
12	A	24	B

Did you have 20 or more correct? If not, review trouble areas. If so, you have completed this text—a job well done!

Printer and Binder: The Murray Printing Company

78 79   9 8 7 6 5 4 3

DATE DUE